Applied Architecture Patterns on the Microsoft Platform

Second Edition

Work with various Microsoft technologies using
Applied Architecture Patterns

Andre Dovgal

Gregor Noriskin

Dmitri Olechko

PUBLISHING

BIRMINGHAM - MUMBAI

Applied Architecture Patterns on the Microsoft Platform
Second Edition

First published: September 2010

Second edition: July 2014

Production reference: 1180714

Published by Packt Publishing Ltd.
Livery Place
35 Livery Street
Birmingham B3 2PB, UK.

ISBN 978-1-84968-912-0

www.packtpub.com

Cover image by Aniket Sawant (aniket_sawant_photography@hotmail.com)

Credits

About the Authors

Andre Dovgal has worked for several international organizations in the course of his 30-year career. Some of his most exceptional accomplishments include building customized solutions for the financial industry, algorithms for artificial intelligence systems, e-business systems for real-estate agents, and IT integration services in the areas of law enforcement and justice. He possesses certifications in different areas of computer science, project management, and finance. He has authored more than 30 publications on IT, computer science, finance, history, and philosophy.

Since the mid 2000s, Andre has been focusing on integration and workflow technologies (BizTalk, SQL Server, and later WF and SharePoint). His current experience includes the latest versions of the BizTalk ESB and SQL Server platforms with all components, such as SSIS and SSRS, and .NET 4.5 pillars (WCF, WF, and WPF).

I would like to thank my coauthors and colleagues for the knowledge they shared with me and the incredible experience they brought to this work. I would like to thank my wife, Elvira, for the inspiration that she has been giving me for this and many other projects.

Gregor Noriskin is a polyglot programmer, software architect, and software development leader. Over the past two decades, he has written a lot of code; designed enterprise, web, and commercial software systems; and led software engineering teams. He has worked with large and small companies on five continents in multiple roles, industries, and domains. He spent nearly a decade at Microsoft, where he worked as Performance Program Manager for the Common Language Runtime and Technical Assistant to the CTO.

I would like to thank my wife, Deirdre, for her ongoing support, and my children, Elle and Aeden, for giving up some of their playtime with me while I was working on this book. I would also like to thank my ex-colleagues at Metalogix for having answered technical SharePoint questions and enlightening me about some of the nuances and idiosyncrasies of the various SharePoint APIs and features. I would particularly like to thank my colleagues Matthew McKinnon, who helped me by technically reviewing the book, and Jay Dave. Lastly, I would like to thank, with much gratitude, respect, and humility, the many brilliant people I have worked with over the years, and who have taught me so much of what I know about software development, the .NET Framework, and SharePoint.

Dmitri Olechko has over 15 years' experience in software project architecture and development using Microsoft products, including Visual Studio .NET, SQL Server, WCF services, SSRS, SSIS, SharePoint, WPF, Workflow Foundation, BizTalk, ASP.NET, and MVC/jQuery.

He has been part of a number of commercial projects for large corporations and government organizations, including Future Concepts, Government of Saskatchewan, The Los Angeles Police Department, Green Dot Corp, and Comcast among others.

Apart from this, he has a keen interest in areas such as dispatching and logistics algorithms, parallel processing, Big Data management, and cloud-based software.

His real-life experiences have enriched him and have given him the confidence to evaluate various business scenarios and find the best-suited product for them.

About the Reviewers

Sriram Cherukumilli is a developer/architect with experience in architecture, design, and development across all application tiers with emphasis on enterprise SOA and real-time backend systems. He works at Argo Data Resources on Windows Workflow Foundation 4.5-based workflow management applications, which abstract developer and platform-specific details to present business-friendly orchestrations running extensible workflows across the company's different verticals. Sriram holds a Bachelor of Science degree in Engineering and a Master of Science degree in Information Technology.

Robert Gaut is a father, husband, martial arts practitioner, musician, photographer, and application developer. He began his life as a programmer in 1979, writing games on a Texas Instruments TI-99/4A computer. After attending college and receiving a degree in music, he went back to programming as an instructor at a technical college. Since then, he has built a career as a software architect focusing on web-based technologies and has helped build several successful start-up companies.

Moustafa Refaat has over 15 years' experience in developing software solutions, leading the architecture, design, coding, and refactoring of many large projects.

He has worked for the City of Vaughan and organizations such as TransCanada Pipelines, Tim Hortons, VMS, Deloitte DMGF, Newfoundland and Labrador, and First Canadian Title Insurance. Moustafa has designed and implemented many systems based on SQL Server and BizTalk. His experience spans the financial, insurance, health, banking, retail, oil and gas, marketing, and telecommunications services automation industries.

He is a published author with books on programming and BizTalk. He also acted as a referee for the IEEE Software magazine. Moustafa runs his own software and consulting company, Genetic Thought Software Inc.

Andrei Sinelnikov is an Information Technology professional, with over 14 years of experience in the design, development, and implementation of the Windows n-tier applications using the TOGAF, RUP, Agile, SCRUM, and Waterfall methodologies. He has also worked on the latest Microsoft technologies and SQL programming. He holds a Master's degree in Computer Science and a variety of Microsoft certifications in the Server, Database, and Developer stack.

He has worked on a variety of projects that apply Microsoft technology in the enterprise environments of various industries and government sectors, such as education, banking, insurance, law enforcement, municipal affairs, provincial government, and healthcare.

Municipal Infrastructure Management System, architected by Andrei, was chosen as a finalist in the 2010 Microsoft IMPACT Award in the Custom Development Solution of the Year and Small Business Specialist of the Year categories.

Smitha Sundareswaran has her PhD from Pennsylvania State University. Her current research focuses on distributed systems of scale, specifically cloud computing. She is very passionate about security systems and has done research in security in social networks, web applications, and cloud computing. She has led over 15 software development research projects as a program manager with over 20 refereed publications.

www.PacktPub.com

Support files, eBooks, discount offers, and more

You might want to visit www.PacktPub.com for support files and downloads related to your book.

Did you know that Packt offers eBook versions of every book published, with PDF and ePub files available? You can upgrade to the eBook version at www.PacktPub.com and as a print book customer, you are entitled to a discount on the eBook copy. Get in touch with us at service@packtpub.com for more details.

At www.PacktPub.com, you can also read a collection of free technical articles, sign up for a range of free newsletters and receive exclusive discounts and offers on Packt books and eBooks.

http://PacktLib.PacktPub.com

Do you need instant solutions to your IT questions? PacktLib is Packt's online digital book library. Here, you can access, read and search across Packt's entire library of books.

Why subscribe?

- Fully searchable across every book published by Packt
- Copy and paste, print and bookmark content
- On demand and accessible via web browser

Free access for Packt account holders

If you have an account with Packt at www.PacktPub.com, you can use this to access PacktLib today and view nine entirely free books. Simply use your login credentials for immediate access.

Instant updates on new Packt books

Get notified! Find out when new books are published by following @PacktEnterprise on Twitter, or the *Packt Enterprise* Facebook page.

Table of Contents

Preface

Once a small company established in 1975, Microsoft is one of the leading software companies in the world today. Over decades, Microsoft has been bringing new technologies to all of us. Some Microsoft products did not have a long life, whereas others became leading software products, supporting a vast number of solutions in the world for many years. Today, Microsoft delivers operating systems for servers, desktops, tablets, and phones. It has dozens of server products, such as SharePoint, BizTalk, Exchange, or SQL Server. It supports a powerful development framework, .NET, as well as development and testing tools. Its Visual Studio is one of the best Integrated Development Environments, and its Team Foundation Server covers all aspects of application lifecycle management. Most of us use applications from the Microsoft Office Suite, and many businesses have deployed Microsoft Dynamics solutions. To make a long story short, the world of Microsoft is huge.

How does an architect, especially a solutions architect, find his way in this world? Typically, architects want to use experience of other architects in the form of patterns and best practices. This book will help you navigate through the ocean of Microsoft technologies and provide guidance to select proper technologies for chosen patterns. We shall look at the patterns from an architect's point of view, focusing on major groups such as data exchange patterns or integration patterns.

This book has significantly changed since its first edition. First of all, it covers the changes that have happened since 2010; for example, new versions of all products, including major changes to the foundational software such as .NET and SQL Server. In addition to this, the second edition discusses .NET and SharePoint, which were not covered before. We also have added some related patterns, including presentation layer patterns.

What this book covers

Chapter 1, Solution Decision Framework, provides an approach to evaluating technologies that is used for different patterns described in the book.

Chapter 2, The .NET Framework Primer, presents an overview of the latest .NET version, and an assessment of the most notable namespaces in .NET based on their maturity, productivity, performance, and availability.

Chapter 3, The SQL Server Primer, discusses the capabilities of SQL Server and presents a typical use case.

Chapter 4, The SSIS Primer, discusses the capabilities of SQL Server Integration Services as an ETL tool and presents a typical use case.

Chapter 5, The BizTalk Server Primer, provides an introduction to the major architectural integration styles, discusses BizTalk essentials, and shows how BizTalk fits in to an integration use case.

Chapter 6, The SharePoint Server Primer, talks about SharePoint Server capabilities as a platform and presents major concepts and notions related to this.

Chapter 7, Other Microsoft Technologies, provides an overview of many Microsoft products that are last but not least; these include operating systems, Microsoft Office and Exchange, software development tools, and cloud computing.

Chapter 8, Integration Patterns and Antipatterns, presents an introduction to the major architectural integration patterns such as federated request and Publish/Subscribe, discusses the problem of guaranteed delivery, and presents use cases corresponding to different patterns.

Chapter 9, Web Services and Beyond, discusses web services, Service-Oriented Architecture, and Enterprise Service Bus.

Chapter 10, Data Exchange Patterns, continues the discussion on integration patterns started in the preceding two chapters. It talks about data synchronization and migration, ETL, multiple master synchronization, data sharing, and data federation. Most complex patterns are presented with use cases and solutions.

Chapter 11, Workflow Patterns, discusses two major types of workflows: fully automated workflows and human workflows.

Chapter 12, Presentation Layer Patterns, presents the variety of Microsoft technologies for building user interfaces and discusses the most popular architectural patterns, such as MVC, MVP, and MVVM.

Chapter 13, Conclusion, wraps up the book discussions and recaps the decision-making process.

What you need for this book

In order to work with the code examples that accompany this book, you need to have the following software:

Windows OS:

- Windows Server 2012
- Windows 7 or newer

MS Servers:

- SQL Server 2012 (including SSIS) or newer
- BizTalk Server 2013 (including the ESB toolkit)
- SharePoint Server 2013

Development tools:

- Visual Studio 2012 or newer
- MS SQL Server Data Tools—BI for Visual Studio 2012

Miscellaneous:

- .NET 4.5 or newer
- AppFabric 1.1

Who this book is for

This book is not a tutorial on Microsoft technologies, nor does it provide code that you can copy-and-paste to your solution to make everything start working miraculously.

This book is intended to be a tool for architects who need to make a decision about the software to use for their solutions. They will also appreciate the presented solution decision framework. The book is also suitable for other IT professionals who want to get an introduction to major Microsoft products and their potential usage.

Conventions

In this book, you will find a number of styles of text that distinguish between different kinds of information. Here are some examples of these styles, and an explanation of their meaning.

Code words in text, database table names, folder names, filenames, file extensions, pathnames, dummy URLs, user input, and Twitter handles are shown as follows: "The System namespace is both the root namespace for the .NET Framework and contains the basic building blocks of the .NET Framework."

A block of code is set as follows:

```
private static int CreateAndEnumerateList(int maxValue)
{
    var list = new System.Collections.ArrayList(maxValue);
    foreach (var val in Enumerable.Range(0, maxValue))
    {
        list.Add(val);
    }
    var total = 0;
    foreach (int val in list) //implicit type conversion
    {
        total += val;
    }
    return total;
}
```

Any command-line input or output is written as follows:

```
EsbImportUtil.exe /f:"<Path to folder with Itinerary>\ SmcOneWaySimple.
xml" /c:deployed
```

New terms and **important words** are shown in bold. Words that you see on the screen, in menus or dialog boxes for example, appear in the text like this: "In order to complete the package to process all input files, we need to go back to the **Control Flow** tab."

 Warnings or important notes appear in a box like this.

 Tips and tricks appear like this.

Reader feedback

Feedback from our readers is always welcome. Let us know what you think about this book—what you liked or may have disliked. Reader feedback is important for us to develop titles that you really get the most out of.

To send us general feedback, simply send an e-mail to feedback@packtpub.com, and mention the book title via the subject of your message.

If there is a topic that you have expertise in and you are interested in either writing or contributing to a book, see our author guide on www.packtpub.com/authors.

Customer support

Now that you are the proud owner of a Packt book, we have a number of things to help you to get the most from your purchase.

Downloading the example code

You can download the example code files for all Packt books you have purchased from your account at http://www.packtpub.com. If you purchased this book elsewhere, you can visit http://www.packtpub.com/support and register to have the files e-mailed directly to you.

Errata

Although we have taken every care to ensure the accuracy of our content, mistakes do happen. If you find a mistake in one of our books—maybe a mistake in the text or the code—we would be grateful if you would report this to us. By doing so, you can save other readers from frustration and help us improve subsequent versions of this book. If you find any errata, please report them by visiting http://www.packtpub.com/submit-errata, selecting your book, clicking on the **errata submission form** link, and entering the details of your errata. Once your errata are verified, your submission will be accepted and the errata will be uploaded on our website, or added to any list of existing errata, under the Errata section of that title. Any existing errata can be viewed by selecting your title from http://www.packtpub.com/support.

Piracy

Piracy of copyright material on the Internet is an ongoing problem across all media. At Packt, we take the protection of our copyright and licenses very seriously. If you come across any illegal copies of our works, in any form, on the Internet, please provide us with the location address or website name immediately so that we can pursue a remedy.

Please contact us at copyright@packtpub.com with a link to the suspected pirated material.

We appreciate your help in protecting our authors, and our ability to bring you valuable content.

Questions

You can contact us at questions@packtpub.com if you are having a problem with any aspect of the book, and we will do our best to address it.

Solution Decision Framework

1

The notion of software architecture has been around for about 50 years; however, only in the 1990s did it become a part of the computer industry dictionary. Since then, it has undergone some evolution, influenced by other areas of software development and project management. In the *Software Architecture and Design* chapter of the *Microsoft Application Architecture Guide, 2nd Edition* document (2009), software application architecture is defined as follows:

> "*Software application architecture is the process of defining a structured solution that meets all of the technical and operational requirements, while optimizing common quality attributes such as performance, security, and manageability*".

Today, the notion of software architecture is typically applied to two major areas of the industry: project development and product development. **Project development** is characterized by the fact that every project has a beginning and an end, which always has a time frame. At the beginning of the project, there is normally a requirements-gathering process, and the solution that is delivered at the end of the project has to satisfy those requirements. Some requirements describe the business functionality of the solution. Other requirements can specify its availability, extensibility, resilience, security, and many other nonfunctional aspects.

In **product development**, businesses focus on developing products according to the initial set of requirements or upgrading them according to the subsequent sets of requirements. In a typical process, the **software development life cycle (SDLC)** has several stages. The stages start from generating an idea of the new product, business analysis, and market research about the coding, testing, delivering to the market, and maintenance. Delivering a new version of a software product can be considered a project itself; however, the entire product development process is cyclic typically, and it does not have a visible end. There are many SDLC methodologies from Waterfall to a whole spectrum of Agile ones; the focus of the architect's role in them is very different from one to another.

In this chapter, we'll consider an architect's approach to a typical software project. We'll discuss the need for an architectural decision framework and sources of information that influence an architect's decisions. We'll talk about evaluating technologies and how organizational context, solution design, implementation, as well as operations have their impact on such an evaluation.

The need for a decision framework

Architects who work on solutions are called **solutions architects**, and solution architecture will be the main focus of this book. A solutions architect is by no means required to be very technical; however, he/she should possess other capabilities such as understanding organizational dynamics, providing leadership, and quite often, fulfilling the role of a translator between the business and technical teams. Regardless of their involvement in the solution delivery, they always need to make decisions about the technologies that will be used.

Here is where frameworks become very helpful. Frameworks truly give architects a structure to build their decisions on. Without such a structure, there are always gaps; some good decisions would be missed and some simple solutions will be overlooked.

The decision framework that we propose in this book is based on the following principles:

- **Gather as much information about the current status or the existing solution**: For product development, if a new version is to be developed, it consists of the knowledge of the existing product. For project development, this will be the knowledge of how the same or similar problems are being solved in the organization. Gather as many requirements as possible (see the next section, *Sources of input*, to get more ideas about requirements gathering). Gather as much context information as possible: existing infrastructure, business purpose for the solution, laws and regulations that might apply in the industry, standards, and so on.

- **Align your decisions with the organizational direction**: The next section discusses this principle in detail.

- **Look for critical and problem areas**: The 80/20 principle suggests that 80 percent of time is spent on 20 percent of problems. Try to identify these problems at the beginning of the architectural work. See whether the problems can be solved using some best practices and patterns.

- **Apply best practices and patterns**: True innovations seldom happen in the world of software architecture; most of the solutions have been thought of by hundreds and thousands of other architects, and reinventing the wheel is not necessary.

- **Capture and evaluate alternatives**: Experts are often biased by their previous experience, which blinds them and does not let them consider alternatives. If a few architects with different experiences (for example, in Java and in .NET) got together in a room, each one would have his/her own strong preferences. The architecture work can then get into "analysis paralysis". To avoid this, capture all alternatives, but evaluate them unbiasedly.

- **Simplify**: Simple solutions are the most elegant and, surprisingly, the most effective. Don't use the pattern just because it's cool; don't add a feature if it is not requested; don't use a technology that is not designed for the problem. Use Occam's razor as it removes the burden of proof.

Sources of input

There are several major sources of input that an architect must consider before making a decision. Four of them are crucial to the solution delivery: organizational direction, functional requirements, nonfunctional requirements, and derived requirements.

Organizational direction

Software development teams often forget that any solution they build is required only because of the business needs. They don't necessarily understand (and unfortunately, often don't want to understand) the details of these needs. Business people also usually don't want to learn the technicalities of the software solution. Nothing is wrong with that. However, since technical and business people speak different languages, there should be a role of a translator between the two groups. And this is, not surprisingly, the role of the solutions architect.

Every solution starts with a challenge. A business creates these challenges — this is the nature of business, this is its driving force, this is the imminent requirement for the business to survive. The solutions are typically executed as projects, with a start date and an end date, which is limited in time. However, most businesses also do not exist as short temporary activities; they plan their existence and strategies for a long period of time.

Business strategies and long-term plans provide the context for time-framed solutions that have to be delivered in order to solve a specific problem or a set of problems. For organizations with mature IT departments, **Enterprise Architecture (EA)** frameworks help architects manage this context. Usually, the organizational considerations are outlined in the EA policies and principles.

Functional requirements and use cases

The next input for the decision-making process is functional requirements. Functional requirements describe the intended behavior of the system. Functional requirements typically come from the business and there are many methods for requirement solicitation, from questionnaires and surveys, to workshops and stakeholder interviews. The requirements can originate in the marketing department or come from existing end users of the product. They can describe the feature baseline necessary for the product to survive competition or can be "nice to haves" produced by the dreamer/owner of the business. The process of gathering, validating, and prioritizing requirements might be quite long and can end up with different artifacts.

When building a solution, architects should pay attention to the priorities assigned to the requirements. Usually, it is impossible to satisfy them all in the first releases of the solution, and the choice of technologies should be flexible enough to extend the solution in the future.

One of the most convenient ways to capture functional requirements is to build **use cases**. Use cases define a focused specification of interaction between actors and the system. **Actors** can be end users, roles, or other systems. Usually, use cases are written in a language that is relevant to the domain, and they can be easily understood by non-technical people. A common way to summarize use cases in a structured way is using the UML notation.

Use cases are also used in the validation of proposed architectures. By applying the proposed architecture to the use cases, architects can identify the gaps in the future solution.

Functional requirements analysis should be aligned with the design of major architectural blocks of the solution. Each requirement must be implemented in one of the solution components. Breaking down functional requirements across components or tiers provides us with a good way to validate the proposed solution architecture.

Nonfunctional requirements

Nonfunctional requirements (NFRs) are often ignored, maybe not completely, but to a significant degree. However, they are as important to the architecture as functional requirements. Moreover, some architects argue that NFRs play a more significant role in the architecture than their functional counterpart. Wikipedia even suggests the following:

> *"The plan for implementing functional requirements is detailed in the system design. The plan for implementing non-functional requirements is detailed in the system architecture."*

We may argue this statement, but NFRs, without a doubt, touch very deep areas of the technology.

There are many different categories of nonfunctional requirements. There is no exact list of these categories; different sources would give you different names, but the major ones would be the following:

- Availability
- Performance
- Reliability
- Recoverability
- Capacity
- Security
- Interoperability
- Maintainability
- Auditability
- Usability
- Scalability
- Expandability

When we discuss the criteria for choosing technologies later in this book, we shall pay very close attention to the NFRs. They will become the major criteria for coming up with a proper solution design.

To summarize the difference between functional and nonfunctional requirements, one can say that functional requirements answer the "what?" questions, and nonfunctional requirements answer the "how?" questions.

Derived (architectural) requirements

Working on the solution architecture, architects might come up with a requirement that was not explicitly stated either as a functional or as a nonfunctional requirement. Architects derive these requirements from initial inputs. The derived requirements have to be validated with the stakeholders and added to the set of functional or nonfunctional requirements.

For example, a functional requirement might state that the system must have real-time monitoring capabilities with an ability to inform the administrator about reaching certain configurable thresholds. To conform to this requirement, a couple more requirements should be added, which are as follows:

- The system must be integrated with a communication channel: e-mail, SMS, or a similar channel

- The system must have a mechanism (XML files and a database with a UI) to change the configuration

Requirements could be simply forgotten during the requirement-gathering process. For example, a Publish/Subscribe system should have a way to manage subscriptions and subscribers, which sometimes become an epiphany later during the design process.

Gathering requirements is an iterative process. Once the architects start working with the requirements, more requirements can be derived. They should be given back to the business stakeholders for validation. The more complete set of requirements the designers get, the less expensive the system development will be. It is well known that a requirement implemented at the end of the solution development costs much more than if it was suggested at the beginning of the process.

Deciding upon your architecture strategy

Once the core requirements are set forth, architects can start working on the building blocks for the solution. The building blocks are like high-level patterns; they specify what major components the system might have. For example, for a middle-tier monitoring solution, building blocks might consist of a message-logging system, a reporting system, a notification system, a dashboard, a data maintenance system, and others. The next step should be to look into a lower level of the architecture; each building block requires patterns to be used. Message logging can be done with the usage of the filesystem, a database, SNMP sending log data into another system, or something else. Before the patterns are selected, evaluated, and thoroughly considered, jumping into a product selection would be a grave mistake. It could cause selecting a tool that might not be fit for the task, a tool that is an overkill, or a tool that requires an enormous amount of configuration effort. Sometimes, building a proof of concept might be required to evaluate the patterns implemented by a technology candidate.

There are many books that have been written on generic patterns, especially patterns of the enterprise application architecture. The most respected series is the series with the Martin Fowler signature. We would recommend *Patterns of Enterprise Application Architecture, Addison-Wesley Professional, Martin Fowler*, and *Enterprise Integration Patterns, Addison-Wesley Professional, Gregor Hohpe, Bobby Woolf*, as the most relevant to discussions in our book.

Technology evaluation dimensions

In the process of evaluating technologies, we will build criteria in the following four dimensions:

- **Organizational context**: Solutions built to function in an organization should be aligned with business needs and directions. Organizational context is usually provided by the enterprise architecture that builds general IT principles and strategies for the organization.

- **Solution design**: These criteria are relevant to the process of designing the system. The design is typically the step that starts after the core architecture is completed. In the Agile development, the design starts sooner, but the architecture keeps the backlog of unfinished business (the so-called **architectural debt**) that is being worked on over time.

- **Solution implementation (development, testing, and deployment)**: These criteria focus on the next stages of solution delivery from the completed design to the deployment in production. Product development might not have a production deployment stage per se; rather, it would have a need to create installation programs and packaging.

- **Operations**: Surprisingly, this is the area that is neglected the most while the architecture is developed. This is because it is all about the business value that the solution is supposed to provide and was built for. A very typical example is giving low priority to buying (or developing) administration tools. We have seen organizations that buy sophisticated and very expensive monitoring tools but don't provide proper training to their staff, and the tools end up simply not being used. As the most ridiculous example, I remember an organization providing SaaS services that allowed intruders to use a back door to their FTP server for eight months simply because they did not use proper monitoring tools.

Organizational context

Organizational context provides us with a big picture. Every organization has its set of principles, implicit or explicit, and the task of the solutions architect is to build systems aligned with these principles. The following table lists some major principles that are typically developed by the organization enterprise architecture team:

Principle	Description
Consider process improvement before applying technology solutions	Although it may sound important, this principle is often not considered. Sometimes, architects (or businesses) rush into building a solution without looking into a possibility to completely avoid it. We put it as the first consideration, just as a warning sign.
The solution should satisfy business continuity needs	Some businesses are more critical than others. A bank, for example, should function even if a flood hits its data center. Disaster recovery is a major part of any solution.
Use vendor-supported versions of products	All Microsoft products (or those of any vendor) have to be supported. Microsoft typically provides at least 10 years of support for its products (including 5 years of mainstream support or 2 years after the successor product is released, whichever is longer).
Automate processes that can be easily automated	Take advantage of information systems; however, think of eliminating unnecessary tasks instead of automating them.
Design for scalability to meet business growth	This is one of the essential points of alignment between business and IT. However, look into possibilities of building flexible solutions instead of large but rigid ones.
Implement adaptable infrastructure	Infrastructure must be adaptable to change; minor business changes should not result in complete platform replacement but should rather result in changing some components of the system.
Design and reuse common enterprise solutions	In the modern enterprise, especially in service-oriented architecture (SOA) environments, enterprise solutions should produce reusable components.
Consider configuration before customization	Changing the configuration takes less technical skills as compared to customizing the solution. It also produces the result much quicker.
Do not modify packaged solutions	Packaged solutions maintained by a vendor should not be modified. Times of hacking into third-party packages are gone.

Principle	Description
Adopt industry and open standards	From the initial assessment and inception phase of the project, you should consider industry and open standards. This will save you from re-inventing the wheel and will bring huge advantages in the long run.
Adopt a proven technology for critical needs	Many enterprises approach technologies from a conservative standpoint. Some, for example, suggest that you should never use the first couple of versions of any product. Whether you want to go with extremes depends on the organization's risk tolerance.
Consider componentized architectures	Multi-tier architecture enables separating concerns in different tiers, allowing faster development and better maintenance. A service-oriented architecture paradigm emphasizes loose coupling.
Build loosely-coupled applications	Tightly-coupled applications might seem easier to develop, but—even when it is true—architects should consider all phases of the solution cycle, including maintenance and support.
Employ service-oriented architecture	Service-oriented architecture is not just a technological paradigm; it requires support from the business. Technologically, SOA services mirror real-world business activities that comprise business processes of the organization. Employing SOA is never simply a technological decision; it affects the entire business.
Design for integration and availability	Every solution might require integration with other solutions. Every solution should provide availability according to the organization's SLAs.
Adhere to enterprise security principles and guidelines	Security, being one of the most important nonfunctional requirements, has to be consistent across the enterprise.
Control technical diversity	Supporting alternative technologies requires significant costs, and eliminating similar components also increases maintainability. However, limiting diversity also sacrifices some desirable characteristics, which may not be ideal for everybody.
Ease of use	Just following the Occam's razor principle, simplify. Remember, at the end of the day, all systems are developed for end users; some of them might have very little computer knowledge.

Principle	Description
Architecture should comply with main data principles (data is an asset, data is shared, and data is easily accessible)	These three main data principles emphasize the value of data in the enterprise decision-making process.
Architecture should suggest and maintain common vocabulary and data definitions	In a complex system with participants from business to technical people, it is critical for experts with different areas of expertise to have a common language.

Solution design aspects

In this section, we look at the characteristics relevant to the overarching design of a solution. The list is certainly not exhaustive, but it provides a good basis for building a second dimension of the framework.

Areas of consideration	Description
Manageability	• Does the system have an ability to collect performance counters and health information for monitoring? (See more about this consideration in the *Solution operations aspects* section). • How does the system react to unexpected exception cases? Even if the system graciously processes an unexpected error and does not crash, it might significantly affect the user experience. Are these exceptions logged at a system level or raised to the user? • How will the support team troubleshoot and fix problems? What tools are provided for this within the system?
Performance metrics	Good performance metrics are reliable, consistent, and repeatable. Each system might suggest its own performance metrics, but the most common are the following: • Average/max response times • Latency • Expected throughput (transactions per second) • Average/max number of simultaneous connections (users)

Areas of consideration	Description
Reliability	• What is the expected mean time between service failures? This metric can be obtained during testing, but the business should also provide some expectations. • How important is it for the system to be able to deal with internal failures and still deliver the defined services (resilience)? For some industries, such as healthcare or finance, the answer would be "critical". Systems in these industries are not supposed to be interrupted by major disasters, such as a flood or a fire in the data center. • Should the failure of a component be transparent to the user? If not, then what level of user impact would be acceptable (for example, whether the session state can be lost)? In the old days, a user often received some cryptic messages in case of an error, such as "The system has encountered an error #070234. Please call technical support". This is not acceptable anymore; even 404 errors on the Web are becoming more user-friendly. • What's the expected production availability? The following is a table of the availability "nines" and corresponding downtown times: <table><tr><td>Uptime</td><td>Unplanned downtime/year</td></tr><tr><td>99%</td><td>3d 15h 36m 00s</td></tr><tr><td>99.9%</td><td>0d 08h 45m 36s</td></tr><tr><td>99.99%</td><td>0d 00h 52m 33s</td></tr><tr><td>99.999%</td><td>0d 00h 05m 15s</td></tr></table> • What is the acceptable duration of a planned outage? Is it also important to know what the planned outage windows are, whether they should be scheduled every week or every month, and what maintenance windows are required for each operation (service upgrade, backup, license renewal, or certificate installation)? • What are the assurances of a reliable delivery (at least once, at most once, exactly once, and in order)?

Areas of consideration	Description
Recoverability	• Does the system support a disaster recovery (DR) plan? The DR plan is typically developed during the architecture stage. It should include the DR infrastructure description, service-level agreements (SLAs), and failure procedures. The system might seamlessly switch to the DR site in the case of a major failure or might require manual operations. • What are the system capabilities of the backup and restore? • What is the acceptable duration of an unplanned outage? Some data losses in case of an unplanned outage are inevitable, and architects should also consider manual data recovery procedures.
Capacity	• What are the data retention requirements, that is, how much historical data should be available? The answer to this question depends on the organizational policies and on the industry regulations as well. • What are the data archiving requirements, that is, when can the data be archived? Some industry regulations, for example, auditing, might affect the answer to this question. • What are the data growth requirements? • What are the requirements for using large individual datasets?
Continuity	• Is there a possibility of data loss, and how much is the loss? Very often, businesses would answer with a "no" to this question, which creates a lot of grief among architects. However, the proper question should sound: "In the case of a data loss, how much data can be restored manually?"

Areas of consideration	Description
Security	• What are the laws and regulations in the industry with regards to security? Organization security policies should be aligned with those in the industry.
	• What are the organization internal security policies? What are the minimal and the optimal sets of security controls required by the organization? The security controls might require zoning, message- or transport-level encryption, data injection prevention (such as SQL or XML injection), data sanitizing, IP filtering, strong password policies, and others.
	• What are the roles defined in the system? Each role should have a clear list of actions that it can perform. This list defines authorization procedures.
	• What are the login requirements, and particularly, what are the password requirements?
	• What are encryption requirements? Are there any certificates? In case of integration with other internal or external systems, is mutual certification required? What are the certificate-maintenance policies, for example, how often should the certificates be updated?
	• What are the authentication and authorization approaches for different components of the system?
Auditability	• What are the regulations in the industry that are affecting the audit? Which data should be available for the audit? Which data should be aggregated?
	• What data entities and fields should be audited?
	• What additional data fields should be added for the audit (for example, timestamps)?
Maintainability	• What architecture, design, and development standards must be followed or exclusions created for? Maintaining the code is a tough task, especially maintaining bad code. Proper documentation, comments inside the code, and especially following standards helps a lot.
	• Which system components might require rapid changes? Those components should be independent from other components; their replacement should affect the rest of the system minimally.

Areas of consideration	Description
Usability	• Can the system in its entirety support **single sign-on (SSO)**? Single sign-on today becomes a feature expected by most of the users and a mandatory requirement by many organizations.
	• How current must the data be when presented to the user? When a data update happens, should the end user see the changes immediately?
	• Are there requirements for multi-lingual capabilities? Are they possible in the future?
	• What are the accessibility requirements?
	• What is the user help approach? User help information can be delivered in many ways: on the Web, by system messages, embedded in the application, or even via a telephone by the support team.
	• Can the system support the consistency of user messages across all presentation layers? For example, how does the system handle messages delivered by the Web and the mobile application presentation layers? They cannot be the same because of the mobile application limitations; how should they be synchronized?
Interoperability	• What products or systems will the target system be integrated with in the future?
	• Are there any industry messaging standards? In the world of web services, many standards have emerged. The most common interoperability set of standards is the **WS-I** set of standards.
Scalability	• What is the expected data growth?
	• What is the expected user base growth?
	• What is the new business functionality that is anticipated in the future?
	• Can the system be scaled vertically (by increasing the capacity of single servers) and horizontally (by adding more servers)?
	• What are the system load balancing capabilities?

Areas of consideration	Description
Portability	• Are there any requirements to support the system on different platforms? This question becomes very important today, especially in the world of mobile and online applications. Several major mobile platforms as well as several browsers are competing in the market.
Data quality	• What are the data quality requirements (deduplication or format standardization)?
Error handling	• Failures within the system should be captured in a predictable way — even unpredictable failures.
	• Failures within connected systems or system components should be handled consistently.
	• "Technical" error messages should not be exposed to users.
	• What are the logging and monitoring requirements? Capturing errors is essential for the analysis and improving the system quality.

Solution implementation aspects

Should design, coding, and other standards be automatically enforced through tooling, or is this a more manual process? Should the source control system be centralized and integrated in a continuous integration model? Should the programming languages be enforced by an organizational policy or be chosen by developers? All these questions belong to the realm of solution delivery. If architects select a technology that cannot be delivered on time or with given skillsets, the entire solution will suffer.

Solution delivery also very much depends on the project management approach. In a modern Agile world, delivery technologies should be chosen to allow for rapid changes, quick prototyping, quick integration of different components, efficient unit testing, and bug fixing. Agile projects are not easier or cheaper than Waterfall projects. In fact, they guarantee rapid and quality delivery but at a cost. For example, it is well known that Agile projects need more skilled (and therefore, more expensive) developers. Some estimate the number of required senior developers is up to 50 percent of the team.

The following table presents some considerations that affect the technology selection:

Areas of consideration	Description
Are skilled developers available in the given timeframe?	• As mentioned previously, rapid quality delivery requires a bigger number of skilled resources. If the technology selected is brand new, it would not be easy to acquire all necessary resources.
What are the available strategies for resourcing?	• There are several strategies for resourcing in addition to in-house development: outsourcing (hiring another organization for the development and testing), co-sourcing (hiring another organization to help deliver the solution), in-house development using contract resources, and any mixture of the above.
Based on the delivery methodology, what environments have to be supported for the delivery?	Typically, there are several environments that are required to deliver a complex solution to the production stage. Some of them are as follows: • **Sandbox environment**: This is the environment where developers and architects can go wild. Anything can be tried, anything can be tested, the environment can be crashed every hour—and it should definitely be isolated from any other environment. • **Development environment**: Usually, every developer maintains his/her own development environment, on the local computer or virtualized. Development environments are connected to a source control system and often in a more sophisticated continuous integration system. • **Testing environments**: Depending on the complexity of the system, many testing environments can exist: for functional testing, for system integration testing, for user acceptance testing, or for performance testing. • **Staging or preproduction environment**: The purpose of this environment is to give the new components a final run. Performance or resilience testing can also be done in this environment. Ideally, it mimics a production environment. • **Production and disaster recovery environments**: These are target environments. • **Training environment**: This environment typically mimics the entire production environment or its components on a smaller scale. For example, the training environment does not require supporting all performance characteristics but requires supporting all system functionalities.

Areas of consideration	Description
Is environment virtualization considered?	• Virtualization is becoming more and more common. Today, this is a common approach in literally all medium and large organizations.
Is cloud development considered?	• Cloud development (supported by Microsoft Azure) might be considered if the organization does not want to deal with complex hardware and infrastructure, for example, when it does not have a strong IT department. Cloud development also gives you the advantage of quick deployment, since creating environments in Azure is often faster than procuring them within the organization.
What sets of development and testing tools are available?	• What programming languages are considered? • What third-party libraries and APIs are available? • What open source resources are available? Open source licensing models should be carefully evaluated before you consider using tools for commercial development. • What unit testing tools are available? • What plugins or rapid development tools are available?
Does development require integration with third-party (vendors, partners, and clients)?	• Will third-party systems test/stage environments be required for development? • Are these systems documented, and is this documentation available? • Is there a need for cooperation with third-party development or support teams?
In case of service-oriented architecture, what are the service versioning procedures?	• Can a service be upgraded to a new version seamlessly without breaking operations? • Can several versions of the same service operate simultaneously? • How do service consumers distinguish between the versions of the same service?
What is the service retirement procedure?	• Can a service be retired seamlessly without breaking operations? • How does it affect service consumers?
What service discovery mechanism is provided?	• Is a service registry available within the proposed technology? • Is an automated discovery available? • Is a standard discovery mechanism available, such as UDDI?

Solution operation aspects

Even after we have satisfied our design and implementation needs, we absolutely must consider the operational aspects of the proposed solution. Although the project delivery team inevitably moves on to other work after a successful deployment, the actual solution might remain in a production state for years. If we have a grand architecture that is constructed cleanly but is an absolute nightmare to maintain, then we should consider the project failed. There are many examples of solutions like this. Consider, for instance, a system that provides sophisticated calculations, requires high-end computers for this purpose, but has a small number of servers. If an architect suggests that the organization should utilize Microsoft System Center for monitoring, it would create a nightmare for the operations team. The System Center is a very large tool, even formal training for the team would take a week or two, and the learning curve would be very steep. And at the end of the day, maybe only 5 percent of the System Center capabilities will be utilized.

Operational concerns directly affect the solution design. These factors, often gathered through nonfunctional requirements, have a noticeable effect on the architecture of the entire system.

Areas of consideration	Description
Performance indicators provide essential information about the system behavior. Can they be captured and monitored?	• What exactly are the metrics that can be monitored (the throughput, latency, or number of simultaneous users)? • What are the delivery mechanisms (file, database, or SNMP)? • Can the data be exported in a third-party monitoring system (Microsoft SCOM, VMware Hyperic, or Splunk)?
Can the hardware and virtual machine health status be captured and monitored?	• What exactly are the metrics that can be monitored (the CPU usage, memory usage, CPU temperature, or disk I/O)? • What are the delivery mechanisms (file, database, or SNMP)? • Can the data be exported in a third-party monitoring system (Microsoft SCOM, VMware Hyperic, or Splunk)?

Areas of consideration	Description
In the case of a service-oriented architecture, can the service behavior be captured and monitored?	• What exactly are the metrics that can be monitored (# of requests for a given time interval, # of policy violations, # of routing failures, minimum, maximum, and average frontend response times, minimum, maximum, and average backend response times, and the percentage of service availability)? • What are the delivery mechanisms (file, database, or SNMP)? • Can the data be exported in a third-party monitoring system (Microsoft SCOM, VMware Hyperic, or Splunk)?
What kind of performance and health reports should be provided?	• Daily, weekly, or monthly? • Aggregated by server, by application, by service, or by operation?
What kind of notification system should be provided?	• What is the delivery mechanism (e-mail or SMS) used? • Is it integrated with a communication system such as Microsoft Exchange?
Are any dashboard and alerts required?	• Does the real-time monitor (dashboard) require data aggregation? • What kind of metric thresholds should be configurable?
What are the backup and restore procedures?	• What maintenance window (if any) is required for the backup? • Do the backup or restore procedures require integration with third-party tools?
What are the software upgrade procedures?	• What maintenance window (if any) is required for the version upgrade? • How does the upgrade affect the disaster recovery environment? • What are the procedures of license changes? Do they require any maintenance window?
What are the certificate maintenance procedures?	• How often are the certificates updated; every year, every three years, or never? • Does the certificate update require service interruption?

Applying the framework

So what do we do with all this information? In each of the "pattern chapters" of this book, you will find us using this framework to evaluate the use case at hand and proposing viable candidate architectures. We will have multiple candidate architectures for each use case and, based on which underlying product is the best fit, go down the path of explaining this specific solution.

So, how do we determine the best fit? As we evaluate each candidate architecture, we'll be considering the preceding questions and determining whether the product that underlies our solution meets the majority of the criteria for the use case. Using the next representation, we'll grade each candidate architecture in the four technology evaluation dimensions. The architecture that is the most compatible with the use case objectives will win.

In the next chapters, we will use the icons presented in the following table to indicate the overall evaluation of the technologies:

Icon	Description
	This icon will indicate that the technology has more pros than cons with regard to a specific dimension, such as organizational, design, implementation, or operations
	This icon will indicate that the technology does not fit with regard to a specific dimension

Summary

A common methodology to evaluate solution requirements against product capabilities will go a long way towards producing consistent, reliable results. Instead of being biased towards one product for every solution, or simply being unaware of a better match in another software offering, we can select the best software depending on its key capabilities for our client's solution.

In the next set of chapters, we'll introduce you to these core Microsoft application platform technologies and give you a taste as to what they are good at. While these primers are no more than cursory introductions to the products, they should give you the background necessary to understand their ideal usage scenarios, strengths, and weaknesses.

Later in this book, when we discuss different Microsoft applications and technologies, we shall build a taxonomy of Microsoft products, which will help architects navigate in the ocean of software tools.

2
The .NET Framework Primer

The **.NET Framework** (**.NET**) is the most popular technology for developing applications for the Microsoft Platform. .NET has been in existence for over a decade and, with the recent release of Version 4.5.1, is in its eighth major release. It is unarguably one of the most comprehensive development platforms in existence today.

The .NET Framework consists of a runtime environment called the **Common Language Runtime** (**CLR**), a standard library called the **Base Class Library** (**BCL**), and a complex hierarchy of higher-level libraries for developing applications that target Microsoft's mobile, desktop, video game console, server, cloud operating systems, products, and services. Third-party versions of the .NET Framework also exist for non-Microsoft platforms, including OS X, iOS, Linux, and Android (`http://xamarin.com`).

The CLR provides a virtual execution environment for all .NET applications; this includes a common type system, self-tuning memory management, optimized just-in-time compilation, exception handling, security, and debugging capabilities. As the name of the CLR implies, .NET applications can be written in one or more of nearly 40 programming languages (refer to the Wikipedia page at `http://en.wikipedia.org/wiki/List_of_CLI_languages`), though some may require additional runtime components, including the Dynamic Language Runtime. Volumes could be, and have been, written about the internals of the CLR and each of the aforementioned programming languages, so these topics will not be covered in any detail in this chapter.

A few lines of code (see the `DotNetStats` code sample) reveal that Version 4.5.1 of the .NET Framework includes some 261 assemblies that contain 627 namespaces; 11,627 classes; 2,297 value types; 1,012 interfaces; 1,929 enumerated types; 439,341 methods; and 113,075 properties. The aforementioned totals do not include private or internal types or members and are based on the .NET 4.5.1 Release Candidate.

Deciding which of these many APIs within the .NET Framework to use in an application or system can be a daunting task. The reason is not only the size of the Framework but also because the Framework often provides multiple mechanisms to deliver the same capability, with each mechanism having different strengths, weaknesses, and idiosyncrasies. There are a lot of well-written, comprehensive publications and materials that exhaustively enumerate and explain the use of every assembly, type, and method in the .NET Framework (and its sometimes-fuzzy periphery). There are also very detailed tomes dedicated to some of the more complex .NET APIs, for example, ASP.NET MVC, Windows Communication Foundation, and Windows Presentation Foundation. The intent of this chapter is not to attempt to replicate them, but to give software architects and developers a framework to evaluate and select the APIs from .NET that are appropriate for the applications that they are developing.

An evaluation framework for .NET Framework APIs

Understanding the .NET Framework in its entirety, including keeping track of the APIs that are available in various versions (for example, 3.5, 4, 4.5, 4.5.1, and so on, and platforms such as Windows 8, Windows Phone 8, and Silverlight 5) is a near impossible undertaking. What software developers and architects need is a high-level framework to logically partition the .NET Framework and identify the APIs that should be used to address a given requirement or category of requirements.

API boundaries in the .NET Framework can be a little fuzzy. Some logical APIs span multiple assemblies and namespaces. Some are nicely contained within a neat hierarchy within a single root namespace. To confuse matters even further, single assemblies might contain portions of multiple APIs. The most practical way to distinguish an API is to use the API's root namespace or the namespace that contains the majority of the API's implementation. We will point out the cases where an API spans multiple namespaces or there are peculiarities in the namespaces of an API.

Evaluation framework dimensions

The dimensions for the .NET Framework API evaluation framework are as follows:

- **Maturity**: This dimension indicates how long the API has been available, how long it has been part of the .NET Framework, and what the API's expected longevity is. It is also a measure of how relevant the API is or an indication that an API has been subsumed by newer and better APIs.

- **Productivity**: This dimension is an indication of how the use of the API will impact developer productivity. This dimension is measured by how easy the API is to learn and use, how well known the API is within the developer community, how simple or complex it is to use, the richness of the tool support (primarily in Visual Studio), and how abstract the API is, that is, whether it is declarative or imperative.

- **Performance**: This dimension indicates whether the API was designed with performance, resource utilization, user interface responsiveness, or scalability in mind; alternatively, it indicates whether convenience, ease of use, or code pithiness were the primary design criteria, which often comes at the expense of the former.

- **Availability**: This dimension indicates whether the API is available only on limited versions of the .NET Framework and Microsoft operating systems, or whether it is available everywhere that managed code is executed, including third-party implementations on non-Microsoft operating systems, for example, Mono on Linux.

Evaluation framework ratings

Each dimension of the API evaluation framework is given a four-level rating. Let's take a look at the ratings for each of the dimensions.

The following table describes the ratings for Maturity:

Rating	Glyph	Description
Emerging		This refers to a new API that was either added to the .NET Framework in the last release or is a candidate for addition in an upcoming release that has not gained widespread adoption yet. This also includes APIs that are not officially part of the .NET Framework.
New and promising		This is an API that has been in the .NET Framework for a couple of releases; it is already being used by the community in production systems, but it has yet to hit the mainstream. This rating may also include Microsoft APIs that are not officially part of .NET, but show a great deal of promise, or are being used extensively in production.

Rating	Glyph	Description
Tried and tested		This is an API that has been in the .NET Framework for multiple releases, has attained very broad adoption, has been refined and improved with each release, and is probably not going to be subsumed by a new API or deprecated in a later version of the Framework.
Showing its age		The API is no longer relevant or has been subsumed by a superior API, entirely deprecated in recent versions of .NET, or metamorphosed\merged into a new API.

The following table describes the ratings for Productivity:

Rating	Glyph	Description
Decrease		This is a complex API that is difficult to learn and use and not widely understood within the .NET developer community. Typically, these APIs are imperative, that is, they expose the underlying plumbing that needs to be understood to correctly use the API, and there is little or no tooling provided in Visual Studio. Using this API results in lowered developer productivity.
No or little impact		This API is fairly well known and used by the .NET developer community, but its use will have little effect on productivity, either because of its complexity, steep learning curve, and lack of tool support, or because there is simply no alternative API.
Increase		This API is well known and used by the .NET developer community, is easy to learn and use, has good tool support, and is typically declarative; that is, the API allows the developer to express the behavior they want without requiring an understanding of the underlying plumbing, and in minimal lines of code too.

Rating	Glyph	Description
Significant increase		This API is very well known and used in the .NET developer community, is very easy to learn, has excellent tool support, and is declarative and pithy. Its use will significantly improve developer productivity.

The following table describes the ratings for Performance and Scalability:

Rating	Glyph	Description
Decrease		The API was designed for developer productivity or convenience and will more than likely result in the slower execution of code and the increased usage of system resources (when compared to the use of other .NET APIs that provide the same or similar capabilities). Do not use this API if performance is a concern.
No or little impact		The API strikes a good balance between performance and developer productivity. Using it should not significantly impact the performance or scalability of your application. If performance is a concern, you can use the API, but do so with caution and make sure you measure its impact.
Increase		The API has been optimized for performance or scalability, and it generally results in faster, more scalable code that uses fewer system resources. It is safe to use in performance-sensitive code paths if best practices are followed.
Significant increase		The API was designed and written from the ground up with performance and scalability in mind. The use of this API will result in a significant improvement of performance and scalability over other APIs.

The following table describes the ratings for Availability:

Rating	Glyph	Description
Rare		The API is available in limited versions of the .NET Framework and on limited operating systems. Avoid this API if you are writing code that needs to be portable across all platforms.
Limited		This API is available on most versions of the .NET Framework and Microsoft operating systems. It is generally safe to use, unless you are targeting very old versions of .NET or Microsoft operating systems.
Microsoft only		This API is available on all versions of the .NET Framework and all Microsoft operating systems. It is safe to use if you are on the Microsoft platform and are not targeting third-party CLI implementations, such as Mono.
Universal		The API is available on all versions of .NET, including those from third parties, and it is available on all operating systems, including non-Microsoft operating systems. It is always safe to use this API.

The .NET Framework

The rest of this chapter will highlight some of the more commonly used APIs within the .NET Framework and rate each of these APIs using the Evaluation framework described previously.

The Base Class Library

The **Base Class Library** (**BCL**) is the heart of the .NET Framework. It contains base types, collections, and APIs to work with events and attributes; console, file, and network I/O; and text, XML, threads, application domains, security, debugging, tracing, serialization, interoperation with native COM and Win32 APIs, and the other core capabilities that most .NET applications need. The BCL is contained within the `mscorlib.dll`, `System.dll`, and `System.Core.dll` assemblies.

The mscorlib.dll assembly is loaded during the **CLR Bootstrap** (not by the **CLR Loader**), contains all nonoptional APIs and types, and is universally available in every .NET process, such as Silverlight, Windows Phone, and ASP.NET. Optional BCL APIs and types are available in System.dll and System.Core.dll, which are loaded on demand by the CLR Loader, as with all other managed assemblies. It would be a rare exception, however, when a .NET application does not use either of these two aforementioned assemblies since they contain some very useful APIs. When creating any project type in Visual Studio, these assemblies will be referenced by default.

For the purpose of this framework, we will treat all of the BCL as a logical unit and not differentiate the nonoptional APIs (that is, the ones contained within mscorlib.dll), from the optional ones. Despite being a significant subset of the .NET Framework, the BCL contains a significant number of namespaces and APIs. The next sections describe a partial list of some of the more notable namespaces/APIs within the BCL, with an evaluation for each.

The System namespace

The System namespace is both the root namespace for the .NET Framework and contains the basic building blocks of the .NET Framework, including System.Object, the mother of all types in .NET. It contains "built-in" types, such as System.Boolean, System.Int32, System.Int64, and System.String, and arrays of these types. It also contains interfaces, classes, and value types / structs that are used throughout the rest of the framework. The direct contents of the System namespace have been stable since the very early days of .NET; are very well known to developers; are highly optimized for performance and resource utilization; and are available on all platforms, though pruned-down a little in some cases.

The following table shows the evaluation of the System namespace:

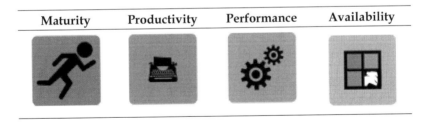

Maturity	Productivity	Performance	Availability

The System.Text namespace

The System.Text namespace contains APIs for converting one text encoding to another, primarily to and from Unicode—the encoding used in .NET strings.

System.Text also contains the StringBuilder class, which—unlike System.String—is mutable. Almost every time you modify a string value in .NET, it results in at least one new string being created. This leaves a lot of garbage around for the Garbage Collector to clean up. Using StringBuilder instead can, therefore, result in significant performance gain and a reduction in memory usage, particularly in string-processing-heavy workloads. The StringBuilder class should be used when strings are being concatenated or manipulated, and particularly when single strings are being modified in each iteration of one of more loops.

The System.Text API is very stable, very well known, was designed with performance in mind, and is available with all versions of .NET, on all platforms. The use of StringBuilder when creating strings is probably the most well-known .NET best practice.

The following table shows the evaluation of the System.Text namespace:

Maturity	Productivity	Performance	Availability

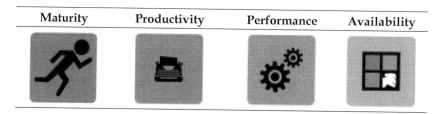

The System.IO namespace

System.IO contains APIs to read and write to and from streams, and perform operations on files and directories in the filesystem. It is the only game in town for doing low-level I/O operations (unless you want to resort to COM Interop or Platform Invoke). The majority of the APIs in this namespace are as old as the .NET Framework, and they are very stable, highly optimized, and very well understood. System.IO is also available in all of the versions of .NET, on all Microsoft platforms, and in all CLI implementations.

The following table shows the evaluation of the `System.IO` namespace:

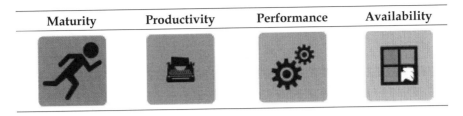

Maturity	Productivity	Performance	Availability

The System.Net namespace

The `System.Net` namespace contains APIs for communicating between network clients and servers. It includes support for several, relatively low-level protocols, including DNS, HTTP, FTP, SMTP, and MIME. It also includes a managed implementation of the Windows Socket API and APIs to perform peer-to-peer networking. Though `System.Net` has been part of .NET since its first release, newer APIs are available, including ASP.NET Web APIs and WCF, which hide many of the details of their communication with other devices over the network. Unless you need to do relatively low-level network operations, implement a custom, high-performance protocol, or do not control both client and server, you should consider using a higher-level API such as WCF.

The following table shows the evaluation of the `System.Net` namespace:

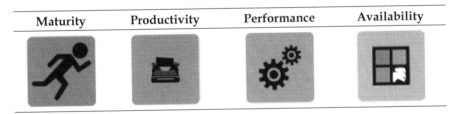

Maturity	Productivity	Performance	Availability

The System.Collections namespace

The `System.Collections` namespace contains nongeneric, non-thread-safe collections, for example, `ArrayList`, `Hashtable`, `Queue`, and `Stack`. These collections only contain objects, so the use of these collections requires implicit or explicit casting when removing or reading items, which requires relatively expensive type checking.

They have been around since the beginning of .NET, so they are very well known, stable, and have been optimized for performance, but they have been entirely subsumed by System.Collections.Generic, and more recently by System.Collections.Concurrent and System.Collections.Immutable, for cases where thread-safety is required.

The following code, from the PerformanceMeasurement sample, demonstrates the performance differences between generic and nongeneric collections. When comparing the performance (average elapsed CPU "ticks") of the methods mentioned in the following code, we see that the CreateAndEnumerateGenericList method performs two to three times faster than CreateAndEnumerateList and uses less memory:

```
private static int CreateAndEnumerateList(int maxValue)
{
    var list = new System.Collections.ArrayList(maxValue);
    foreach (var val in Enumerable.Range(0, maxValue))
    {
        list.Add(val);
    }
    var total = 0;
    foreach (int val in list) //implicit type conversion
    {
        total += val;
    }
    return total;
}


private static int CreateAndEnumerateGenericList(int maxValue)
{
    var list = new List<int>(maxValue);
    foreach (var val in Enumerable.Range(0, maxValue))
    {
        list.Add(val);
    }
    var total = 0;
    foreach (var val in list) //no type conversion required
    {
        total += val;
    }
    return total;
}
```

Unlike their generic counterparts in `System.Collections.Generic`, all of which implement the `IEnumerable<T>` interface, the collections in `System.Collections` do not work directly with **Language Integrated Query (LINQ)**. Therefore, unless you are targeting the .NET Framework with a language that does not support parametric polymorphism (generics) and does not provide its own collections, you should avoid using `System.Collections` and use `System.Collections.Generic` instead.

Downloading the example code

You can download the example code files for all Packt books you have purchased from your account at `http://www.packtpub.com`. If you purchased this book elsewhere, you can visit `http://www.packtpub.com/support` and register to have the files e-mailed directly to you.

The following table shows the evaluation of the `System.Collections` namespace:

Maturity	Productivity	Performance	Availability
🏃	⌨	(⚙)	⊞

The System.Collections.Generic namespace

The `System.Collections.Generic` namespace contains collections that are customized at the time of JIT compilation for the type that they are going to contain. Also in this namespace is the `IEnumerable<T>` interface; generic collections implement it and it is the interface that most LINQ methods operate on.

As was demonstrated earlier, these generic collections are more efficient than their nongeneric counterparts. The only thing to be aware of when using generic collections, in general, is that they result in an increase in overall code size, since the JIT has to compile a unique version of the code for each combination of types that are passed as arguments to the generic type or method. This is very rarely an issue in light of the other gains associated with using generics.

The collections contained within the System.Collections.Generic namespace are not thread-safe; if they are going to be accessed from multiple threads, the developer has to explicitly use synchronization primitives, for example, a **monitor** (used in the C# lock statement) or an instance of the ReaderWriterLockSlim class to ensure that the contents of the collections remain in a coherent state. As of Version 4.0, .NET includes the System.Collections.Concurrent API, which contains inherently thread-safe collections.

The collections in the System.Collections.Generic API are as mature, stable, and well understood as their nongeneric counterparts, but they provide significant performance benefits. They should be your default choice for collections if thread-safety is not an issue. This API is available with .NET 2.0 and above and on all platforms.

The following table shows the evaluation of the System.Collections.Generic namespace:

Maturity	Productivity	Performance	Availability

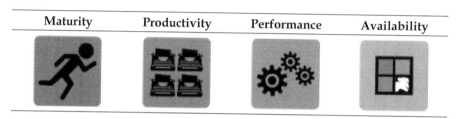

The System.Collections.Concurrent namespace

Multithreaded, task- and data-parallel programming has become very common in this age of multicore and many-core, but it still remains one of the more difficult, error-prone areas of software development. Microsoft has gone to great lengths to make the writing of multithreaded code easier, including adding **Task Parallel Library (TPL)** and **Parallel LINQ (PLINQ)** to .NET. To make the data parallelism part that much easier, it has also added a library of inherently thread-safe, generic collections and the building blocks to build your own. These collections are contained within the System.Collections.Concurrent namespace and include a lock-free, concurrent Queue and Stack and a number of other concurrent collection types that use lightweight locking internally.

Though this API was only added in .NET 4.0, it is already being used fairly extensively in new applications because of its obvious benefits in multithreaded code. Despite their novelty, using these APIs will save developers a lot of potential headaches and time related to debugging multithreaded **Heisenbugs** (http://en.wikipedia.org/wiki/Heisenbug).

Also, if used correctly, these collections will result in a significant performance gain when compared to using `System.Collections.Generic` collections with a thread synchronization primitive from `System.Threading`, for example, `Monitor` or `ReaderWriterLockSlim`.

The following table shows the evaluation of the `System.Collections.Concurrent` namespace:

Maturity	Productivity	Performance	Availability

Another approach to thread-safety, borrowed from **functional programming**, is to use read-only or immutable collections. Read-only collections have been available for a while in the `System.Collections.ObjectModel` namespace, but Microsoft has recently introduced **modifiable immutable collections** to .NET in the `System.Collections.Immutable` namespace.

The term "modifiable immutable collections" may seem to be a contradiction, but it is not; these collections can be modified, but those modifications are always local to the current thread and are, therefore, inherently thread-safe. From each thread's perspective, they have their own snapshot of the collection that they can safely operate on. Programming with immutable types turns out to be very useful in multithreaded programming, as the emerging functional programming fad has demonstrated.

Immutable collections are currently a **release candidate** (**RC**) and available via NuGet, but will probably be formally included in an upcoming release of .NET.

The System.Linq namespace

The `System.Linq` namespace contains the LINQ API. LINQ, introduced in .NET 3.5, brings some very useful features from functional programming to historical object-oriented languages (such as VB.NET and C#), and also adds novel query capabilities to all .NET languages. This includes multiple, handy extension methods that implement the `IEnumerable<T>` and `IQueryable<T>` interfaces, lambda expressions, and a generalized expression-processing mechanism that allows query expressions to be transformed into technology-specific queries at runtime, for example, T-SQL.

Using LINQ results in very pithy code, but developers should be aware that the convenience of using LINQ usually comes at a significant performance cost.

A demonstration of the potential performance impact of using LINQ has been included in the `PerformanceMeasurement` sample. This sample includes a number of tests that measure the performance of various approaches to iterating over a collection of collections using LINQ, a `foreach` loop, an incremented `for` loop, and a decremented `for` loop. Running the sample shows that the decremented `for` loop (which is the fastest) is about five times faster than the LINQ implementation. Though you may get slightly different numbers, they should still reveal the potential performance cost of using LINQ, so carefully consider this before using it in performance-sensitive code paths! There are some cases where using LINQ will result in faster code, but this is an exception rather than the rule.

When doing performance measurement, remember that, if a debugger is attached to a .NET process, *even a Release build*, the JIT compiler will not emit optimized code. Nonoptimized code will yield very different results. As an experiment, try running the Release build of the `PerformanceMeasurement` sample in Visual Studio with the *F5* key (**Start Debugging**) and then with *F7* (**Start without Debugging**), and notice the difference in the results produced.

The `System.Linq` namespace also includes the PLINQ API, which provides extension methods to perform concurrent operations over collections that implement `IEnumerable<T>`. PLINQ is implemented using the **Task Parallel Library** (**TPL**). This API is a very powerful tool to improve the performance of code using parallelization, but its mere use does not guarantee performance improvement; the naïve use of PLINQ or naïve data partitioning can significantly worsen performance.

LINQ is now an integral part of the .NET Framework and is used in many .NET, third-party, and custom APIs. It is mature and stable, and its use is almost ubiquitous in the .NET developer community, though a deep knowledge of its inner workings is rare. It is also available on most versions of .NET and on all platforms.

The following table shows the evaluation of the `System.Linq` namespace:

Maturity	Productivity	Performance	Availability

The System.Xml namespace

When the first version of the .NET Framework was released into the wild in 2002, XML was already the lingua franca of the Internet, so support for the human-readable markup language was woven deeply into the very fabric of .NET. The `System.Xml` namespace contains APIs that have been around since the original release, though they have been highly optimized over the many releases of .NET, and new capabilities have been added continually.

The popularity of XML has been slowly waning for some time. It used to be that developers were prepared to pay the relatively high cost of serialization to a human-readable format. It is now generally the volume of data that makes it practically unreadable by humans, rather than that data's formatting. That said, XML is going to be with us for a while; so if your application is XML heavy, then `System.Xml` contains the APIs that you need.

Though `System.Xml` is relatively well understood in the .NET developer community, provides highly performance optimized APIs, and is available everywhere, it is more imperative than declarative and does not shield the developer from the complexities and subtleties of XML, XSD, XSLT (a Turing-complete language in its own right), XPath, and the DOM. These subtleties can result in buggy code and reduced developer productivity. If developer performance is not a major concern, and developer productivity is key, then `System.Xml.Linq` provides XML APIs for you.

The following table shows the evaluation of the `System.Xml` namespace:

Maturity	Productivity	Performance	Availability

The System.Xml.Linq namespace

The `System.Xml.Linq` namespace contains the **LINQ to XML** API. This relatively new API, added in .NET 3.5, gives developers the power and expressiveness of LINQ when working with XML. This includes novel types and methods to create, query, manipulate, and transform XML. LINQ to XML also enables a very pithy syntax to Visual Basic to work with XML; the VB compiler now natively understands literal XML. Unfortunately, similar additions were not made to C#, perhaps because angle brackets were already being used for generics, though using `System.Xml.Linq` still results in significantly reduced code when compared to an equivalent implementation that just uses `System.Xml` APIs.

The following code snippet shows how simple is it to create a new XML document using the LINQ to XML API:

```
XDocument doc = new XDocument(
    new XDeclaration("1.0", "utf-16", "true"),
    new XElement("ParentNode",
        new XElement("ChildNode",
            new XAttribute("name", "child1"),
            new XElement("decription", "Child Node 1")),
        new XElement("ChildNode",
            new XAttribute("name", "child2"),
            new XElement("decription", "Child Node 2")),
        new XComment("Child Node 2 is special.")
        ));
```

This generates the following XML code when written to a string or file:

```
<?xml version="1.0" encoding="utf-16"?>
<ParentNode>
  <ChildNode name="child1">
```

```
      <decription>Child Node 1</decription>
    </ChildNode>
    <ChildNode name="child2">
      <decription>Child Node 2</decription>
    </ChildNode>
    <!--Child Node 2 is special.-->
  </ParentNode>
```

Creating the same document with `System.Xml.XmlDocument` would require twice the number of lines of code! It is also interesting to note that the LINQ to XML code is faster than the `System.Xml` equivalent.

Also, see the preceding code in the `XmlApiComparison` sample. Note how the structure of the code recapitulates the structure of the resulting XML document.

LINQ to XML is a relatively new API, but it has been very widely adopted and has proven itself in many real-world applications. It should significantly improve developer productivity because of its simplified syntax; though it may have a small negative impact on performance in some cases, this is well worth the other gains.

The following table shows the evaluation of the `System.Xml.Linq` namespace:

Maturity	Productivity	Performance	Availability

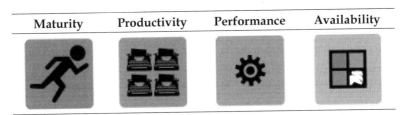

The System.Security.Cryptography namespace

It is almost a golden rule that one should strongly resist the temptation to write custom thread synchronization primitives or cryptography; one is bound to get it subtly wrong, and it generally leads to catastrophe. The `System.Security.Cryptography` namespace contains the **Cryptographic Services** API; if you need to do cryptographic operations, including hash, encrypt or decrypt data, or generate strong random numbers in your application, then you should definitely use this API.

`System.Security.Cryptography` is mature and stable, is relatively well known in the developer community, has been optimized for performance, and is available on all versions of .NET on all platforms. If you are targeting .NET for Windows Store Apps, then a subset of the API is available in the `Windows.Security.Cryptography` namespace.

The following table shows the evaluation of the `System.Security.Cryptography` namespace:

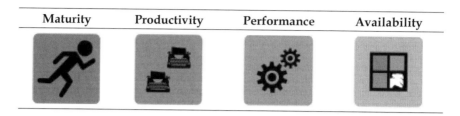

Maturity	Productivity	Performance	Availability

The System.Threading namespace

`System.Threading` is one of the most "dangerous" namespaces in the .NET Framework, and it contains everything you need to add concurrency (and hopefully performance and scalability) to your application or break it in completely mind-boggling ways. It contains classes to create your own threads, queue work to run on/in the thread pool, and synchronize activity across threads.

Multithreaded programming can be hard to get exactly right, and Microsoft has gone to great lengths to provide a number of abstractions to make data- and task-parallel programming easier and safer. So, unless you need fine-grained control of concurrency in your application, you should consider avoiding creating and managing your own threads directly using the APIs in the `System.Threading` root namespace; instead, make use of the Task Parallel Library, PLINQ, and `System.Collections.Concurrent` APIs.

The following table shows the evaluation of the `System.Threading` namespace:

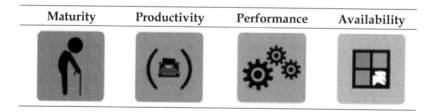

Maturity	Productivity	Performance	Availability

The System.Threading.Tasks namespace

The `System.Threading.Tasks` namespace contains the TPL API. It was introduced in .NET 4.0 and provides APIs that significantly simplify the tasks associated with writing multithreaded applications by hiding most of the messy details of task- and data-parallel programming.

The TPL API, which queues work for the thread pool under the covers, dynamically optimizes its concurrency based on the capabilities of the processor that the code is running on and automatically partitions data based on the number of threads available to operate on it. TPL is also extensible, so you can customize the scheduling and partitioning if you need to.

This new API will save developers a lot of headaches writing, debugging, and maintaining multithreaded code and, if used appropriately, it will result in significant performance gain. It is available in .NET 4.0 and above on all platforms, including Mono.

The following table shows the evaluation of the `System.Threading.Tasks` namespace:

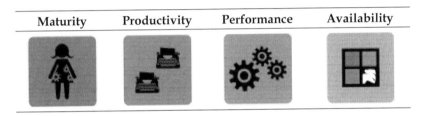

Maturity	Productivity	Performance	Availability

The System.ServiceProcess namespace

The .NET Framework offers a myriad of ways to host your code: a console application, a rich client application, Silverlight, **Windows Process Activation Service (WAS)**, **Internet Information Server (IIS)**, AppFabric (Windows Azure and Windows Server), or a Windows Service. If your application is long-running, its lifetime is tightly linked to its host operating system, it doesn't need the sophisticated services provided by a host such as IIS, and it doesn't need to interact with the desktop, then a good place to host it is in a Windows Service; the `System.ServiceProcess` namespace contains all of the APIs you need to do so.

The `System.ServiceProcess` API has been in .NET since the very beginning, so it is mature, stable, and very well known in the developer community. The API is relatively simple, so its use should result in improved developer productivity. Windows Services are a good place to host performance-critical code, but it is entirely the developer's responsibility to ensure that their service delivers the performance that they need. The `System.ServiceProcess` namespace is available in all versions of .NET on most platforms that include Mono but not Silverlight, Windows Phone, or .NET for Windows Store Apps.

The following table shows the evaluation of the `System.ServiceProcess` namespace:

Maturity	Productivity	Performance	Availability

The System.ComponentModel.Composition namespace

The `System.ComponentModel.Composition` namespace contains the **Microsoft Extensibility Framework** (**MEF**), which provides lightweight dependency injection for .NET applications. MEF, which was first introduced in .NET 4.0, was originally limited to an attribute-based programming model. However, as of .NET 4.5, you can either use the simple Import and Export attributes to inject instances based on type, contract, or both, or you can use an explicit API to inject types based on whatever criteria you choose.

Historically, MEF lacked some of the features of more mature dependency injection or **Inversion of Control** (**IoC**) containers, such as Castle Windsor, Ninject, or Unity; however, with the release of .NET 4.5, MEF has played some catch-up. Though MEF is a relatively new API, it has proven that it is ready to be used in real-world applications; since the .NET 4.5 release, it should be considered a mature API.

MEF adoption has been relatively limited to date, but many developers are familiar with similar dependency injection APIs and will understand MEF immediately. MEF has a negligible performance impact in most cases, and it improves developer productivity since it simplifies code and enforces **Separation of Concerns** (**SoC**). MEF is available in .NET 4.0 and above and on most platforms, including Mono. For .NET for Windows Store Apps applications, an explicit import of the `Microsoft.Composition` (`NuGet`) package is required to use MEF, and the API is located in the `System.Composition` namespace rather than `System.ComponentModel.Composition`.

The following table shows the evaluation of the `System.ComponentModel.Composition` namespace:

Maturity	Productivity	Performance	Availability

The System.ComponentModel.DataAnnotations namespace

The `System.ComponentModel.DataAnnotations` namespace, which was introduced in .NET 3.5, provides a primarily attribute-based API for adding metadata to types. One of its primary uses is to express validation criteria for properties that can be evaluated by consumers of that type at runtime. The API includes attributes to indicate required values, valid value ranges, string lengths, regular expressions, and even credit card and phone numbers. It also includes APIs to evaluate the validity of types that are decorated with these attributes.

ASP.NET, WPF, Silverlight, and Entity Framework use these data annotations in their validation controls and logic. You can also use `DataAnnotations` in your own framework, but you will have to wire up the validation yourself even though this is relatively simple.

This is a relatively mature, stable API, and many developers are familiar with its use. This API makes for very clean code and improved developer productivity since developers do not need to write or maintain complex validation logic for every type or use case. The use of this API should have a negligible impact on performance. The `DataAnnotations` API is available in .NET 3.5 and above on all platforms, including Mono.

The following table shows the evaluation of the `System.ComponentModel.DataAnnotations` namespace:

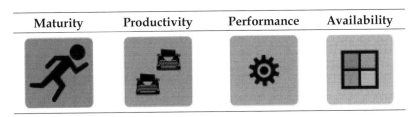

Maturity	Productivity	Performance	Availability

ADO.NET

Most computer programs are meaningless without appropriate data to operate over. Accessing this data in an efficient way has become one of the greatest challenges modern developers face as the datasets have grown in size, from megabytes, to gigabytes, to terabytes, and now petabytes, in the most extreme cases, for example, Google's search database is around a petabyte. Though relational databases no longer hold the scalability high ground, a significant percentage of the world's data still resides in them and will probably continue to do so for the foreseeable future. ADO.NET contains a number of APIs to work with relational data and data provider APIs to access Microsoft SQL Server, Oracle Database, OLEDB, ODBC, and SQL Server Compact Edition.

The System.Data namespace

Sometimes referred to as "classic ADO.NET", the `System.Data` namespace contains APIs to access data in relational databases. It is primarily an imperative API and exposes many of the underlying relational database concepts, including tables, columns, rows, relationships, T-SQL, and stored procedures.

Classic ADO.NET is very stable, is very well known in the developer community, has been highly optimized for performance, and is available in all versions of .NET on all platforms. The API does, however, require that a developer write custom code to transform relational data to and from objects; this can be very time-consuming and error-prone, and the resulting code can be brittle in the face of changes to the underlying relational schema. Therefore, it is costly to maintain. Classic ADO.NET still has it uses, particularly if high performance is a requirement, but in the vast majority of cases, developers should strongly consider using the Entity Framework API instead.

The following table shows the evaluation of the `System.Data` namespace:

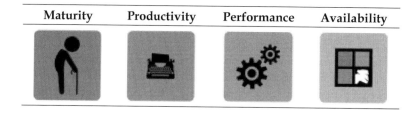

Maturity	Productivity	Performance	Availability

The System.Data.Entity namespace

The `System.Data.Entity` namespace contains the ADO.NET **Entity Framework (EF)** API. For many years, .NET developers had to write (or borrow) an application-specific **data access layer (DAL)** for their applications using "classic" ADO.NET and were forced to think about tables, relationships, T-SQL, and the relational algebra, while the rest of their application was composed of object-oriented types written in C# or VB.NET. Entity Framework is an API that hides all of the relational algebra from developers and allows them to think in terms of objects and LINQ queries.

Though third-party **Object-Relational (O/R)** mapping technologies have been around since the early days of .NET, Entity Framework was only released in Version 3.5 SP1 of the .NET Framework and has only achieved community acceptance and broad adoption fairly recently. Frameworks such as ASP.NET MVC use Entity Framework as their default data access technology as it is very convenient to store model data.

Entity Framework is now relatively mature, stable, and provides relatively high performance. It provides excellent tooling and makes creating new databases or using existing ones very simple, though low-level access is always available to mappings if required. EF is available in .NET 3.5 SP1 and above and on all platforms, including Mono.

 As of Version 6.0, Entity Framework has been made open source. It will ship out-of-band with the .NET Framework and will be available as a NuGet package. This change has necessitated a number of namespace changes.

The following table shows the evaluation of the `System.Data.Entity` namespace:

Maturity	Productivity	Performance	Availability

The System.Data.Linq namespace

The System.Data.Linq namespace contains the **LINQ to SQL** API. This API, was introduced in .NET 3.5, provides an alternate O/R mapping API to EF. Despite being very slightly older than Entity Framework (by only a single service pack) and becoming quite popular in the developer community, it has been almost entirely eclipsed by Entity Framework. Though not officially deprecated by Microsoft, no significant enhancements have been made to the API in recent releases of .NET. Despite how popular it has become, it is best avoided for new applications, given its uncertain future. Microsoft is making significant investments in Entity Framework, and it is now a far more mature and feature-rich API than LINQ to SQL; EF is clearly the better choice.

The following table shows the evaluation of the System.Data.Linq namespace:

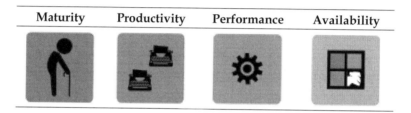

Maturity	Productivity	Performance	Availability

The System.Data.Services namespace

The System.Data.Services namespace contains the **Windows Communication Foundation (WCF)** Data Services API, which provides APIs to create, query, and consume data using the RESTful **Open Data (OData)** protocol. The OData protocol, which was originally designed by Microsoft, has become an OASIS standard protocol for data exchange on the Web. More can be read about the OData protocol at http://www.odata.org.

The WCF Data Services API, which used to be called ADO.NET Data Services, has been part of .NET since Version 3.5. Despite its standardization and growing adoption, particularly in the public sector, a deep knowledge of this API is relatively rare in the developer community. OData, and its .NET implementation, trade off performance for openness and accessibility, so don't expect lightning performance from this protocol and API. The OData client APIs are available on all recent versions of .NET and all Microsoft platforms. The server APIs are available on fewer Microsoft platforms, and neither client nor server is available for third-party CLI implementations; that said, a number of third-party, CLI-compliant OData Client APIs do exist.

If you simply want to expose your data via a RESTful API, and don't need OData, the ASP.NET Web API is probably a better choice.

The following table shows the evaluation of the System.Data.Services namespace:

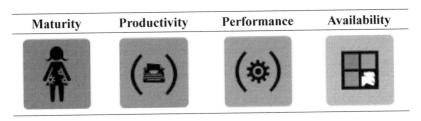

Maturity	Productivity	Performance	Availability

Windows Forms

Windows Forms (WinForms) was the original API for developing the **user interface (UI)** of Windows desktop applications with the .NET Framework. It was released in the first version of .NET and every version since then.

The System.Windows.Forms namespace

The WinForms API is contained within the System.Windows.Forms namespace. Though WinForms is a managed API, it is actually a fairly thin façade over earlier, unmanaged APIs, primarily Win32 and User32, and any advanced use of WinForms requires a good understanding of these underlying APIs. The advanced customizations of WinForms controls often require the use of the System.Drawing API, which is also just a managed shim over the unmanaged GDI+ API.

Many new applications are still developed using WinForms, despite its age and the alternative .NET user interface APIs that are available. It is a very well understood API, is very stable, and has been optimized for performance (though it is not GPU-accelerated like **WPF** or **WinRT**). There are a significant number of vendors who produce feature-rich, high-quality, third-party WinForms controls, and WinForms is available in every version of .NET and on most platforms, including Mono.

WinForms is clearly showing its age, particularly when its capabilities are compared to those of WPF and WinRT, but it is still a viable API for applications that exclusively target the desktop and where a sophisticated modern UI is not necessary.

The following table shows the evaluation of the `System.Windows.Forms` namespace:

Maturity	Productivity	Performance	Availability

Windows Presentation Foundation

Windows Presentation Foundation (**WPF**) is an API, introduced in .NET 3.0, for developing rich user interfaces for .NET applications, with no dependencies on legacy Windows APIs and with support for GPU-accelerated 3D rendering, animation, and media playback. If you want to play a video on a clickable button control on the surface of an animated, 3D rotating cube and the only C# code you want to write is the button click event handler, then WPF is the API for the job. See the `WPFSample` code for a demonstration.

The System.Windows namespace

The `System.Windows` namespace contains the Windows Presentation Foundation API. WPF includes many of the "standard" controls that are in WinForms, for example, `Button`, `Label`, `CheckBox`, `ComboBox`, and so on. However, it also includes APIs to create, animate, and render 3D graphics; render multimedia; draw bitmap and vector graphics; and perform animation. WPF addresses many of the limitations of Windows Forms, but this power comes at a price. WPF introduces a number of novel concepts that developers will need to master, including a new, declarative UI markup called **Extensible Application Markup Language** (**XAML**), new event handling, data binding and control theming mechanisms, and a variant of the **Model-view-controller** (**MVC**) pattern called **Model View ViewModel** (**MVVM**); that said, the use of this pattern is optional but highly recommended.

WPF has significantly more moving parts than WinForms, if you ignore the underlying native Windows APIs that WinForm abstracts. Microsoft, though, has gone to some lengths to make the WPF development experience easier for both UI designers and developers. Developers using WPF can choose to design and develop user interfaces using XAML, any of the .NET languages, or most often a combination of the two. Visual Studio and Expression Blend provide rich WYSIWYG designers to create WPF controls and interfaces and hide the complexities of the underlying XAML. Direct tweaking of the XAML is sometimes required for precise adjustments.

WPF is now a mature, stable API that has been highly optimized for performance—all of its APIs are GPU accelerated. Though it is probably not as well known as WinForms, it has become relatively well known within the developer community, particularly because Silverlight, which is Microsoft's platform for developing rich web and mobile applications, uses a subset of WPF. Many of the third-party control vendors who produce WinForm controls now also produce equivalent WPF controls. The tools for creating WPF applications, predominantly Visual Studio and Expression Blend, are particularly good, and there are also a number of good third-party and open source tools to work with XAML.

The introduction of WinRT and the increasingly powerful capabilities of web browser technologies, including HTML5, CSS3, JavaScript, WebGL, and GPU-acceleration, raise valid questions about the long-term future of WPF and Silverlight. Microsoft seems to be continuing to promote the use of WPF, and even WinRT supports a variant of the XAML markup language, so it should remain a viable API for a while.

The following table shows the evaluation of the `System.Windows` namespace:

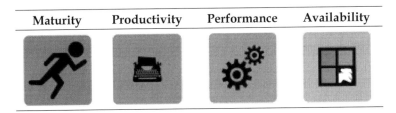

Maturity	Productivity	Performance	Availability

ASP.NET

The .NET Framework was originally designed to be Microsoft's first web development platform, and it included APIs to build both web applications and web services. These APIs were, and still are, part of the ASP.NET web development framework that lives in the `System.Web` namespace. ASP.NET has come a very long way since the first release of .NET, and it is the second most widely used and popular web framework in the world today (see `http://trends.builtwith.com/framework`).

The ASP.NET platform provides a number of complimentary APIs that can be used to develop web applications, including Web Forms, web services, MVC, web pages, Web API, and SignalR.

The System.Web.Forms namespace

The System.Web.Forms namespace contains the ASP.NET **Web Forms** API. The original goal of the design of this API, which has been in .NET since its very first release, was to give developers a familiar, symmetrical (across client and server) WYSIWYG web programming model. Web Forms is a predominantly server-side technology that used relatively expensive HTTP "post-backs", and more recently, less-expensive AJAX calls to communicate with the browser and the now-infamous View State to maintain state across round trips. Web Forms has evolved along with the Web and has been significantly optimized; despite its popularity, however, it is beginning to show its age. Modern web developers mostly prefer fine-grained control, clean abstraction, and high performance from their web frameworks rather than WYSIWYG web development and a symmetrical programming model.

Web Forms is a very well-known, stable, and mature API, with a substantial, third-party control ecosystem and excellent WYSIWYG design tools, so developers can be very productive with it. Web Forms is a good choice if you need to quickly create relatively-simple web applications, but if you are designing an application for web scale and performance that provides a high-fidelity experience on all devices, then Web Forms is probably not the best choice, and you should consider one of the other ASP.NET APIs.

The following table shows the evaluation of the System.Web.Forms namespace:

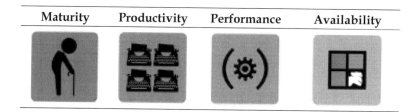

Maturity	Productivity	Performance	Availability

The System.Web.Mvc namespace

The System.Web.Mvc namespace contains the ASP.NET **MVC** API. The model-view-controller pattern is possibly the most ubiquitous software design pattern in use today, and it is very appropriate for developing maintainable and testable web applications. ASP.NET MVC is a strict MVC web application development framework for .NET that favors convention over code. This API will feel very familiar to Ruby on Rails developers, which is also based on the MVC pattern and uses conventions rather than code to improve developer productivity and reduce the complexity of the code.

ASP.NET MVC is a mature, stable API, and is relatively well understood.

ASP.NET has also recently been made open source, though it is expected that Microsoft will continue to enhance and optimize it, given its emerging popularity.

The following table shows the evaluation of the `System.Web.Mvc` namespace:

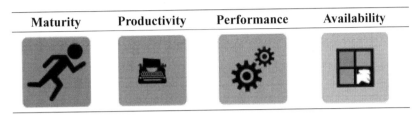

The System.Web.WebPages namespace

The `System.Web.WebPages` namespace contains the relatively new ASP.NET **Web Pages** API. The Web Pages API provides a simplified programming model that mixes markup and code in a single file using the **Razor** syntax. This API will feel familiar to developers who have worked with PHP, but it leverages the power of the ASP.NET platform and Razor syntax. The WebPages API is available on all platforms that support ASP.NET, including Mono.

The following table shows the evaluation of the `System.Web.WebPages` namespace:

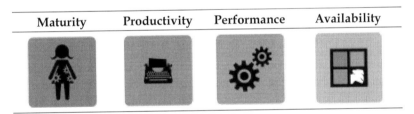

 As of Version 4.5, the `System.Json` namespace is included in .NET. This namespace includes APIs to convert to and from the **JSON** format and query JSON documents with LINQ.

The System.Web.Services namespace

The System.Web.Services namespace contains the original ASP.NET **Web Services** API. Despite being an important API in the first few versions of .NET (.NET was sold as the first web services platform, after all), and despite the fact that you can still add new ASMX services to an ASP.NET project in Visual Studio 2013, this API is well beyond its "use by" date, and it has been entirely subsumed by WCF; its use should generally be avoided (other than to make simple AJAX services for Web Forms applications, perhaps). If you need to create sophisticated, SOAP-based web services, then you should use WCF, and if you need to create lightweight REST services, then you should use the ASP.NET Web API.

The following table shows the evaluation of the System.Web.Services namespace:

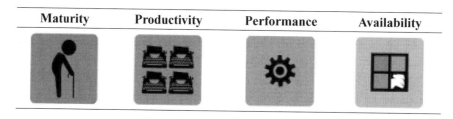

The Microsoft.AspNet.SignalR namespace

Though technically not part of the .NET Framework yet, **SignalR** is a promising new technology that is part of ASP.NET and deserves a mention here. SignalR is an ASP.NET API for real-time communication between web servers and clients. The API provides a robust implementation of long polling and other newer technologies to send web notifications, including WebSockets.

The following table shows the evaluation of the Microsoft.AspNet.SignalR namespace:

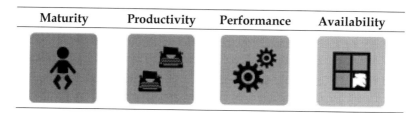

Windows Communication Foundation

One of the major selling points of the first release of .NET was that the platform had support for web services baked in, in the form of ASP.NET Web Services. Web Services have come a very long way since SOAP was invented in 1998 and the first release of .NET, and WCF has subsumed the limited capabilities of ASP.NET Web Services with a far richer platform. WCF has also subsumed the original .NET Remoting (`System.Runtime.Remoting`), MSMQ (`System.Messaging`), and Enterprise Services (`System.EnterpriseServices`) APIs.

The System.ServiceModel namespace

The root namespace for WCF is `System.ServiceModel`. This API includes support for most of the WS-* web services standards and non-HTTP or XML-based services, including MSMQ and TCP services that use binary or **Message Transmission Optimization Mechanism** (**MTOM**) message encoding.

Address, Binding, and Contract (**ABC**) of WCF are very well understood by the majority of the developer community, though deep technical knowledge of WCF's inner workings is rarer. The use of attributes to declare service and data contracts and a configuration-over-code approach makes the WCF API highly declarative, and creating sophisticated services that use advanced WS-* capabilities is relatively easy. WCF is very stable and can be used to create high-performance distributed applications. WCF is available on all recent versions of .NET, though not all platforms include the server components of WCF. Partial support for WCF is also available on third-party CLI implementations, such as Mono.

REST-based web services, that serve relatively simple XML or JSON, have become very popular, and though WCF fairly recently added support for REST, these capabilities have now evolved into the ASP.NET Web API.

You can read a lot more about WCF in a later chapter of this book.

The following table shows the evaluation of the `System.ServiceModel` namespace:

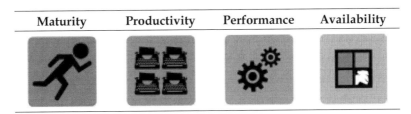

Maturity	Productivity	Performance	Availability

Windows Workflow Foundation

Windows Workflow Foundation (WF) is a workflow framework that was introduced in .NET 3.0, and that brings the power and flexibility of declarative workflow or business process design and execution to .NET applications.

The System.Activities namespace

The `System.Activities` namespace contains the Windows Workflow Foundation API. WF includes a workflow runtime, a hosting API, a number of basic workflow activities, APIs to create custom activities, and a workflow designer control, which was originally a WinForms control but is now a WPF control as of .NET 4.0. WF also uses a variant of the same XAML markup, which WPF and WinRT use, to represent workflows; that said, an excellent designer, hosted by default in Visual Studio, should mean that you never have to directly modify the XAML.

The adoption of the first few versions of the WF API was limited, but WF was completely rewritten for .NET 4.0, and many of the shortcomings of the original version were entirely addressed. WF is now a mature, stable, best-of-breed workflow API, with a proven track record. The previous implementation of WF is still available in current versions of the .NET Framework, for migration and interoperation purposes, and is in the `System.Workflow` namespace.

WF is used by SharePoint Server, Windows Server AppFabric, Windows Azure AppFabric, Office 365, Visual Studio Team Foundation Server (MSBuild), and a number of other Microsoft products and services. Windows Server AppFabric and Windows Azure AppFabric enable a new class of scalable SOA server and cloud application called a **Workflow Service**, which is a combination of the capabilities of WCF and WF. WF has a relatively small but strong following within the .NET developer community. There are also a number of third-party and open source WF activity libraries and tools available.

Though applications composed using workflows typically have poorer performance than those that are implemented entirely in code, the flexibility and significantly increased developer productivity (particularly when it comes to modifying existing processes) that workflows give you are often worth the performance price. That said, Microsoft has made significant investments in optimizing the performance of WF, and it should be more than adequate for most enterprise application scenarios.

Though versions of WF are available on other CLI platforms, the availability of WF 4.x is limited to Microsoft platforms and .NET 4.0 and higher. The evaluation of the System.Workflow namespace shown in the following table is for the most recent version of WF (the use of versions of WF prior to 4.0 is not recommended for new applications):

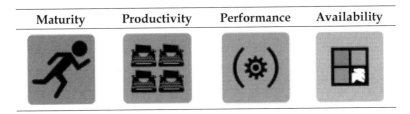

Maturity	Productivity	Performance	Availability

Summary

There is more to the .NET Framework than has been articulated in this primer; it includes many useful APIs that have not even been mentioned here, for example, System.Media, System.Speech, and the Windows Identity Framework. There are also a number of very powerful APIs developed by Microsoft (and Microsoft Research) that are not (yet) officially part of the .NET Framework; for example, Reactive Extensions, Microsoft Solver Foundation, Windows Azure APIs, and the new .NET for Windows Store Apps APIs are worth looking into.

In the next chapter, we will provide an overview of the many capabilities and features of Microsoft SQL Server — Microsoft's Relational Database Management System.

3
The SQL Server Primer

In 1970, when E. F. Codd came up with his seminal work *A Relational Model of Data for Large Shared Data Banks*, his approach sounded like a purely theoretical one. Computers were not powerful enough to implement the relational database concepts in a manner that would suffice the needs of the consumers. However, in a few years, different corporations, such as IBM and Oracle, started building relational database management systems, and in a few more years, Oracle (known as Relational Software at that time) came up with the first RDBMS in 1979.

Microsoft jumped on to the bandwagon significantly later, after 10 more years had passed, partnering with Sybase, and developed their original version of SQL Server. In the beginning of 1990s, Microsoft negotiated exclusive rights to the SQL Server versions written for Windows; in 1998, they came up with SQL Server v7, which was the first version written in-house.

Over the years, Microsoft SQL Server has undergone a significant transformation from being simply a database management system to a full-blown development platform with a rich set of capabilities. Started as a relational database management system, SQL Server now has full-text, spatial, and XML support as well as the ability to store unstructured data, such as documents and images, on the filesystem. Assuming that almost all significant projects would require data in some format, one may argue that SQL Server should always be on an architect's list of development tools, besides .NET.

SQL Server also plays an important role as a foundational piece of software for many other Microsoft server products. BizTalk, SharePoint, Team Foundation Server, Dynamics CRM, and others use SQL Server as a reliable data engine.

Hundreds of books have been written on Microsoft SQL Server, but we are not going to regurgitate that information. In this chapter, we'll prove that SQL Server is indeed a powerful development platform. We'll discuss its capabilities, which will help us as architects to take proper decisions in the future.

What is included in SQL Server 2012?

SQL Server 2012 is the latest released commercial version; however, SQL Server 2014 **Community Technology Preview 2 (CTP2)** was also available at the time of writing this book. We shall base our discussion and examples on SQL Server 2012, but we'll provide a brief overview of the new capabilities available in SQL Server 2014 at the end of the chapter.

SQL Server editions

Each time Microsoft comes up with a new version of SQL Server, there are several editions of it with different capabilities and often confusing licensing models. SQL Server 2012 is definitely not an exception. There are three principal editions (Enterprise, Business Intelligence, and Standard), one specialized web edition, and two breadth editions (Developer and Express). All the editions come in 64-bit and 32-bit flavors.

The Developer edition of SQL Server traditionally has all the functionalities of the Enterprise edition but is licensed for development and testing only.

SQL Server components and tools

The following table provides a brief description of the different SQL Server components and tools:

Components	Description
Database Engine	Database Engine is the core service used to store, process, and secure data. It provides features such as replication and full-text searches, and tools to manage relational and XML data. It also has the Data Quality Services, introduced in the 2012 version. SQL Server Service Broker, also a part of Database Engine, did not become very popular since its introduction in SQL Server 2005 and was not updated much in the 2012 version.
Analysis Services	**SQL Server Analysis Services (SSAS)** is a server-based platform used to develop and manage **online analytical processing (OLAP)** and data mining applications.
Reporting Services	**SQL Server Reporting Services (SSRS)** is a server-based platform used to develop and manage interactive, tabular, graphical, or free-form reports from relational or XML-based data sources. SSRS also provides the ability to develop ad hoc reports.

Components	Description
Integration Services	**SQL Server Integration Services (SSIS)** is a server-based platform used to develop and manage data integration and workflow applications. One of the main uses of SSIS is the development of the **extract, transform, load (ETL)** applications in order to support data warehousing and data migration. From our standpoint, the significance of SSIS (especially for integration solutions) is such that we have devoted a separate chapter to SSIS.
Master Data Services	**Master Data Services (MDS)** plays a significant role in data integration projects and is also used to synchronize, validate, and sanitize data as well as to remove duplicates. Therefore, MDS reduces redundancies across all data processing applications.

The SQL Server tools are described in the following table:

Tools	Description
SQL Server Management Studio	SQL Server Management Studio (sometimes abbreviated as SSMS) is an integrated environment used to develop, manage, access, and configure components of SQL Server. Database development can be done using Visual Studio. However, note that SQL Server Management Studio provides a variety of other features, especially to access, configure, and manage databases.
SQL Server Configuration Manager	SQL Server Configuration Manager is a tool that provides basic configuration management for the SQL Server services. It is also used to configure network protocols and to manage the network connectivity configurations for client computers.
SQL Server Profiler	SQL Server Profiler is a tool that captures the SQL Server events in a trace file. Later, the trace file, via a graphical user interface, is used for analysis and troubleshooting. Using SQL Server Profiler, one can monitor an instance of Database Engine; in particular, one can analyze the SQL Server code, monitor performance, or audit security.
Database Engine Tuning Advisor	Database Engine Tuning Advisor is a tool that, via a graphical user interface or the dta command prompt utility, examines how queries are processed and helps to create optimal sets of indexes, indexed views, and partitions.
Data Quality Services Client	Data Quality Services, introduced in SQL Server 2012, comprises a server and a client part. They provide the ability to perform data cleansing operations as well as to centrally monitor various activities performed during these operations.

Tools	Description
SQL Server Data Tools	**SQL Server Data Tools** (**SSDT**), introduced in SQL Server 2012, provides an integrated development environment to build Analysis Services, Reporting Services, and Integration Services. SSDT is also a feature of Visual Studio (starting with VS 2010), used to develop database projects.
Connectivity Components	These consist of components, responsible for communication between clients and servers, and network libraries for DB-Library, ODBC, and OLE DB.

SQL Server 2012 abilities

As discussed in *Chapter 1, Solution Decision Framework*, solutions architecture deals a lot with "abilities": availability, reliability, manageability, and many others, coming primarily from nonfunctional requirements. Well, it's certainly arguable—for a developer, availability may sound completely nonfunctional, but a service center operator will most likely have a different point of view. Architects should keep this in mind and address different user groups in different ways.

Let's see how SQL Server 2012 addresses some of those abilities.

High availability

Traditionally, high availability in SQL Server had been achieved by database mirroring and log shipping. The downside of database mirroring was the necessity to deal with databases individually if the solution required several databases.

SQL Server 2012 introduced the **AlwaysOn** availability groups that provide all the benefits of database mirroring and a number of new ones, for example, multiple database failover, built-in compression and encryption, flexible failover policy, PowerShell automation, dashboards, automatic page repairs, several failover modes, active secondary replicas, and many others.

An availability group is a container that defines a set of user databases—availability databases—to failover as a single unit and a set of availability replicas to host copies of each availability database.

AlwaysOn availability groups will eventually replace database mirroring in the future versions of SQL Server.

Manageability

SQL Server Management Studio is the principal tool that enables the database management capabilities of SQL Server. Originally released with SQL Server 2005 almost 10 years ago, Management Studio became an essential component of the everyday life of database administrators. Today, many solutions rely on this component instead of building a specialized database management solution.

In SQL Server 2012, a few small changes have been made to the dynamic management views, Transact-SQL debugging and IntelliSense, startup procedures, and the usage of PowerShell. A detailed description of the SQL Server PowerShell components, tasks, and cmdlets can be found at `http://technet.microsoft.com/en-us/library/hh245198.aspx`.

 A **cmdlet** (command-let) is a single-feature command in PowerShell. One can recognize cmdlets by their name format—a verb and a noun separated by a dash. `Invoke-Sqlcmd` or `Encode-Sqlname` are examples of the SQL Server PowerShell cmdlets.

Database Recovery Advisor is a new feature of SQL Server that simplifies the restoration of databases, improves user experience, and, in general, makes the entire process more manageable.

Programmability and maintainability

Since the days of Edgar F. Codd, SQL has been the main language for relational database development. In 1986, it became an ANSI standard and has been evolving since then. Note that the pronunciation of SQL in the name of the language and that in SQL Server are different. The language is pronounced as "es-que-el," which is declared by the standard, but in SQL Server, the same word is pronounced as "sequel."

Microsoft's version of SQL is called **Transact-SQL (T-SQL)** and it is not fully ANSI-compliant. Architects have to be aware of this fact if solutions require that you generate SQL statements automatically to further process SQL Server.

Sometimes, .NET developers, with a lot of object-oriented development experience, find it difficult to start coding in SQL. Database development uses a different paradigm and requires that you look at the task from a different perspective. However, development in T-SQL is no less powerful or productive as development in C# or VB.NET.

Over the years, there has been some deviation from the original relational database development paradigm and some convergence between the SQL and .NET languages, for example, the ability to use XML data or the TRY-CATCH blocks in SQL. In SQL Server 2012, the THROW statement has been finally added to the TRY-CATCH blocks.

In SQL Server 2005, Microsoft introduced SQL **Common Language Runtime (CLR)** — a component that integrates a SQL Server solution with .NET. This technology allows you to perform limited development in SQL Server using the .NET languages such as C# or VB.NET. For this development, SQL Server 2012 requires .NET Version 4.0 and not Version 4.5.

The new **FileTables** feature of SQL Server 2012 built on top of the file streams enables the integration of application storage and data management components. It provides SQL Server services (including full-text search and semantic search) over unstructured data along with easy policy management and administration. FileTables are special tables in SQL Server that hold files and documents and are accessible from Windows applications as they are stored in the filesystem.

Significant enhancements were made to the capability of text search. **Statistical Semantic Search** is a new feature of SQL Server 2012 that enables you to find key phrases in a document, identify similar or related documents, and identify the key words or phrases that make these documents related. Full-text search was updated in the part of the word breakers and stemmers, and a property search was added.

> We are familiar with the properties of Microsoft Office documents. For example, *Author*, *Title*, or *Company* are valid properties of Word documents.

Spatial features have been significantly updated in SQL Server 2012. New subtypes, methods, and aggregates have been introduced. One of the changes that we, as architects, have been waiting a while for is a significant improvement of performance characteristics.

Another improvement is related to pagination. In the previous versions, if a developer wanted to apply pagination to large result sets, they had to be creative. In SQL Server 2012, pagination can be implemented using OFFSET and FETCH.

Scalability

In terms of scaling out, SQL Server 2012 supports up to 15,000 partitions versus 1,000 in the previous versions.

In terms of scaling up, it enables scalability up to 320 logical processors and 4 TB of memory with Windows Server 2012. It also allows SQL Server virtual machines to use up to 64 virtual processors and 1 TB of memory.

Performance

Performance considerations have always been the key in SQL Server solution development. Performance analysis and the consequent optimization can be achieved by means of SQL Server Management Studio and Resource Governor.

The new, powerful columnstore index feature optimizes the way data columns are stored within pages. Instead of being split between pages, when a columnstore index is selected, the data from one column is stored on the same page. According to Microsoft, this improves the data warehouse query performance by hundreds to thousands of times in some cases.

Another important new feature is the **selective XML index**. XML indexes based on the entire content of XML data were hard to use in the previous versions of SQL Server because of the huge size of the index tables and the resultant performance degradation. A selective XML index allows developers to index the XML data using XPath definitions relative to the queries performed on the XML data. This minimizes the size of the index and improves the database performance significantly.

Security

Microsoft has been constantly improving the security of SQL Server at all levels, from data encryption to the policy-based management.

SQL Server 2012 did not bring dramatic changes with regard to security; rather, there were small improvements in most security-related areas, that is, new permissions and new role management, audit enhancements, hashing algorithms, certificate keys, service master key and database master key encryption, and certificates. You can find the details in the presentation at `http://technet.microsoft.com/en-us/video/whats-new-in-sql-server-2012-database-engine-management-and-security`.

Data quality

In data warehousing, a lot of time and effort is spent building transformations that take raw, "dirty" data from different sources and transform it into a more appropriate format. What if the data comes from many different sources and data cleansing has to be applied to each ETL package?

One of the new, powerful features introduced in SQL Server 2012 is **Data Quality Services (DQS)**. DQS assists data administrators to build a knowledge base that can be used later for data cleansing. The knowledge base helps to define validation and correction rules. Once defined, the rules can be used against the database.

Building the payroll processor application

Over the next few pages, we shall present some essential aspects of SQL Server development. We'll see how we can work with different data sources, structure them, and present them through the report engine. We'll see how we can display the data using the web user interface.

Let's analyze the following use case and see how we can use SQL Server to implement our solution.

Use case

Reliable Payroll Pro Inc. (RPP) is a payroll processor for a large number of small- to medium-sized companies. The core business workflow may be described in the following steps:

1. Collect the employee and payroll data from the client.
2. Process data to produce the following:
     ◦ Tax forms and checks
     ◦ Payroll checks and direct deposit requests
     ◦ Client reports
3. Send tax forms and payments to the respective government agencies.
4. Send payroll checks to the employees and submit direct deposits.
5. Bill the client for the following:
     ◦ Payments issued on the client's behalf
     ◦ RPP services

Recently, RPP started experiencing a significant growth in its client base due to economic downturn, of all things. Many medium-sized businesses found that hiring a professional services company for payroll management is much cheaper than keeping extra full-time accountants in-house.

To keep up with the demand and restrain itself from hiring more employees, RPP is looking for a solution to automate major tasks in its business workflow. The most challenging task is data collection. RPP's clients come from a variety of industries and use different accounting systems. Most of them have no IT departments and would be unwilling to participate in any significant data integration projects. In other words, it is up to RPP to decide how they want to handle the various data formats they receive.

RPP does its business in several US states and plans to expand further. This presents another challenge, as different states, counties, and municipalities require you to file a variety of tax forms. The solution should be able to produce these forms as output. It also needs to be flexible enough, so that new forms can be added with relative ease to the system.

RPP also wants to automate as many of their tasks as possible. It wants to be able to set up schedules for the delivery of data files, forms, and reports to its employees, clients, financial institutions, and government agencies.

RPP is also looking to have a web portal for its clients. It should deliver customized reports to its clients, both on schedule and on demand.

Yet another requirement, as with any financial system, is auditing. RPP is required by law to keep all of its data in order to be able to present the source of any transaction it issues on behalf of its clients.

It is also worth mentioning that RPP has no IT department of its own or IT project experience. It has to rely on hired consultants to build the system, maintain it, and develop any future upgrades or additions.

As banks and government agencies are increasingly exchanging data in the digital form, rather than on paper, RPP is looking for a system that would allow exporting the data in a variety of formats. Ultimately, the company would want to train its employees to create new data formats as a system output on an "as needed" basis.

Last but not least, RPP is keen to keep up with present and future technologies. It wants to make sure that the system will be easy to expand and accommodate new technologies, without restructuring the core platform.

Key requirements

If we try to translate the previously mentioned scenario into a language that is appropriate for an IT solution, we will end up with two lists of requirements—functional and nonfunctional. Let's start with the functional requirements to examine what our solution should be able to do.

Functional requirements – first draft

The first draft of the functional requirements is a result of a few workshops with business stakeholders. The requirements are stated as follows:

1. Ability to import client payroll data of various formats and store it in the system.
2. Ability to process client payroll data and produce payroll checks.
3. Ability to process client payroll data and produce tax forms.
4. Ability to process client payroll data and produce reports for clients.
5. Ability to process client payroll data and RPP employees' data (hours of work for each client) as well as generate bills to clients.
6. Ability to export data out of the system in various formats as required.
7. Ability to present reports to the clients through a secure web interface.
8. Ability to deliver data output and reports on schedule.
9. To store unmodified source data for audit purposes.

These functional requirements are somewhat simplified even for the first draft. Typically, the stakeholders would provide more details, but our focus now is on the process.

Requirements analysis

What is the story emerging here? We need to import data in many different formats and process it. We shouldn't create a separate data processing program for each client's data format; we want to make the data processing generic. We also need reports. Our system should consist of the following major components:

- **The data conversion component**: This will import the client's data and convert it into the tables designed to suit RPP purposes. Can the component be implemented using the BizTalk Server? Or, will a number of SSIS packages suffice? Let's decide later. At the moment, we are just gathering requirements.

- **The data processing component**: This component will process the converted data to perform a number of functions. It will implement the required business rules, that is, calculate taxes and other deductions for each employee. It will fill up tax forms, print checks, and prepare data for reports. We can code it in C# or VB.NET; again, let's decide later.

- **The reporting component**: We need to produce reports; therefore, we need a reporting engine. This component should come with a web interface since RPP wants to expose the UI to its clients.

- **The user interface**: The system needs a user interface for RPP employees; they should be able to execute system functions. Since RPP wants to keep up with modern technology, our first choice would be a web interface. Desktop interfaces are being phased out, aren't they?

Did we cover everything? No, we are missing data output, which is mentioned in the functional requirements as well. We'll add this function to the data processing component. It will fill up tax forms, process them, and generate data output.

What about data storage? In the Microsoft world, our choices are limited. It simply cannot be a filesystem; our data requires some structure. Can you use MS Access or FoxPro? FoxPro is well on its way to retirement. Access does not have the tools and capabilities required for data conversion and for seamless integration with many different data sources. So, the choice is simple: SQL Server.

Let's look into data conversion. If we decide to use BizTalk, RPP will also need BizTalk programmers for data conversion. Also, they will need programmers to design reports. Hopefully, we can find consultants who can do all of this. RPP will need to get licenses for BizTalk and SQL Server. Or, maybe just SQL Server if we stick with SSIS packages for data integration.

Great! We have a picture emerging now. It looks like we can cover all the functional requirements with a solution such as this. It will surely be robust and scalable, as we will use the latest technologies. We just need to find the right resources for the job. Oh and there's a minor detail. We need to put a project plan together, come up with the cost estimate, and sell it to RPP. This shouldn't be a problem, we think.

Somehow, we haven't decided which reporting technology we will use, as yet. Ok, let's look at that now. We can use SAP reporting tools (also known as Crystal Reports, of course), or we can use SSRS. SSRS comes with SQL Server, so the total cost of licensing is lower. However, Crystal Reports have been in the market way longer. We think that this is a mature technology that has more features. It also has a web reporting engine. However, Crystal Reports will require developers with specific knowledge. Therefore, SSRS is our choice. For our needs, it has just enough capabilities.

See how easy it is to put a solution together if one knows enough about the technologies that can do the job. Should the system interface be ASP.NET WebForms or ASP.NET MVC?

Wait a second. We were just about to start the requirements analysis, and somehow, we ended up designing a solution and throwing technologies around. Let's roll back a little and look at our functional requirements list one more time.

What strikes the eye is that points 2 to 5 start with "Ability to process client data." Maybe we can consolidate these? Let's make a single list of the outcomes of that data processing. These are checks, tax forms, reports to clients, and bills to clients.

What do we need to produce these? We shall generate some data. Namely, payroll and deductions data and RPP's own services data (employee work hours). We also want to print this data on paper. This will produce checks, tax forms, and reports to clients. Can checks and tax forms also be printed as reports? Surely they can. Can client bills be reports? Just as well. So, we can say that the system will generate data according to the business rules and produce reports.

Our requirements list just got shorter. Let's rewrite it.

Functional requirements – second draft

To gather more specific requirements, we decided to conduct targeted interviews with business stakeholders rather than conduct workshops. The requirements thus observed are as follows:

1. Ability to import client payroll data of various formats and store it in the system.
2. Ability to process data (client payroll data and RPP data) and generate data according to business rules.
3. Ability to produce reports. The reports will include payroll checks, tax forms, and reports for clients as well as bills to clients.
4. Ability to export data out of the system in various formats as required.
5. Ability to present reports to the clients through a secure web interface.
6. Ability to deliver data output and reports on schedule.
7. To store unmodified source data for audit purposes.

Well, it looks so much simpler now.

Let's look at points 1 and 6. If we import client data and store it in the system, can we keep the unmodified version for audit? Yes, we can. We don't have to convert the data to the output format immediately. As a best practice, we are going to have an area where the source data will be kept in the raw (initial) format.

When we think about data processing requirements, we find that we don't need to verify or sanitize the source data. The requirements don't say that RPP must check whether the data is correct and fix errors. It is the RPP clients' responsibility to supply accurate information about their employees. RPP will use this data as a source and generate a different set of data as an output, according to the business rules. Then, it will use the output dataset as the basis for reports.

Let's try to depict this system workflow in the following diagram:

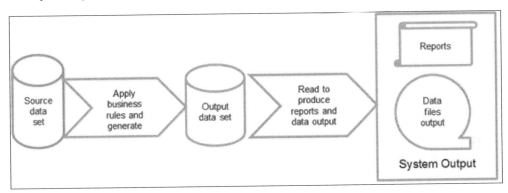

You may notice that we have combined **Reports** and **Data files output** in the same box. Well, the system performs the same operation to produce both. It presents data, that's it. No data modification takes place to either produce reports or generate the data file.

Nonfunctional requirements

We started analyzing the functional requirements by keeping SQL Server in mind.

Now, let's look at the following system that uses the NFRs that we discussed in *Chapter 1, Solution Decision Framework*. This is a good way to make sure that we are not building for more than we were asked to do.

- **Availability**: Does the system need to be available 24/7/365? Actually, the answer is "No." Maybe some parts of the system, such as the client-facing reports. It is reasonable to say, however, that the system should be available during business hours. It can also tolerate some downtime for maintenance and troubleshooting.

- **Performance**: Most of the functionality in the system is to perform batch processing, not transaction processing. End users will most likely deal with the reports generated by the system. Since the reports will use the data that is already processed, it is more important to make sure that all the batch processing and report generation is done before the user needs to access them.

- **Reliability**: There are no special considerations for reliability outside of the general consensus that the system should do what it is supposed to do. One important point to make though is that, like all financial systems, it should generate alerts whenever things don't work as planned.

- **Recoverability**: As with all data processing systems, the recoverability of the system is the ability to restore the system to the previous known state and to rerun the transactions made after that. With SQL Server, there are plenty of tools for a database administrator to ensure that system is backed up regularly, perhaps offsite, to plan for disaster recovery scenarios. An excellent description of backing up the SQL Server database is provided on Microsoft's site at `http://technet.microsoft.com/en-us/library/ms187048.aspx`.

- **Capacity**: As described before, SQL Server has a lot of space to grow. For our scenario, RPP will hardly outgrow its potential. It is a question of planning hardware requirements, which will satisfy a reasonable period of the business growth.

- **Security**: Security is paramount in the systems that operate with personal and financial data. Among other security features of SQL Server, we should specifically consider the column-based encryption of sensitive data. It allows you to store data securely encrypted in the database without compromising on database performance.

- **Interoperability**: We will consider this when we discuss processing data input. We don't have any special requirements concerning interoperability with other systems.

- **Maintainability**: SQL Server provides a lot of tools for system monitoring and maintenance. The rule of thumb that we will use is "the fewer bicycles we invent, the easier it will be to maintain them."

- **Auditability**: There is a special requirement for auditability in this use case. We will follow the following rules to ensure that the system is properly audited:
  - No modifications to the source data are made by the system
  - Any output data can be traced back to its source easily
  - Any operation that produced output data from the source can be rerun to produce the same result

- **Usability**: There is a requirement that RPP employees should be able to create ad hoc reports with little technical training. We will try to address it.

- **Scalability**: We have the requirement that the system should allow business expansion. For this, it is very much a question of capacity that we discussed before.

The database design

We can start thinking about how to implement the basic blocks now. Let's start with the source dataset. Earlier, we said that we wanted to convert the client's data into a single format. We also said that we needed to keep the raw data for auditing purposes. Why do we need to convert the data? Well, the program that will process the data to produce the output dataset needs a single format of the data to work with. Does that really require data from different clients to be stored in the same set of tables? Probably not. Remember that we are not modifying the source data; we are just reading it. Also, RPP can reasonably expect the client to supply the data that has all the necessary pieces in it.

Maybe, instead of converting the client's raw data, we can have a different way of looking at it? In SQL Server, it's called a **view**. SQL views enable you to select data and transform it at the same time. We can create views on top of the client data tables. Then, our processing component will select data from various clients' formats as if it were in the same table. This approach has its pros and cons. It is quite elegant and enables rapid design. On the other hand, it will cause the database to grow very fast, with the addition of new clients. In the future, when we may have more clients, it would be advantageous to split the database.

Let's continue with this thought in mind and, for the moment, pretend that we don't care about the various input client data formats. In fact, we don't know much about them from the requirements to even care. We'll design the database for the job and get back to populating it later on.

Based on the requirements and IRS tax forms, we will need the following entities:

- `Client`: This will keep a track of the RPP clients and store the data necessary to file taxes, for example, the address, the Employee Identification Number, and so on.

- `ClientEmployee`: We will store the client's employee data here, including tax-related information.

- `ClientPayPeriod`: This entity will keep a track of the client pay periods. Our system will use it to know when to process the next payroll for each client.

- `ClientEmployeeEarning`: This entity will store an employee's gross earnings in the pay period.

- `ClientEmployeeDeduction`: This is where the system will store the results of the taxes and other deductions from the employee's earnings. It will also serve as the basis for payments to tax agencies or other sources of deductions.

- `ClientEmployeePayment`: This entity will keep a track of the payments paid to employees.

There are also a few reference tables that we need to create in order to ensure the proper normalization of the database. The final design is presented in the following screenshot:

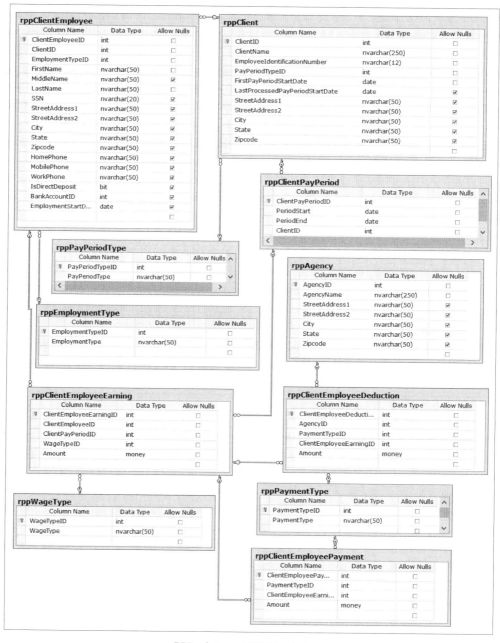

RPP solution – DB tables design

The input dataset design

Now, let's design our ideal dataset that we will need for a client's payroll processing. We make an assumption that RPP will have its client's data already populated in the Client table.

We also require the pay period data, that is, the start and end dates of the period.

For each of the employees, we need the following data:

- First and last name
- Employment type (full-time, part-time, or contractual)
- Date of birth
- Social Security Number
- Income base (for tax calculations)
- Pay period earnings

The application prototype design

Let's imagine that we have a table containing all of the input data. We can implement this table in SQL Server, as shown in the following screenshot:

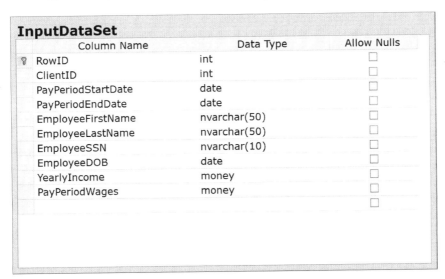

RPP solution – input dataset design

We will process this table by performing the following steps:

1. Insert into or update the `ClientEmployee` table. We will use the `SSN` field to identify whether the employee record is already in the table.

2. Insert into the `ClientEmployeeEarning` table.

For the purpose of the `SELECT` statement, SQL views behave pretty much like tables. Therefore, instead of creating a table, we can use a view to get the data from various sources. We are going to consider data sources from two different clients of RPP, ABC and XYZ.

The ABC client design

This client of RPP sends the data in a simple Excel spreadsheet, as presented in the following table:

FirstName	LastName	SSN	DOB	DateHired	YearlySalary	SalaryPaidYTD
Michael	Smith	123123123	1/1/1977	2/10/2012	$ 50,000.00	$ 41,666.67
Angela	Johnson	321321321	5/3/1980	11/19/2012	$ 58,500.00	$ 48,750.00
Robert	Hastings	999888777	12/11/1976	1/15/2011	$ 35,300.00	$ 29,416.67

We also know that all of the ABC client employees work full-time. The ABC client pays them weekly, and their last pay period was from 10/19/2013 to 10/25/2013. We can conclude that we are processing the next pay period from 10/26/2013 to 11/1/2013. There is sufficient data to populate our input dataset.

We will create a SQL Server table-valued function to return the data about the client and the next pay period. This function will select the last pay period for the client from the `rppClientPayPeriod` table and calculate the next pay period based on the pay period type associated with the client.

The following code snippet presents this function:

```
CREATE FUNCTION dbo.ufnClientNextPayPeriod
    (@ClientName nvarchar(250)  )
RETURNS TABLE
AS
RETURN (
SELECT TOP 1 C.ClientID, NextPeriodStart = DateAdd(d,1,PP.PeriodEnd),
NextPeriodEnd = CASE PT.[PayPeriodType]
    WHEN 'Weekly' THEN DateAdd(d,7,PP.PeriodEnd)
    WHEN 'Bi-weekly' THEN DateAdd(d,14,PP.PeriodEnd)
```

```
        WHEN 'Monthly' THEN DateAdd(MONTH,1,PP.PeriodEnd)
END
FROM [dbo].[rppClient] C
INNER JOIN [dbo].[rppClientPayPeriod] PP ON C.ClientID=PP.ClientID
INNER JOIN [dbo].[rppPayPeriodType] PT ON PT.PayPeriodTypeID=C.
PayPeriodTypeID
WHERE C.ClientName=@ClientName

ORDER BY PP.PeriodEnd DESC )
```

Since the source of the data is an Excel spreadsheet, we can use the OLEDB provider to extract data from it by the OPENROWSET query. We can combine the data from the client's spreadsheet with the data returned by the SQL Server function we have just created:

```
CREATE VIEW ABCClientDataInput
AS
SELECT ufn.ClientID, ufn.NextPeriodStart,
ufn.NextPeriodEnd, excel.FirstName,
excel.LastName, excel.SSN,CAST(excel.DOB as date) as DOB,
excel.YearlySalary, (excel.YearlySalary/(365/7)) as PayPeriodWages
  FROM OPENROWSET('Microsoft.ACE.OLEDB.12.0',
    'Excel 12.0;Database=C:\Project\RPP\Data\ABC\ABC-Client-Employees.
xlsx',
    'SELECT * FROM [Employees$]') excel
    INNER JOIN dbo.ufnClientNextPayPeriod('ABC Client') ufn ON 1=1
```

The result set, as shown in the following table, is exactly what we need for the data source. Since this is a rather simple SELECT statement, the reader may note that we made it a SQL view to use for further payroll processing.

ClientID	NextPeriodStart	NextPeriodEnd	FirstName	LastName	SSN	DOB	Salary	PayPeriodWages
2	10/26/2013	11/1/2013	Michael	Smith	123123123	1/1/1977	50000	961.5384
2	10/26/2013	11/1/2013	Angela	Johnson	321321321	5/3/1980	58500	1125
2	10/26/2013	11/1/2013	Robert	Hastings	999888777	12/11/1976	35300	678.8461

The XYZ client design

Input data from the XYZ client's spreadsheet can be retrieved in a similar fashion, as illustrated in the following code snippet:

```
CREATE VIEW XYZClientDataInput
    AS
SELECT ufn.ClientID, ufn.NextPeriodStart, ufn.NextPeriodEnd,
C.[First Name] as FirstName, C.[Last Name] as LastName, C.SSN,
```

```
CAST(C.DateOfBirth as date) as DOB,
SUM(C.HourlyRate * T.[Hours]) * 26 as YearlySalary,
SUM(C.HourlyRate * T.[Hours]) as PayPeriodWages
FROM
(select * FROM OPENROWSET('Microsoft.ACE.OLEDB.12.0',
'Excel 12.0;Database=C:\Project\RPP\Data\XYZ\XYZcontractors.xlsx',
'SELECT * FROM [Contractors$]') ) C
INNER JOIN
(select * FROM OPENROWSET('Microsoft.ACE.OLEDB.12.0',
'Excel 12.0;Database=C:\Project\RPP\Data\XYZ\XYZcontractors.xlsx',
'SELECT * FROM [Timesheets$]') ) T
ON C.[Contractor Number]=T.[Contractor Number]
INNER JOIN dbo.ufnClientNextPayPeriod('XYZ Client') ufn ON 1=1
GROUP BY ufn.ClientID, ufn.NextPeriodStart, ufn.NextPeriodEnd,
C.[Contractor Number], C.[First Name], C.[Last Name],
C.SSN, CAST(C.DateOfBirth as date)
```

The data structure for the XYZ client's payroll is completely different. It has two worksheets; one worksheet has the list of contractors and their hourly pay rate, and the other worksheet has the hours worked during the pay period. However, we came up with a view that retrieves the data of the same structure as the first one. Now, we can combine the worksheets into a single view as follows:

```
CREATE VIEW ClientDataInput
AS
 SELECT * FROM ABCClientDataInput
 UNION ALL
SELECT * FROM XYZClientDataInput
```

If we select data from the ClientDataInput view, we may get all the data for both the clients. In fact, this is not what we shall necessarily need in the future, because we will process them individually. It is, however, good to check whether the data sources are fully compatible.

We can now proceed to the next step in our simple workflow diagram, that is, **Data Processing**. We need to use this data input to populate the tables we have designed for the database. As mentioned before, there are two steps: updating the ClientEmployee table and populating the ClientEmployeeEarning table for the next pay period. Even before that, we need to generate the current pay period's record. We'll do all of this with a few SQL queries.

We are going to continue our example using the ABC client. Since we already have a function to calculate the client's next pay period, we'll use it here, as shown:

```
INSERT INTO [dbo].[rppClientPayPeriod]
    ([PeriodStart], [PeriodEnd], [ClientID])
SELECT [NextPeriodStart], [NextPeriodEnd], [ClientID]
    FROM dbo.ufnClientNextPayPeriod('ABC Client')
```

We can now proceed with updating the ClientEmployee table and creating the pay period records in ClientEmployeeEarning. We'll use a SQL cursor for all the records that we select from the client-specific view:

```
DECLARE ClientEmployeeCursor CURSOR FORWARD_ONLY READ_ONLY
    FOR
SELECT DISTINCT FirstName, LastName, SSN, CAST(PayPeriodWages as
money)
    FROM ABCClientDataInput
-- Process client's employee payroll
OPEN ClientEmployeeCursor
FETCH NEXT FROM ClientEmployeeCursor
INTO @FirstName, @LastName, @SSN, @PayPeriodWages

WHILE @@FETCH_STATUS = 0
BEGIN
    DECLARE @ClientEmployeeID INT
    -- Insert or update client employee record
    IF EXISTS(SELECT 1 FROM rppClientEmployee
        WHERE ClientID = @ClientID AND SSN = @SSN)
    BEGIN
        UPDATE [dbo].[rppClientEmployee]
            SET  [FirstName] = @FirstName,[LastName] = @LastName
             WHERE ClientID = @ClientID AND   SSN = @SSN
        SELECT @ClientEmployeeID = ClientEmployeeID FROM
rppClientEmployee
            WHERE ClientID = @ClientID AND SSN = @SSN
    END
    ELSE
    BEGIN
        INSERT INTO [dbo].[rppClientEmployee]
        ([ClientID],[EmploymentTypeID],[FirstName],[LastName],[SSN])
        VALUES
```

```
            (@ClientID,@EmploymentTypeID,@FirstName,@LastName,@SSN)
        SELECT @ClientEmployeeID = SCOPE_IDENTITY()
    END
        -- Insert employee wages
    INSERT INTO [dbo].[rppClientEmployeeEarning]
            ([ClientEmployeeID]
            ,[ClientPayPeriodID]
            ,[WageTypeID]
            ,[Amount])
        VALUES
            (@ClientEmployeeID
            ,@ClientPayPeriodID
            ,@WageTypeID
            ,@PayPeriodWages)

        FETCH NEXT FROM ClientEmployeeCursor
            INTO @FirstName, @LastName, @SSN, @PayPeriodWages
    END
```

We are getting close. The next step in payroll processing is to calculate the taxes. We will assume that there are two tax levels: federal and state taxes. They are represented by the agency records in the Agency table, Internal Revenue Service and State Tax Service. We assume that the federal tax rate is 20% and the state tax rate is 7%.

We need to process each employee's earnings record and create records in the ClientEmployeeDeduction table (for taxes) and ClientEmployeePayment (for the remainder of the earnings after taxes). The following code will need to be incorporated in the SQL cursor fetch block after the ClientEmployeeEarning record is created:

```
INSERT INTO [dbo].[rppClientEmployeeDeduction]
([AgencyID],[PaymentTypeID],[ClientEmployeeEarningID],[Amount])
VALUES
(@IRSAgencyID,1,@ClientEmployeeEarningID,@PayPeriodWages * 0.2)

 INSERT INTO [dbo].[rppClientEmployeeDeduction]
([AgencyID],[PaymentTypeID],[ClientEmployeeEarningID],[Amount])
VALUES
(@StateAgencyID,1,@ClientEmployeeEarningID,@PayPeriodWages * 0.07)

INSERT INTO [dbo].[rppClientEmployeePayment]
([PaymentTypeID],[ClientEmployeeEarningID],[Amount])
VALUES
(1,@ClientEmployeeEarningID,@PayPeriodWages * 0.73)
```

Now, we have all the data to proceed with the payments. To make sure that this payroll processing is executed on schedule, we'll create a SQL Agent job. The job will be scheduled to run each Friday at 2:00 P.M. The assumption is that by this scheduled time RPP employees will receive the payroll spreadsheet from their clients and save them in a specially designated folder where SQL Server can access and process it.

The last step in the system is to make the actual payments. We will print checks to the client's employees and tax agencies as SSRS reports.

SSRS allows us to fulfill another important requirement—provide reports to customers. More than that, SSRS has a ready-made web interface. By providing access to customer-specific reports over the Internet, RPP may save a lot of development effort.

In fact, SSRS has the ability to save the report as a spreadsheet, comma-separated, or XML data. This covers the requirement to be able to generate data files. In fact, there is not much extra development required once the reports are developed for the specific format.

Lessons learned

With this example, we were trying to point out that SQL Server in itself is a development platform for complex integrated systems. The tools and services that are provided with SQL Server should be diligently considered by solution architects.

Just to reiterate the important points of when we have used SQL Server:

- To retrieve data from multiple non-SQL data sources by using the OPENROWSET() function.
- To create a single structured view of various data sources by using the SQL views.
- To run data processing and report generation on schedule using the SQL Server Agent scheduled job.
- To create a web-based, client-facing reporting interface without writing any web application code. This was done using the SSRS reporting web portal.
- To extract data files of various data formats using the SSRS reporting web portal.

New features of SQL Server 2014

To conclude this chapter, let's take a look at what the **Community Technology Preview 2 (CTP 2)** of SQL Server 2014 presents us with. The commercial release of SQL Server 2014 will most likely happen in early 2014.

So far, the following new features of SQL Server 2014 have been revealed:

- Enhanced **In-Memory OLTP** that gains significant performance by moving the most-used tables into memory. According to Microsoft, the performance gains will average 10 times and can even reach 30 times. This is achieved via a new engine with a code name **Hekaton**.

- In SQL Server 2012, Resource Governor allowed you to adjust the amount of CPU and memory resources, but with SQL Server 2014 **IO Resource Governor**, we can manage and limit the I/O utilization. That enables more effective I/O management across multiple databases.

- Improved resilience with Windows Server 2012 R2 using **Cluster Shared Volumes**.

- The **Buffer Pool Extension** (**BPE**) feature that enables caching frequently used data on **Solid State Disks** (**SSDs**). BPE deals only with "clean" data, so there is no risk of data loss.

- Enhancements of the **AlwaysOn Availability Groups**; now, they support up to eight secondary replicas (versus four in SQL Server 2012).

- Updatable clustered **columnstore indexes** for faster retrieval.

- BI enhancements, that is, **Power Query** and **Power Map**.

- Azure support enhancements, that is, simplified backup and disaster recovery.

Just before this book was published, Microsoft released SQL Server 2014. All the features that we listed in this section are present in the release. The initial benchmarking that we performed showed that the performance characteristics are even better than what we have seen with the CTP. It is also worth mentioning that SQL Server 2014 supports up to 640 logical processors and 4 TB of memory in a physical environment. It can also scale up to 64 virtual processors and 1 TB of memory when running on a virtual machine.

Summary

MS SQL Server is a robust and powerful technology that also works as the basis for many other Microsoft products. Having a long history, SQL Server is a leading database management system today, with the ability to support different data formats; it is a powerful and secure tool.

In the next chapter, we will discuss a tool that comes as a part of the SQL Server offering, **SQL Server Integration Services (SSIS)**. SSIS plays a significant role in integration technologies, particularly supporting the **Extract, Transform, Load (ETL)** pattern.

4
The SSIS Primer

When the ancestor of **SQL Server Integration Services (SSIS)** — **Data Transformation Services (DTS)** — was initially released with SQL Server 7.0, database administrators were extremely pleased. DTS not only replaced old data transformation and loading tools, but also added new features that significantly simplified their lives. However, only in SQL Server 2000 did DTS become a modern **Extract, transform, load (ETL)** tool, which set up a foundation for SQL Server Integration Services.

SSIS was originally released with SQL Server 2005 with the intention of replacing DTS. SSIS 2005 was a full-featured data integration engine and development environment to build high-performance solutions. After several more versions, SSIS became a development platform to build quality data integration, migration, and transformation solutions. Typical scenarios for the usage of SSIS include the following:

- ETL tasks to support data warehousing
- Data migration as part of legacy system migration tasks
- The integration of different data sources
- The merging of data from heterogeneous data sources
- Data cleansing

SSIS includes capabilities such as the accessing of data in different formats, the extraction of data from different databases, and the sending of e-mails in response to events. It also enables the building of packages with its graphical user interface without a single line of code or creating sophisticated custom packages programmatically.

We consider SSIS to be one of the most important tools in the SQL Server offering. It is almost impossible to imagine a large, enterprise-wide project that does not use SSIS. That's why we have devoted a separate chapter to it. In this chapter, you will read about the features of SSIS 2012 and 2014; you will consider a use case that requires moving data, and learn how SSIS fits into the picture.

What's new in SSIS 2012

Every new version of SQL Server and its components, including SSIS, present a significant number of changes. The number of improvements in SSIS 2012 is too big to even be listed in this book. Therefore, the following list only mentions the most significant among these:

- In this release, SSIS has new features related to the integration with external data sources. Among them, integration with Hadoop is probably the most interesting one. Hadoop is an open source Apache project with a distributed filesystem. SSIS supports data transfer between SQL Server databases and the Hadoop filesystem, and it also can transfer data between Hadoop and other data sources.

- SSIS 2012 has introduced the project deployment model. In this model, parameters are used to assign values to package properties, and they create a project together with the packages. A project is deployed to the SSISDB catalog on an instance of SQL Server. One can validate projects and packages before execution. Package execution takes place on the database engine.

- Related to the project deployment model is the concept of server environments. Environments are created to specify the runtime values for packages in the project. These values are mapped to the project parameters.

- The SSISDB catalog is a feature of SSIS 2012 used to store SSIS solutions and much more; it provides an integrated environment for SSIS project deployment, maintenance, execution, and monitoring.

- During package execution, events are captured automatically and stored in the catalog. They can be analyzed later, which improves package troubleshooting.

- In this release, SSIS provides an improved developer experience, for example, an updated user interface, visual improvements to the data flow, new functions and scripting features, and much more.

- Connection managers can be created at the project level. Now, they can be shared between the packages in the project.

- The SSIS team did not forget about architectural "abilities". The data quality capability is now enhanced with the **DQS Cleansing transformation**. Performance is improved by reducing the memory usage for the **Merge** and **Merge Join** transformations.

Building the payroll processor application

We will be working with the use case from the previous chapter, the solution for Reliable Payroll Pro Inc.—also known as RPP. Refer to *Chapter 3*, *The SQL Server Primer*, for the full details of this use case.

To briefly refresh your memory, we were building a system to process payroll data from the various sources and clients of RPP. We built a solution using the capabilities of MS SQL Server alone. We created SQL scheduled tasks that are running T-SQL scripts to import data from Excel spreadsheets into the RPP database and process it as required.

Adding more details to the RPP use case

Let's imagine that we have an additional requirement in our use case. We made a tacit assumption that our scripts would work because the input data filenames would be the same each and every time. Now, it appears that this is not how RPP wants it to happen. For RPP, saving the datafiles into a location where SQL Server can find them is a manual task. RPP employees receive files from the clients by e-mail, or they download them from an FTP site or bring them on CDs. They are instructed to save them into client-specific folders on the network that SQL Server can access. However, RPP management feels that renaming the files is too much of a task for the employees. Additionally, some of the clients may need to process several payment files for one payroll.

Therefore, RPP has requested that the system be intelligent enough to find all of the data files in the client-specific data source folder. It need not know the filename so long as this file is the last one that was dropped into that folder.

Requirements analysis

We have to get back to the architectural drawing board now. The programming language we used for the data processing scripts is **T-SQL**—the language of SQL Server queries. This language has been specifically designed to manage all of the possible data manipulation tasks imaginable. However, it was never meant to substitute the application programming languages, such as C# or Visual Basic. For example, it does not have the means to manage the filesystem.

To deal with the new requirement, we need to find a way of bringing this ability into the system. Still, we don't want to change the architecture completely because of it. That would mean starting the project from scratch because of something that appeared when we were almost done. We should look inside SQL Server for the tools that would work for the task.

Luckily, SSIS packages provide just the capability to add custom logic to the data manipulation tasks developed as T-SQL scripts. Let's see how we can build an SSIS package to satisfy the RPP requirement.

SSIS package design

To develop SSIS packages for SQL Server 2012, **SQL Server Data Tools for Business Intelligence Studio (SSDT BI)** must be installed. The SSDT BI installation package can be downloaded from the Microsoft website at `http://www.microsoft.com/en-us/download/confirmation.aspx?id=36843`.

 At the time of this writing, SSDT BI is only available in the 32-bit version. When installing SSDT BI on the 64-bit SQL Server, choose **New Server Instance** during installation.

Also, there is presently no support for BI projects in Visual Studio 2013.

We will create a new SSIS package in the SSDT BI 2012 environment. In fact, SSDT BI uses the familiar Visual Studio 2012 environment, with several extra project templates specific to SSIS, SSRS, and SQL Server BI projects. When creating a new SSIS package project, navigate to **Business Intelligence | Integration Services** and select **Integration Services Project** template.

First off, we need to create a new Flat File connection manager (we will import data from comma-separated `*.csv` files in this example). Let's select any existing file in the `ABC` directory under `/RPP/Data/` in the RPP project sample, as shown in the following screenshot:

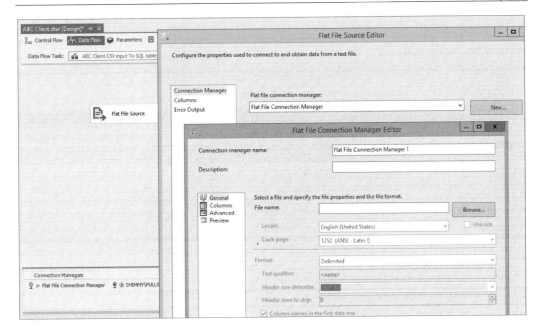

We will also create two variables. The first one called `ABClientDataPath` will have the static value pointing to the directory with the data files for the ABC client. It is set to `C:\Project\RPP\Data\ABC`.

The other one called `ABCClientProcessingFilePath` will hold the value for the `.csv` file that we are currently processing.

SSIS allows the creation of system and user-defined variables. System variables are defined by Integration Services and user variables are defined by developers. You can create as many user-defined variables as you need.

We will add a Foreach Loop container to the control flow and call it ABC Input Files Foreach Loop container. We will set the value of **Folder** to the location of the ABC client's input files and the value of **Files** to `*.csv`.

The adding of the Foreach Loop container to process each data source file is presented in the following screenshot:

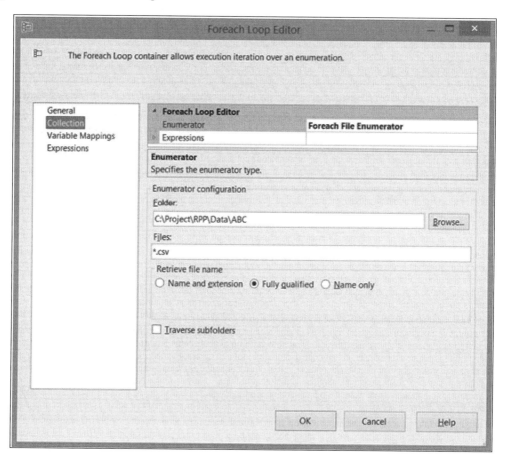

We will assign the output value parameter to the ABCClientProcessingFilePath variable.

Next, we will need to create a data flow task to transfer the data from the input file to the Client table in the SQL Server database. This is done on the **Data Flow** tab in the SSIS **Package Designer**. We will create a Flat File data source and SQL Server destination with data mapping between them.

We will build an expression for the Flat File data source connection string and assign it the value of the `ABCClientProcessingFilePath` variable, which we used in the Foreach Loop to iterate through the files in the input directory, as shown in the following screenshot:

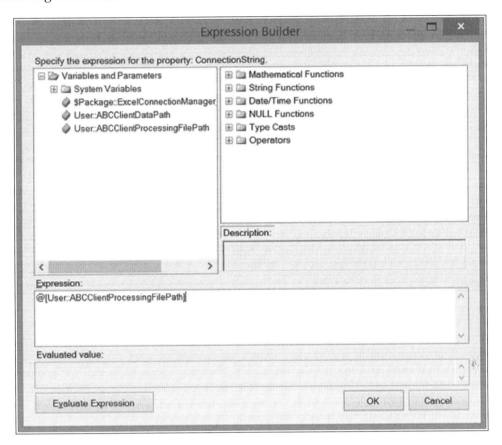

Now, we need to create a mapping between the columns in the source file and the destination SQL table, as illustrated in the following screenshot:

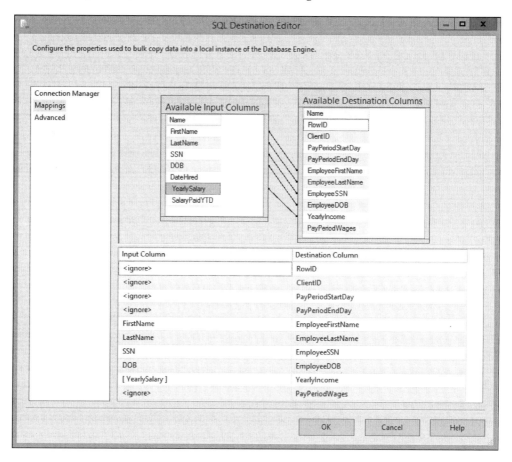

We built the **Data Flow** task. In order to complete the package to process all input files, we need to go back to the **Control Flow** tab and drag the **Data Flow** task inside the Foreach Loop container.

This is shown in the following screenshot — our package is now ready for execution:

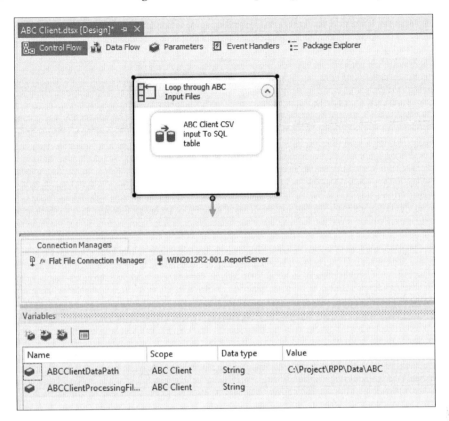

Lessons learned

The most important lesson that we should have learned is to have confidence in SQL Server Integration Services. Certainly, the task that we had was way easier than real-life integration or data migration tasks. With this confidence, we can approach solutions that require the moving around of thousands of SQL Server tables, transformation from dozens of different sources, and the loading of data warehouses of petabytes of data.

What's new in SSIS 2014

Well, in terms of the new functionality, not much. However, the 2012 release is significant enough to be the base for future, small improvements.

Performance improvements in SQL Server 2014 affect SSIS as well. Enhanced, in-memory OLTP (**Hekaton**); improved resiliency; and updatable, clustered columnstore indexes all have an impact on processing SSIS packages.

Integration with non-Microsoft sources will continue, and one of the most important initiatives is working with Hadoop, and releasing solutions based on Microsoft Hadoop for Windows, now called **MS HDInsight Server**.

And finally, there is a promise to include SSIS and other BI templates in Visual Studio 2013.

Summary

SSIS is a highly reliable, proven tool for data integration. It can be used in different ETL scenarios, such as during data migration from a legacy database to a new one or when building a data feed for a data warehouse. Over the years, SSIS has been improved, new features have been added, and the development interface has become a truly enjoyable one.

We will talk more about SSIS in *Chapter 10, Data Exchange Patterns*. In the next chapter, we will present another integration tool, Microsoft BizTalk Server. Where SSIS is a valuable tool for data integration solutions, BizTalk is more helpful when there is a need for application integration. Read more about integration architecture in the next few chapters.

5
The BizTalk Server Primer

Among the Microsoft servers today, BizTalk Server is one of the most complex products. In its 13-year history, it went from being a clumsy tool that was made to support XML messages to an enterprise-quality integration server with a variety of features and a large technical community around it.

In the year 2000, when the first version of BizTalk was launched, EDI was dominating the market. XML messaging was in its infancy, but seemed very promising. Many technology corporations were looking into it, and Microsoft was no exception.

The original version, and even the following version of BizTalk, was totally different from the BizTalk we know today. They were built using some code from other servers, had very poor orchestration abilities, and did not provide much functionality. They supported EDI, HTTP, MSMQ, SMTP—and that was pretty much it. The 2002 version was also influenced by the concept of web services.

BizTalk 2004 was a completely new product. The code base was changed, and the product was rewritten from scratch. Orchestrations and message transformation abilities became similar to what we can see in BizTalk now, content-based routing was introduced, and security features were improved (`http://msdn.microsoft.com/en-us/library/dd547397(v=bts.10).aspx`). BizTalk started looking like an enterprise-level server.

The next versions, originally released every second year, added more and more critical functionalities to BizTalk. With every release, developers got more tools and richer development environments; they built a community of BizTalk lovers and developed a large number of tools. Some of these tools would become a part of the official BizTalk package.

With every version, Microsoft has expanded support for integration with a popular line of business applications, such as SAP, JD Edwards, and Microsoft Dynamics CRM. BizTalk works with EDI, HL7, HIPAA, SWIFT, and other standards. RFID support was introduced in 2007. Third parties have been developing different adapters, and there are several hundreds of BizTalk adapters available on the market.

Initiated as a tool for Enterprise Application Integration, today BizTalk can implement an ESB. It has **Business Activity Monitoring (BAM)** capabilities, web services, and WCF support. In this chapter, we'll touch on some of its major features, introduce BizTalk essentials, and talk about the new improvements made in BizTalk 2013. We'll discuss BizTalk Server editions and see how BizTalk capabilities support general, nonfunctional requirements. Finally, step by step, we will build a BizTalk application to cover a simple use case and introduce you to the BizTalk development process.

Using BizTalk in an integration architecture

Generally speaking, BizTalk is for system integration. However, the notion of integration itself is a complex subject. With a variety of computer technologies, platforms, data formats, and standards, integration opens a door into the endless world of solutions. Let's discuss the high-level taxonomy of the integration domain.

Within the spectrum of integration solutions, two major paradigms emerged by early 2000: EII and EAI. **Enterprise Information Integration (EII)** provides a unified view of enterprise data. The data can be moved into a data warehouse or presented to end users via a federated search in disparate sources. **Enterprise Application Integration (EAI)** provides message exchange between applications in order to have them work together. In reality, there is always a mixture of these in large systems. Later in the book, we will talk about integration patterns and approaches in detail.

Another term, **Business-to-Business (B2B)**, is also popular. However, using the notion of an extended enterprise, we shall consider B2B as an extended EAI. In the modern world, with multinational enterprises, there is no significant difference between the two.

In enterprises, there are more integration needs than data and application integration. Business processes and workflows can be integrated as well. The notion of business services found its technological counterpart in the new paradigm: **service-oriented architecture (SOA)**. SOA has brought a new dimension to the integration world; problems that were traditionally solved by EAI and EII can also be solved today using SOA.

Integration approaches vary. File transfers, data replication, point-to-point solutions, direct calls to different APIs, web services, and enterprise service buses all serve integration purposes. Which are the most appropriate ones that use BizTalk?

BizTalk is a complex tool. One can use it for literally anything, from data replication to advanced integration with heterogeneous data sources. However, the majority of BizTalk use cases traditionally belonged to the domain of EAI. BizTalk is a messaging tool; it routes messages to different applications and can send messages back, providing feedback from these applications. However, in the last several years, the SOA paradigm has emerged, supported by Web service technologies. Although it had support for web services and WCF, BizTalk was missing a significant SOA tool: an enterprise service bus. The concept of ESB finally reached the BizTalk community in the mid 2000s, and the first ESB toolkit was developed as an open source product on CodePlex. Only in BizTalk 2010 did ESB become a part of the official release, that made BizTalk SOA solutions a reality.

BizTalk essentials

Let's briefly describe several important notations that we will use in this book—consider this little section as an introduction to the BizTalk terminology. They are as follows:

- **Message Box**: There are many books written on the topic of messages. We shall not discuss its details; let's assume that, intuitively, we understand what a message is. BizTalk operates with messages; they are the basic units of information that floats between connected applications. Once a message enters BizTalk, it is persisted in the Message Box, which consists of one or more SQL Server databases. This is essential for businesses that require highly reliable solutions. Also, persisting messages help with debugging, tracing, monitoring, and working with long transactions. Does it come with a price? Definitely. As architects, we have to realize that BizTalk is optimized for throughput rather than low latency; when we work on an integration solution, we have to assess that.

- **Publish/Subscribe**: The moving of messages to and from the Message Box is based on the Publish/Subscribe pattern. (An excellent introduction to integration patterns is given in the book *Enterprise Integration Patterns: Designing, Building, and Deploying Messaging Solutions*, *Gregor Hohpe* and *Bobby Wolf, Addison Wesley*). Different BizTalk components have the ability to publish a message or insert it in the Message Box. Subscribers specify the criteria to be used to retrieve messages from the Message Box.

- **Orchestrations**: Orchestrations are executable components of BizTalk solutions that can subscribe and publish messages through the Message Box as well as create new messages. Orchestrations run workflows to support business processes. BizTalk Orchestration Designer is an intuitive visual tool that automates complex messaging patterns and system workflows.

- **Transformations**: In system integration, it never happens that incoming and outgoing data have the same format. Even in similar systems—such as record management systems, for example—the data is always presented in different formats. One system may have one field that combines a first name and a last name; another system may have two separate fields; a third system may have a first name, a second name, a last name, and a name suffix; and so on. Therefore, data transformation became a mandatory and very important task in system integration. In BizTalk, maps are used to transform XML messages, and BizTalk Mapper is the tool used to create and edit these maps.

- **Adapters**: BizTalk adapters extend the functionality of BizTalk Server, enabling connectivity to other applications. Adapters usually implement a commonly recognized standard, such as SMTP, POP3, FTP, or MSMQ. The BizTalk edition includes a number of so-called, "native" adapters, such as WCF adapters. There are hundreds of third-party adapters on the market; in addition to this, developers can also create their own adapters using the BizTalk Adapter Framework (`http://msdn.microsoft.com/en-US/library/bb798080(v=bts.80).aspx`).

- **Accelerators**: The BizTalk accelerator is an industry-specific solution that comes with data schemas that follow industry standards, tools, and procedures.

- **Business Rules Engine** (BRE): This provides a central repository to manage business rules.

- **Business Activity Monitoring**: The Business Activity Monitoring component of BizTalk provides a framework to track the activities of a particular business process. For example, for a sales system, it can provide information about how many purchase orders were completed during a given hour and what types of products were ordered. It can be used to monitor financial transactions in a banking system or to track claims in an insurance system. Sounds good, right? However, the complexity of BAM scares many business people away, and it is very common that, since it is a desirable feature during the envisioning phase, BAM gets completely abandoned in production.

Architects who are considering using BAM for their solutions should pay special attention to the operational requirements. Also, all reports and procedures have to be developed and "sold" to the IT and business, ideally even before the final deployment. When the business sees the advantages of BAM from the early days of the system's life, it becomes a strong supporter.

- **Business Process Management**: Today, BizTalk orchestrations can be used to implement very complex business processes. These processes can consume data from different sources via different adapters. If we add BAM to this picture, we can consider BizTalk as a tool for Business Process Management solutions. This is certainly true, but we should be very careful when implementing BizTalk in different workflows. Let's not forget that BizTalk is primarily a messaging tool and that the workflows are only to support message processing.

New features of BizTalk Server 2013

BizTalk Server 2013 works with the latest technologies and standards. They are listed as follows:

- Windows Server 2012, Microsoft Visual Studio 2012, Microsoft SQL Server 2012, Microsoft System Center 2012, and the latest version of Microsoft Office
- .NET Framework 4.5
- SAP 7.2 and 7.3, Oracle Database 11.2, Oracle E-Business Suite 12.1, and Oracle Siebel 8.1
- Health Level Seven (HL7) 2.5.1 and 2.6
- Society for Worldwide Interbank Financial Telecommunication (SWIFT) 2012 Message Pack
- X12 5030 and EDIFACT D05B

BizTalk Server 2013 has a new SFTP adapter to transfer messages to and from a secure FTP server using the SSH protocol. It has updated SharePoint Services. If you are using SharePoint 2013, SharePoint Online, or SharePoint 2010, it is recommended that you use the new client-side object model.

One of the great and long-awaited features is the REST support that is now included out of the box in BizTalk . BizTalk Server 2013 includes a WCF-WebHttp adapter that you can use to both invoke a REST endpoint as well as expose BizTalk artifacts as RESTful resources.

Another significant improvement has been made in the area of integration with BizTalk Azure (`http://azure.microsoft.com/en-us/services/biztalk-services/`). BizTalk Server 2013 provides new adapters, such as the SB-Messaging adapter, WCF-BasicHttpRelay adapter, and the WCF-NetTCPRelay adapter, for Azure integration.

The integrated ESB Toolkit that is included as part of the BizTalk core offering has a much easier installation and configuration.

The development and maintenance experience is simplified. BizTalk Server Administration Console now includes a Dependency Tracking panel that provides the ability to track dependent BizTalk artifacts.

One very important change is the introduction of the per core license model of BizTalk Server 2013. All previous versions of BizTalk were licensed per processor. The introduction to Per Core Licensing can be downloaded from the Microsoft site at `http://www.microsoft.com/licensing/about-licensing/briefs/licensing-by-cores.aspx`.

BizTalk Server editions

BizTalk Server 2013 comes in the following four editions:

- **Enterprise edition**: This has been designed for customers with enterprise-level requirements for high volume, reliability, and availability. It allows an unlimited number of applications and supports failover for multiple Message Boxes.

- **Standard edition**: This has been designed for customers with moderate volume and deployment scale requirements. It allows five applications and uses a single Message Box. Both the Enterprise and Standard editions support complete EAI, B2B, and Business Process Management functionalities. They include industry accelerators for RosettaNet, HIPAA, HL7, and SWIFT.

- **Branch edition**: This has been designed for customers with hub and spoke deployment scenarios, including RFID. It allows only one application.

- **Developer edition**: This traditionally has all of the functionalities of the Enterprise edition, but it has been licensed for development and testing only.

BizTalk Server abilities

As we mentioned previously, BizTalk Enterprise edition was designed for customers with enterprise-level requirements for high volume, reliability, and availability. While addressing all of these nonfunctional "abilities" of BizTalk, we primarily consider the Enterprise edition.

High availability

BizTalk Server lets you separate hosts and run multiple host instances to provide high availability. In large implementations, it is considered best practice to separate the receiving of messages, processing of orchestrations, and sending of messages into three separate groups of hosts. BizTalk automatically distributes the workload across multiple computers through host instances. However, the hosts running receive handlers for the HTTP and SOAP adapters require a load balancing mechanism to provide high availability; hosts running receive handlers for FTP, MSMQ, POP3, SQL, and SAP require a clustering mechanism to provide high availability.

A high availability configuration for the BizTalk databases typically consists of two or more SQL Server databases in an active/passive server cluster configuration.

Master secret server is used by BizTalk to obtain the encryption key. If it fails, each BizTalk Server will continue to use a cached-in memory copy of the master secret. However, if the SSO service has been restarted on that BizTalk Server, the latter will need to contact the master secret server. To provide high availability for the master secret server, Windows clustering can be used.

Reliability

As mentioned before, every message in BizTalk is persisted in the Message Box. In addition to this, every message is immutable. In other words, once the message is in the Message Box, it does not change and does not disappear until it is consumed by all subscribers. This provides extremely high resiliency even in complex scenarios, such as long-running or distributed transactions.

Manageability

Most administration and operation tasks are performed in the BizTalk Server Administration Console. The Administration Console has a graphical user interface. Additionally, there is the **BTSTask** command-line tool that is used for all administration tasks and can be run from a command line and used in batches. Extensive monitoring can be developed using BAM, and additional administrative tasks can be programmed with the use of **WMI Object Model**.

However, the Administrative Console is not very rich in features; coding additional tasks requires significant effort.

The BizTalk community realized the lack of proper tools a long time ago, and several products to administer BizTalk have been developed. The most popular and most stable and rich-in-features product is **BizTalk360** (http://www.biztalk360.com).

Programmability

BizTalk is not your usual Microsoft product. If you install Microsoft Exchange or Microsoft Office, Windows or Visual Studio, you will be able to immediately perform some tasks right after the installation. When you install BizTalk, it does nothing. The BizTalk solution has to be designed and programmed. In fact, BizTalk is a development tool, pretty much like SQL Server, one would say. Therefore, programmability in BizTalk is one of the main abilities, and every new release has some significant improvements in this area.

However, that said, we should always remember that BizTalk is a tool for developers. In its early years, one could gauge that BizTalk — if not yet, but very soon — would be a tool that even nontechnical people could use. There were even promises that eventually a business analyst would be able to magically sketch a solution via a mighty user interface and no coding would be involved. Well, these dreams did not come true. However, the product today is certainly one of the most powerful Microsoft development tools, the caliber of SQL Server and Visual Studio.

Scalability

Scalability can be achieved by adding more hosts and host instances to the group as well as more servers. Additional servers pull work items off the queues independently. The more the number of servers in the group, the more work can be performed. There is no limit to the number of servers that can be added to a BizTalk Enterprise edition. However, there are two things to keep in mind. The first one is **sequencing**. If you want to process messages in a sequence, you need to implement special means. The second one is **licensing**. More servers require more licenses; even if there is no technical limit, the budget restrictions will limit your solution.

Performance

We mentioned earlier that BizTalk is optimized for throughput rather than for low latency. In general, the latency of BizTalk is higher than the latency of its competitors that don't persist messages. However, for the majority of industries, including financial and health care, BizTalk is a proven integration tool. BizTalk generally relies on the performance of SQL Server, and there are multiple ways to optimize the performance of both products. Unfortunately, there are no simple solutions; improving the performance is routine work that requires some skills and experience. Microsoft has great recommendations for performance and capacity planning at `http://msdn.microsoft.com/en-us/library/aa577523(v=bts.80).aspx`.

Security

There are several ways to increase message security in a BizTalk solution. One is to authenticate senders either by a certificate or using **Windows Integrated Security**. Another approach is to authorize the receiver of the message. Messages can be also encrypted. Needless to say that access control can be achieved by means of Windows or SQL Server.

Using SQL Server as its underlying engine, BizTalk relies on its **Transparent Data Encryption (TDE)** feature. Using TDE is necessary to comply with industry standards such as PCI (find more about this at `https://www.pcisecuritystandards.org/security_standards/index.php`).

Building the BizTalk application

We will now proceed to see how a BizTalk application can be utilized in the business scenario. The use case given in the next section highlights the primary functionality of BizTalk—the interoperability of several subsystems within the enterprise.

The use case of a web hosting company

All Things Internet (ATI) is a domain registrar company that decided to start offering e-mail hosting (MS Exchange) and website hosting services to its customers. ATI had put a significant effort into building the infrastructure for the provisioning of these services. They have been built and tested by separate teams of subcontractors and are scheduled to be launched soon. Together with the existing systems, ATI will have the following business applications on board:

- A **Domain name registration (DNR)** service
- Customer subscription management

- Customer billing
- An MS Exchange server cluster and MS Exchange provisioning application
- A web hosting server cluster and web hosting provisioning application

ATI is looking to build a system that will manage new customer provisioning. Such a system needs to send provisioning requests to various provisioning applications based on the level of service the customer has subscribed to. In essence, it will become a dispatcher that routes orders to the departments that will serve them.

ATI is optimistic about its business prospects and wants to make sure it has the ability to expand its services further in the future. In particular, it is considering adding SharePoint site services and cloud-based storage from third-party providers. The system that handles the provisioning should be capable of adding these, and possibly other services in the future, without breaking existing workflows.

Requirements analysis

First of all, we want to mention that, for this use case analysis, we are not concerned with the actual functionality of the provisioning systems. In fact, it is to our advantage not to take it into consideration. From a high-level architectural point of view, all of these subsystems just send and receive messages. The object of our analysis is the system that delivers these messages to and from those subsystems to ensure the smooth operation of the business as a whole.

If we look at all of the various operations in the provisioning of the new customer for ATI, we may notice one thing that they have in common. Each of them takes a relatively long time to execute. DNS registration takes anything from a few minutes to several hours to propagate across DNS servers. The provisioning of the MS Exchange server and web hosting typically involves the allocation of storage space, among a lot of other things that also take a significant amount of time. In short, for all of the business transactions that constitute the provisioning of a new customer, we cannot expect an immediate response. So, performance for our case is really not a significant consideration.

What is important, then? The primary consideration in this scenario is reliability. No doubt, the provisioning of new customers is mission-critical for any business. Failure to start the service that the customer has subscribed for will very likely impact the company image negatively and possibly deter future customers from signing up in the first place.

Similarly, the ability to be alerted is important if failures are still occurring. No system is bulletproof, and things go wrong sometimes. However, a quick reaction and the ability to respond and recover is what distinguishes an outstanding service provider and makes it look good in its customer's eyes.

By abstracting ourselves from the technical details of the implementation, in this manner, we will see that BizTalk Server is the primary candidate for this solution. It is a specialized server built for the reliable dispatch and delivery of messages. It has a lot of built-in adapters that cover most of the mainstream data storage and delivery technologies. It has the ability to configure alerts and notifications that the customer service and support can be built around.

Also important for this use case, as for a number of real-life scenarios, is the fact that the BizTalk Server solution architecture is easy to upgrade in line with business needs. In contrast with many other technologies, a new consultant who is working with BizTalk solution a few years into its production lifetime does not need to understand the details of the implementation. For our use case scenario, if ATI implements a BizTalk solution and then decides to add SharePoint Services to its customer offering, the existing system will not be significantly impacted. The addition of a new subsystem will require the configuration of a new location, message types, and ports, whereas the existing system functionality will likely stay untouched.

BizTalk Server installation and setup

Setting up BizTalk Server might be a challenge. The following steps provide detailed instructions to install and set up BizTalk Server 2013 on Windows Server 2012. For more information, read the description of the BizTalk Server 2013 installation on MSDN (`http://msdn.microsoft.com/en-us/library/jj248688(v=bts.80).aspx`). However, we would like to briefly repeat the steps and focus on some major ones.

 Excellent, step-by-step instructions to install and configure Microsoft BizTalk 2013 with the ESB Toolkit are presented in Sandro Pereira's blog at `http://sandroaspbiztalkblog.wordpress.com/2013/05/05/biztalk-2013-installation-and-configuration-important-considerations-before-set-up-the-server-part-1/`.

1. Install all Windows updates. It is also a good idea to check for updates after installing each major component (such as SQL Server or BizTalk).

   You need to be an administrator to install and configure BizTalk Server.

2. The computer name has to be 15 characters or shorter. Otherwise, the BizTalk configuration will not work properly. Change the computer name, if necessary, from the Server Manager Dashboard.

3. BizTalk 2013 does not fully support IPv6 yet. For our purposes, let's disable IPv6 as shown the following screenshot:

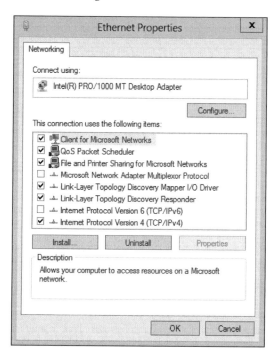

4. You may decide to configure Windows Firewall as described on MSDN after the installation. However, if you need BizTalk for development and aren't using it in the production environment, you can simply disable Windows Firewall.

5. Install IIS 8 by navigating to **Manage | Add Roles and Features**. Include the following features:

   ° .NET Framework 3.5 features

   ° The SMTP server (if you want to use alerts)

   ° Windows Identity Foundation 3.5 (if you want to use the SharePoint adapter)

6. Include the following role services:

    ○ **Common HTTP features**: Default Document, Directory Browsing, HTTP Errors, Static Content

    ○ **Health and Diagnostics**: HTTP Logging, Logging Tools, ODBC Logging, Request Monitor, and Tracking

    ○ **Performance**: Static Content Compression and Dynamic Content Compression

    ○ **Security**: Request Filtering, Basic Authentication, Digest Authentication, and Windows Authentication

    ○ **Application Development (all)**: Select all of the options

    ○ **Management Tools**: IIS Management Console and IIS 6 Management Compatibility (all)

7. Installing BAM is optional. The BAM portal runs only in 32-bit mode. For 64-bit environments, you need to set IIS to 32-bit mode. In order to do this, run IIS Manager and enable 32-bit applications in **Advanced Settings** for the default application pool, as shown in the following screenshot:

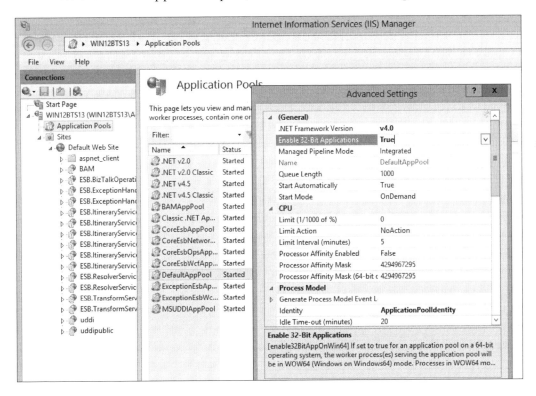

8. Setting up SMTP is optional if you want to set up BAM alerts, and WIF is optional if you want to use the SharePoint adapter. We do not require either for our purposes.

9. If you want to use BAM, you will need to install Microsoft Office Excel 2013. Remember that BizTalk supports only the 32-bit version of Office. You will need to select VBA when installing Excel.

10. If you are installing Visual Studio, you need to perform the following two steps:

    1. BizTalk 2013 is currently not compatible with Visual Studio 2013. Microsoft is planning to publish an upgrade in 2014. If the upgrade is not available by the time this book is published, install Visual Studio 2012 with BizTalk 2013.

    2. Microsoft SQL Server Express is incompatible with BizTalk. To avoid problems, remove the following features from **Windows Program and Features** after installing Visual Studio: Microsoft SQL Server 2012 Express LocalDb and Microsoft SQL Server Compact 4.0 SP1 x4 ENU.

11. Install SQL Server 2012 and select the following features:

    - Database Engine Services such as SQL Server Replication, Full-text, and Semantic Extractions for Search
    - Analysis Services
    - Reporting Services: Native
    - SQL Server Data Tools
    - Client Tools Connectivity
    - Integration Services
    - The Basic and Complete options of Management Tools

12. Install BizTalk 2013 and select all components.

13. Configure BizTalk using Basic Configuration.

14. Install Microsoft BizTalk Adapter Pack and add the adapters to the BizTalk Administration Console. Perform the complete installation of all of the adapters.

15. If you plan to install BizTalk ESB Toolkit, install UDDI services, add all components, and configure a UDDI service from the BizTalk Configuration tool. Use Basic Configuration.

16. Run Windows Updates, just in case.

Implementing the BizTalk solution

For this use case implementation, we will use three SQL databases:

- `Customers`: This database will be used as the source of incoming messages. The incoming messages will be modelled by new records in the `Customer` table with `IsProvisioned = 0`.

- `DNR`: This database will be used as the destination for the **Domain name registration (DNR)** service and **Hosting** service. Customer domains will be provisioned by inserting new records into the `Domain` table. Web hosting for customers will be provisioned by inserting new records into the `Hosting` table.

- `Billing`: This database will be used as the destination for the `Billing` service. Customer billing records will be added to the `Customer` table.

> In order to develop BizTalk 2013 projects in Visual Studio 2012, the reader needs to install WCF LOB Adapter SDK 2013 on the development server with BizTalk Server 2013 and Visual Studio 2012 installed. The download is available from Microsoft Download Center at `http://www.microsoft.com/en-us/download/details.aspx?id=39630`.

Perform the following steps to walk through the creation of a BizTalk project for this use case:

1. Restore the `Customers`, `DNR`, and `Billing` databases from the backup files on the code bundle included with this book.

2. For each of the restored databases, add a current Windows user login to the database logins. Specify `Default Schema = 'dbo'`.

3. Open Visual Studio 2012 and navigate to **New | Biz Talk Projects | Empty BizTalk Server Project**. Enter `ATI` as the name of the project.

4. Right-click on the `ATI` project in **Solution Explorer**, then navigate to **Add | Add Generated Items**.

5. In the **Add Generated Item Wizard** screen, select **Consume Adapter Service**:

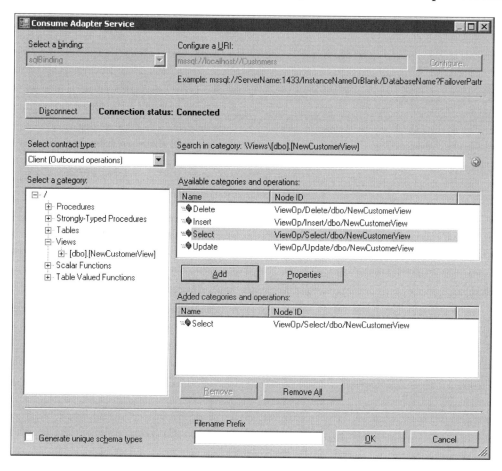

6. Within the **Consume Adapter Service** window (as shown in the preceding screenshot), perform the following steps:

   1. Select `sqlBinding` from the **Select a binding** dropdown.

   2. In the **Configure a URI** box, enter `mssql://localhost//Customers`. Change `localhost` to the named instance of SQL Server if necessary.

   3. Click on the **Configure** button to the right of the **Configure a URI** box. Change the value of **Client Credential Type** from **None** to **Windows**.

4. Click on the **Connect** button. If a connection to SQL Server is successful, the **Select a Category** window will be populated with SQL object types.

5. In the **Select a Category** window, expand **Views**. Click on dbo. NewCustomerView.

6. In the **Available Categories and Operations** window, click on the **Select** operation. Then, click on the **Add** button.

7. Click on **OK**.

7. Repeat steps 4 to 6 for the following database objects:

    ○   The Customer table of the Billing database: Select the **Insert** operation from the **Available Categories and Operations** list

    ○   The Domain table of the DNR database: Select the **Insert** operation from the **Available Categories and Operations** list

8. Right-click on the ATI project in the **Solution Explorer** view and navigate to **Add | Add New Item**. Select **BizTalk Orchestration** from the list of BizTalk templates. Enter New Customer Provisioning Orchestration as the orchestration name.

9. In the **Orchestration View** pane, right-click on the Port Types folder and select **New One-Way Port Type**.

10. Click on PortType_1. In the **Properties** pane, change the value of **Identifier** to PortType_Incoming. Expand the PortType_Incoming node.

11. Expand Operation_1. Click on the Request_1 node. In the **Properties** pane, click on the **Message Type** dropdown. Expand the Schemas node. Click on ATI.newViewOperation_dbo_NewCustomerView.Select.

12. In the **Orchestration Editor** window, right-click on the **Port Surface** pane and select **New Port** from the pop-up menu. The Port_1 icon will appear in the pane.

13. Click on the Port_1 icon. Then, in the **Properties** view, perform the following steps:

    1. Change the value of **Identifier** to NewCustomerPort.

    2. Click on the **Port Type** dropdown. Select PortType_Incoming.

14. Repeat steps 8 to 13 to add **Port Types** to **Orchestration** for the following schema objects:

    ○ `ATI.TableOperation_dbo_Customer.Insert`

    ○ `ATI.TableOperation_dbo_Domain.Insert`

15. In the **Orchestration View** pane, right-click on the `Messages` folder. Select **New Message**.

16. Change the identifier for `Message_1` to `Msg_CustNotification`. Change the value of **Message Type** to `ATI.newViewOperation_dbo_NewCustomerView.Select`.

17. Repeat steps 15 and 16 to create the following two message types:

    ○ **Identifier**: `Msg_InsBilling` and **Message Type**: `ATI.TableOperation_dbo_Customer.Insert`

    ○ **Identifier**: `Msg_NewDomain` and **Message Type**: `ATI.TableOperation_dbo_Domain.Insert`

18. Drag-and-drop the **Receive** component from the **Toolbox** pane to the center of the orchestration.

19. Click on the `Receive_1` icon. In the **Properties** pane, change the value of **Operation** to `NewCustomerPort.Operation_Get_New_Customers.Request`. Change the value of **Message** to `Msg_CustNotification` and the value of **Name** to `NewCust_Notification`.

20. In the toolbox, double-click on **Transform Component**. The Transform Component icon will appear under the **Receive** component.

21. Double-click on the Transform Component icon to open **Transform Configuration** window. Then, perform the following steps:

    1. In the **Transform** pane, click on **Source**. In the **Source Transform** grid, select `Variable Name = Msg_CustNotification`.

    2. In the **Transform** pane, click on **Destination**. In the **Destination Transform** grid, select `Variable Name = Msg_InsBilling`.

    3. Check the **When I click OK, launch the Biztalk Mapper** option.

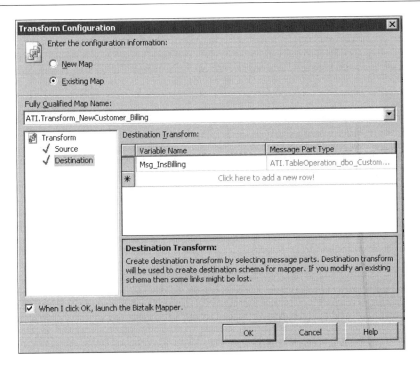

22. In **BizTalk Mapper**, create links between the **Source Columns** (in the left-hand pane) and **ns3:Customer** (in the right-hand pane) nodes.

23. Drag-and-drop the **Send** component from the toolbox into the **Orchestration** window. Repeat steps 18 to 22 to create the following two operations:

    ○ The operation `Insert Billing.Configure` with the `ATI.TableOperation_dbo_Customer.Insert` message type

    ○ The operation `Insert Domain.Configure` with the `ATI.TableOperation_dbo_Domain.Insert` message type

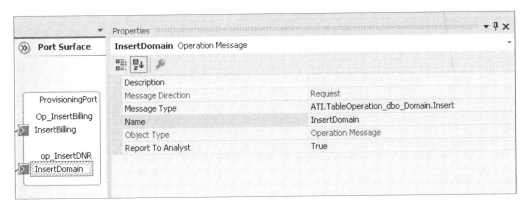

24. The orchestration should now look as shown in the following screenshot:

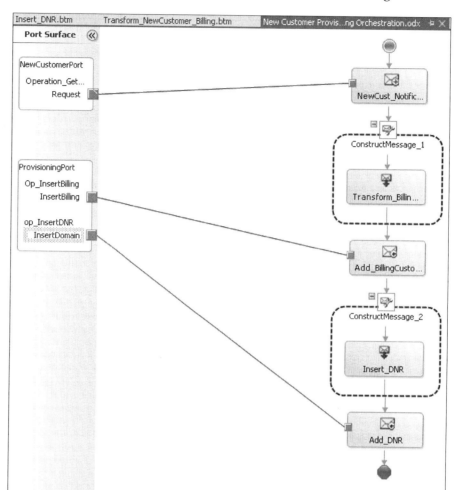

Lessons learned

We have defined, analyzed, and implemented a simple use case scenario for the BizTalk implementation. From this example, it is easy to see how a BizTalk solution can be expanded to handle very large and complex business scenarios—involving multiple systems, both in-house and third party—using various technologies. BizTalk's primary role is to serve as a messaging hub that orchestrates the communication between various systems and ensures reliable delivery.

Summary

In the world of software system integration, MS BizTalk Server plays a significant role. It provides reliable delivery and is the ultimate tool for Enterprise Application Integration scenarios delivered using Microsoft technologies.

In the next chapter, we will present another complex tool that has become the ultimate solution for many enterprise scenarios, such as content and document management, enterprise collaboration, and even for building social networks: Microsoft SharePoint Server.

6
The SharePoint Server Primer

Perhaps you have read the parable about the three blind men and the elephant (http://en.wikipedia.org/wiki/Blind_men_and_an_elephant). This story is very apropos when describing **Microsoft SharePoint Server** (**SharePoint**) and its many capabilities. If you ask three software architects what SharePoint is, they will each give you a different answer, depending on the specific features and capabilities of SharePoint that they have used. It is very rare indeed that you will meet an architect or developer who has experience with all of the capabilities of SharePoint. The first architect might claim that SharePoint is an enterprise content management, document management, or even a business process management product. The second will insist that SharePoint is a collaboration and social networking product. And the last will say that it is an Intranet-In-A-Box. And they would all be partially correct; SharePoint is all of the mentioned features (and much more), but it is not a product; it is a **business application platform**, and it is both wide and deep. SharePoint should be viewed as a toolbox for developing very powerful business applications, often with little or no requirement to write any custom code (though rich APIs are available when you need deeper customization).

Choosing whether to use SharePoint in a system or application and then choosing which of SharePoint's myriad capabilities to use in that system can be challenging. It is the goal of this primer to give architects and developers enough information to get the most out of SharePoint, while avoiding some of the possible pitfalls and antipatterns.

The latest version of SharePoint is **SharePoint 2013**, and this primer focuses on the features and capabilities of this most recent version. Most of the topics are highly applicable to SharePoint 2010, though less so to SharePoint 2007 and its predecessors.

The SharePoint editions

SharePoint comes in a number of editions, including **Foundation**, **Standard**, **Enterprise** and **Online**:

- **Foundation edition**: This edition (formally known as Windows SharePoint Services) offers only the core capabilities of SharePoint and is available as a free download from Microsoft (`http://www.microsoft.com/en-us/download/details.aspx?id=35488`). SharePoint Foundation's only licensing requirement is that each user has a valid Windows **Client Access License (CAL)**.

- **Standard edition**: This includes all of the capabilities of Foundation and adds many capabilities targeted at small- to medium-sized organizations and departments, including additional site templates, and collaboration, enterprise content management, and Search capabilities.

- **Enterprise edition**: This includes all of the capabilities and services that the SharePoint platform has to offer and is targeted at larger organizations. These additional capabilities include the Office services, that is, Access, Excel, InfoPath, Visio Services, as well as Power View and PerformancePoint Services.

> The Standard and Enterprise editions of SharePoint have different licensing requirements depending on whether the farm is being used to host intranet, extranet, or Internet sites. For SharePoint 2013, a server license is always required for each server running the SharePoint software, and internal users require either a Standard or Enterprise SharePoint CAL, depending on the SharePoint capabilities that they are using. External users do not require a CAL and are licensed under the server license. Microsoft has a document that describes the new SharePoint 2013 licensing model at `http://download.microsoft.com/download/3/D/4/3D42BDC2-6725-4B29-B75A-A5B04179958B/Licensing_Microsoft_SharePoint_Server_2013.pdf`.

- **Online edition**: This is one of the hosted services (along with Exchange and Lync) available in Microsoft's **Office 365 (O365)** cloud platform. Microsoft provides multiple subscription plans that provide either the Standard edition or Enterprise edition capabilities, on either single- or multi-tenant/shared servers. Online edition is licensed per user, as is all of O365.

The specific edition of SharePoint that your application or organization will need will depend on the specific capabilities that you require; a detailed feature comparison of the SharePoint 2013 editions and their capabilities is available at `http://technet.microsoft.com/en-us/library/sharepoint-online-service-description.aspx`.

The SharePoint platform

At its very core, SharePoint is a distributed, multi-tiered, Microsoft **Internet Information Server (IIS)** application, comprising unmanaged, COM-based ISAPI extensions (`OWSSRV.DLL` being the most important) and APIs; .NET Framework-based APIs hosted in ASP.NET, XML, HTML, CSS, JavaScript, and image files stored in the Windows filesystem; and configuration and content stored in Microsoft SQL Server. Though much of SharePoint's core capabilities are implemented in native/unmanaged COM objects, and though calls to those COM objects are allowed (either directly or through HTTP RPC calls to the ISAPI extensions), all of those capabilities are also exposed by the .NET Framework-based "wrapper" APIs, which include SOAP and REST web services.

SharePoint is a very complex system, and its architecture has many layers of abstraction above IIS, COM, ASP.NET, and SQL Server. Luckily, understanding COM is not necessary for understanding SharePoint, but having a good knowledge of IIS and ASP.NET will certainly help in gaining a deep understanding of SharePoint. Most of the metadata, configuration, and user content (including documents) associated with SharePoint are stored in Microsoft SQL Server, but direct manipulation of raw SharePoint data is almost never required, nor is it encouraged.

The rest of this chapter will discuss the levels of abstraction within SharePoint that a developer or architect will need to understand in order to design and develop solutions for and with SharePoint.

The SharePoint server topology

A typical SharePoint installation consists of a single SharePoint farm. All servers in the farm operate, and are managed, as a single logical system, and most SharePoint services are farm-bound (though some can operate across farms). An entire farm can be installed on a single physical or virtual server, or can be installed on many servers, each in one or more SharePoint Server roles (not to be confused with Windows Server roles).

For an Enterprise-scale SharePoint 2013 farm, Microsoft recommends the use of 32 physical servers hosting 59 virtual servers! See `http://go.microsoft.com/fwlink/p/?LinkId=271929`. SharePoint also supports multi-farm installations if high-scalability is the principal requirement of the installation, or if strict departmental isolation is required, because of significant differences in policy or security requirements. See `http://go.microsoft.com/fwlink/p/?LinkId=267619`.

The exact topology and number of servers that will be needed for a system or organization will depend on the required performance, scalability, and capabilities (and your hardware and software budget). Microsoft provides good guidance on how to design an appropriate farm topology for an organization or system. See `http://go.microsoft.com/fwlink/p/?LinkId=257304` and `http://go.microsoft.com/fwlink/p/?LinkId=286978`.

The SharePoint server roles

There are three primary server roles within a SharePoint farm: the Web Server role (referred to as a Web Front End explained in next section server), the Application Server role, and the Database Server role. A server role simply describes the specific SharePoint services that are running on the server and that are being actively used as part of the overall SharePoint installation; the SharePoint components and services installed by default for the Web Server and Application Server roles are identical. A physical or virtual server may be in more than one role and, in the case of a single-server installation, will be in all three roles. The hardware and software requirements for each server role for SharePoint 2013 can be found at `http://technet.microsoft.com/en-us/library/cc262485.aspx`.

The Web Server role

The **Web Server role**, or **Web Front End (WFE)** server, describes a physical or virtual server in a SharePoint farm that is primarily directly handling HTTP(S) requests made by users, typically using a web browser, or from external client applications using SOAP or REST web services. A server in a Web Server role is typically configured with exactly the same base services and components as a server in the Application Server role, but is then configured to only actively run those services associated with the Web Server role. In SharePoint 2013, both roles are installed by simply selecting **Complete** as the value of **Server Type** in the installation wizard.

Adding WFE servers is one of the primary **scale-out** strategies for increasing the number of simultaneous user requests the SharePoint farm can accommodate with a user-acceptable response time for every response. See `http://www.nngroup.com/articles/response-times-3-important-limits/` for the currently accepted definition of "user-acceptable response time". WFE servers are essentially "stateless" web servers, and scale-out can be achieved by load-balancing requests across all the servers using hardware or software load balancing, for example, Windows Server **Network Load Balancing (NLB)**.

> By default, IIS has HTTP Keep-Alive response headers enabled, which will cause the HTTP connection between the client browser or application and IIS on the WFE server to remain open across multiple HTTP requests. Although this setting does reduce the response time of each of the HTTP requests made over a single connection, it also guarantees server affinity while the connection is kept alive, and therefore reduces the efficiency of a per-request, round-robin load-balancing strategy. Also note that disabling HTTP Keep-Alive response headers in IIS will render Integrated Windows Authentication with NTLM inoperable.

The Application Server role

The SharePoint **Application Server role** describes a physical or virtual server in a SharePoint farm that is *primarily* hosting one or more SharePoint **service applications**. In SharePoint 2013, there are 17 service applications, which include the Search, Access, Business Data, Excel, Visio Graphics, and App Management Service applications, to name just a few. You can see a full list of all of the service applications at `http://go.microsoft.com/fwlink/p/?LinkId=259425`.

Typically, unless SharePoint is installed on a single server, users should not be making direct HTTP(S) requests to a server in the Application Server role, and the SharePoint (Foundation) Web Application service should be disabled. If a service application is started on multiple physical or virtual application servers in a SharePoint farm, SharePoint will automatically load-balance between them using Application Discovery and Load Balancer (or simply, Topology) services.

The Search Application Server role is a subset of the Application Server role that is dedicated to running SharePoint Search-specific services. In large-scale deployments, there can be two Search Application Server roles: one focused on indexing and query processing, and the second on crawling, administration, analytics, and content processing. Because of the importance of Search in SharePoint, and the often-high computational costs associated with Search, it is often necessary to put the Search services and components on dedicated application and database servers.

The SharePoint Application Server role should not be confused with the Windows (Server) Application Server role, which is required to be installed on servers configured for both the SharePoint WFE and application roles.

The Database Server role

The SharePoint Database Server role describes a physical or virtual server in a SharePoint farm that is running Microsoft SQL Server, often in a SQL cluster, and is hosting one or more of the many databases created and used by SharePoint.

If a farm is using all of the services in SharePoint 2013, there will be as many as 24 databases or more hosted in SQL Server. In large-scale SharePoint installations, there will be servers in the Database Server role dedicated to storing only Search-related data, and others dedicated to storing content and other service data. Microsoft provides a diagram detailing all of the SharePoint databases at `http://go.microsoft.com/fwlink/p/?LinkId=257370`.

SharePoint does not provide any special scale-out capabilities for servers in the Database Server role other than those provided by SQL Server itself (see `http://msdn.microsoft.com/en-us/library/aa479364.aspx`).

Administration and management

Administration and management of a SharePoint farm is done using the SharePoint Central Administration website, Windows PowerShell for SharePoint cmdlets, or through custom applications written using the SharePoint Server Object Model. Site-level administration is done within the SharePoint user interface. There are also a number of very good third-party tools that ease the administration and management of SharePoint.

Know your limits

It is always good to know what the documented limits for a technology or product are before including it in the design of a system. Fortunately, Microsoft provides a detailed document of the software boundaries and limits for SharePoint 2013 at `http://technet.microsoft.com/en-us/library/cc262787.aspx`. Having a good knowledge of these limits will help you to avoid a number of common SharePoint antipatterns, for example, deeply-nested site/subsite hierarchies.

Core concepts and capabilities of SharePoint

As mentioned before, SharePoint should be viewed as a platform rather than a product, and as such, offers an architect an extensive toolbox of capabilities and services that can be used as or in a solution. Understanding those capabilities and services, and how they can be composed, is key to getting the most out of SharePoint. The following section describes many, though not all, of the core concepts and capabilities of the SharePoint platform. This section also indicates the specific SharePoint APIs that are available for programmatically accessing each entity or capability. The broader SharePoint APIs are described in a later section.

SharePoint web applications

A **SharePoint web application** is the logical root container in the SharePoint Content Hierarchy. A web application provides logical service, feature, policy, user, and content isolation. Site collections and their sites and lists and all their items and documents are contained within a SharePoint web application.

A web application is not just a logical abstraction, however; it also represents a number of identical IIS web applications running on all WFE servers in the farm. IIS web applications provide configuration, content, security and lifetime isolation, by running each application in a dedicated or shared **application pool** (which is just a .NET application domain under the covers). These ASP.NET applications are the host environments for the SharePoint runtime components associated with handling HTTP(S) user and web service requests for content contained within the SharePoint web application.

SharePoint web applications are created and administered in the SharePoint Central Administration web interface, and the associated IIS applications are created or modified on each WFE server in the farm automatically.

In the SharePoint **Server Object Model (SOM)**, the web application is represented by the `SPWebApplication` class in the `Microsoft.SharePoint.Administration` namespace. The web application is not exposed in the SharePoint .NET SharePoint **Client-side Object Model (CSOM)** or SharePoint **JavaScript Object Model (JSOM)** APIs.

SharePoint content database

SharePoint web applications are associated with one or more **SharePoint content databases**, which are SQL Server databases used to store one or more site collections and all of the content associated with them. A content database can only be associated with a single web application, though multiple site collections can be stored in a single content database.

In the SOM, the content database is represented by the `SPContentDatabase` class in the `Microsoft.SharePoint.Administration` namespace. The content database is not exposed in the CSOM or JSOM APIs.

Though a user with appropriate permissions can access and modify a SharePoint content database directly, it is not advisable; the intrinsic databases should not be considered valid extensibility points for SharePoint. The SharePoint SQL schema is highly normalized and abstract, and it is easy to break it in such a way that all your data becomes inaccessible. Modifying the database schema directly is also unsupported by Microsoft (`http://support.microsoft.com/kb/841057`), and any changes you make might be overwritten by a service pack or update. It is best to treat the database as a black box and access it through one of the many SharePoint APIs.

SharePoint site collections

Every SharePoint web application has one or more **site collections** contained within it. A site collection represents a root SharePoint site and all of its content, which almost always includes a hierarchy of nested subsites. Site collections are accessed via a distinct URL, which can be either a unique subpath of the web application root URL, for example, `http://www.acme.com/sites/finance`, or in 2013, can be a distinct hostname, for example, `http://finance.acme.com/`.

Typically, all of the sites in a site collection represent a logical grouping of content along organizational or functional lines, for example, a business unit or cross-cutting business function. Subsites inherit the configuration, capabilities, and branding of the root site in the site collection by default, which allows the entire site collection to be managed as a single logical entity. A site collection is stored in one of the content databases associated with the site collection's parent web application.

In SOM, the site collection is represented by the `SPSite` class in the `Microsoft.SharePoint` namespace. The site collection is not exposed in the CSOM or JSOM APIs (though the root site of the site collection is).

Warning!

The naming in the SOM can get a little confusing, primarily because the class names do not always have an immediately intuitive relationship with the SharePoint logical entity that they represent. For example, SPSite encapsulates functionalities related to the site collection, while SPWeb encapsulates the functionalities related to a site. There is also `SPSiteCollection`, which is actually an `IEnumerable<SPSite>` collection containing all of the site collections in a web application!

SharePoint sites

A **SharePoint site** is the primary container (available to non-administrator users) for partitioning content and functionality within SharePoint. A site can typically be created by any user with appropriate permissions using the regular SharePoint web interface. When creating a new site, a title and a URL name are required; the latter is used to produce the canonical URL used to access the site. You can also configure alternate URLs for the site using the *alternate access mappings* feature.

A site is created from a site template, which defines the site's initial structure, functionality, and appearance, and also the templates available for creating subsites. In SharePoint 2013, a new site collection is created with either the 2013 experience version or the 2010 experience version, and this governs which version of the templates will be available when creating new sites in that site collection. A site collection created with the 2010 experience version can be upgraded to the 2013 version at a later time, though not all of the 2010 templates have a 2013 equivalent. Unless you are upgrading from SharePoint 2010, it is recommended that you use the 2013 experience version templates.

There are three categories of the SharePoint 2013 experience version site templates: **Collaboration**, **Enterprise**, and **Publishing**. The Collaboration category includes templates for blogs and team, community, and project sites. The Enterprise category includes templates for document, eDiscovery, records, business intelligence, and enterprise search centers. The Publishing category includes templates for publishing portals, sites, and enterprise wikis. SharePoint also supports creating and using custom site templates. You can read about all of the site templates available in SharePoint 2013, and their capabilities at `http://technet.microsoft.com/en-us/library/cc262410.aspx`.

In SOM, the site is represented by the `SPWeb` class in the `Microsoft.SharePoint` namespace. In CSOM, the site is represented by the `Site` class in the `Microsoft.SharePoint.Client` namespace, and in the JSOM is represented by the `SP.Site` object in `sp.js`.

SharePoint lists

The **SharePoint list** is the workhorse of the SharePoint platform, and most SharePoint capabilities and features use the list in some way. If there is one SharePoint concept (and its implementation) that every SharePoint developer or architect must master, it's list. A **list** is a table (similar to a SQL table or Excel worksheet), with typed and named columns (or **fields**), and rows (or **list items**), which contain the actual list data. A user can create a **custom list** or use one of the built-in **list templates**, for example, announcements, contacts, events, tasks, and so on. Whether an appropriately permissioned user creates a custom list, or uses one of the aforementioned templates to create one, they can customize or modify the list at any time, typically by adding columns, content types, or views.

 SharePoint lists can also be configured to contain data that is external to SharePoint, using external content types and **Business Connectivity Services** (**BCS**). BCS is a very powerful way to seamlessly integrate line-of-business data into SharePoint. You can read more about BCS at `http://technet.microsoft.com/en-us/library/ee661740.aspx`.

In SOM, the list and list items are represented by the `SPList` and `SPListItem` classes in the `Microsoft.SharePoint` namespace. In CSOM, they are represented by the `List` and `ListItem` classes in the `Microsoft.SharePoint.Client` namespace, and in the JSOM are represented by the `SP.List` and `SP.ListItem` objects in `sp.js`.

SharePoint columns

Columns are first-class SharePoint entities; they are named, typed, and scoped to a site and its subsites, or a specific list. A number of column types are available, including the **choice type**, which allows the user to provide a list of possible values for the column, and the **managed metadata type**, which requires that the value come from a specific taxonomy or set of tags. A user can create both site- and list-scoped columns through the SharePoint user interface. Site columns are stored in the site column gallery, though adding a site column to a list *copies* the column to the list. A user needs to explicitly propagate changes made to a site column to all lists that are using that column.

In SOM, the column is represented by the `SPField` class in the `Microsoft.SharePoint` namespace. In CSOM, it is represented by the `Field` class in the `Microsoft.SharePoint.Client` namespace, and in JSOM is represented by the `SP.Field` object in `sp.js`.

SharePoint content types

Lists can also be configured to allow the management of content types. **Content types** can be thought of as a named collection of site columns, but there is far more to them than that; content types can also include a document template, forms, workflows, information management policy, and other resources. Content types are essentially a mechanism for *encapsulating* related data, policy, and behavior. Some examples of built-in content types are announcement, contact, event, and task (note the relationship to the list templates mentioned previously).

Content types are scoped to the site they are created in and that site's subsites, and are stored in the site content type gallery. Content types, such as site columns, also support a weak form of inheritance; a new content type is always based on an existing content type. That base type can be one of the built-in content types, for example, document or item, or another in-scope custom content type. Like site columns, propagation of changes from a base content type to derived content types is not automatic; a user has to explicitly choose to propagate the changes. A list may be configured to contain multiple content types, though there is always a default content type associated with the list.

In SOM, the content type is represented by the `SPContentType` class in the `Microsoft.SharePoint` namespace. In CSOM, it is represented by the `ContentType` class in the `Microsoft.SharePoint.Client` namespace, and in the JSOM is represented by the `SP.ContentType` object in `sp.js`.

SharePoint views

A list can also have multiple user-specific or public views that define how the list items in that list will be displayed in the browser. **Views** allow for the inclusion of specific columns and also allow custom sorting, filtering, grouping, summing, and layout. When a list is created, a default public view is automatically created for the list, and possibly multiple other views, based on the template that was used to create it. Multiple new views can be created and any public view can be set as the default view for the list by a user with appropriate permissions.

In SOM, the view is represented by the `SPView` class in the `Microsoft.SharePoint` namespace. In CSOM, it is represented by the `View` class in the `Microsoft.SharePoint.Client` namespace, and in JSOM the view is represented by the `SP.View` object in `sp.js`.

SharePoint document libraries

A **document library** is a specialized SharePoint list that is customized for storing documents and files. Each item in the library *is* a document, though the item can also have additional columns. All lists support attachments and major versioning, but document libraries also support check-in/out, property promotion/demotion, minor versioning, WebDAV accessibility, and a number of other document-centric capabilities. Libraries also enable the "New Folder" command by default so that files can be easily arranged into folder hierarchies.

In SOM, the document library is represented by the `SPDocumentLibrary` class, which derives from `SPList`. The documents in the library are just `ListItem` instances, and the actual file is represented by the `SPFile` class, an instance of which is returned by the `ListItem.File` property accessor. Folders are represented by the `SPFolder` class. In CSOM and JSOM, there is no special class or object for the document library, and an instance is treated as a `List` class instance or `SP.List` object instance respectively. A folder is represented by the `Folder` class in CSOM and by the `SP.Folder` object in JSOM.

SharePoint web parts

Web Parts are a server-side ASP.NET technology for creating web pages whose layout and behavior are user-modifiable within the browser. Web Parts can be dynamically placed in **Web Part zones**, which are contained within a **Web Part page**. This ability to dynamically compose Web Parts can be used for either single-user personalization or customization of a page or portion thereof for all users. You can read more about ASP.NET Web Parts at `http://msdn.microsoft.com/en-us/library/hhy9ewf1.aspx`.

SharePoint uses primarily ASP.NET Web Parts for the composition of its web user interface to give administrators and users the highest degree of flexibility in how the SharePoint UI looks and behaves. Web Parts are embedded in SharePoint pages and are most often used to display list data, but because Web Parts are server-side controls, they can be configured to have access to all of the capabilities of SharePoint through the server object model (though it is always best to follow the *principle of least privilege*).

Because almost every SharePoint UI element is either a Web Part or part of one, SharePoint has a large number of built-in Web Parts. The exact Web Parts that a site will have available will depend on the edition of SharePoint installed/licensed and the site template that was used to create the site. There are also a large number of free and paid-for, third-party Web Parts for SharePoint. Web Parts are stored in the Web Part gallery of the site and are scoped to the site they are installed in and its subsites, though they can be deployed to an entire site collection or farm.

Web Parts also provide developers with a powerful and convenient mechanism for extending SharePoint's user interface and experience. Custom Web Parts are typically developed with Visual Studio, which includes multiple project and item templates for designing, coding, and packaging custom Web Parts for SharePoint, including Web Parts based on Silverlight. You can read more about creating custom Web Parts for SharePoint 2013 at `http://msdn.microsoft.com/en-us/library/ee231579.aspx`.

ASP.NET Web Parts are represented by the `WebPart` class in the `System.Web.UI.WebControls.WebParts` namespace. In CSOM, it is represented by the `WebPart` class, and in JSOM it is represented by the `SP.WebPart` object.

There is a second API for developing SharePoint Web Parts; the confusingly named SharePoint Web Parts API. This API, which is in the `System.SharePoint.WebPartPages` namespace, is actually based on the ASP.NET Web Parts API. However, unlike Web Parts created with the ASP.NET Web Parts API, SharePoint Web Parts cannot be run outside of the context of SharePoint. There are very few cases where this API will be required.

Apps for SharePoint

In SharePoint 2013, Microsoft has added the new **Apps for SharePoint (SharePoint Apps)** capability to the platform. SharePoint Apps introduces a new, predominantly cloud-based, development model, which enables extending SharePoint using standard-based web technologies, for example, HTML5, CSS, and JavaScript, and a new execution model where Apps generally run outside of SharePoint and access SharePoint capabilities using one of the web-based client APIs (see the *SharePoint APIs* section later in this chapter). SharePoint 2013 also introduces a new mechanism for publishing and sharing these Apps; Apps can be published to on-premises app catalogs hosted in SharePoint 2013, or to Microsoft's Office Store. You can read more about Apps for SharePoint at `http://msdn.microsoft.com/en-us/library/office/fp161507(v=office.15).aspx`.

SharePoint workflows

A SharePoint workflow is an automated, often human-driven, business process executed in, and managed by, SharePoint. SharePoint workflows primarily operate over lists, libraries, list items, documents, folders, and forms, but can also respond to SharePoint events, send e-mails, interact with other SharePoint service applications or external services, and even start other workflows. There are three types of SharePoint workflows: **site workflows** are site features and are scoped to a site and its subsites; **reusable workflows** are associated with a content type and can be associated with multiple lists within a site; **list workflows** are only associated with a specific list and its contents. Workflows can be added to lists, list items, folders, and content types. Workflows can be started manually, or automatically based on an event, for example, the event of a new list item being added to the list.

An example of a commonly used SharePoint workflow is the **Approval workflow**, which notifies approvers that a document is ready for approval and then notifies the author once the document is approved or rejected. SharePoint 2013 has a number of other built-in workflows, including **Collect Feedback**, **Collect Signatures**, **Three-State**, and **Publishing Approval**. Custom workflows can be created in either SharePoint Designer or Visual Studio. Both tools support visual editing of the workflow flowchart, but only Visual Studio supports adding custom activities and code to workflows. Both tools also support the creation of custom workflow forms, though InfoPath may also be required depending on the SharePoint edition that the workflow will be deployed to. Visio can also be used to edit or modify workflow flowcharts, but SharePoint Designer is required to deploy them to SharePoint.

SharePoint workflow is based on **Windows Workflow Foundation (WF)**, which is the workflow API in the .NET Framework. Prior to SharePoint 2013, workflows were implemented using WF 3.x (3.0 or 3.5), and workflows ran in the SharePoint web application process. SharePoint 2013 has added a new workflow model called **Windows Azure Workflows** based on the new WF 4.0 API, which is ostensibly a complete rewrite. In the 2013 workflow model, the workflows run in the Workflow Manager process, which is external to SharePoint, and uses Windows Azure Service Bus to communicate with SharePoint. You can read about the SharePoint 2013 workflow model at `http://msdn.microsoft.com/en-us/library/jj163181`. SharePoint 2013 supports both workflow models and provides a mechanism to interoperate between them.

SOM provides programmatic access to SharePoint workflows through the new `Microsoft.SharePoint.WorkflowServices` API and the older `Microsoft.SharePoint.Workflow` API. Since the new API is compatible with both WF 3.x and 4.x workflows, it should be the API of choice for all new development. Workflows are also accessible in CSOM using the `Microsoft.SharePoint.Client.WorkflowServices` API, and in JSOM in the `SP.WorkflowService.js` API.

SharePoint forms

Forms are used to edit and display data that typically resides in SharePoint lists. There are perhaps too many options for creating forms in SharePoint 2013, including list forms, custom ASP.NET Web Forms, Access, Excel, HTML/CSS/JavaScript, InfoPath, and Silverlight forms.

It is also not always immediately evident which of these should or is being used for any given form. As an example, the default list forms use the `ListFormWebPart` class embedded in ASPX pages to render a list item as a simple form for displaying or editing. But you can customize them with InfoPath, which adds new default forms based on InfoPath documents (`.xsn`) that are seamlessly rendered in the browser (in a different Web Part). Alternatively, you can add your own custom forms in SharePoint Designer, which uses a Data View (Web Part) and a combination of XSLT, HTML, JavaScript, and possibly CSS. It can get quite confusing.

In January 2014, Microsoft announced that they will be retiring the InfoPath client and InfoPath Forms Services in SharePoint and are working on a replacement forms technology (see `http://blogs.office.com/2014/01/31/update-on-infopath-and-sharepoint-forms/`). As of this writing though, they have not announced what that technology will be, so for the moment InfoPath (Version 2013 for SharePoint 2013) is the most deeply-integrated, feature-rich, and flexible option for creating forms in SharePoint and, therefore, it is the obvious choice when considering a SharePoint forms technology.

The APIs you will use to access and manipulate forms will somewhat depend on which technology you choose. However, a form associated with a list is typically represented by the `SPForm` class in SOM. In CSOM, it is represented by the `Form` class, and, in JSOM it is represented by the `SP.Form` object.

SharePoint service applications

SharePoint **service applications** are shared services that are available to all sites within a SharePoint farm, and in some cases, across multiple farms. SharePoint provides a number of out-of-the-box service applications with each edition of SharePoint; for example, **Business Connectivity Services** (**BCS**) is a service application that is available in all editions of SharePoint, while the Access, Excel, and Visio Services are only available in the Enterprise edition. SharePoint Enterprise search is also implemented as a service application.

Service applications are yet another extensibility point for SharePoint, though they are also one of the most complex to implement, and are poorly documented. SOM includes all of the necessary APIs to create custom service applications that reside in the `Microsoft.SharePoint.Administration` namespace.

SharePoint Search

Perhaps the most important capability of SharePoint is the ability it gives
users to search data and documents stored within it, and also to search external
line-of-business data, or data that resides in external data sources, all within a single
web-based user interface. All editions of SharePoint include some Search capabilities,
though they are very limited in SharePoint Foundation. The Standard and Enterprise
editions of SharePoint include full SharePoint Search, which is a platform in its own
right. SharePoint Search has been designed for massive scalability, and is also highly
extensible. You can read about the SharePoint 2013 Search platform at `http://msdn.`
`microsoft.com/en-us/library/office/jj163300.aspx`. Search APIs are available
in SOM, CSOM, and JSOM, and through REST web services.

SharePoint extensibility

If the built-in templates, content types, Web Parts, pages, features, service application
and so on, are not adequate for your organization or system, then the SharePoint
platform offers many extensibility points and APIs that you can use to develop your
own. In SharePoint 2013, there are two primary models for extending the platform:
the **SharePoint Solutions model** and the new **SharePoint (Cloud) Apps model**.
The major difference between these models is that SharePoint solutions run in a
SharePoint process and leverage SOM, while SharePoint Apps run in a separate,
isolated process, which can be hosted in SharePoint, in Azure, or wherever the
architect wants, and use one of the SharePoint client APIs; for example, CSOM,
JSOM, or REST.

The SharePoint Apps model is very convenient for building small SharePoint
applications and widgets, but any significant customizations of SharePoint
will require a SharePoint solution, including building custom site or list templates,
complex workflows, administration tools, branding, service applications, and so on.
The SharePoint solutions model can also be used to create **sandbox solutions**, which
run in a SharePoint process but are isolated from the SharePoint web application
process. You can read more about the differences between the models at
`http://msdn.microsoft.com/library/office/jj163114.aspx`.

SharePoint APIs

SharePoint offers multiple APIs for extending the capabilities of the platform. Each of these APIs has different use cases and limitations. Choosing the appropriate API for a given use case can sometimes be challenging and, in many cases, a custom SharePoint solution or application will require the use of more than one. There is a good paper on choosing the appropriate API(s) for a specific SharePoint customization on MSDN at `http://msdn.microsoft.com/en-us/library/jj164060.aspx`, but the following few paragraphs give a summary of the APIs, their common use cases, and limitations.

SharePoint Server Object Model

The SharePoint **Server Object Model (SOM)**, which predominantly resides in the `Microsoft.SharePoint` namespace and identically named assembly, provides the broadest and deepest programmatic access to SharePoint. It can be used to create custom ASP.NET pages and user controls, web services, Web Parts, complex workflows, central admin extensions, and extensions that have pretty much complete access to every aspect of the SharePoint platform. The SOM API has one major restriction though; it only works if the code that references the SOM assemblies is executing on a WFE or Application Server. The capabilities of SOM are also governed by the edition of SharePoint that you are using, for example, if you have SharePoint Foundation 2013 installed, SOM exposes far fewer types and methods than if you have SharePoint Server 2013 installed.

 SOM can also be used in conjunction with **LINQ to SharePoint**, which transforms LINQ queries on lists into **Collaborative Application Markup Language (CAML)** queries. Removing the necessity to learn CAML, which is a fairly complex XML-based query language, is justification enough to use LINQ to SharePoint.

SharePoint web services

SharePoint 2013 exposes its data and functionality through a number of web service APIs. These include WCF-based **RESTful OData services** and **WCF Data Services** (previously **ADO.NET Data Services Framework**), which give you strongly-typed queries over list data. SharePoint also supports WebDAV-based access to SharePoint documents over HTTP/S, which also happens to be the service that is used to open a SharePoint site or document library in Windows Explorer.

The legacy SOAP-based SharePoint ASP.NET Web Services, for example, `Lists.asmx` or `Sites.asmx`, and direct **Remote Procedure Calls (RPCs)**, which are HTTP Posts to the `OWSSVR.dll` ISAPI extension, are still supported in SharePoint 2013, but have been deprecated. Their use should be avoided.

SharePoint .NET Client-side Object Model

The **Client-side Object Model (CSOM)** can be used to develop .NET desktop, server, web, and cloud applications that integrate with SharePoint. CSOM exposes the capabilities of SharePoint that typically can be done through the SharePoint web user interface but *excludes* those capabilities available in the SharePoint central administration site. Under the covers, CSOM uses the RESTful OData web service, as do all the other client object models.

CSOM was originally introduced for SharePoint 2010, but had very limited capabilities; the SharePoint 2013 version of the API exposes significantly more of SharePoint's capabilities. CSOM is available from Microsoft in the SharePoint Server 2013 Client Components SDK or as part of the SharePoint 2013 installation. The 2010 version is available in the SharePoint Foundation 2010 Client Object Model Redistributable, which can be found at `http://www.microsoft.com/en-ca/download/details.aspx?id=21786`.

CSOM is designed in such a way that the developer has to explicitly load data into the object model from the server. To reduce the overhead of communicating with the server, load operations can be executed in a batch, and LINQ expressions can be used to specify specific properties to load. Though this does improve performance, it is not always clear what data will be retrieved when load operations are executed.

SharePoint Silverlight Client Object Model

Though the future of Silverlight is uncertain, Microsoft has provided a version of CSOM tailored to this technology. It is almost identical to the .NET CSOM, though it is optimized for keeping the user interface responsive. The Silverlight Client Object Model assemblies are also available from Microsoft in the SharePoint Server 2013 Client Components SDK or as part of the SharePoint 2013 installation.

A version of the Silverlight Client Object Model also exists for Windows Phone. It includes additional phone-specific APIs but only supports the core SharePoint feature set. This version of the API is available as part of the SharePoint 2013 installation.

SharePoint JavaScript Object Model

For those developers who are developing client or server (for example, Node.js) applications where .NET is not a choice, and a JavaScript runtime is available, Microsoft also provides **JavaScript Object Model (JSOM)**. The capabilities of JSOM are equivalent to those of CSOM. JSOM is available as part of the SharePoint 2010 and 2013 installations.

SharePoint development tools

Though you can do a great deal with SharePoint using just a web browser — gain access to the site settings and SharePoint central admin (and appropriate permissions of course) — if you need to make significant customizations, you will need a more powerful tool. Microsoft provides excellent tools for power users, designers and developers to extend and customize all aspects of SharePoint.

SharePoint Designer

SharePoint Designer is a free, lightweight development tool, targeted primarily at SharePoint power users, designers, and developers, to customize SharePoint sites and create SharePoint applications without the need to write .NET code (though a good working knowledge of HTML, CSS, and JavaScript is definitely required for customizing the SharePoint user interface).

A user can customize almost every aspect of a SharePoint site collection or site, including creating new, or modifying existing lists, columns, content types, master pages, site groups, and so on. One of the more useful capabilities that SharePoint Designer provides is the ability to create and modify custom SharePoint workflows. SharePoint Designer also integrates with Visio, to design workflows, and Infopath, for designing complex SharePoint forms.

The version of SharePoint Designer is tightly coupled to the version of SharePoint that is being customized, that is, SharePoint 2010 requires SharePoint Designer 2010 and SharePoint 2013 requires SharePoint Designer 2013. SharePoint Designer 2013 is available from Microsoft as a free download at http://www.microsoft.com/en-ca/download/details.aspx?id=35491.

In versions of SharePoint Designer prior to 2013, WYSIWYG editing of pages was supported, but in the latest release, this functionality has been removed. Microsoft claims that this is because the underlying technology that provided the WYSIWYG editing capabilities in previous versions has not kept up with advances in web technologies such as HTML5 and CSS3. Microsoft recommends that designers use Visual Studio or another third-party web development tool to develop or modify web pages.

Office Developer Tools for Visual Studio

Visual Studio is the primary tool for developing advanced SharePoint solutions. It includes SharePoint-specific project templates and features, which give developers the ability to rapidly customize or build extensions for every aspect of SharePoint.

These capabilities have been added to Visual Studio by installing the Microsoft Office Developer Tools for Visual Studio, which also adds templates and features for developing Microsoft Office solutions, including Office add-ins and the new apps for Office (2013) solutions. The Microsoft Office Developer Tools for Visual Studio are only available in the Professional, Premium and Ultimate editions of VS. Depending on the version of VS that is installed, this add-in may be available as part of the VS installation package or as a separate download.

In order to create new projects from the SharePoint solution templates, the target SharePoint version will need to be installed on the workstation; this is not true for the app for the SharePoint template, though a valid SharePoint site is required for debugging.

Examples of the SharePoint project templates that are included in Visual Studio 2013 are **App for SharePoint 2013**, **Silverlight Web Part**, and **Empty Project** for both SharePoint 2010 and 2013. These project templates include capabilities for packaging related files into **SharePoint Features** and then packaging one or more features into a **SharePoint Package** (WSP file), which can be directly deployed to and installed on a SharePoint farm.

Microsoft has created an MSDN Dev Center dedicated to developing for SharePoint 2013 (and earlier versions) at `http://msdn.microsoft.com/en-US/office/dn448478`.

Visual Studio 2012 and Visual Studio 2013 include the ability to create LightSwitch apps for SharePoint. LightSwitch provides a simplified programming model and environment, hosted with Visual Studio, for rapidly developing business applications. These apps can be hosted directly in SharePoint and Office 365, though integration with SharePoint is through the Client-side Object Model.

"Napa" Office 365 Development Tools

"Napa" Office 365 Development Tools (Napa) is a new online service for developing Office and SharePoint Apps for O365 inside a browser-based development environment. Napa specifically targets applications developed from the apps for SharePoint and apps for Office. You can read more about Napa and its capabilities at `http://msdn.microsoft.com/library/jj220038.aspx`.

Summary

It is impossible to do the SharePoint platform justice in the few pages dedicated to this primer. The SharePoint platform is massive, and there are a number of SharePoint capabilities and services that are not mentioned here but that are worth looking into, for example, the new social computing features in SharePoint 2013. It is probably not necessary or practical to attempt to master all of SharePoint's intricacies, but hopefully, this chapter has given you some starting points that will guide the rest of your discovery of this powerful business application platform.

In the next chapter, we shall provide an overview of some other major Microsoft technologies that mostly affect administration, office automation, and infrastructure. We'll talk about operating systems, Microsoft Office and Exchange, and Azure.

7
Other Microsoft Technologies

In the previous chapters, we considered several Microsoft technologies that would be essential for our discussion of architectural patterns. We talked about .NET, SQL Server, SSIS, BizTalk, and SharePoint. However, there are many more applications and technologies within the Microsoft domain. In this chapter, we would like to provide a brief overview of some important ones.

In this chapter, we shall talk about technologies that require more configuration than development. We'll discuss the MS operating systems, enterprise packages such as MS Office and Exchange, and technologies that support their development; finally, we'll bring cloud computing into the picture.

Operating systems

The architect's journey starts with the selection of operating systems. This step, although sometimes neglected, specifies the foundation for the entire solution. As we discussed in *Chapter 1*, *Solution Decision Framework*, there are two ways to approach the challenge: via product development or via project development.

When an organization develops a product for future distribution to customers, it is mandatory to understand what platform the customers are going to use, whether they would be using personal computers or tablets, whether they would prefer Windows or Linux, or whether the solution should be based in the cloud or on the corporate network. Microsoft offers a variety of approaches covering the entire spectrum of software development, from mobile applications with data stored in the cloud to systems serving the needs of corporations that support several data centers.

As we said earlier, we would be focusing on project development. Project constraints are heavily influenced by an organization's history. If the company has been in business for decades, it has a lot of legacy even in the smallest IT department. It starts with the operating systems in use. One of the toughest decisions architects need to make is about switching from one operating system to another or adding a new operating system to the mix. Solution maintenance and support should be the first challenges to consider. Even if the mixed solution looks less expensive at first glance, in reality, it could be very costly. Imagine, for example, that a corporation that runs its software completely on the Windows platform decides to switch from MS Exchange to a free Linux-based e-mail server. What looks free on the surface, becomes quite expensive if one considers the cost of maintaining a new server, training an employee to support Linux or hiring one who would be able to do it, changing backup and restore procedures, maintaining patches and upgrades in two different ways, and so on.

Microsoft Windows operating systems bring a lot of functionalities and "abilities" to solutions. Let's take a look at some of them in the upcoming sections.

Windows Server

The latest release of the Windows Server family consists of four editions: Windows Server 2012 R2 Datacenter, Windows Server 2012 R2 Standard, Windows Server 2012 R2 Essentials, and Windows Server 2012 R2 Foundation.

The Datacenter and Standard editions provide the same features, and they are the most feature-rich editions in the Windows Server family. The two editions are differentiated by virtualization rights only. A Standard edition license enables two virtual **operating system environments (OSEs)** on up to two processors; a Datacenter edition license enables an unlimited number of virtual OSEs on up to two processors.

[An operating system environment is an instance of an operating system, including any application configured to run on it.]

The Datacenter and Standard editions have a full-blown set of essential services: Active Directory, Web Server (IIS), Remote access, DHCP and DNS, virtualization, print services, and much more.

The Essentials and the Foundation editions target small businesses; they have a limited number of features and have a 25-user and 15-user limit, respectively. The Foundation edition is available through OEM only.

Virtualization

Microsoft Hyper-V technologies come in two flavors: a free standalone Hyper-V Server 2012 R2 and a Hyper-V role in Windows Server 2012 R2. Hyper-V became an integral part of the operating system technology starting from Windows Server 2008 and has been constantly improving since then. However, until the latest version, Hyper-V was behind the virtualization products of Microsoft's main competitor—VMware. VMware got a significant market share over the years; today, many organizations, even though they are "Microsoft shops," use VMware as their virtualization solution. Organizations new to virtualization are more likely to select Hyper-V over VMware products.

Let's take a look at the main benefits of virtualization:

- It uses hardware better. Using virtualization, organizations can move from a typical 15 percent server utilization to 55 to 60 percent when they get a true increase in efficiency. However, according to Gartner, even for the companies that adopted virtualization, only about 25 percent of available processing power is utilized.

- With better use of hardware, it reduces IT operational costs. It reduces the total number of servers and power consumption.

- It simplifies administration work, not only because of reducing the number of machines, but also because of the simplified administrative procedures, for example, to create backups and to clone. It is also easier to isolate virtual machines and encapsulate processes and applications.

- Cloud computing benefits from using virtualization for severs in the cloud. It significantly simplifies the delivery of services.

- It simplifies the support of heterogeneous models and legacy applications.

- It improves development and deployment processes by isolating applications. Systems can be fixed instantaneously after severe crashes by simply copying virtual images. In more complex cases, snapshots can be taken at different points of system execution, and the system can be rolled back to these snapshots if needed.

- It improves development and deployment processes by isolating environments, that is, development, testing, integration, preproduction, and others. It enables the creation of preconfigured test environments, focusing on different issues. Being isolated, these environments help identify specific problems.

Desktop operating systems

Microsoft desktop operating systems have a long history. The latest OS, Windows 8 (currently 8.1), was designed having tablets and touch PCs in mind. Its user experience was shocking for most of the average users... same as it was when switching from Windows 3.1 to Windows 95. Moving from Windows 7 to Windows 8 was a paradigm change, and most users are still going to experience a certain level of inconvenience.

However, for a business, and especially for a large business, there are many reasons other than user experience to upgrade an operating system or to stay with a current one. There are inevitable expenses related to OS upgrade: licenses, training, data migration, and so on. Most corporations are conservative when it comes to performing a system upgrade; some of them have even invented rules that suggest migrating to every second version of Windows (presumably, being more stable). In addition to this, a better user experience often requires hardware changes, for example, getting monitors with a better resolution. Despite promises of software vendors, there are always inevitable challenges in running old software on new platforms. On a corporate scale, moving to the next version is always expensive.

Today, most corporations have not accepted Windows 8 yet. Well, some of them are still moving to Windows 7 from Windows XP. Corporate strategy issues have always been major constraints in solutions architecture.

The Windows Phone OS

In the highly competitive market of smartphones, Windows Phone (as well as its predecessor, Windows Mobile) doesn't have a large share. In a complex solution that requires the usage of smartphones, it is important to provide the ability to support several platforms through the development of either native or browser-based applications.

In this book, we will not focus on the native applications for Windows Phone but rather on generic solutions.

The Microsoft Office software

What kind of software does a business office need? Most businesses deal with documents; they create, modify, and print them. They also perform some calculations, starting from simply recording expenses to maintaining more sophisticated spreadsheets full of stock exchange information. Businesses often require to keep track of inventory, likely in the form of a database with a user interface. Oh, they send e-mails, tons of e-mails. They send e-mails to their customers and business partners, and they exchange documents within the organization. The employees spend a lot of time in meetings, so they need some software to track and schedule meetings. In these meetings, they do presentations.

If you make a list of essential office software, you will inevitably list a document processor, spreadsheet/tables software, a simple database-management system, e-mail client... sounds familiar? That's what Microsoft Office provides.

Microsoft Office 2013 consists of the following core applications:

- **Word**: A document processor
- **Excel**: A spreadsheet program
- **PowerPoint**: A presentation tool
- **Outlook**: A personal information manager; it consists of an e-mail client, calendar, task manager, and address book
- **OneNote**: A free-form note-taking program
- **Lync**: Formerly Communicator, an instant messaging client used with Microsoft Lync Server
- **Access**: A database-management system
- **Publisher**: An entry-level desktop publishing application
- **Project**: A project-management tool
- **Visio**: A diagramming tool
- **InfoPath**: A form editor, typically used as a frontend for SharePoint

In 1990, Microsoft Office was released as a set of three nonrelated applications: Word, Excel, and PowerPoint. Many other tools have been added and removed from the Office suite during its more than 20-year history. Original applications were completely rewritten; today, the suite presents a set of cohesive tools.

Microsoft Office applications are closely related to SharePoint (see *Chapter 6, The SharePoint Server Primer*). The SharePoint offering includes Excel Services, InfoPath Forms Services, and Project Server, among other tools.

In late 2000s, Microsoft launched SkyDrive—a cloud-based storage that was renamed to OneDrive in 2014. In 2008, Office Web Apps (Word, Excel, PowerPoint, and OneNote) were released, enabling file editing in the cloud and providing a limited functionality of the familiar desktop applications. Recent versions of the products allow simultaneous editing and synchronization of the desktop and web documents.

In 2011, Microsoft launched a cloud version of the Office, called Office 365. In February 2013, Office 365 was updated to match the Office 2013 applications. For a monthly fee, Microsoft provides a cloud solution to your organization. Some of them are as follows:

- **Exchange Online Service**: This removes the operational burden of managing the server on-premises; in addition to this, Office 365 enables the Exchange Online Archiving Service, also available for organizations using Exchange 2013 or Exchange 2010 (with SP2 or later)

- **Exchange Online Protection Service**: This enables e-mail filtering for the cloud-based or on-premises solutions

- **SharePoint Online Service**: This provides solutions to build team-focused or project-focused sites as well as full-blown organization-wide portals

- **Lync Online Service**: This provides solutions for collaboration, such as instant messaging, audio and video conferencing, and information sharing

- **Office Web Apps Service**: This allows us to work with web-based versions of Word, Excel, PowerPoint, and OneNote

- **Office Application Service**: This provides the latest versions of the core Office applications to be run on the desktop; the files are synchronized to the cloud

- **Project Online Service**: This enables team members with an Internet connection to collaborate on their project literally from anywhere

- **Yammer Service**: This provides a private enterprise social network to organizations

Office 365 comes in many different plans, typically in the form of a monthly subscription based on the number of users. The plans are different for small and midsize businesses, large enterprises, government organizations, and educational institutions.

One of the huge benefits of using Office 365 is that you can cancel your subscription any time, but your work will not get lost. All files are available via OneDrive.

Without a doubt, Microsoft Office is a very popular suite of office applications. According to Microsoft, over 1 billion people use Office. Partially, it is a result of the popularity of Windows in homes and organizations. Microsoft Office is developed primarily for Windows and has a consistent user experience. Architects should remember this when it comes to integrating the solution with office software.

 When this book was almost complete, Microsoft launched Office applications for iOS. This quiet event may actually have very significant consequences. In the next few years, we may see an increasing amount of office workers using iPads instead of laptops.

Visual Basic for Applications — the MS Office programming language — enables customization of Office applications and their integration with other tools. In addition, .NET provides a number of namespaces to support interoperability with the Office.

Microsoft Exchange Server 2013

We already mentioned Microsoft Exchange a few times, but it certainly deserves more attention.

There is no organization in the modern world that does not use e-mail. We rely on e-mail probably more than on any other communication tool in business. This is the main reason why we, as architects, should pay attention to the e-mail capabilities of our solutions.

Compared to many other e-mail servers, MS Exchange Server — whether it is deployed on-premises or as part of the Office 365 in-cloud solution — provides more nonfunctional "abilities". Some of them are listed as follows:

- MS Exchange has an internal component called **Active Manager** that is responsible for failure monitoring and corrective actions through failover within a database availability group.

Database availability group (DAG) is a group of up to 16 Exchange 2013 Mailbox Servers that host a set of replicated databases.

- Introduced in Exchange 2010, automatic recovery from storage failures has been improved in Exchange 2013 by adding more supported cases.

- Architectural changes made in Exchange 2013 have significantly improved site resilience.

Software development tools

In many software-related projects, with any project-management methodology, whether it's Waterfall or Agile, there is a development phase sooner or later. For architects, the development is an exciting moment; seeing the software emerging from architectural blueprints is similar to seeing a house being built. Selecting the right development tool and the right development process is essential for architects. Even if the architect does not have enough power to make the choice, they should have enough influence and respect to suggest the right approach.

One may say that the choice of development tools is limited for the solution based on the Microsoft platform, and the decision is obvious. This is true only at first glance. Yes, Visual Studio is the key development tool used for literally any development on the Microsoft platform. However, it comes in several different editions, from free Express editions to the heavily priced Ultimate edition. After the installation, Visual Studio can be customized, and tons of plugins are available for download. Which ones should be used for the development process, and what should this development process be?

Let's take a closer look at the editions of Visual Studio and other related tools, and see why architects are interested in all this.

Visual Studio 2013 is the latest release that became available in October 2013. Since the first version released in mid 1990s, Microsoft has been releasing new versions approximately every 2 years.

Visual Studio 2013 has several editions: Professional, Premium, Ultimate, and Test Professional, as well as several Express editions. Among paid editions, Visual Studio Professional is an entry point for developers; it provides enough tools to perform rapid development, whether it is for a web, desktop, or cloud application.

However, if you decide to take it up a notch, you should consider the Premium edition. Why? Let me ask you a question: as an architect, how do you know that the developers have implemented the design matching your architecture? Well, you don't, unless you perform design review and code review sessions. In addition, code reviews show the code quality of the solution, which you and your team certainly strive to achieve.

The Visual Studio Premium edition provides a whole spectrum of tools that improve the code quality and help conduct code reviews; you can assess the code coverage with unit tests, view code metrics that show unnecessary complexity of the code, profile the code to find out performance or memory-usage issues, and run code analysis to identify security holes. The Premium edition has a range of test tools that were previously available in the Ultimate edition; starting from VS 2012, developers can suspend and resume their work, and it also has better support for Agile development.

The Visual Studio Ultimate edition is quite pricey, but it is the only one that provides an ability to build architecture diagrams to validate the built code against. In addition, it has web load- and performance-testing tools (which are not available even in the Test Professional edition), IntelliTrace, and other features.

 IntelliTrace provides a picture of the application, showing events that occurred in the past and the context of these events. This reduces the number of restarts compared to traditional debugging and enables debugging of errors that are otherwise nonreproducible.

The Test Professional edition targets testers rather than developers; all of its features are available in the Premium edition.

Free Express editions of Visual Studio 2013 target specific development: Web, desktop, or phone. Microsoft released these editions primarily for learners and nonprofessionals; however, some small businesses use them for actual development to save money. Limitations of the Express editions usually stop development teams from using them on larger projects that require significant collaboration and quality control.

Finally, Microsoft provides an ability to develop in the cloud. Visual Studio Online (formerly, Team Foundation Service) enables developers to host projects in the Microsoft cloud for a monthly fee.

Since the dawn of programming, there has been a need for developer collaboration. Two major factors drove this need: working on larger projects and developing better quality code. **Software development lifecycles (SDLCs)** have been formalized; hundreds of books have been written on different development methodologies, and many tools have been developed to support these methodologies.

In the collaborative team-development environment, Visual Studio comes hand in hand with **Team Foundation Server (TFS)**. TFS 2013 covers the entire software-development process and can be used with Visual Studio, Eclipse, or other development environments.

As an on-premises tool, TFS 2013 runs on SQL Server and provides source code management and application-lifecycle management; additionally, it can support automated builds and automated testing. Its online version is included in the Visual Studio Online offering.

It is difficult to imagine any development without a source-control system (also called a revision-control system). **Source control systems** such as TFS are used as source code repositories, but any document or any piece of information can be also stored there. It will not only store and back up this information, it will also allow us to share it between different team members, provides version control, reuses the information for different projects, and supports the entire change management.

One of the new features in TFS 2013 is providing an option of using Git—a distributed version-control system that became extremely popular in the last few years. Any Git-compatible client can now connect to TFS.

There are dozens of source-control tools on the market, and TFS is not the only choice even for .NET developers. However, TFS 2013 comes with many other features that make it the ultimate choice for those developing on the Microsoft platform.

One of the most important features of TFS is the ability to support the SDLS, whether it is built on Agile or on more traditional principles. There are three process templates that come with TFS 2013: Microsoft Visual Studio Scrum 2013, MSF for Agile Software Development 2013, and MSF for CMMI Software Improvement 2013. With Team Foundation Build, a component of TFS, you can automatically compile applications, run associated tests, perform code analysis, release continuous builds, and publish build reports. The authors of this book have seen a team that published the build results to an LED display in the office hallway for all company projects. We could imagine that, in a highly competitive environment, one would even be able to display the name of the developer whose code broke the build.

Cloud computing

The history of cloud computing goes back to the 1950s, when mainframe resources in Academia and large corporations became available via terminal computers used for communication rather than for their internal processing capacities. They were given the name **thin terminals** for this reason.

Thin terminals enabled two very important features: sharing resources of the central computers and minimizing expenses on the client side. These two features became the main drivers of the cloud computing that started evolving in 2000s. Some companies, called **Application Service Providers (ASPs)**, began offering software-based services over the Internet in several ways.

Imagine a small business that required lead management or accounting software to support their sales. Acquiring such applications might not be costly, but this was not even an issue. The challenge that these businesses faced was in running an IT department just to support a few applications. For a small company, outsourcing their IT work helped build their competitive advantage. Being able to access applications via the Internet was a definite bonus. Not only did it allow people to work from home and eliminated the need for an office, but it also allowed them to get results anywhere. Now, sales people could access and share documents, work on presentations, and exchange their lead information on the road.

Several factors have a visible impact on the evolution of cloud computing. First of all, it was the speed of communication. Accessing a server in the cloud with a speed of 300 bps, as it was in the early days of the Internet, and even with a speed of 56 Kbps, as it was in the early 1990s, would not produce any decent results. Only when the communication rates started using Mbps as their units did accessing cloud services became achievable.

The second factor that influenced cloud computing was the decreasing cost of client computers. Computers, especially personal computers, became affordable. Now, a small business could buy a computer for each sales person who could use them on the road instead of having just one or two PCs in the office.

The third important factor was the power of the Internet systems, particularly, the Web. The simplicity of HTTP resulted in the general adoption of the Web and services that could be delivered via it. We certainly use other protocols, for example, to deliver videos and audios, but HTTP remains one of the most utilized delivery tools. SOAP Web services, RESTful applications, all use HTTP as the underlying protocol.

In essence, cloud computing simply means delivering services over the Internet. The services can provide access to different resources, from applications to data centers.

The services can be delivered in different formats. They are as follows:

- **Software as a Service (SaaS)**: This is the successor to the original ASP model. Software applications that run in the cloud are accessible remotely via the Internet (and most likely, via a web browser). The organizations that use the service don't need to support it and have an IT department for this purpose. They just sign up (usually, in the form of a subscription) and can start using it immediately. The service provider is responsible for software and data maintenance. If the client organization grows, the cloud solution supports the growth by simply adding more subscriptions. Well, building a scalable SaaS solution is a challenge that the provider's architects face—to the benefit of the client.

- **Platform as a Service (PaaS)**: If you want to develop and maintain your own application in the cloud but don't want to buy and manage underlying hardware, operating systems, and database management systems, the PaaS approach is for you. Service providers provision hardware and a solution stack such as LAMP (Linux, Apache, MySQL, Perl/PHP) or WISA (Windows, IIS, SQL Server, ASP.NET).

- **Infrastructure as a Service (IaaS)**: If you don't want to invest in your own infrastructure but prefer to rent it, you may want to consider IaaS. You don't need to have an office space for the servers and data storage, and you can get as much infrastructure as you want. Later, you may decide to increase or reduce your needs, and you can get out of the contract at any time. You also have access to your cloud network via the Internet, anytime, anywhere.

You may have noticed while reading this chapter that placing solutions in the cloud is becoming a more common trend. Shifting the responsibility (and the headache!) to the cloud provider seems to have become an attractive option. The only caveat is the provider has to be trusted. Even if the provider claims 99.5 or 99.9 percent availability, will they guarantee it? Will the data be completely safe? Once in a while, we see power outages and other disasters that affect cloud providers.

Well, if you have your data and systems on-premises, there is no guarantee that your data center will have no power outages. You simply believe that your disaster-recovery process is more mature than that of the cloud provider.

When choosing a cloud solution, there is another aspect to consider—legal. One of the critical concerns is the privacy and security of the data. For example, in financial institutions, maintaining customer data may become tricky. The data may be required to be deleted immediately or after a certain period of time when the customer is no longer with the business. Even more, federal, provincial, or state laws may require to keep the customer data within the country borders. How can you do it if large cloud providers tend to be multinational corporations?

These concerns should be addressed in the very beginning of the project. It is the responsibility of the solutions architect to make the right recommendation.

Windows Azure

The `windowsazure.com` site states the following:

> *"Azure is an open and flexible cloud platform that enables you to quickly build, deploy, and manage applications across a global network of Microsoft-managed datacenters. You can build applications using any language, tool, or framework. And you can integrate your public cloud applications with your existing IT environment."*

Windows Azure provides all kinds of cloud services and seems to be far from its final state. The services, approach, terminology, even the entire paradigm have rapidly evolved over the last few years. Some links from the main Azure-management screen point to community resources that are quickly getting outdated. Some information on the Windows Azure website is incorrect or contradictory. However, without a doubt, Azure has become one of the significant players on the cloud market.

Windows Azure provides a number of services at IaaS, PaaS, and SaaS levels. They are as follows:

- You can simply set up and get access to Windows or Linux virtual machines using a variety of preconfigured templates. There is a choice of Windows Servers from 2008 R2 SP1 to 2012 R2, and a Linux family of servers such as Ubuntu, CentOS, SUSE, or Oracle Linux. In addition to this, you can choose SharePoint, SQL Server, or BizTalk Server, as well as Oracle Database or WebLogic Server.

- You can build a website using a number of tools and applications: ASP.NET, PHP, Lemoon, WordPress, MediaWiki, and many more. The list of tools is constantly updated. The website will be hosted in a Microsoft data center that will provide quite competitive SLAs.

- You can set up storage for your structured or unstructured data. You will be able to access your data from your virtual machines, from your cloud applications, or from your applications on-premises. Azure provides a few services and an API to help with them. You can also download utilities for your storage.

- Windows Azure provides services to work with Big Data. The concept of Big Data assumes that the amount of data is so big that it cannot be managed by usual means. In order to manage Big Data, Windows Azure provides the HDInsight service based on Hadoop, an open source Apache framework.

- Visual Studio Online mentioned earlier in this chapter comes as a part of Azure offering. This enables end-to-end cloud development using familiar programming languages.

- Windows Azure Active Directory provides access management for your cloud solution. It can be synchronized with your on-premises identities if you chose to use the hybrid solution, mixing your on-premises applications with your cloud services.

- Windows Azure BizTalk Services became available to the general public in November 2013. You certainly can run a BizTalk instance on a virtual machine, but using BizTalk Service takes the managing overhead from you. If you run BizTalk Server on a virtual machine, you are still responsible for configuring your server for high availability, for example.

- At the time of writing this book, Windows Azure Service Bus provided cloud-based messaging solutions for three patterns: message queues, Publish/Subscribe, and two-way synchronous messages. Service Bus provides a number of connectivity options, including WCF and RESTful services.

- Windows Azure Media Services enable the creation, management, and delivery of media to a variety of devices on different platforms, from Xbox to iOS.

With cloud computing, we should add one more "ability" to our nonfunctional requirements. This is elasticity, an ability to grow and shrink as necessary. For a traditional on-premises model, we usually talked about scalability and ability to grow. This was a requirement desirable for many businesses. When the business slowed down, the IT assets were already capitalized, and there was no big advantage in removing them. The cloud model makes these expenses operational, and minimizing these expenses became a desirable option.

We have mentioned that Windows Azure is rapidly changing. New services are being built; the old ones are being updated. By the time this book is published, this chapter may become obsolete. However, we can make some recommendations based on our experience in dealing with new technologies over the last 3 decades.

If you are architecting a solution for a large corporation, stay conservative. Large corporations don't change quickly, and applying new technologies usually cannot be done in an agile manner. You can get stuck with technologies that were very promising for some time and then disappeared forever. It might take years to replace the technology with something new. When it comes to using the cloud, thoroughly calculate the total cost of ownership and compare it with the **total cost of ownership (TCO)** of the on-premises solution. Don't forget that barriers to exit can be a source of significant expenses.

When building a solution for a small business that does not have an IT department, the cloud model should be always considered. However, the barriers to exit still exist; therefore, calculate your TCO before jumping into new technologies.

The cloud approach is not very new, and some patterns have already emerged. When choosing a long-lasting solution, rely on the proven patterns.

Summary

We cannot discuss all Microsoft technologies in this small chapter, but we would like to mention some of them. For example, developing in .NET often requires the use of Enterprise Library—a set of reusable application blocks. Enterprise Library simplifies coding for logging, exception handling, data access, and many other areas. AppFabric that supports hosting WF workflows in the form of WCF services and caching data in memory is another tool that we would consider in .NET development.

There are small applications, such as Microsoft Streets and Trips, and much larger suites, such as Microsoft Dynamics. Keeping an eye on the evolution of these packages and on new Microsoft offerings is the responsibility of solution architects.

Microsoft also offers a variety of software packages to maintain and support corporate infrastructure. System Center is a group of server applications aimed at helping system administrators manage corporate infrastructure. From a set of disconnected products, it has evolved into an elaborate suite of administrative tools. Host Integration Server enables integration with IBM host systems. Forefront Protection Suite is a set of security software products designed to protect corporate networks, servers, and workstations.

Some of these products we may consider later in this book when we talk about specific patterns.

This is the last chapter that provides a technology overview and primers. In the next chapter, we shall start talking about actual architectural patterns and antipatterns. Our first patterns will be the patterns of integration.

8
Integration Patterns and Antipatterns

The purpose of any system integration is to bind two or more different systems together to work as a whole. You can find system integration tasks in any area of business or technology. In this chapter, we'll discuss integration by means of software technologies.

The history of software-intensive system integration is almost as old as the history of computer systems themselves. Even in the early days of computers, people experienced a need to connect systems developed on different hardware platforms, operating systems, and systems that used different data formats and ran in different locations. Early methods of integration were as simple as taking printouts from one computer to another and entering the data manually. Today, we have integration tools and processes as big as the Internet itself.

In this chapter, we shall provide an introduction to software-intensive system integration from an architect's point of view. We shall discuss different architectural styles and talk about the difference between data integration and application integration. The patterns presented in this chapter belong to application integration. We'll continue with more integration patterns in the next two chapters.

Integration styles and challenges

Connecting different systems is just one part of an integration task. Any type of connection is done for a purpose, and the main purpose of integrating systems is to get them to work together as a part of a single process. In a sense, all integration tasks are based on process integration. To get two or more systems to work together, one also needs to enable the flow of information from one system to another.

Integration can be data-focused when the data that belongs to one system is made available to another system. It can be done by moving the data or providing shared access to the data. This type of integration is usually called **data integration**. Another term that is often used in this regard is **Enterprise Information Integration (EII)**. We are going to discuss data integration in *Chapter 10, Data Exchange Patterns*.

If the information is sent from one system to another in order to initiate an action by the means of another application, this is usually called **application integration** or **Enterprise Application Integration (EAI)**. EAI and EII are the two major integration styles. We have to admit that all this terminology is somewhat vague, and the boundary between data integration and application integration is blurred. Often, a significant amount of data to be processed is sent from one system to another and presented in a different format, which can also initiate some new actions.

Evolution of system integration goes hand in hand with the evolution of programming. First, computer programs were monolithic and ran in the memory area allocated for that purpose on a single computer. Integration with other programs could be only done by means of file exchange, which sometimes was semiautomatic.

 File exchange, or data export/import, can be considered to be one of the first data integration patterns.

Future improvements in software and hardware caused programs to be created in a more modular way with the ability to run components at different locations. Different standards, such as CORBA or Microsoft COM, were designed to support interoperability. However, the standards, even for products designed on the same platform, can help only to a certain extent. Software vendors don't necessarily want to follow rules.

With the advance of the Internet and the means of connecting literally anything to anything, new integration solutions emerged. Sometimes we take our ability to access our bank accounts from mobile phones, or to purchase online from shops overseas, for granted. However, building these solutions is usually a process full of challenges; most of the challenges are faced while integrating independently-built components. The following are the main challenges of integration architecture:

- First off, we need to establish connectivity. Can two integration participants even talk to each other? What hardware, what networks can we use? Do we want to use wireless technologies or not? Can we? Answering all these questions is the initial step towards building the integration architecture.

- On the lines of the previous questions, the question of protocols arises. In the modern world, especially when we start building a system from scratch, we would think about web services, SOAP, or RESTful services. However, in many cases, integration has to be performed between already existing applications; quite often, these applications have been around for a while. It means that these applications often do not understand new standards. Take, for example, the financial industry. Financial networks have existed for decades, and some standards, such as ISO 8583, have not significantly changed in the last 10 to 15 years; applications that use them are not going away in the nearest future.

- The most common task of integration systems is data transformation. Why? Because all systems are different—and some are even more different than others. The data formats used by one system have to be understood by the other system. There are two ways to deal with this challenge. One way is to change the data format of one application to the data format of the other, but this has to be done for each pair of applications in the system. Another way is to transform data into a standard format. The latter approach is more common in modern systems; we'll talk about it later in this chapter.

- With the evolution of standard protocols and data formats, the challenges of integrating different operating systems or different database management systems are not as significant as they were 10 years ago. But still, once in a while, you may face the need to convert small endian data into big endian data; this kind of challenge will never go away.

- However, when some challenges become easier to solve, other challenges become more complex and more important. And one of those is the challenge of establishing proper security to the integrated system. Imagine that you need to securely connect your house to your neighbor's house across the street. You want to make sure that the entire system is secure. You build a tunnel under the road, you put sophisticated locks on your doors, and you reinforce your windows just to find out that your neighbor never locks his back door. The same thing happens with systems; for example, if an online application is prone to SQL injection attacks, it can damage your database.

- If the integration solution is developed in order to connect applications already existing in production that do not require modification, it can be developed in isolation and later added to the mix. However, if the applications are also developed at the same time, testing becomes a significant challenge. The testing process will include a phase of the system integration testing, where each component is a moving target.

To deal with these and other challenges, architects have established certain patterns to be implemented in integration solutions. One of the most famous books on this topic is *Enterprise Integration Patterns: Designing, Building, and Deploying Messaging Solutions, Gregor Hohpe* and *Bobby Wolf, Addison Wesley*. It very well describes design patterns for integration solutions, but does not provide a proper level of detail for architectural patterns. In this chapter, we shall focus on architectural patterns that we use for building solution architecture.

 If you want to compare architectural patterns and design patterns, you can think of architecture as a skeleton of a system — its core. Architectural patterns are intended to provide "abilities" that we discussed in *Chapter 1, Solution Decision Framework*. System design describes implementation of its architecture, and design patterns are intended to provide building guidance at the lower levels.

Point-to-point integration

Point-to-point integration is a very common solution that you can find in literally every organization.

Point-to-point is an overloaded term that is used in many areas, such as communication, networking, and messaging. In system integration, by point-to-point architecture we usually mean direct connection between applications. The calling application should know the exact address of the application it invokes and the parameters to pass. All this information is usually configured or even hard-coded. The applications can be located on the same computer or in datacenters on different continents.

In a small corporation that uses a few applications that require integration, such as a payroll application, a lead management system, a customer relation management system, and a few others, this approach seems to be the simplest one. These rarely change their interfaces, and new applications are not acquired often. Therefore, connecting an application to another one using a native API is the most logical choice.

Decades ago, this approach was popular also because of its efficiency, as it did not require any intermediary software in order to provide address translation, which might not even exist. However, as time went on, some problems emerged.

First of all, many applications were physically moved to a different location. They were moved to another computer or another network; alternatively, their names were simply changed. In any case, their addresses changed. It meant that all calling applications had to change their code or at least configuration parameters. Imagine a government database that provides information to hundreds of clients. If the access point changes, all client applications have to incorporate the changes. This has to be coordinated and tested before the changes are put in production.

Secondly, all client applications have to comply with the data formats used by data providers. Changing a data provider in a point-to-point architecture requires each application to make changes to use new data formats. Replacing a data provider with another one is usually a big undertaking by itself, and this certainly adds to the overall complexity.

In addition to this, if the number of providers increases, the architecture becomes very cumbersome. The number of connections increases exponentially, and the system maintenance becomes a nightmare.

The point-to-point pattern becomes an antipattern.

In the next chapter, we will discuss building web services and **service-oriented architecture (SOA)**. SOA and its most common implementation, **Enterprise Service Bus (ESB)**, has become a popular alternative to point-to-point solutions. SOA is often built using web services. However, don't assume that just using web services will automatically move your solution away from the point-to-point architecture. If the web services are called directly using the URI from WSDL, the solution is still point-to-point.

And one last thing, the book on enterprise integration patterns, mentioned earlier, presents the **point-to-point channel pattern**. This design pattern is something different. It ensures that only one receiver consumes any given message. The channel can have multiple receivers that can consume multiple messages concurrently, but only one of them can successfully consume a particular message. This design pattern is suggested not as a direct connection between applications, but rather as an alternative to multicasting or broadcasting at the messaging level. Confusing? Welcome to the world of integration.

The federated request pattern

Most point-to-point systems work using a simple **request-response pattern**. The calling application (let's call it a **sender**) sends a message to another application (let's call it a **receiver**) and expects a response. The response can simply return a code that indicates success or failure. It can also return a complex set of data. However, in either case, the sender gets back the result of actions performed by the receiver.

Let's consider a system that connects several applications and requires some logic in order to properly send the message. Take, for example, a traffic document processing system that works with two types of documents: traffic tickets and collision reports. Once a police officer creates a traffic ticket on his or her laptop, it has to be sent to the police department and the court. The collision report, on the other hand, has to be sent to the police department and the state department of transportation. In some cases, the documents have to be sent to the state department of licensing. Which application has to make this decision? If we use a point-to-point approach, the decision becomes the sender's responsibility. The sender application has to implement all routing logic, and it becomes quite heavy. What if the responses from the message receiving applications also have to be routed? In this approach, they have to be sent back to the sender (even if the sender does not need that response), who will make another decision.

A common architectural solution to this problem is building a component in the middle that takes the responsibility for these decisions. All senders send messages to this component, and it routes the messages based on the business rules. It also processes responses from receivers and decides what to do with that information: whether to send it straight back to the sender or perform some workflow in order to gather more information for instance.

One of the very popular workflows in this type of systems is the response aggregation workflow that we shall discuss in the next section.

Working with the use case – purchasing power calculation

Instant Stock Trades Inc. (IST) is a stock broker that provides its clients with the online ordering system. Until recently, its clients were only able to trade stocks within the limits of their deposits on an IST account. IST management decided that they should allow their clients to increase the limits of their purchasing power.

They came up with the following simple policies:

- Clients can sign an agreement with IST to leverage their other assets, such as bank account balances and stock holdings, for the purpose of placing stock trade orders with IST
- IST will approve the limit of the client's purchasing power as the sum of 80 percent of the balance in their bank account and 50 percent of the current market value of their stock holdings

To provide clients with real-time trade order approval, IST has signed an agreement with several major banks and investment brokers. The agreement allows IST to retrieve their clients' financial information. Now, IST needs to implement a solution that would retrieve clients' financial data from several sources and calculate the purchasing power based on the aggregate value of various client assets.

The existing online trading system has been custom-built by IST as a .NET and SQL Server solution. The management does not want to replace this solution or redesign it in the near future. It will consider minimal changes in the trading system to determine how the client's purchasing power is calculated. It, however, makes it clear that any problem with this new system should not affect its regular business. In other words, if the purchasing power solution is unavailable for any reason, it should not affect the client's ability to place orders within the limits of their deposit on the IST account.

Key requirements

While analyzing the use case, we can identify the following key requirements:

- The proposed solution shall be a standalone system.
- The proposed solution is not a mission-critical business system. Catastrophic failure of the system should not lead to interruptions in business.
- The solution will need to interface with multiple external systems. Failure to connect to one source of data shall not lead to the system response failure.

The federated request pattern description

To discuss this pattern more, let's review the terminology mentioned in the following list:

- In application integration, the data that is sent between connected systems is sent for a reason; the data is supposed to initiate some action. In messaging systems, **messages** typically conform to some standard that describes message parts. Messages usually have a header, which describes the data being transmitted and provides some information to the messaging system and the body.

- The application that sends messages is called a **sender**, and the one that receives messages is called a **receiver**. In a system with a complex workflow, a receiver may become a sender; and these terms then stop being straightforward.

- Another approach to describing the participants in the messaging system is defining information consumers and providers. An application that provides information, for example, an e-commerce catalog, is called an **information provider**. An application that uses this information, a browser-based application in this example, is called an **information consumer**.

- However, with the introduction of the service-oriented approach, particularly with the usage of web services, we started talking about service consumers and providers. And that's where we have to be very careful; a service consumer can play the role of an information provider. Consider, for example, a payroll application that sends employee information to the application that prints checks. The payroll application that provides information about employees is an information provider. On the other hand, it sends requests for services of the check printing application, and therefore it is a service consumer.

- The **message hub** is an application that is connected to all other applications as a hub, connected to spokes. All message traffic runs through the hub.

In our use case, we consider the federated request pattern. In its simplest form, the pattern is executed in the following steps:

1. The sender (consumer) sends a request to several recipients through the message hub.

2. The message hub decides where the request has to be passed based on certain criteria. The criteria can be very simple, for example, specified in the message header. They can be quite complicated as well, to the point where the hub has to analyze the message body in order to make the routing decision.

3. The recipients receive the request and process it. Each recipient works as a service (and information) provider. Typically, all of them may have information that the consumer is interested in.

4. The recipients send their responses back to the hub along with success/failure codes.

5. The hub aggregates all responses into a single response and sends it back to the sender.

The steps are presented on the following diagram:

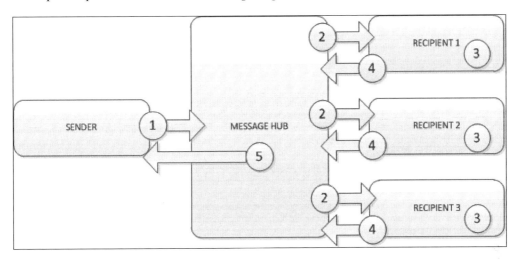

Candidate architecture for federated requests #1 – BizTalk

BizTalk is our first choice since that's what it is designed for — being a hub in the hub-and-spoke architecture. Let's see how it fits into the picture of our use case.

Solution design aspects

BizTalk is an enterprise class product designed for scalability and reliable delivery. It acts as a hub (or rather as a message broker that we'll discuss a little later on) in complex integration architectures, and it perfectly fits the solution from the design perspective.

Extensibility and loose coupling are also important to this solution. We may have new or changed endpoints in the future and want to be able to isolate those changes.

BizTalk orchestration also can perform simple workflows, and direct the traffic based on a set of criteria. It also works well when the endpoints are static, which is our case: we want to connect to the exiting external systems that would seldom change.

We have a need to talk to existing databases and potential web services. BizTalk has a series of adapters that make connectivity to many protocols a code-generation and configuration task, instead of a custom coding or scripting task.

We can leverage BizTalk mapping capabilities to deal with different data formats.

Using BizTalk would save some effort on designing for scalability and high availability. In a typical financial project, reliable delivery is critical as well. If BizTalk cannot reach its providers, it would be able to perform retries and alert the system administrator if the number of retries is exhausted.

However, we should note that, despite the fact that we are building the solution for a financial institution, high reliability is not crucial. The system is not supposed to perform financial transactions; it is planned to be informational only.

Solution implementation aspects

Instant Stock Traders Inc. is not currently a BizTalk shop, so they will need to both acquire and train resources to effectively build their upcoming solution. Their existing developers, who are already familiar with Microsoft's .NET Framework, can learn how to construct BizTalk solutions in a fairly short amount of time. The tools to build BizTalk artifacts are hosted within Visual Studio, and BizTalk projects can reside alongside other .NET project types.

Because the BizTalk-based messaging solution has a design paradigm (for example, Publish/Subscribe and distributed components to chain together) different from that of a typical custom .NET solution, understanding the toolset alone will not ensure delivery success. If the organization decides to bring in a product such as BizTalk Server, it will be vital for them to engage an outside expert to act as a solutions architect and leverage their existing BizTalk experience while building this solution.

Solution operations aspects

BizTalk is a complex tool that requires significant training for the system administrator. It is based on SQL Server, may require third-party adapters, and installing and supporting it would be a challenge for the organization that has no previous BizTalk experience. BizTalk Server Administration Console has limited capabilities, and many organizations purchase additional third-party tools, such as BizTalk 360.

Organizational aspects

BizTalk Server would be a new technology to the organization; therefore, there is some risk involved. It becomes necessary to purchase licenses, train developers and system administrators, provision environments, and hire experts. With a fairly low use of BizTalk, this may become too expensive.

This also indicates a significant upfront cost. If the organization had solid long-term plans in using BizTalk and extending the system to perform financial transactions, this investment would be feasible. In the current scenario, there are no significant advantages investing in BizTalk.

Solution evaluation

As before, we shall evaluate the solution using four different dimensions: design, implementation, operations, and organizational aspects. For each dimension, we shall give a "thumbs up" or "thumbs down," as shown in the following table

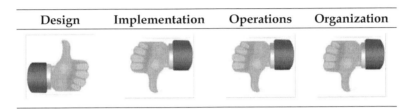

Design	Implementation	Operations	Organization

Candidate architecture for federated requests #2 – .NET Service (WCF)

Since the organization has valuable experience in developing .NET applications, our second choice would be to develop the message hub as a WCF service. This service will provide connectivity to the external systems as well as the aggregation of the responses.

Solution design aspects

Currently, the organization expects about 10,000 requests per day. In future, the number of customers is expected to increase by 10 percent every five years. This will require designing for scalability and availability.

The solution will require building a web farm using several IIS servers. The number of servers can be increased if needed. The availability will be achieved by using native load balancing for the IIS server farm with **Application Request Routing (ARR)**.

Solution implementation aspects

Development of the solution will be done using Visual Studio, which is familiar and should be no challenge for the organization's development team. The service will be built using WCF, which allows developers to add more security measures in future. Initially, security will be implemented at the transport level using TLS (SSL). Later, WS-* standards can be applied to the service.

Solution operations aspects

The solution is based on a lightweight WCF service that does not require a lot of server resources. Instant Stock Traders Inc. anticipates that the number of requests to this service will increase by 10 percent in five years, proportionately with the increase in the number of customers.

Maintenance of the solution does not create a challenge since IST is a Microsoft shop and has enough skilled resources with the ability to modify and improve the code.

Scalability of the solution is achieved by building the web farm from several IIS servers, callable horizontally by adding more servers. Windows provides native load balancing to the IIS that increases the solution availability.

Organizational aspects

Instant Stock Traders Inc. already has an experienced team of developers with a lot of .NET knowledge. Building the solution on .NET will not require additional learning and can be started immediately.

Also, at this point, the organization does not have clear plans about building future integration solutions. They believe that service-oriented architecture is the paradigm to be used in their future architectures, but are not sure what technology they would use to implement it. If they develop .NET WCF services, they can reuse them with any Microsoft technology in future without much modification.

Solution evaluation

The following table shows all thumbs up! This is definitely our choice!

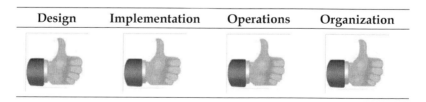

Design	Implementation	Operations	Organization
👍	👍	👍	👍

Architecture selection

In the following table, we shall compare the architectures of two candidates, their risks, and benefits

BizTalk Server	WCF Service
Benefits	**Benefits**
• This perfectly fits the solution from the design perspective • This is designed for scalability and supports future needs	• The in-house staff develops, maintains, and supports the solution • This is an extensible solution that can satisfy future needs • This provides adequate scalability and extensibility for the organization needs
Risks	**Risks**
• This has additional licensing and training costs • There is no in-house expertise with BizTalk • Solutions that are too heavy will require inadequate effort to support and maintain	• This may require modifications for future integration solutions

Even if BizTalk is a perfect tool for hub-and-spoke architecture, for this solution it will be too heavy. The organization will have to spend far too much money and expend too much energy to build such a lightweight solution. Even though it is extensible, the BizTalk solution would require significant up-front costs that do not seem feasible since the organization does not have solid plans for future system development.

The .NET WCF solution, on the other hand, does not require significant up-front costs, and the organization also has enough skilled resources to start the development immediately. The WCF solution is also scalable for the organization's needs. In case IST decides on future integration architecture, the WCF services can fit most of the solutions without significant modifications.

Our choice is .NET WCF services.

Building the solution

We will start solution implementation by creating three SQL Server databases. Two of them, Bank and InvestFund, will represent sources of financial data. The third database, StockTrader, will represent Instant Stock Trades' online trading system, which is the client of the solution we build.

We will now walk through creating a WCF Service Application project for this use case.

1. Restore the Bank, InvestFund, and StockTrader databases from the backup files in the code samples.

2. For each of the restored databases, add the current Windows user login to the database logins. Specify Default Schema = 'dbo'.

3. Open Visual Studio 2012 and navigate to **New** | **Templates** | **Visual C#** | **WCF** | **WCF Service Application**. Enter Chapter8_WCF for the name of the project, as shown in the following screenshot:

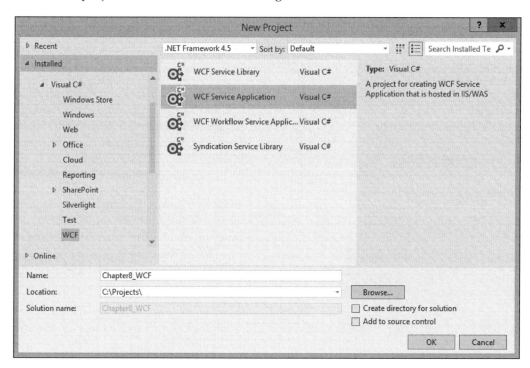

4. Open the **Server Explorer** pane. Right-click on **Data Connections** and select **New** from the menu. Select or enter your development SQL Server instance name. Select **Bank** in the **Select or enter database name** dropdown, as shown in the following screenshot:

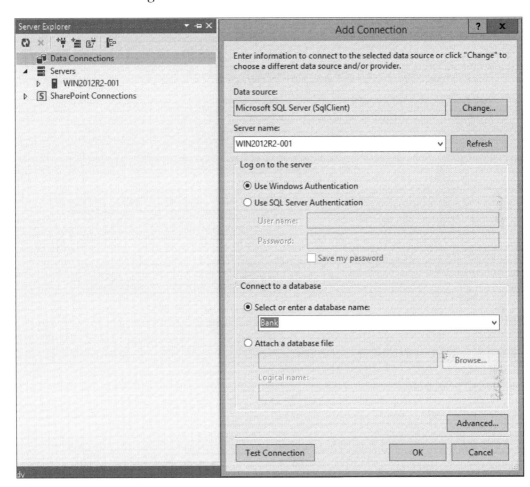

5. Repeat step 4 for the `InvestFund` and `StockTrader` databases.

6. Right-click on the **Chapter8_WCF** project in the **Solution Explorer** window. Navigate to **Add | New Item | Data | LINQ to SQL Classes**. Enter `Bank.dbml` in the **Name** box, as shown in the following screenshot:

7. Open the `Bank.dbml` file. In the **Server Explorer** window, expand **Data Connections | BankConnectionString | Tables**. Drag the `Account` table into the data model designer surface. Drag the `Customer` table into the data model designer surface, as shown in the following screenshot:

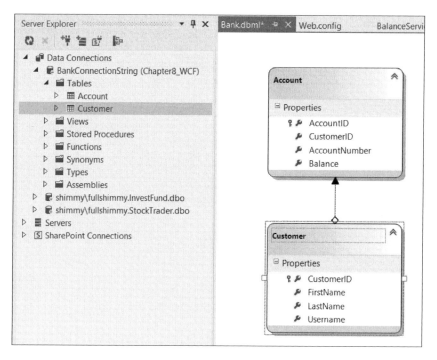

8. Repeat steps 6 and 7 for the `InvestFund` and `StockTrader` databases. Add all tables from these databases to their respective data models.

9. The notable point about the service method implementation is the two `try{}` `catch{}` blocks in the code. They represent attempts to connect to various data sources. If either of those connections fail, service will still return the result that is meaningful for the use case scenario, as shown:

```
public decimal GetClientPurchasingPower(string LastName)
    {
    decimal ClientPurchasingPower = 0.0M;
        //Try to retrieve bank account balance
    try
    {
        decimal BankAccountsSummaryBalance = 0.0M;
        using (BankDataContext bankContext = new
BankDataContext())
        {
            List<Account> accounts = (from a in bankContext.
Accounts
                                      join c in bankContext.
Customers
                                      on a.CustomerID equals
c.CustomerID
                                      where c.LastName == LastName
                                      select a).ToList();

            foreach (Account account in accounts)
            {    .
                BankAccountsSummaryBalance += (account.Balance ==
null) ? 0 : (decimal)account.Balance;
            }
            ClientPurchasingPower += BankAccountsSummaryBalance *
0.8M;
        }
    }
    catch
    {
        //Error handling here
    }
        //Try to retrieve stock holdings balance
    try
    {
        decimal InvestFundSummaryBalance = 0.0M;
```

```
        using (InvestFundDataContext investContext = new
InvestFundDataContext())
        {
         List<Holding> holdings = (from h in investContext.
Holdings
                            join c in investContext.Clients
                            on h.ClientID equals c.ClientID
                            where c.LastName == LastName
                            select h).ToList();
        foreach (Holding holding in holdings)
        {
        InvestFundSummaryBalance += (holding.Shares == null ||
            holding.PurchasePrice == null) ? 0 : (decimal)holding.
Shares * (decimal)holding.PurchasePrice;
        }
        ClientPurchasingPower += InvestFundSummaryBalance * 0.5M;
      }
        }
    catch
    {
        //Error handling here
    }
    return ClientPurchasingPower;
}
```

The important aspect of this implementation is the robustness of service. We have ensured that service always returns the response, even in situations when one or more data sources are unavailable for any reason.

In our simple solution, we have achieved this by creating independent code blocks that connect to the two data sources, represented in the solution by SQL databases. Readers may note that, in real life, implementing this approach should be enhanced by the following:

- Most likely, remote data sources from third parties will be represented by web services (SOAP, WCF, or REST) rather than direct access to SQL databases. Direct access to SQL databases should only be allowed to the services and applications hosted in-house for security purposes.

- Implementation of code that connects to different data sources in parallel threads. This will reduce overall service response time to the slowest response using any of the underlying data sources.

- Implementation of error logging and alerts when any of the underlying data sources fail to respond.

- Enhancing the interface. In addition to returning the business data (that is, the client's purchasing power as a numeric value), it should also return the response code that indicates whether the attempt to connect to all data sources was successful.

Lessons learned

In this example, we have introduced the notion of using data aggregation in the request/response scenario. A WCF service was chosen to act as a message hub since we did not want to invest in the heavy BizTalk solution. This scenario will be elaborated later in this book, providing true integration between external data sources. We will also show how this solution can improve its security capabilities that are currently limited to the **Transport Layer Security (TLS)**.

The message broker pattern

In the request-response example, we have built a WCF service that acts as a hub in the hub-and-spoke architecture, which connects different integration participants. The workflow we presented is quite simplistic; the only action it performs is aggregating the results of requests that are sent to providers.

In a more sophisticated solution, more actions can be required. The most typical ones are **message validation**, **message transformation**, and **message routing** (they are explained in the following list). Message hubs that perform these actions are called **message brokers**.

- **Message validation**: This is performed using a set of validation rules. Placing message validation in the middle tier enables having a centralized set of rules that are consistent across the entire system. Message validation can be centralized as a service called by other processes in the message broker.

- **Message transformation**: This is one of the most essential functions of the message broker, since data in different systems are typically presented in different formats. In order to perform message transformation consistently, message brokers usually support canonical schemas. Transformations are performed to or from the canonical schema. Schema mappings are performed at the design stage, and the maps are stored with the message broker.

- **Message routing**: This is performed to direct messages to the appropriate recipients. The routing algorithm can analyze the message header as well as the message body.

Message broker versus point-to-point integration

Many companies that increase in size due to organic or acquisition growth find themselves in a position where the new enterprise consists of a large number of disparate systems that are responsible for managing their various products. Many times, this causes inefficiency in the organization as sales representatives/agents must log in to multiple systems in order to get the answers to their questions. This increases time and effort and the likelihood of mistakes. Over time, they may discover that this is inefficient, so they may decide to implement a point-to-point integration. For example, one can create a consolidated web application GUI that calls system A, B, or C, as appropriate. One of the challenges for this is that, as new GUI applications are added, each of them needs to perform this connectivity between the systems. In the majority of cases, the environment will be heterogeneous; even if they do manage to make all the applications work together, any change could stop it from working. For example, what happens if one of the systems is down, or if a system is upgraded or replaced? These two scenarios are illustrated in the following diagram:

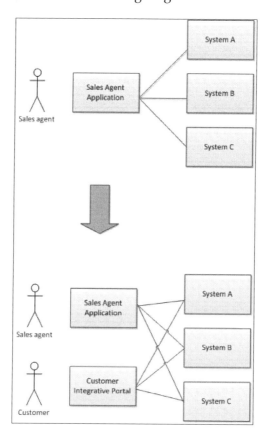

They can consider integrating the frontend application to all required backend systems, but this would dramatically increase the complexity of the application; moreover, if any other systems need to connect to the same systems, this logic would need to be duplicated and maintained.

Rewriting all of a business's applications on a common platform is unrealistic and impractical from a financial point of view. Therefore, the message broker pattern is an approach that is commonly implemented. This provides a communication infrastructure, adapter connectivity, and common command set. Companies that implement message broker can use a universal connector between their various systems. A key requirement of a message broker is that it must be flexible and must be able to respond to change quickly, such as the addition of a new system or an upgrade of a system. While the features of GUI systems may differ, the logic necessary to connect each of the backend systems is common and is encapsulated in the message broker. Therefore, it can be reused by each GUI application. This enables applications to represent a unified view of their organization to their users, for example, sales agents, end customers, management, and so on.

By leveraging the message broker architecture, the organization will be able to provide an integration architecture that provides a common communication and messaging infrastructure to support communication between all systems across the enterprise. Let's revisit our previous diagram and demonstrate in the following diagram how a message broker can be used:

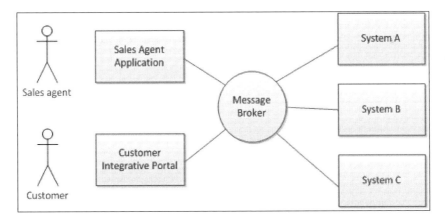

Here, we have two applications that are communicating with the message broker; the complexity of the integration that is required to connect to systems A, B, and C is handled by the message broker. The message broker is now responsible for routing messages to the appropriate systems and handling any necessary transport or transformation issues. This avoids the prohibitive costs of performing point-to-point (otherwise known as "spaghetti") integration. It also avoids the need for users to log on to multiple systems, thereby increasing productivity. The message broker acts as an intermediary across all enterprise applications.

The workflows of the message broker are implemented by orchestrations. Orchestrations represent the entire process that is required to successfully deliver messages between integration participants. Orchestrations arrange the sequence on message validations, message transformations, and routing. They may implement ordered delivery, use asynchronous processes, and rely on a set of services internal to the message broker. All modern integration tools, including BizTalk, provide means to use the standard **Business Process Execution Language (BPEL)**.

By standardizing this approach and developing this integration capability, organizations are able to reduce the time invested to include new applications and offer new innovative composite services to their customers. This enables them to quickly react to changes driven either from customer demand or internal mergers, acquisitions, or reorgs.

When organizations move away from point-to-point architectures, they want to find a close fit for the message broker architecture. A more sophisticated solution will require an Enterprise Service Bus, which we shall discuss in *Chapter 9, Web Services and Beyond*.

In the Microsoft world, BizTalk is the major tool for implementing message brokers. The way in which it can be used is shown in the next use case.

The guaranteed delivery problem

Exchanging information between different applications in order to integrate business processes is a common task for any enterprise. However, the requirements given by different organizations reflect different needs. Let's discuss one aspect of reliability. The question that seems very important is how much data can you afford to lose? Well, our initial reaction is, None! However, after some thinking, we realize that this is not necessarily true. Take an e-commerce system, for example. What if the customers don't receive all items in the catalog due to some network problems? Will the business be ruined?

No, especially if the catalog has hundreds or thousands of items. Certainly, if the catalog search system returns just 50 percent of all items, then that would create a problem. However, if it returns 99 percent of items, the majority of the users will be satisfied.

However, there are industries that cannot afford losing even one percent of information. Financial institutions or health care organizations, for instance, have a much lower tolerance for data loss. For these organizations, we need to build systems with guaranteed delivery. Whether they truly need it or not is a different question, but the perception exists and the organizations are willing to spend enough money to achieve it.

Working with the use case – health care industry

LarHans Pharmaceuticals is a multinational health sciences company with a special focus on the human immune system. Because of the nature of their work, the company is subject to regulations set by governmental agencies around the world (for example, the Food and Drug Administration in the United States or the National Institute for Health and Clinical Excellence in Great Britain). As a result, LarHans Pharmaceuticals has strict guidelines that it adheres to, regarding product safety and alerting the public about changes in a product's safety profile.

When there is a product recall or change to the product's label, the LarHans team must immediately communicate with at least the following three distinct locations:

- **Federal agencies**: A notice of product recall or label change must be distributed to governmental bodies within a very short period of time. This interval may differ by country, but companies face harsh fines if they delay the communication of this information.

- **Internal sales teams**: The LarHans sales force must be notified in a timely fashion to make sure they provide physicians with the latest and most accurate information regarding product safety.

- **Public website news feed**: LarHans conveys product changes to the consumer population through their public-facing website.

Today, when such an event occurs, the LarHans organization fills out a series of paper forms to fax to each governmental body, crafts and sends out e-mail messages to various sales organizations, and creates a work order with the website ownership team. This process has proved to be arduous, and LarHans has nearly missed several filing deadlines because of the frantic coordination of resources and document preparation.

Moving forward, LarHans Pharmaceuticals wants to establish an automated process, which allows a single label change or product recall event to trigger notifications to all interested parties. Each of the three communication targets outlined before has some sort of technology interface that can be leveraged by this solution. Each governmental body has either a secure web service interface or the FTP drop spot that can receive these safety notifications. The directors of the company sales teams are willing to create e-mail templates that get populated by an automated solution instead of hand-crafting these customized notices. Finally, the team that runs the public website is willing to open a channel to the news feed database so that entries can be added without requiring website administrator interaction.

Because of the sensitivity and impact of this solution, the LarHans team has placed high importance on the quality of service and guaranteed delivery. They want to make sure they do not lose or skip notices to government agencies, or open themselves up to fines or penalties for failure to notify the public.

LarHans Pharmaceuticals is primarily a Microsoft shop with existing investments in SQL Server, SharePoint Server, BizTalk Server, and .NET development. While LarHans has entered early adopter programs for some Microsoft applications, they typically wait until a service pack is released prior to deploying new software in the environment.

We have summarized this discussion in the key requirements given in the next section.

Summarized key requirements

The following are the key requirements for a new software solution:

- Automated distribution of the same message to multiple interested parties
- Guaranteed delivery of messages or, at a minimum, notice of failed delivery
- Flexibility to support future data recipients without reengineering the process

Additional facts

There are some additional details gathered after the initial use case was shared with the technical team. These include the following facts:

- This is a low-volume solution that puts a higher priority on reliable delivery than raw throughput or load.

- The solution must initially address the three known types of notification targets (government agencies, sales team, and public websites), but there may be future internal and external parties interested in acting upon product recall or label change events.

- There are multiple sales teams, and not all teams receive e-mails for all events. Product recalls or label changes may be specific to a particular country (or set of countries), so we need the flexibility to notify only the teams that are directly impacted.

- Similarly, not all governmental agencies need all notifications. Based on the scale of the recall or label change (and at whose request that change was made), only some agencies require notifications.

- While there is an industry-standard data format for these notifications, not all countries currently accept data in this format. This means that a transformation strategy is needed.

- If a transmission to a governmental agency fails, the LarHans team must proactively be notified so that they can perform manual publications within the legally required time window.

Pattern for guaranteed delivery

The guaranteed delivery scenario comes as a result of resiliency and reliability requirements when losing data is considered unacceptable. Guaranteed delivery can come in many flavors; a particular message may be required to be delivered exactly once or, for idempotent systems, at least once.

 Idempotence is a feature of an operation; it means that the operation can be applied many times without changing the result beyond the initial application.

A set of messages may be required to be delivered in order; this would have an additional impact on the scenario.

Regardless of this, an implementation of the guaranteed delivery requires two things:

- Data persistence, which is the ability to store data in a persistent form. The data should be stored in such a way that it is resilient to external impact. For example, in case of a power outage, the data should not be damaged and the system should have the ability to recover it.

- An ability to resubmit the data in case of failed delivery.

The simplest way to satisfy both criteria is to keep data at the source and resubmit them in case of a failure. However, there are a couple of problems that make this solution less than ideal. First, if the source system needs to get a confirmation from the destination about successful message delivery, which requires a full message round trip, this affects performance. Secondly, in a complex integration scenario, we want the system to have minimum dependence on each other. Sometimes, especially when the systems are built by independent organizations, having them loosely coupled is the only way to integrate them.

This offers suggestions us about the pattern when the data persistence happens in the middle tier that separates data or service providers and consumers. This middle tier is also responsible for resubmitting data in case of failure.

Candidate architectures

There are three ways in which we decided to tackle this problem. Each possible solution brings with it some benefits and risks, which we can see in the next sections.

Candidate architecture for guaranteed delivery #1 – Windows Azure Service Bus

Although going with a Windows Azure solution may be a bit aggressive for a more traditional IT shop, there are strategic benefits to seriously considering a guaranteed delivery solution hosted in the cloud.

Solution design aspects

While not dealing with an enormous load, the solution does require us to deal with a varied usage profile and bursts of changes. A cloud-based infrastructure is an asset when we have an inconsistent load and wish to design a solution that scales up or down based on our needs. Likewise, our clients need to pay only for their data usage instead of setting up hardware that is sized for the peaks, but remains idle during the valleys.

One of the unique aspects of the Windows Azure candidate proposal is the ability to decentralize the attachment of listeners from the router administrator. NetEventRelayBinding, special to Windows Azure Service Bus, provides a way to do a one-way multicast to multiple applications that listen on a single endpoint. Each listener attaches itself to the endpoint by starting up their listener service and providing proper authentication to Windows Azure Service Bus.

This technique provides a very loosely coupled routing infrastructure where data consumers can be rapidly provisioned and decommissioned without the intervention of a central administrator. The downside of this mechanism is that it becomes difficult to perform impact analysis and have a central console that manages the data flow.

So how do we achieve reliable delivery and automatic retries in the cloud? Windows Azure Service Bus has the concept of **buffers**, which act as temporary queues with limited lifetime and message storage. However, these buffers are not meant to be a durable store that sits between cloud routers and service listeners. Instead, we need to build reliability into our listener service, which fronts the backend systems. This means you can use a durable queue or repository that can store messages in the event that the target system is unavailable or overloaded.

Service Bus is a lightweight router and thus does not have a rich set of services for data quality or error handling. However, it can leverage Access Control Service to cleanly and efficiently allow both internal and external parties to authenticate to our service. Exception handling and auditing will need to be managed at the individual service layer.

Solution implementation aspects

Windows Azure solutions are built using a mix of Visual Studio components and Azure administration interfaces. Developers who are comfortable building WCF projects in Visual Studio can easily extend their toolbox to new Azure WCF bindings and configuration options.

Solution operations aspects

A cloud-based solution means that we have fewer physical infrastructure concerns and can confidently predict the ability of the shared cloud platform to perform under load. This will also help us successfully maintain failover in the event of a node malfunction.

The tooling for Azure administrators is still relatively immature, so solution administrators will have to establish their own best practices and governance to monitor the active router and perform effective troubleshooting.

Organizational aspects

LarHans Pharmaceuticals prefers to invest in existing products and minimize their exposure to fully custom-built solutions. While components of the Windows Azure solution would require custom code, the core routing infrastructure, security, and usage patterns are already well-defined and ready to use.

The organization can use their existing .NET resources to build Windows Azure projects, and they can be confident that such a solution can be very rapidly provisioned and deployed. However, there is clearly a risk involved in going with a new offering, and LarHans would have to examine the strategic value in moving to the cloud and decide whether it is worth accepting newfound operational and solution risks.

Solution evaluation

The following table presents the results of our assessment. When it is obvious that implementation and operations get the "thumbs up", questions may arise with regard to the design. On one hand, the design seems to be quite simple; Azure will take care of many things. However, Azure by itself does not solve our main concern—reliability. In order to provide it, we need to perform additional development that does not look obvious.

Design	Implementation	Operations	Organization

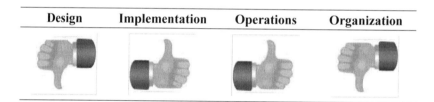

Candidate architecture for guaranteed delivery #2 – BizTalk Server

A loosely coupled service bus such as BizTalk Server can offer unique quality-of-service capabilities that closely match the needs of this customer.

Solution design aspects

A BizTalk solution offers us a few key benefits during the design of this solution. First and foremost, we get an enterprise-scale infrastructure built around reliable delivery. When we send a product recall message to the Food and Drug Administration (FDA) in the United States, we can configure our solution to retry the message in the case of failure, and we can proactively alert an administrator if a defined set of retries is exhausted.

The BizTalk architecture assures us that messages get queued in the case of downstream unavailability. If this customer can tolerate a solution where a message may get missed (for example, a stock ticker message where another will be coming along later), then nondurable solutions could be a fit. However, for "can't miss" solutions that demand delivery guarantees, BizTalk is the leading choice.

We have a need to talk to existing web services, databases, and e-mail systems. BizTalk has a series of adapters that make connectivity to these protocols a code generation and configuration task, instead of a custom coding or scripting task. Each message target may accept a different data format for product recalls and label changes, so here we would want to leverage BizTalk's mapping capability to transform data at the point of delivery.

Extensibility and loose coupling is also important to this solution. We may have new or changed endpoints in the future, and we may want to be able to isolate those changes. BizTalk's Publish/Subscribe architecture means that a single publisher can stay decoupled from all the independent consumers of a message. There will be zero impact on other subscribers if an existing subscriber needs to be modified (for example, URI address change or an alteration to the endpoint's message format) or a completely new subscriber is added. If this solution needs a very fluid, dynamic set of subscribers that change with regularity, then the Azure cloud offering might be a prime choice. However, if you have a static set of endpoints and find central management and impact analysis to be critical, then BizTalk is the right fit.

Finally, we see that our customer has a very time-sensitive transmission schedule, so failures need to be captured and handled in a consistent, actionable manner. Our BizTalk solution could actually subscribe on any exceptions thrown by the delivery service and initiate an additional process, or it can simply notify a group or a person where the manual delivery of a message may be needed to beat the required deadlines. BizTalk has a number of options for handling exceptions and, after a reasonable number of automated attempts (through configurable retry intervals), alternative options (for example, fax) are required.

Solution implementation aspects

The LarHans IT organization has enough skills in working with BizTalk Server, so they have a pool of available developers who can design and implement this solution. These developers currently store their BizTalk artifacts in an open source Subversion source control repository. While BizTalk Server is not installed on all developer workstations, the organization invests in project-specific virtual machines that are accessed by developers through remote access.

Solution operations aspects

The time-sensitive nature of the data being distributed by this solution means that a robust and rich monitoring environment is needed. Also, we need to have confidence in the infrastructure such that it supports this new application on top of all the existing solutions deployed in the BizTalk environment. Our solution has a small load requirement, but the project stakeholders want to make sure that bursts of data from other applications do not block the server from processing our mission-critical messages. BizTalk provides built-in load balancing, and we can even segment our solution into its own processing space to help ensure that it maintains a high priority for processing.

BizTalk Server comes with a dashboard for monitoring and interacting with failed messages. This allows us to proactively resume failed transmissions or delete them if the data ends up being submitted manually to its targets.

Organizational aspects

The BizTalk-based proposal can serve as a long-term solution that meets the needs of LarHans Pharmaceuticals for years to come. It has built-in extensibility points that allow us to add, change, or remove endpoints, without impacting the rest of the solution. This solution leverages the existing organizational investment in BizTalk and the developers who are trained in the tool. It also complies with their preference of configuring applications, instead of building them, and helps them rely on the solution to transition a critical manual process to an automated one.

Solution evaluation

The following table shows the solution evaluation which shows all "thumbs up"!

Design	Implementation	Operations	Organization

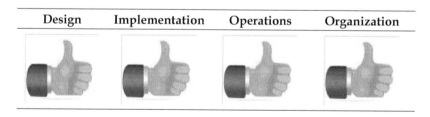

Candidate architecture for guaranteed delivery #3 – SQL Server Service Broker

The third scenario requires a shift of perspective for most database professionals, as we tend to think of Publish/Subscribe scenarios as replication issues. Here we are pushing data to diverse routes. These routes are controlled by folks outside the control of LarHans Pharmaceuticals. It is difficult enough to maintain route definitions when the enterprise controls the start and end points. The loss of end-point control and the diversity of potential protocols and message formats will create administrative issues that we will need to account for in any application.

SQL Server Service Broker (SSSB) is, at first glance, a potentially useful matching technology nonetheless. We are faced with a situation where specific data must be sent with guaranteed delivery in a specific format to a specific service. That is a sweet spot for the Service Broker.

SSSB provides native support for messaging and queuing operations. With SSSB, you can build asynchronous, loosely-coupled applications. However, unlike traditional message queues, the queue is handled through the databases involved, and messages can be coordinated, grouped, and prioritized. It requires no additional software. An understanding of Transact-SQL (T-SQL) and its basic services is all that you need for SSSB.

 Transact-SQL (T-SQL) is a Microsoft version of the SQL language that is designed for Microsoft SQL Server. You can read more about T-SQL and SQL Server in *Chapter 3, The SQL Server Primer*.

Using asynchronous processing can yield big performance gains, particularly when you can prioritize messages. Consider the classic order-entry example that is so often used in books such as this one. When an order is placed, certain systems must get data immediately to confirm an order. For example, you need to commit data that concerns the customer, the product ordered, and the number of units purchased. On the other hand, the accounts-receivables system and the order-fulfillment system do not need this data to confirm the order. You can send the data that those systems need asynchronously, using SSSB, and even prioritize the messages based on the order priority (rush orders first, for example). In short, you do the minimum work you need to do to—accept the order and complete the rest at your leisure.

Solution design aspects

It is rare that one has an out-of-the-box solution in any SQL Server-based technology. This pattern is particularly illustrative of that fact. We require setting up the following:

- User interfaces to allow input of data (for example, input of details around product recalls).

- Some form of notification to relevant sales staff (for example, SQL Mail to predefined relevant teams stored in tables).

- Service Broker conversations with multiple end points, each of which requires different data, in different formats, and potentially different languages. These would include the following:

    ○ Transmissions to regulatory agencies

    ○ External publication to the consumer and medical communities

All of this would require a fairly complex and custom solution and is not something easily achieved in SQL Server tooling.

Solution implementation aspects

One of the key requirements of this application will be to handle **Call Your Attorney (CYA)** situations. Failure to notify can give rise to expensive regulatory and, at least in the United States, tort liabilities. We need to track precisely when, where, and how each message was sent and when (or whether) it was delivered. Moreover, if the message is not delivered within the predetermined time frame, it must allow for human intervention. For example, we may want to account for a central FTP server being unavailable to receive messages for some time period. Beyond that time period, we may want someone to call the regulatory agency in question or fall back on alternative methods of delivery.

A second key consideration will be the long-term evolution of data that must be sent. We are dealing with multiple regulatory authorities in multiple countries, each of which will have their own required format for the data. Of course, each will want the data in their own national language. As a part of this solution, therefore, we will need a user interface and database schema that will provide the flexibility for performing the following tasks:

- Capturing the data that is required at present

- Sending the data in an appropriate format

- Allowing edits to that format; hopefully, with minimal IT involvement
- Storing that data in a way that allows someone to reconstruct what was sent, the format used, and when it was sent

Using SSSB presents advantages for these requirements. First, both physical and logical access to this data is always under the control of the enterprise. It is also very easy to relate the data that we leverage in this application with the data stored in other enterprise databases. For example, recall data can be linked to quality control, order fulfillment, and manufacturing systems to make it easier to obtain a complete view of the recall process or to respond to any request for further information sent in by regulatory agencies. We can even place this ability in the hands of power users using PowerPivot technologies available in Microsoft Office.

The LarHans team has extensive SQL Server development experience and can build this solution, but they are relatively new to SQL Server Service Broker and typically do not construct SQL solutions that communicate with nondatabase endpoints.

Solution operations aspects

For this application, IT can never be a bottleneck for getting data out the door. It is not only regulatory and liability issues that dictate this requirement, sufficient though they may be. Real harm, even death, can come to real people from ingesting potentially defective medications. As architects, we should be very well aware of the real-world consequences our designs may impose on people.

Once in operation, this application must allow business users to get appropriate data, at the appropriate place, in a correct format, and in a timely manner. Formats, data, and potentially even the definition of "timely" can change rapidly over time and according to a given situation. The application must be flexible enough to handle such requirements and allow for easy updates to formats, business rules, and the data stored in the application to meet these requirements. So, in addition to the creation of an SSSB application, we would also need to provide user frontends to handle these requirements or an IT staff person whose primary role would be to create and send these messages via SSSB.

Organizational aspects

As noted earlier, LarHans Pharmaceuticals prefers to invest in existing products and minimize their exposure to completely custom-built solutions. An SSSB solution will require significant investment in the custom code or a DBA dedicated primarily to operating this system.

Solution evaluation

As you can see in the following table, this would not be our preferred solution:

Design	Implementation	Operations	Organization
👎	👎	👍	👎

Architecture selection

Let's look at how these candidate architecture technologies stack up while evaluating the risks and benefits of each, with the help of the following tables:

Windows Azure Service Bus

Benefits	Risks
• This provides rapid provisioning of endpoint listeners • No new hardware is needed to host message routing function • Internet-based hosts allow for secure access for internal and external endpoints	• No durable component to store failed messages • No centralized management of data subscribers • This requires endpoints to be able to integrate with Service Bus

BizTalk Server

Benefits	Risks
• It has a reliable messaging engine that can ensure delivery of critical data • It has a diverse set of adapters that can natively communicate with all the protocols your client demands • It has a loosely coupled infrastructure that allows us to add/remove/change endpoints in a nondisruptive fashion • It leverages existing organizational investment in BizTalk	• BizTalk Server does not have an out-of-the-box business dashboard for monitoring and resubmitting failed messages. The monitoring tools are very technical. • This requires additional modules or code.

SQL Server	
Benefits	**Risks**
• There is reliable delivery of data between database systems • The in-house staff develops and maintains the solution	• This requires significant coding effort to communicate with diverse endpoints • The solution would have to be made up of multiple components woven together • Nontrivial efforts to modify or create new endpoints

In evaluating these options against the problem scenario, BizTalk Server is the most appropriate choice. BizTalk provides us with a quality-of-service guarantee through persistent storage, automatic retries, and flexible exception handling mechanisms. We also have a static set of endpoints, so the powerful, distributed Azure model is not needed here.

Building the solution

For this solution demonstration, we will publish two of the desired endpoints: the FDA web service endpoint and the LarHans website database endpoint. This gives us a chance to evaluate BizTalk's capabilities to communicate with standard web services as well as database platforms.

One key aspect of our solution architecture is to keep our design as loosely coupled as possible. In our case, this means embracing canonical formats while performing routing operations instead of polluting our message processing rules with endpoint-specific formats. Also, we want our endpoints to be as distinct and separate from each other as possible so that changes to one endpoint have little to no impact on existing message consumers.

Setting up the development foundation

Perform the following steps to set up the development foundation:

1. We start off by creating a new database named `Chapter9` on a SQL Server 2012 instance.

2. After the database is created, execute the `Chapter9.sql` database script in the `Begin` folder under `<Installation Directory>\Chapter9\`, and install the tables in your new database. This is the database that holds the public website's company news feed entries.

3. Now open the `Chapter9.sln` Visual Studio solution located in the `Begin` folder under `<Installation Directory>\Chapter9\`. In this solution, you will find a single WCF service that represents the destination endpoint of the FDA.

4. Build the solution and add this to IIS as a new web application named `Chapter9.FDA.SafetySubmissionService`. Testing this service via the WCF Test Client application should yield a result that consists of a tracking number and timestamp. The directory structure is shown in the following screenshot:

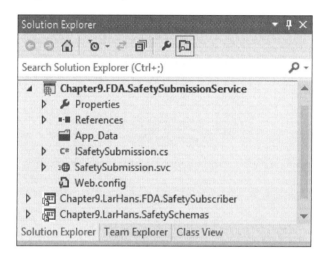

Building the canonical solution artifacts

Now that our foundational database and services are in place, we are ready to develop the canonical solution components that are independent of any particular downstream system. Perform the following steps to do so:

1. Launch Visual Studio 2012 and open the `Chapter9.sln` solution under `<Installation Directory>\Chapter9\Begin`. You will find a single WCF service already in place.

2. The first BizTalk project is needed to hold enterprise canonical schemas.

The canonical schema is an intermediary schema that utilizes a common data model.

Specifically, these are the standard schemas that represent a product recall notice, a label change, and a government agency response. Regardless of the data formats required by various subscribers, our core messaging solution only routes canonical formats.

3. Right-click on the solution in Visual Studio and choose **Add | New Project**. Choose the **BizTalk Projects** category and select **Empty BizTalk Server Project**. Name the project `Chapter9.LarHans.SafetySchemas`, as shown in the following screenshot:

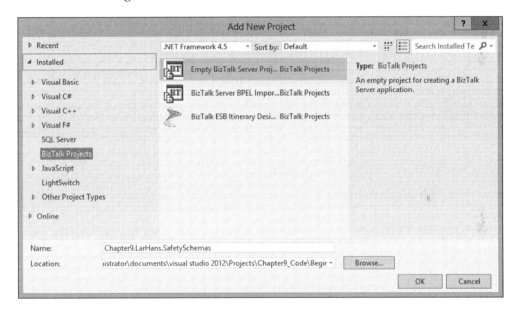

4. Immediately after creating the BizTalk project, right-click on the project, select **Properties**, highlight the **Signing** tab, and set a strong name key. If you do not have an existing strong name key to reference, select **New...** from the **Choosing a strong name key** drop-down box. In the **Create Strong Name Key** dialog box, set the parameters for your new key. Finally, switch to the **Deployment** tab and set the value of **Application Name** to `Chapter9`.

5. Now, right-click on the BizTalk project again and choose **Add | New Item**. Under the **Schema Files** category, select **Schema** and name it `ProductRecall_XML.xsd`, as shown in the following screenshot:

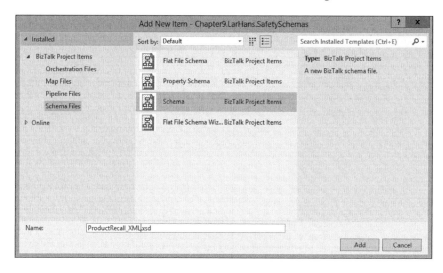

6. Click on the topmost node in the schema named **<Schema>** and look in the Visual Studio **Properties** window for the **Target Namespace** property. Change this value to `http://Chapter9.LarHans.SafetySchemas`. Use this value as the target namespace for all canonical schemas in this project.

7. Define the schema so that it looks like the following screenshot. Note that all elements are of a string data type, and the **Lot** and **Incident** nodes are marked with an unbounded maximum occurrence in the Visual Studio **Properties** window. This is because our recall notice may impact multiple lots of the product, and we can have any number of reported incidents associated with a recall.

8. Next, right-click on the BizTalk project and add another schema named `ProductLabelChange_XML.xsd`. Rename its target namespace to the same value designated in step 6. This schema should look like the following screenshot. Note that all elements are of the `string` type, and there are no changes to the default node properties.

9. Now we need a schema to hold the acknowledgements that we receive from each government agency. Right-click on the BizTalk project and add an XML schema named `AgencySubmissionAcknowledgement_XML.xsd`. Once again, alter its target namespace as per the value we identified earlier. This schema has a simple structure that looks like the following screenshot:

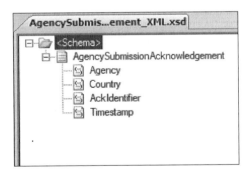

10. We want to have the option to filter our subscriptions for product recalls and label changes based on some of the values in the messages. Specifically, a particular subscriber may only wish to receive notifications for a particular product or for those affecting a specific country. To perform content-based routing in BizTalk solutions, we need to promote message nodes via property schemas. Right-click on the BizTalk project and add a new **Property Schema** named `SafetyRouting_PropSchema.xsd`.

11. This schema has two nodes for the country and product as shown in the following screenshot:

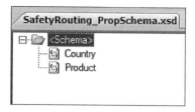

12. We now need to get our product recall and label change schemas to point to this property schema so that we can perform content-based routing on each message type. Open the `ProductRecall_XML.xsd` schema, right-click on the root **<Schema>** node, and navigate to select **Promotions | Show Promotions**. On the **Property Fields** tab, choose **Add a Property Schema** by pointing to our previously built property schema. Then, create the relationship between the **Country** and **Product** nodes, and their corresponding property schema nodes, as shown in the following screenshot:

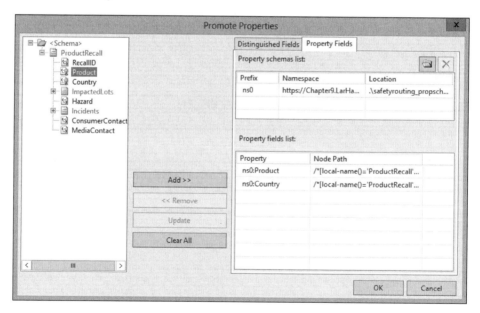

13. Save the schema and then repeat this same process on the `ProductLabelChange_XML.xsd` schema. At this point, you should have a BizTalk project with four complete schemas in it, as shown in the following screenshot:

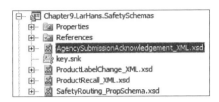

Building the FDA subscriber solution artifacts

With our canonical objects in place, we can now define subscriber-specific artifacts. Each subscriber will have its own BizTalk project to hold any schemas and maps associated with that particular endpoint. Why not bunch them together in a single project? We want a clear separation of concern and to allow the isolation of change. If one subscriber changes their endpoint schema, why should it impact all the other unchanged endpoints as well? By separating the projects, we establish a very modular solution with a clear extension pattern.

1. In Visual Studio, right-click on the solution and choose to add a new project. Select the **Empty BizTalk Project** type and name the project `Chapter9. LarHans.FDA.SafetySubscriber`. Upon project creation, right-click on the project, select **Properties**, and set a strong name key and **Application Name** to `Chapter9`.

2. This project will hold the artifacts needed to communicate with the FDA service. Right-click on the project and navigate to **Add | Add Generated Items**. Select the **Consume WCF Service** menu option, as shown in the following screenshot:

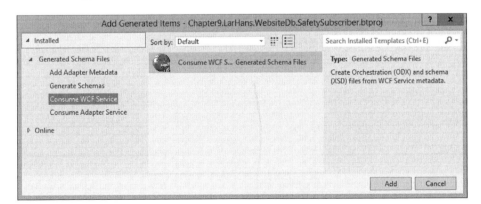

3. The **BizTalk WCF Service Consuming Wizard** launches; when prompted, choose **Metadata Exchange Endpoint** as the service source.

4. For the metadata URL, use the URL of the service you installed into IIS during the earlier solution setup (for example, `http://localhost/Chapter9.FDA.SafetySubmissionService/SafetySubmission.svc`), as shown:

5. Keep the default namespace on the next wizard page and click on the Import button.

6. This wizard creates a host of artifacts in our BizTalk project, including an orchestration, multiple schemas, and two send port binding files, as shown in the following screenshot:

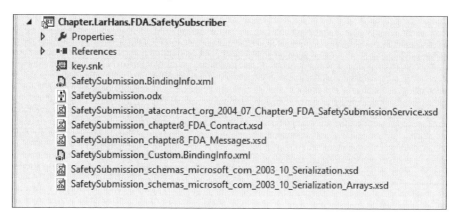

7. Now we need to add the following three maps to this project:

    ○ The canonical product recall format to the FDA input format

    ○ The canonical label change format to the FDA input format

    ○ The FDA acknowledgement format to the canonical government agency response format

8. Right-click on the BizTalk project and choose to add a reference. Point to the **SafetySchemas** project so that we can access the canonical schemas defined there.

9. Then, right-click on the BizTalk project and navigate to **Add | New Item**. Select the **Map** type and name it `ProductRecall_To_FDASafetyIssue.btm`.

10. On the left-hand side of the map, click on the **Open Source Schema** link, go to the `References` folder, and open the `SafetySchemas` project. Find and select the **ProductRecall** message.

11. Click on the **Open Destination Schema** button on the right-hand side of the map, and navigate directly to the **Schemas** node to pick the `SafetySubmission_chapter8_FDA_Contract` type. Select the **PostSafetyIssue** type from the pop-up box. The map should now look similar to the one shown in the following screenshot:

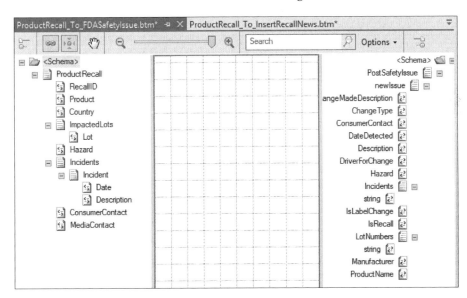

12. Create the mapping as follows:

Source	Destination	Comments
Product	ProductName	
ImpactedLots/Lot	LotNumbers/string	
Hazard	Hazard	
Incidents/Incident/Date	Incidents/string	Use the Concatenate functoid to combine source nodes
Incidents/Incident/Description		
ConsumerContact	ConsumerContact	
	isLabelChange = false	Hard code **Value** property
	isProductRecall = true	Hard code **Value** property
	Manufacturer = LarHans	Hard code **Value** property

13. The mapping visualization is presented in the following screenshot:

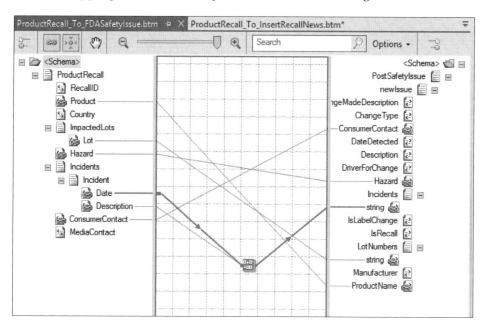

14. It is a good practice to test the map when you complete it, so create an instance file of the source schema (by right-clicking on the **ProductRecall** schema in the **SafetySchemas** project and choosing **Generate Instance**), and set it as an input to this map via the **Properties** window. Then, right-click on the map and select **Test Map**. Your output should show all the relevant source data values in the destination schema.

15. Next, we need the map from the label change to the FDA safety issue. Right-click on the BizTalk project and navigate to **Add | New Item**. Select the **Map** type and name the map `LabelChange_To_FDASafetyIssue.btm`.

16. For the source schema, navigate to the **References** node and select the **ProductLabelChange** type in the **SafetySchemas** project.

17. The destination schema should be the same `SafetySubmission_chapter8_FDA_Contract` type as before. Select the **PostSafetyIssue** type from the pop-up box.

18. Create the mapping as follows:

Source	Destination	Comments
Product	ProductName	
ContactDetails	ConsumerContact	
ChangeDetails/ChangeType	ChangeType	
ChangeDetails/ReasonForChange	DriverForChange	
ChangeDetails/ContentChanged	ChangeMadeDescription	
	isLabelChange = true	Hard coded **Value** property
	isProductRecall = false	Hard coded **Value** property
	Manufacturer = LarHans	Hard coded **Value** property

19. The mapping visualization is presented in the following screenshot:

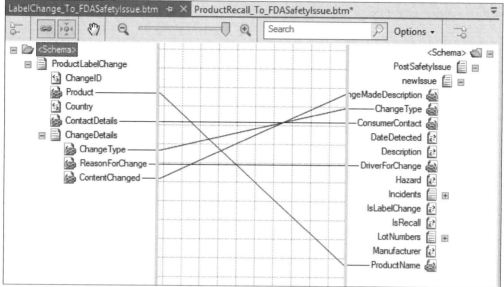

20. Create an instance of the `LabelChange` message and confirm that the map functions as expected.

21. Our final map for this subscriber is for the acknowledgement message. Add a new item to the BizTalk project, choose the **Map** type, and name it `FDAResponse_To_AgencySubmissionAcknowledgement.btm`.

22. Select the `SafetySubmission_chapter8_FDA_Contract` type for **Schema Source** and choose the **PostSafetyIssueResponse** option from the pop-up window. For the destinations schema, navigate to the **References** node and choose the **AgencySubmissionAcknowledgement** schema, as shown in the next screenshot.

23. Create the mapping as follows:

Source	Destination	Comments
AckID	AckIdentifier	
Timestamp	Timestamp	
	Agency = FDA	Hard coded **Value** property
	Country = USA	Hard coded **Value** property

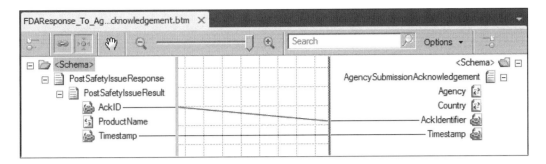

24. Build all the projects currently in the Visual Studio solution.

25. Right-click on `Chapter9.LarHans.SafetySchemas` and select **Deploy**. This will load this project's assembly into the **GAC** and register the relevant artifacts with BizTalk Server.

26. Once that operation succeeds, right-click and deploy the `Chapter9.LarHans.FDA.SafetySubscriber` project.

27. Open the **BizTalk Administration Console** and navigate to the `Chapter9` application. You can confirm the deployment by opening a node such as **Maps** to confirm that our recently built maps appear.

Configuring the data publisher and FDA subscriber

Now that we have the schemas and maps necessary for exchanging information with the FDA, we can construct the actual endpoint that transmits data. Before we can build the endpoints that consume the data, we have to set up the publisher that pulls data to the BizTalk Server. To do this, we configure a BizTalk receive port and location that publish the product recall and label change messages in the bus. In this scenario, we are picking up the canonical message via a BizTalk FILE adapter. Note that we could very well use any adapter to send messages into BizTalk Message Bus.

1. Within **BizTalk Administration Console**, navigate to the `Chapter9` application, and create a new, one-way receive port named `Chapter9.LarHans.ReceiveProductRecall`.

2. Add a receive location named `Chapter9.LarHans.ReceiveProductRecall.FILE` to our new receive port.

3. Select the **FILE** adapter and set the value of **Receive Pipeline** to the **XMLReceive** pipeline. Choose to configure the **FILE** adapter and set the polling location to `<Installation Directory>\Chapter9\Filedrop\PickupRecall`.

4. Create another one-way receive port named `Chapter9.LarHans.ReceiveProductLabelChange` with a FILE receive location named `Chapter9.LarHans.ReceiveProductLabelChange.FILE`. That receive location should also use the **XMLReceive** pipeline and point to `<Installation Directory>\Chapter9\Filedrop\PickupLabelChange`.

5. Note that there are no maps here as we receive the canonical format and do not want to translate to subscriber formats until the latest point possible (send ports).

Now that our publisher is built, we can move on and create the FDA subscriber. We do this by building BizTalk send ports and pointing them to our destination web service.

1. We can create the FDA send port manually; however, when we referenced the WCF service in our Visual Studio project, the BizTalk wizard autogenerated the binding files for the send port. Right-click on the BizTalk application in **Administration Console** and choose **Import** followed by **Bindings**.

2. Navigate to the `Chapter9.LarHans.FDA.SafetySubscriber` project and choose the `SafetySubmission_Custom.BindingInfo.xml` file.

3. When the import is complete, you can go to the `Send Ports` folder in **Administration Console** and see your new send port pointing to our WCF service, as shown in the following screenshot:

4. Remember that this single send port accepts data for either recalls or label changes. So, we need to apply both maps here so that, regardless of which message comes in, the correct message goes out. Go to the **Outbound Maps** tab and select both the maps that result in a **FDASafetyIssue** format, as shown in the following screenshot:

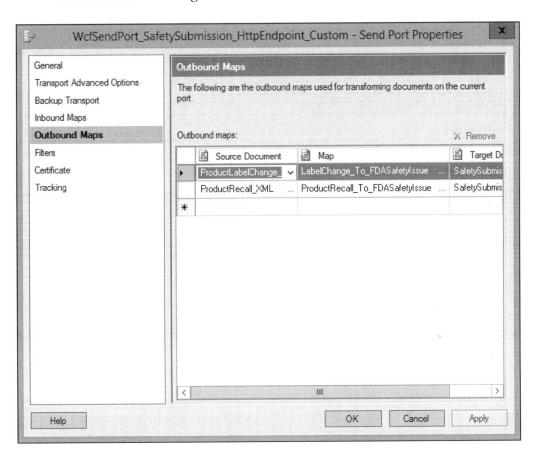

5. Next, we have to add **Inbound Map** so that the acknowledgement that comes back from the FDA maps to our canonical format, as shown in the following screenshot. Recall that "inbound" in this context refers to messages coming back into BizTalk from this send port (that is, the response value from the service call):

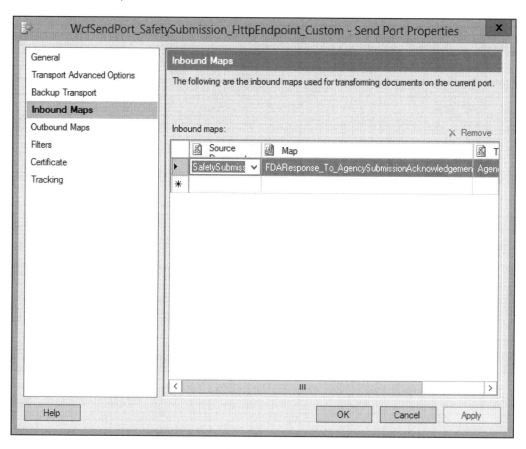

6. Finally, we have to create our subscriptions so that this port picks up the correct messages from the BizTalk Message Box. Specifically, we want an OR condition where the value of `BTS.MessageType` is equal to either `http://Chapter9.LarHans.SafetySchemas#ProductRecall` or `http://Chapter9.LarHans.SafetySchemas#ProductLabelChange`. However, as this is a United States agency, we want to make sure to send notices that relate only to US recalls or label changes. So, here we add a filter based on the country as well, as shown in the following screenshot:

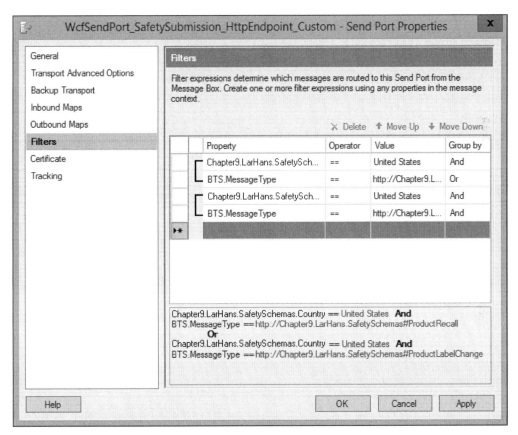

7. All that is left is to create a send port that listens for the synchronous acknowledgement back from the FDA service and publishes the canonical format to disk. Create a new one-way, static send port named `Chapter9.LarHans.SendAgencyAck.FILE`. Set the file adapter's destination location to `<Installation Directory>\Chapter9\Filedrop\DropOffAck\` and use a filter subscription of `BTS.MessageType = http://Chapter9.LarHans.SafetySchemas#AgencySubmissionAcknowledgement`.

8. Start both the receive locations and send ports.

9. Drop a product recall and a label change message to their respective pickup folders.

10. If everything is configured correctly, then the FDA service should be called twice, and you should see two files sent to your acknowledgements folder. The content of the files would be similar to the one shown in the following screenshot:

```
- <ns0:AgencySubmissionAcknowledgement
    xmlns:ns0="http://Chapter9.LarHans.SafetySchemas">
    <Agency>FDA</Agency>
    <Country>USA</Country>
    <AckIdentifier>9bfc6d8f-a6d1-41b8-970b-f44256b343ed</AckIdentifier>
    <Timestamp>2010-01-15T14:02:56.4981344-08:00</Timestamp>
  </ns0:AgencySubmissionAcknowledgement>
```

Building the website database subscriber solution artifacts

With our first subscriber working, we can now build the pieces necessary to share data with our second subscriber—the LarHans website database. Perform the following steps to do so:

1. Return to Visual Studio, right-click on the solution, and add a new **Empty BizTalk Project** named `Chapter9.LarHans.WebsiteDb.SafetySubscriber`.

2. Right-click on the project and choose **Properties** to set its strong name key and **Application Name** parameters.

3. Right-click on the new project and navigate to **Add | Add Generated Items**. Select the **Consume Adapter Service** menu option, as shown in the following screenshot:

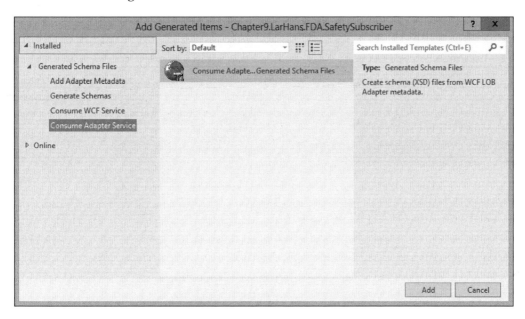

4. When the **Consume Adapter Service** window opens, choose **sqlBinding** from the bindings menu. Note that the following screenshot shows only a portion of the large wizard window that pops up:

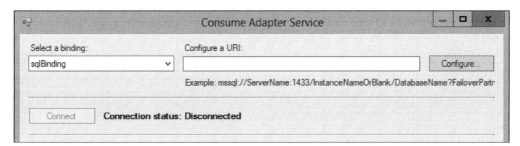

5. Click on the **Configure** button next to the **Configure a URI** textbox.

6. Select **Windows** as the **Client Credential** type on the **Security** tab.

7. On the **URI Properties** tab, set the value of **Initial Catalog** to `Chapter9` and the **Server** to `"."`, as shown in the following screenshot:

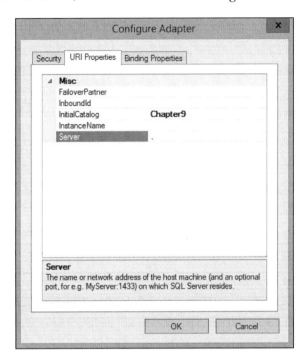

8. Click on **OK** to exit the URI configuration window, and click on the **Connect** button on the **Consume Adapter Service Wizard** page to establish a connection to our database.

9. We are adding records to a table; thus, after choosing **RecallNews** under the **Tables** node, select the **Insert** operation, and add it to the list of operations to generate.

10. After clicking on **OK**, the wizard generates the artifacts necessary for BizTalk to communicate with this database table. The BizTalk project in Visual Studio should now have schemas and a send the port binding file, as shown in the following screenshot:

11. A single map is needed from the canonical product recall schema to the database specific format. Right-click on the BizTalk project and navigate to **Add | New Item**. Choose the **Map** type and name the map `ProductRecall_To_InsertRecallNews.btm`.

12. Add a reference to the **SafetySchemas** project so that we can point to our canonical product recall schema.

13. Once the reference is in place, set the map's source schema to the **ProductRecall** type found in the **References** node.

14. Set the value of **Destination Schema** equal to the `TableOperation.dbo.RecallNews` type and choose **Insert** from the pop-up window.

15. Create the mapping as follows:

Source	Destination	Comments
RecallID	ItemID	
Product	Product	
Hazard	HazardDescription	
ConsumerContact	ConsumerContact	
	DatePosted	Date and time functoid
	Lots	Scripting functoid leveraging Inline XSLT

16. The **Lots** destination field holds all of the possible lots listed in the recall, so we need a way to mash up all the source node values. As mentioned in the preceding table, a scripting functoid was leveraged. The Inline XSLT used is as follows:

```
<Lots xmlns="http://schemas.microsoft.com/Sql/2008/05/Types/
Tables/dbo">
<xsl:for-each select=" /*[local-name()='ProductRecall' and
namespace-uri()='http://Chapter9.LarHans.SafetySchemas']
/*[local-name()='ImpactedLots' and namespace-uri()=''] /*[local-
name()='Lot' and namespace-uri()=''] ">
[<xsl:value-of select="." />]
</xsl:for-each>
</Lots>
```

17. The completed map looks like the following screenshot:

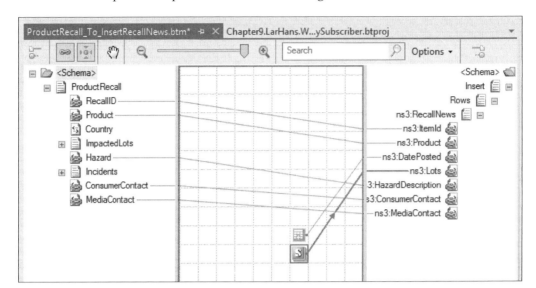

18. This BizTalk project can now be deployed to the BizTalk Server by right-clicking on the project and choosing **Deploy**.

19. Confirm that the deployment was successful by locating our new assembly and components in the `Chapter9` application found in the BizTalk **Administration Console**.

Configuring the website database subscriber

Our final activity is to configure the necessary messaging components to distribute product recall messages to the LarHans website database. Because of the way we have architected our solution, we can achieve this simply by adding a single new send port to the application. There is no need to change anything about our publisher, and there is no impact on our existing FDA service subscriber. Perform the following steps to configure the website database subscriber:

1. While the Consume Adapter Service did produce a binding file (much as when we consumed a WCF service), we do not want to use it. The binding file generated was for a two-way send port, but we are not interested in the result of the database insert operation. So, create a new, one-way static send port named `Chapter9.LarHans.WebsiteDb.SendRecall.Sql`.

2. Choose the **WCF-Custom** adapter type and click on **Configure**.

3. Switch immediately to the **Binding** tab and choose **sqlBinding**.

4. Move back to the **General** tab and enter an address value of
   `mssql://.//Chapter9?`.

5. For the **SOAP Action** header, use the following XML configuration:

```
<BtsActionMapping xmlns:xsi="http://www.w3.org/2001/ XMLSchema-
instance" xmlns:xsd="http://www.w3.org/2001/XMLSchema">
<Operation Name="Insert" Action="TableOp/Insert/dbo/RecallNews" />
</BtsActionMapping>
```

This is shown in the following screenshot:

6. Click on **OK** to save the adapter configuration settings.

7. Next, we need to set the single outbound map that takes the canonical product recall format and transforms it to the data structure expected by the database adapter. View the send port's **Outbound Maps** tab and set the map to ProductRecall_To_InsertRecallNews.

8. Now go to the **Filters** tab so that we can set the subscription for this send port. The filter should look for any BTS.MessageType equal to http:// Chapter9.LarHans.SafetySchemas#ProductRecall.

9. After saving and starting the send port, drop a new product recall message into BizTalk, and you should observe both an acknowledgement file on the disk (from the FDA subscriber) and a database record (from the website database subscriber), as shown in the following screenshot:

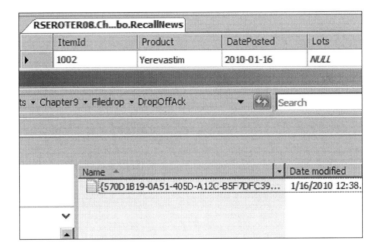

10. If you publish a product recall message that targets a country besides the United States, you'll find that the FDA subscriber does not pick it up, but the website database subscriber does. This is because our FDA subscriber is only interested in recalls targeted at the United States, while the website subscriber is grabbing any recall message that it encounters.

Lessons learned

In this pattern, we looked at a customer who needed the rights to send a single event to a varied list of subscribers. There was no need for tight coupling of the sender and receiver(s), so the injection of a service broker in the middle was a sensible way to leverage asynchronous routing between endpoints.

By clearly isolating our subscription endpoints, we were able to make the addition, modification, or deletion of endpoints a straightforward task. The Publish/Subscribe pattern is a powerful way to transmit data, and the use of canonical message formats and BizTalk Server gave us enterprise-grade quality-of-service attributes that were demanded by this scenario.

The Publish/Subscribe pattern

It is also worth mentioning that message brokers quite often implement Publish/Subscribe patterns. The Publish/Subscribe model together with using a persistent message storage improves reliability of the solution.

In the Publish/Subscribe pattern, message senders do not send messages directly to recipients. They send their messages to a message broker who performs message routing based on subscriptions. Let's introduce some important notions for the Publish/Subscribe pattern:

- **Publisher:** This is a participant in the Publish/Subscribe architecture, that sends messages to the message broker.

- **Subscriber:** This is a participant in the Publish/Subscribe architecture, that retrieves messages from the message broker based on the subscriptions. The message retrieval can use **polling**, when the subscriber periodically inquires about the messages, as well as **pushing**, when the message broker sends messages to the subscriber based on its own schedule.

- **Subscription:** This is a filter that is used by the message broker to match messages to subscribers. Subscriptions are predefined and configurable; they can describe filtering based on the message header as well as the message body.

The Publish/Subscribe model usually requires a persistent data storage to keep the messages that cannot be delivered instantaneously. It also requires additional tools to create and manage subscriber and subscription data, typically in a database.

Note that BizTalk itself is implemented using the Publish/Subscribe mechanism along with the Message Bus for persisting messages. However, this is done at the lower level and does not limit BizTalk to the use of the Publish/Subscribe model. Even more, using BizTalk to implement Publish/Subscribe architecture happens much more rarely than one can think.

Moving to Enterprise Service Bus

With the paradigm of service-oriented architecture that we shall explore later in the book, the Messages Broker pattern started showing some disadvantages.

First off, Message Brokers have been always implemented as a monolithic application that performs all required functionalities of a hub in the hub-and-spoke architecture. They implement routing, validation, and transformation, as well as error handling, logging, and all other message processing activities. This made the message broker a single point of failure in the solutions.

In early 2000s, the notion of **Enterprise Service Bus (ESB)** emerged, which used the bus paradigm instead of the hub. Bus architecture relies on distributed services that can be added and removed seamlessly, making it more dynamic. Significant componentization makes ESB more reliable than message hubs.

The notion of ESB has been changing constantly since its appearance on the market. It is still an evolving notion, and its definitions vary. We'll try to compare ESB with Message Broker based on a generally accepted view with the help of the following table:

	Message Broker	**ESB**
Architecture topology	Hub-and-spoke	Bus
Componentization	A monolithic solution adopted to minimize the number of connections in the point-to-point architecture.	A dynamic set of components in the form of services.
Scalability	This is scalable horizontally by implementing load balancing—limited. This is scalable vertically by increasing the server capabilities.	This is scalable horizontally by adding more services or even by connecting to another bus. This is scalable vertically by increasing the server capabilities.
Connectivity	This uses adapters in order to provide connectivity to different participants.	This uses services and generally complies with messaging standards.
Expandability	Static solution with participants required to be directly connected to the hub.	Dynamic solution based on the set of services that can be rearranged.
Discoverability	Participants have to know the data formats and the endpoints.	Services and contracts are discoverable.

Generally, ESB provides a more dynamic and therefore manageable solution by using a componentized architecture rather than a monolithic one.

Summary

In this chapter, we talked about integration architecture, specifically about application integration. We discussed point-to-point antipattern, request/response with workflow, guaranteed delivery, and message broker patterns. For guaranteed delivery and the request/response with aggregation patterns, we compared different candidate technologies from several perspectives. We have chosen the leading technology and provided working examples.

We introduced the notion of the ESB.

In the next chapter, we'll talk about web services and RESTful services. We shall also see how ESB can provide the basis for service-oriented architecture.

9
Web Services and Beyond

Anecdotal evidence has it that the first time web services, in the context of XML-structured messages, were mentioned by Bill Gates was at the Microsoft Professional Development Conference in Orlando, Florida, on July 12, 2000. By that time, many organizations, including Microsoft, Sun, and IBM, had been working on XML Schema and SOAP specifications. Don Box, in his article named *Brief History of SOAP*, (`http://www.xml.com/pub/a/ws/2001/04/04/soap.html`) presents an excellent overview of issues, more political than technical, surrounding that development.

The invention of XML was critical to web services development. **Electronic Data Interchange (EDI)**, which dominated the market at that time, presented a quite complex data exchange format. Also, despite the fact that it was published as a standard, EDI was influenced by virtually every software vendor that used it. XML looked much simpler and more generic.

The concept of web services is fluid. There are many things that are called web services. XML is not necessarily the only format to be used with web services; for example, JSON is gaining more and more popularity. RESTful services are also often considered web services by some authors.

To start this chapter, we shall discuss XML web services.

The **World Wide Web Consortium (W3C)** defines web services in the following manner:

> *"A Web service is a software system designed to support interoperable machine-to-machine interaction over a network. It has an interface described in a machine-processable format (specifically WSDL). Other systems interact with the Web service in a manner prescribed by its description using SOAP messages, typically conveyed using HTTP with an XML serialization in conjunction with other Web-related standards."*

WSDL originally stood for Web Services Definition Language. In Version 2.0, the meaning of the acronym was changed to the Web Services Description Language. WSDL is XML based, and most WSDL documents are automatically generated. The documents are machine- and human-readable.

SOAP originally stood for Simple Object Access Protocol. Later, the long name was dropped, and only the short acronym was left in Version 1.2. SOAP is typically built on top of HTTP; however, this is not mandatory. A SOAP message has a relatively simple structure consisting of an optional `<Header>` and a mandatory `<Body>` element inside the root element `<Envelope>`. In case of an exception, SOAP returns the `<Fault>` element in the response.

Microsoft was promoting the concept of XML web services built with the ASP.NET framework. Since the file extension for services was `.asmx`, Microsoft called them **ASMX Web services**. After a few beta releases, ASP.NET was finally launched in January 2002.

In the beginning of the web services history, their automatic discoverability seemed to be extremely important. In order to support it, the **Universal Description, Discovery, and Integration (UDDI)** approach was proposed. UDDI registries were considered an essential part of any web services infrastructure. Web services seemed to show the way to complete web automation—the idea that started the entire Semantic Web initiative.

Today, the value of UDDIs is questionable; and in many cases, the existence of a registry that provides automatic discovery is not required. After Windows 7, Microsoft stopped shipping UDDI SDK with Microsoft Windows. Future releases of the SDK will be included with Microsoft BizTalk Server (see `http://msdn.microsoft.com/en-us/library/windows/desktop/aa966237(v=bts.10).aspx`).

Meanwhile, standard bodies such as W3C and OASIS were restlessly working on new standards. The web services domain was not an exception. A lot of new standards, especially around security, were proposed. The set of web service-related standards, the so-called **WS-*** standards, was published over the years.

Almost immediately, these standards found their way into .NET. Microsoft developed **Web Services Enhancements (WSE)**, a set of classes to implement some of the WS-* specifications. WSE provided extensions to SOAP utilizing **WS-Security**, **WS-Addressing**, **WS-SecureConversation**, and others.

In 2006, Microsoft released .NET v3.0 that included Windows Communication Foundation (WCF). WCF superseded WSE; today, it is the main Microsoft approach to building web services.

Service-oriented architecture

Service orientation is a design paradigm that became popular in the last decade and continues to be appreciated by different organizations worldwide. Its popularity resulted in numerous discussions, articles, and books. As an introduction to the topic, we would recommend books written by Thomas Erl, particularly *SOA Design Patterns* and *SOA Principles of Service Design* both by *Prentice Hall*.

Service-oriented architecture (SOA) is an architectural style based on the concept of a service. Since there is no industry-standard describing services, let's talk about features and principles that make service a service. The following describes the features and principles:

- **Service granularity** refers to the size and scope of the functionality. Roughly, a service exposes functionality to cover one business unit of work. During every SOA design, building services of the right granularity is a challenge. If you think of balancing between science, art, and craft, achieving the right granularity is more craft or art than science.

- Related to service granularity is service **encapsulation**. A service encapsulates solution logic providing an interface to its **operations**.

- Service **autonomy** requires that service contracts express a well-defined functional boundary. Services exercise a high level of control over their environment. Service autonomy refers to the service's independence from its environment during the entire life cycle: from designing to retiring the service.

- One of the most important features of services and of the entire service-orientation paradigm is **loose coupling**. Loosely coupled components of a system have very little or no knowledge of each other. Information about services is provided through their **contracts**, which increases independence of the components and interoperability.

- Another reason to build service-oriented architecture is service **reusability**. If properly designed, the same service can be used again and again in different solutions. Designing reusable services is not as simple as it might seem. The service has to be expandable, has to encapsulate solution logic that covers related business units of work, and still not be too coarsely granular.

- A service should not expose too much functionality, especially when it is not really required for invocation of the service. The design principle that suggests building services as black boxes and hiding the details from service consumers other than what's required for their invocation is called service **abstraction**.

- **Location transparency** means the ability of consumers to use a service without knowing its exact location. This is usually achieved by using a registry (with or without UDDI).

Building a system as a set of services helps several architectural challenges such as scalability and extensibility.

Enterprise Service Bus

Probably the most dominant architectural pattern used to implement the middle-tier for service-oriented architectures is the **Enterprise Service Bus (ESB)**. This pattern works particularly well when the number of service consumers is limited and their behavior is predictable. A typical example would be building an ESB for services within one enterprise, where the service providers and consumers are well known, predictable, and are limited in number.

On the next few pages we'll present and analyze a use case of a trading firm, which will require building an Enterprise Service Bus.

Use case – a commodity trading firm

Sam MacColl Commodities is a rapidly expanding commodity trading firm, which is a leader in the production of sustainable and ethical palm oil. Through rapid expansion and acquisition over the last 10 years, they have grown to be the largest palm oil plantation and milling operator in Papua New Guinea. Their core activity is the cultivation and processing of palm oil raw products into various derivatives for sale to domestic and international markets. The primary derivative they trade in is **Crude Palm Oil (CPO)**, which accounts for 70 percent of their yield. Their total output of CPO is approximately 500,000 tones.

Sam MacColl Commodities prides itself on being an environment-friendly and efficient company; they only participate in sustainable production. Through strict adherence to international standards, they have also been able to increase the quality of their products. They were recently recognized for the low fatty acid levels of their palm oil.

Three years ago, the company floated on the Alternative Investment Market in the UK, and with these funds, they were able to accelerate their acquisitions and growth. By increasing size and through appropriate diversification, Sam MacColl Commodities were able to become the single supplier of choice for a number of large multinational corporation customers. Coordinating the order and delivery of large amounts of commodities across the supply chain has been very challenging. Many of the individual units have their own individual supply chain systems. In one case, a huge order could not be fulfilled because the commodity had already been sold by the subsidiary unit to another customer. Sam MacColl Commodities were threatened with legal action in this case.

Managing the credit limit of a large pool of customers has been another challenge. Previously, the individual sales reps in each subsidiary unit would approve transactions and seek unit-director-level approval above a certain amount. Scaling this to a large organization is challenging, and recently, there have been a number of large transactions for which Sam MacColl Commodities did not receive payment.

This results in costly legal action and is extremely damaging to immediate cash flow and the firm's operations.

The company management realizes that they need to improve the quality of their customer experience to continue their long-term growth strategy. They understand the need to consolidate onto a single set of processes and systems to avoid the direct and indirect costs associated with the issues that we have highlighted. By addressing these challenges, they will be able to establish deep customer loyalty, which in turn, creates a barrier to the entry of others and reduces their exposure to price sensitivity, which is notorious in the commodities industry.

The company has brought in a new IT Director who has a lot of real-world experience building enterprise systems. His first priority is to ensure that all Customer PO Requests can be fulfilled with the existing inventory before an acknowledgement is sent to the customer. His second priority is to establish a credit limit system. He intends to gradually migrate individual business units to this system.

Sam MacColl Commodities has grown through normal organic growth and acquisition as a company and therefore has a fairly homogenous set of core technologies. They are primarily a Microsoft "shop" utilizing ASP.NET for their web platform. They have numerous .NET developers on staff. Their primary database platform is SQL Server. They run a mixture of consolidated and dedicated environments depending on the business and technical requirements of the application. Some of their line-of-business applications require, or run best on, Oracle. Therefore, they also have a specialist Oracle support center. Because of the rapid growth of the organization and the margins that it provides, software purchases are often done in a best-of-breed manner instead of building or buying technology that cohesively integrates.

Sam MacColl Commodities need to streamline their system development and come up with a generic architecture to support future growth. Let's consider the requirements and additional facts for building such a system in the next sections.

Key requirements

The following are the key requirements for a new software solution:

- Providing an expandable, scalable, robust solution using the concepts of SOA
- Providing transport and transformation capabilities to connect to and consume multiple sources of data
- Implementing a loosely coupled design, which can adapt over time

Additional facts

There are some additional details gathered after the initial use case was shared with the technical team. These include the following:

- The project will need to demonstrate the Purchase Order request/response and credit checking capabilities in an individual subsidiary unit of the company first.

- Over time, the management would like to include additional functionality into the system and have a single primary processor of transactional data. Therefore, the system must be able to scale to support up to 1 million business transactions per day (24-hour period).

- Sam MacColl Commodities is looking for a flexible solution that can talk to a variety of systems.

- Along with immediate functionality for customer service needs, the company would also like to understand how the system can be extended in the future to service additional customer and business needs that are identified.

- Reliability and speed are equally important here. Customers expect a response within 20 seconds for a real-time order, as prices are volatile and they want to lock these in. A faster system will increase customer satisfaction but only if reliability is not compromised.

- Sam MacColl Commodities is facing a challenge. Every time they add a new application, a number of connections between them increases. They realize that, after a while, the integration topology will become too convoluted and not easily maintainable. The following diagram depicts the addition of one application (Customer Interactive Portal) to already existing applications:

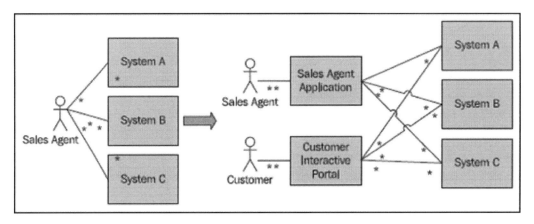

Pattern description

Hub and spoke solutions, which were popular in **enterprise application integration (EAI)** systems, did not fit in SOA. From early 2000, a notion of ESB emerged. The term was initially used by the Gartner Group to define a new type of the emerging integration middleware. As SOA was more and more replacing traditional EAI, ESBs were replacing rigid hub and spoke architectures.

In 2005, competing with several other vendors, Microsoft was trying to position BizTalk as their ESB solution. However, BizTalk lacked certain features that ESB required, and soon after that, several independent groups started working on ESB packages on the Microsoft platform. One of the teams produced **ESB Guidance**—a solution on top of BizTalk. The solution was originally available on CodePlex, a Microsoft open source project hosting site. Later, it was included in the general distribution under the name BizTalk ESB Toolkit. In BizTalk Server 2013, it is a part of the official distribution kit.

The following are the features of ESB that make it different from hub and spoke architectures:

- One of the prominent features is **service orientation**. Enterprise Service Bus is supposed to expose services for consumption. The services are often exposed in the form of web services; however, protocol transformations are supported by all major ESBs.
- The services should support SOA principles and are expected to be **loosely coupled**, **autonomous**, and **reusable**.
- One of the key abilities of ESB is **runtime dynamic routing**, which may take the form of content-based, context-based, or itinerary-based routing.
- **Dynamic message transformation** is not new to ESB; it is an essential part of most messaging middle-tiers. However, in ESB, it takes a new twist—dynamic transformation is encapsulated as a service.
- ESB is a bus of services. To support dynamic routing, translation, and other runtime features, several services may be executed: routing service, message transformation service, logging service, exception service (in case of exceptions), and others.
- ESB can host services that support common tasks for the enterprise. For example, it can be a service that supports a common dictionary for the enterprise. The dictionary can be used to consistently present information on the presentation layer for all enterprise applications. It can be a service specific to the business, for example, in a financial institution, it can be a currency rate convertor.
- To support SOA, ESB has to be expandable. Services should be added or updated seamlessly, ideally, without interruption of production cycles.

If Sam MacColl Commodities continue to use the point-to-point approach, it would dramatically increase the complexity of the application. If any other system needs to connect to the same systems, that logic would need to be duplicated and maintained.

With an ESB implementation, Sam MacColl Commodities will be able to provide an integration architecture for a common communication and messaging infrastructure across the enterprise. Let's revisit our previous example and demonstrate how an ESB can be used.

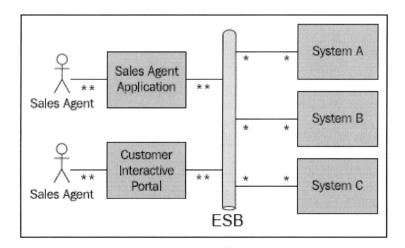

In the preceding diagram, we have two GUI applications communicating with **ESB**; the complexity of the integration that is required to connect to Systems A, B, and C is handled by ESB. The Bus is now responsible for message routing, data transformation, exception handling during message processing, and possibly many more common features. The Bus acts as an intermediary across an enterprise's applications, enabling them to be connected in a loosely coupled fashion.

What Sam MacColl Commodities is looking to do is a close fit for the Enterprise Service Bus architecture. They have what are typically independent business applications built on top of heterogeneous systems. By establishing a common integration solution between them, they can achieve a business objective — establishing customer brand loyalty and demonstrating superior customer service during a period of growth, which in the long term will reduce their price sensitivity and will be a key source of competitive advantage. A key point of what they need is the ability to automate proper due diligence when confirming and fulfilling customer purchase orders so as not to dishearten customers.

Candidate architecture – BizTalk ESB

Microsoft BizTalk Server 2013 comes with the ESB Toolkit Version 2.2.

Solution design aspects

One of the key requirements of this solution is the ability to quickly and reliably process and provide pseudo-real-time responses to purchase orders. The ESB needs to determine where to route the message and what transformations to apply to it. The ESB Toolkit resolvers extend the native BizTalk capabilities and make connectivity more dynamic. We will be dealing with lots of individual orders and a large number of backend systems. We need to assume that many of these factors can change over time; therefore, the chosen solution must provide enough flexibility and expandability.

The services that the ESB Toolkit provides should be used as appropriate for specific customer implementation. The Toolkit contains the following services:

Service	Description	Uses in the solution
Itinerary services	Accept external messages and submit them for processing.	Composes the appropriate business logic depending upon the message received. Provides flexibility in the coupling of components. Itineraries are updateable without recompile.
UDDI service	Provides the capability to query UDDI repositories dynamically from other ESB services including Itinerary services.	Dynamically updates the endpoint information for new and existing systems as they are brought online in the Sam MacColl Commodities environment. This will remove unnecessary configuration relating to other systems in LOB applications.
Exception handling service	Accepts standard fault messages, adds additional metadata, and provides a central portal for investigation and root cause resolution.	Provides a single unified framework and portal for the company to manage exception data.

Service	Description	Uses in the solution
Transformation service	Provides the ability to execute BizTalk maps without using the underlying BizTalk messaging infrastructure (without the overhead of Message Box persistence).	Exposes transformations that BizTalk provides via an endpoint that LOB applications can call independently of other BizTalk services.
Resolver service	Looks up ESB endpoints (using UDDI, Business Rules Engine, and others, including custom resolvers) and provides all details of those endpoints.	Enables flexibility and determination of the route of a message within Sam MacColl Commodities at runtime. This is particularly useful when deploying a new version or onboarding new systems.
BizTalk Operations service	Provides runtime details about BizTalk hosts and deployed artifacts.	Provides uptime stats or dashboards to the business based on the information provided.

The following diagram illustrates how these services work together:

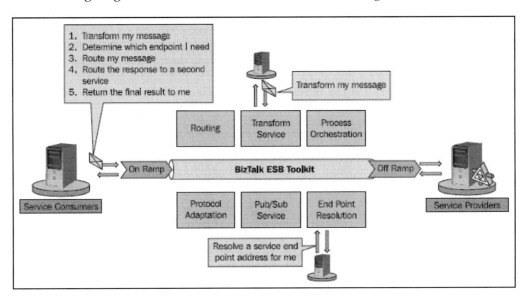

The message is received On-Ramp and is processed by a set of services performing specific tasks, such as transformation or resolving itinerary. At the end of the process, the message is sent Off-Ramp, which is a dynamic BizTalk send port, and then to its final destination to a service provider, as shown in the following diagram:

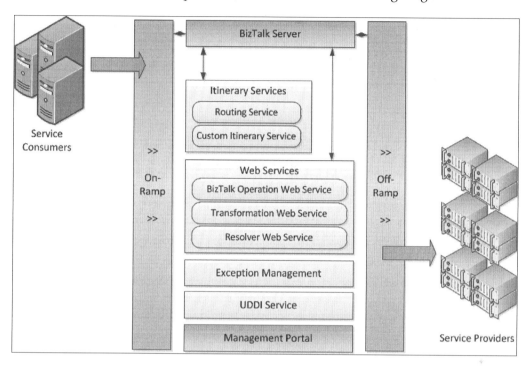

BizTalk Server is built to provide efficient, Publish/Subscribe (pub-sub) messaging capabilities. By building on top of this platform, the ESB Toolkit inherits this. Benchmarking on average hardware has shown that BizTalk Server can scale 1000 to 2000 tps (transactions per second), which results in 86 to 172 million messages in a 24-hour period. Given that Sam MacColl Commodities requires 1 million messages per day, we are confident that BizTalk Server provides a sufficient margin of safety even with the overhead that the ESB Toolkit components will introduce.

We also need the ability to connect to a wide variety of sources in order to produce event streams. BizTalk Server has a well-understood adapter model where developers are free to use out-of-the-box adapters for transport or LOB system connectivity. BizTalk's wide variety of out-of-the-box and available-to-buy adapters mean that the majority of connectivity in the company's system should be possible without writing their own custom code or adapters. The fact that the company can leverage the existing .NET capability if they do need to build adapters is a huge plus for them.

The loose coupling of BizTalk and the ESB Toolkit enables a clean separation of artifacts and minimizes dependencies. The itinerary model also allows new and updated business processes to be deployed rapidly, and for many BizTalk customers, this capability has been a long time coming.

Solution implementation aspects

The ESB Toolkit is built on top of and leverages existing BizTalk functionality. It provides extensibility at all key points. The existing .NET skills that the organization has are applicable as .NET or web service knowledge is applied at all extension points.

Despite the fact that the Toolkit is built on top of BizTalk Server, there is a learning curve. The ESB way of doing things is a paradigm shift for many developers. Traditional BizTalk development uses the Message Broker architecture that is more static in nature. Building an ESB requires a more dynamic approach with itineraries resolved during the process, sometimes based on the content of the message. Developers learning the ESB Toolkit should leverage the Microsoft-provided documentation and samples, as well as ad hoc Internet searches to return relevant answers to problems.

Sam MacColl Commodities already has a small team of developers who have developed BizTalk Server applications, so they can build on and expand the capability of this team by choosing the ESB Toolkit. BizTalk developers are familiar with messaging concepts, so they will find it easier to learn how to build solutions using the ESB services, when compared to someone with no integration experience. Over time, they will be able to effectively determine which ESB services to use and where. As with BizTalk, developers can install the ESB Toolkit and operate it locally on their existing BizTalk development installations before deploying the finished product to a more robust environment. As everything in an ESB Toolkit solution is contained within .NET projects, they can manage their code using the existing source-control repository that BizTalk uses.

Solution operations aspects

This is an area where the BizTalk Server product is well established. There are no concerns over its ability to handle load and gracefully manage the required amounts of data. The story around high availability and support tooling is very strong. The ESB Toolkit's Exception Management portal provides the capability to determine how the engine is running. The portal interface can be extended and customized to display information specific to Sam MacColl Commodities.

Organizational aspects

The company is looking for something that can fulfill the immediate need while serving as a viable long-term solution. BizTalk is an established product; the ESB Toolkit has been released for a while now and has been successfully adopted by a number of customers. We can only expect it to improve as it matures further in the marketplace. It leverages existing developer skill sets. The licensing costs for BizTalk are non-trivial, but are not an adoption blocker for the organization. The extensibility that BizTalk and the ESB Toolkit provides enables creating a well-thought-out Enterprise Service Bus deployment, which can grow to meet future requirements. Building this functionality themselves would require a lot of architectural and development time and would pose a significant challenge for the organization.

Solution evaluation

Despite some implementation concerns, BizTalk seems to be a good technology for our solution.

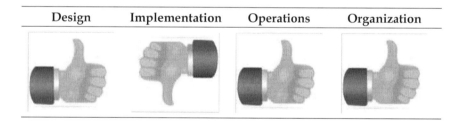

Architecture selection

In the first edition of this book, the authors considered two candidate architectures for the Enterprise Service Bus: BizTalk ESB and WCF/WF with AppFabric. It is obvious now that Microsoft considers BizTalk ESB as its flagship technology for building Enterprise Service Buses on premises. The ESB Toolkit 2.2 is included in the BizTalk Server 2013 installation kit and is officially supported. Over several years, the BizTalk ESB Toolkit has experienced several significant improvements to truly deliver an SOA solution.

The other option of building the ESB by means of Microsoft technologies would be to build it by hand. We would have to use SQL Server as a database for messages in progress, WF (to provide workflows), and WCF (to build all necessary services). We would have to build all services that a typical ESB requires, including itinerary services, exception handling, and transformation services. The BizTalk ESB Toolkit already has them all. In addition to that, the Toolkit includes the ESB Management Portal, which is definitely a nice additional component.

Enterprise Service Bus is a complex architecture. Developing it from scratch would take quite a long time, and the cost of development could skyrocket. Therefore, using the BizTalk ESB Toolkit for the solution is really our only choice.

Building the solution

In this solution, we will be implementing a single message flow. Our system will be loosely coupled and will use WCF-BasicHttp and WCF-WSHttp as the transport adapters of choice.

We will use the WCFTestClient tool to initiate PO Requests, which will then be processed by the ESB. Our ESB will query the inventory server and customer server to determine whether the items requested are in stock and the customer meets the required credit limit. The credit limit is fixed across all customers and will be implemented within BizTalk. Based on the information received, BizTalk will approve/reject the initial case appropriately.

In order to install the solution, we need to install the ESB first. For the purposes of our examples, we will make the installation on a single machine. We would assume that, initially, the machine does not house anything other than the operating system.

BizTalk ESB Toolkit installation and setup

We discussed the BizTalk Server installation in *Chapter 5, The BizTalk Server Primer*. The ESB Toolkit comes as part of the BizTalk installation kit. Perform the following steps to install and set up the BizTalk ESB Toolkit:

1. Select all components, install the ESB Toolkit.

2. To configure the Toolkit, run the ESB Configuration Tool as an administrator. You can use default values for most of the settings.

3. Sometimes **BizTalk Itinerary Designer** is not installed properly, and you cannot see it in Visual Studio. If this happens, from the Visual Studio command prompt, run `devenv.exe /setup`. It forces Visual Studio to merge the resource metadata from all available VS Packages, including the one with the Itinerary Designer.

4. Install the BizTalk ESB Toolkit sample applications as described on the Microsoft site at `http://msdn.microsoft.com/en-us/library/ee236708(v=bts.10).aspx`.

Solution setup

Download the solution from the Packt Publishing website. It is located in the `SMCSupplyChain` folder.

The central part of our solution is ESB Server. The first thing that we will do is define the message schemas that will be used to represent the following types:

*   `PORequest`
*   `POResponse`
*   `InventoryCheckRequest`
*   `InventoryCheckResponse`

These schemas have already been defined for you. They can be found in the `SMCSupplyChain` folder. Open the `SMCSupplyChain.sln` solution file and you will see the `SMCSupplyChain.Schemas` subproject. Within this, you will see schemas representing each of the types in the previous list.

Deploying and using a monolithic solution

We will now walk through and examine a monolithic implementation of this broker scenario. We will deploy this and use the **BizTalk WCF Service Publishing Wizard** to expose a monolithic implementation of this process as a WCF Service that we can consume. Once we have done this, we will demonstrate how the ESB Toolkit can use the same artifacts in an agile manner through Itinerary. From the SMCSupplyChain solution, open the SMCSupplyChain.Orchestrations project, and then open the PurchaseOrderBroker.odx orchestration.

Your screen should now look like the following screenshot:

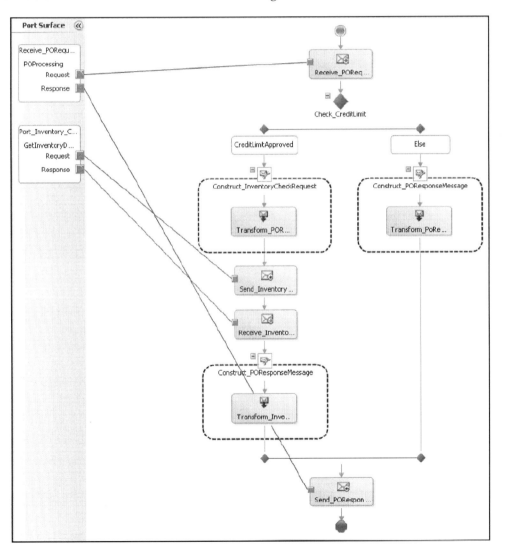

This is an example of a monolithic implementation of this use case. In particular, please note the following and examine these in Visual Studio:

1. The Decision Shape `Check_CreditLimit` has a conditional branch `CreditLimitApproved`, which uses the following static condition:

   `poRequest.TotalDue<=500`

2. Map usage is embedded into Construct/Transform shapes within the Orchestrations. See the `Construct_InventoryCheckRequest`, `Construct_POResponseMessage`, and `Construct_POResponseMessage` shapes.

3. The logical port `Port_Inventory_Check_Request` contains the operation name for the WCF Service. Note that this is the Identifier property of the port; the value in this case is `GetInventoryData`.

4. Now, let's deploy the required WCF Service contained in the `SMCSupplyChain.InventoryCheckService` project and then the BizTalk assemblies.

5. Right-click on the `SMCSupplyChain.InventoryCheckService` project in Visual Studio and select **Publish**. In the **Publish WCF Service** box that appears, click on the ellipsis button, as shown in the following screenshot:

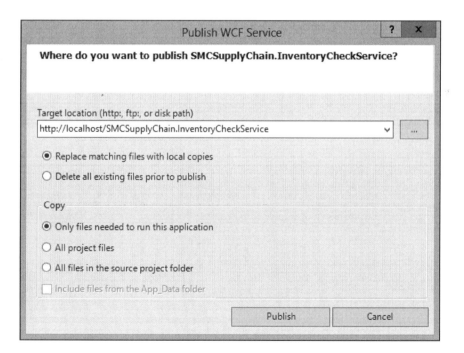

6. Select the local IIS and create a new virtual directory called `SMCSupplyChain.InventoryCheckService`.

7. Follow the remaining steps of the wizard. Check whether the target location is configured as `http://localhost/SMCSupplyChain.InventoryCheckService`, and then click on **Publish**.

We will now publish the BizTalk application and configure it using the following steps:

1. Right-click on the `SMCSupplyChain` solution and click on **Deploy Solution**. Check that no error messages appear and that the deployment is successful.

2. Open the BizTalk Administration Console, and verify that the solution is deployed in the `SMCSupplyChain` application.

3. To create the port required, import the `InventoryCheckService_Customer.BindingInfo.xml` binding file, which is contained within the `SMCSupplyChain.Orchestrations` folder. This will create a WCF-Custom send port called `WcfSendPOrt_InventoryCheckService_WSHttpBinding_IInventoryCheckService_Custom`.

4. We now need to expose our `PurchaseOrderBroker.odx` orchestration as a WCF Service. Go back to your Visual Studio with the `SMCSupplyChain` solution open. Navigate to **Tools | BizTalk WCF Service Publishing Wizard** from the **Tools** drop-down menu.

5. On the first **Welcome to the BizTalk WCF Service Publishing Wizard** screen, click on **Next**.

6. On the next screen, select the following options:
   ○ **Service endpoint**
   ○ **Adapter Name [Transport type]** (set its value as **WCF-WSHttp**)
   ○ **Enable metadata endpoint**
   ○ **Create BizTalk receive locations in the following location:**
   ○ **BizTalk application name** (set its value as **SMCSupplyChain**)

7. On the next screen, select **Publish BizTalk orchestrations as WCF service** and click on **Next**.

8. Now select the `SMCSupplyChain.Orchestrations.dll` file from the build output location for the `SMCSupplyChain.Orchestrations` project. Click on **Next**.

9. Leave the default settings on the next screen (**Orchestrations and Ports**).

10. On the next screen, **WCF Service Properties**, leave the default target namespace `http://tempuri.org`.

11. On the next screen, **WCF Service Location**, leave the default location `http://localhost/SMCSupplyChain.Orchestrations`. Mark **Allow anonymous access to WCF Service** as **true**, and click on **Next**.

12. On the final **WCF Service Summary** screen, click on **Create**. Verify that there were no errors.

13. In the BizTalk Administration Console, open up the **SMCSupplyChain** application and its **Receive Locations** section. You should see a new receive location that has been created.

14. Select the **Orchestrations** section, right-click on `SMCSupplyChain.Orchestrations.Broker` and select **Properties**. Then click on **Bindings** and configure the **Host**. For **Receive Ports**, specify the item generated by the **Publishing Wizard;** for **Send Ports**, specify the WCF-Custom Send Port created by the binding file that was imported. Click on **OK**. Right-click on the `SMCSupplyChain` application and click on **Start**.

> You will need to check that the `SMCSupplyChain.Orchestrations` Virtual Directory that was generated, runs in an application pool whose identity (service account) is a member of the BizTalk Isolated Host Users Group.

15. We will now test this using the WCF Test Client. Open the `WCFTestClient.exe` located under `<Program Files Location>\Microsoft Visual Studio 11.0\Common7\IDE`.

16. Right-click on the root node **My Service Projects** and select **Add Service**. Enter the endpoint address that points to the receive location you exposed as a WCF Service. Click on **OK** to generate the proxy classes that the test client will use.

17. Expand the exposed service contract and double-click on the **POProcessing** operation.

18. Enter the details for the Request as follows:

Field	Value
PurchaseOrderID	2
CustomerID	2
TotalDue	499
Details	Length=1 Note: This will allow you to enter one product detail. Use values below:
ProductID	1
Quantity	1
ItemPrice	1

PO status codes

The following status codes apply to the overall PO:

Code	Meaning
200	Approved
400	Rejected

Item inventory check status codes

The following status codes apply to the overall status of each Detail, that is, each item:

Code	Meaning
200	Approved
400	Not in stock
600	Not checked

600 is implemented for the scenario where the total due exceeds the permitted credit limit. In this case, the inventory status for each item is not checked. When implementing systems, it is best practice to avoid unnecessary expensive service calls by using this technique.

Current behavior of the system

The following details describe the current behavior of the system:

- The maximum value of `TotalDue` is statically defined in the `PurchaseOrderBroker` orchestration as `500`. Any `TotalDue` value greater than or equal to 500 will return a response code of 400, and each Detail, that is, item in that PO, will have a Status of 600.

- If `PurchaseOrderID` is an even number and the value of `TotalDue` is less than or equal to 499, then the PO Status will be 200, and each item will be 200. This logic is implemented in the `SMCSupplyChain. InventoryCheckService` project.

Experiment by submitting the same request but changing the following:

- `PurchaseOrderID`: Change its value to 3. The PO status should be 400 and each individual item Status should be 400, that is, Not in stock.

- `PurchaseOrderID`: Change its value to 2 and change the value of `TotalDue` to 501. The PO status should be 400, and each individual item Status should be 600, that is, Not Checked, due to `TotalDue` exceeding the statically defined credit limit.

 The rudimentary logic for the Inventory Service is implemented in the `SMCSupplyChain. InventoryCheckService` project.

Utilizing the ESB Toolkit

So far we have seen one way to implement this solution and will now look at how the ESB Toolkit can make this solution more agile.

Using existing transformations within an ESB Itinerary

We will now extend this and use some of the existing BizTalk artifacts that were developed to meet this solution and demonstrate how the maps that we previously created can be utilized as an itinerary. To keep things simple, the itinerary will be implemented using file drops to facilitate easier testing. We will begin by implementing one of the transformations step by step, then expand and use another itinerary, which replicates the functionality of the orchestration. This itinerary is transport-independent, so it can be utilized from a different On-Ramp and Off-Ramp.

The purpose of this section is to show you how the ESB Toolkit can be leveraged to use existing components. Let's start by performing the following steps:

1. From the `<BizTalkESB>\SMCSupplyChain\` folder, copy the `filedrops` folder and all subfolders to the root of `C:\`. This structure will be used to receive and send files for the itinerary examples. If access to this location is not permissible on your system, adjust the location in the following instructions appropriately.

2. In the `BizTalk` Administration Console, open up the `SMCSupplyChain` application. Right-click on **References**, and add a reference to the Microsoft. `Practices.ESB` application.

3. Open the **Receive Ports** section. Right-click and create a new one-way Receive port named `SMCOnRamp.OneWay`; this will be the On-Ramp that BizTalk uses.

4. Within the **SMCOnRamp.OneWay Receive Port Properties** window, click on the **Receive Location** tab and select **New**.

5. Enter the name `SMCOnRamp.File` and specify the transport type as **FILE**. Click on **Configure**, set the **Receive Folder** location to be `C:\filedrops\ SMCIn`, and leave the default **File mask** of `*.xml`.

6. Select the appropriate value for **Receive handler** (default is **BizTalkServerApplication**). Select the value of **Receive pipeline** as **ItinerarySelectReceiveXml**, as shown in the following screenshot:

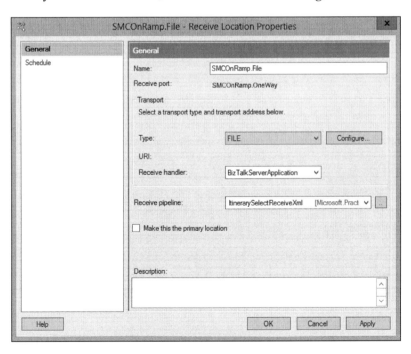

7. Click on the ellipsis button to configure the **ItinerarySelectReceiveXML** pipeline. You should set the value of **ItineraryFactKey** to Resolver. Itinerary and of **ResolverConnectionString** to ITINERARY:\\ name=SMCOneWaySimple. This means that the resolver will look up the value of the **SMCOneWaySimple** itinerary from the Itinerary store (which is a configured SQL Server database).

> Note that there are other resolvers that can use the Business Rules Engine or UDDI v3 to resolve the itinerary. In this case, we decided to specify this explicitly. As the itinerary resides in the database, we can change this at any time.

8. We now need to create a Dynamic Send Port within our application, which can subscribe to the messages that will be published by this Receive Port. Note that the ESB terminology for this is Off-Ramp. Expand **Send Ports** in the SMCSupplyChain application, and create a **Dynamic One-Way** port called SMCOffRampDynamicOneWay. Set the value of **Send Pipeline** to ItinerarySendPassthrough.

9. Click on **Filters** for this port and configure the following filters:

    ○   Microsoft.Practices.ESB.Itinerary.Schemas.ServiceName == SMCOffRampDynamicOneWay

    ○   Microsoft.Practices.ESB.Itinerary.Schemas. IsRequestResponse == false

    ○   Microsoft.Practices.ESB.Itinerary.Schemas.ServiceState == Pending

    ○   Microsoft.Practices.ESB.Itinerary.Schemas.ServiceType == Messaging

> The BTS.ReceivePortName property can be used in the filter expression to match an Off-Ramp with a particular On-Ramp. Typically, I do not include this, as it keeps the Off-Ramp generic and reusable across different itineraries. Note that the GlobalBank ESB sample application also provides generic reusable On-Ramp and Off-Ramp.

10. Now we will examine the itinerary **SMCOneWaySimple**, which we specified we would use in our On-Ramp. Open up the SMCSupplyChain.ItineraryLibrary project that is contained within the solution. Open SMCOneWaySimple.Itinerary to open the **Itinerary Designer** window, which was introduced in ESB Toolkit 2.0. Your screen should look like the following:

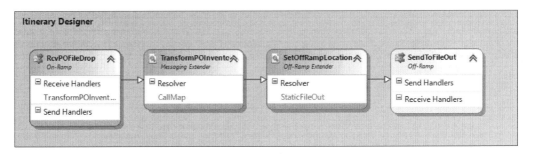

The itinerary broadly consists of the following:

- **On-Ramp**: **RcvPOFileDrop** receives the message.

- **Messaging Extender**: **TransformPOInventoryRequest** executes during the receive pipeline stage (the container object specifies the BizTalk processing stage: either receive pipeline, orchestration, or send pipeline) and invokes the previously defined map to transform the **PORequest** to an **InventoryCheckRequest**.

- **Off-Ramp Extender**: **SetOffRampLocation** uses a static resolver to specify the output location of C:\filedrops\SMCOut\%MessageID%.xml.

- **Off-Ramp**: **SendToFileOut** specifies the Dynamic Send port that we created earlier (our Off-Ramp). The previous resolver shape provides the transport type and location configuration in its static resolver.

11. First, export the itinerary by clicking on the **Itinerary Designer** surface and selecting **Export Model**. Save this in a convenient location as SMCOneWaySimple.xml, and verify that it exports successfully.

12. We will now deploy this by opening a command prompt and changing to the directory C:\Program Files\Microsoft BizTalk ESB Toolkit 2.2\Bin.

13. We will use the tool **ESBImportUtil**, which is provided to deploy itineraries. The **ESBImportUtil** is located in the Bin subfolder of the Microsoft BizTalk ESB Toolkit folder. Run the following command:

```
EsbImportUtil.exe /f:"<Path to folder with Itinerary>\
SmcOneWaySimple.xml" /c:deployed
```

14. Verify that you get the message The Itinerary <Itinerary location xml> was imported successfully to database ….

15. Now check whether the receive locations, send ports, and required hosts have been started.

16. Open the PORequest_output.xml file from the SampleMessages folder; once you have done this, copy it to C:\Filedrops\SMCIn.

17. Navigate to C:\filedrops\SMCOut, and verify that the folder contains a new message whose format is of type **POResponse**.

Congratulations! You've now successfully deployed and used your first itinerary. Note that the deployment of the itinerary was able to occur while BizTalk was still running. This means that your itineraries can change on the fly with zero downtime, which is one of the biggest benefits of ESB Toolkit for BizTalk Server.

Using the itinerary service broker pattern

In this next example, we will show a way to use an itinerary to implement similar broker functionality to the PurchaseOrderBroker orchestration that we used earlier by leveraging the ESB Toolkit. First, let us take a step back and recap on the functionality that we implemented in the PurchaseOrderBroker orchestration to meet our requirements:

1. Receive a PORequest message.

2. Evaluate the TotalDue promoted property.

3. If the value of TotalDue is greater than 500, a map is called to construct a POResponse message with a status code that indicates that the order has not been approved. This response is sent to the appropriate location.

4. If the value of TotalDue is less than or equal to 500, the following steps are taken:

   1. An InventoryCheckRequest is constructed by using a BizTalk map.

   2. A call is made to the Inventory WCF Service GetInventoryData operation.

   3. From the InventoryCheckResponse, which contains details of all the items requested in the original PORequest, a map is called to construct the appropriate POResponse.

   4. Send POResponse to the appropriate location.

The BizTalk Orchestration engine is robust and proven. BizTalk is primarily targeted at and designed for integration scenarios; therefore, each orchestration represents a tight coupling of components; it encapsulates a set of functionalities from transformations to external system calls. Changing the order of invocation of transformations we implemented in the `PurchaseOrderBroker` orchestration would require recompilation and redeployment, which is not acceptable for some systems. Pub-sub messaging is configuration based, so it can be changed without recompilation and redeployment, but implementing the mentioned logic in pub-sub would be challenging and would lose view of the message flow that orchestration provides. What we would really like is the functionality of orchestration, with the flexibility and ease of configuration.

In Version 1.0 of the ESB Toolkit, itineraries were a sequential set of steps modeled in an XML file. When the value of **Export Mode** is set to **Default** for an itinerary, it is created compatible to Version 1.0. If this mode is changed to **Strict**, a number of items change in the XML output of the itinerary. This includes the addition of a number of attributes in the file that correspond to itinerary designer properties, specifically, a `Stage` attribute, which corresponds to the **Container** itinerary designer property; a `PropertyBag`; and a `businessName` attribute, which corresponds to the **Name** designer property. Each Service also contains an `id` and a `nextId` value, as shown in the following screenshot. This reflects internal changes that were made from ESB 2.0; the runtime now processes the itineraries as a linked list.

```
id="d90a2f8622b24aab8e9a3167cd441963"  nextId="49953ce104ec40d491dc926ad301017e"  businessName="TransformPOInventoryRequest"

id="49953ce104ec40d491dc926ad301017e"  nextId="0763ddcc59b24b209f308052028fb9bd"  businessName="ItineraryService6" />
```

The Itinerary Broker Service allows you to take advantage of this and implement rudimentary routing scenarios without an orchestration. It is represented as two shapes in the toolbox: the Itinerary Broker Service and the Itinerary Broker Outport. The **Itinerary Broker Service** shape can be used with the **Context Resolver**, which enables us to access the BizTalk internal and schema-promoted properties of the message. Recall that in our scenario `TotalDue` is a promoted property. We've already demonstrated transformation from within an itinerary, coupled with the access to the message context and the ability to route on it; this looks promising.

In order to call the WCF Service, we will require a two-way Off-Ramp, which we will implement as a BizTalk Dynamic Solicit-Response Port:

1. In the BizTalk Administration Console open the `SMCSupplyChain` application. Right-click on **Send Ports**, select **New**, and then **Dynamic Solicit-Response Send Port**.

2. In the **Send Port Properties** window, set values for properties, as follows:

   ○ **Name**: SMCOffRampDynamicTwoWay

   ○ **Send Pipeline**: ItinerarySendPassthrough

   ○ **Receive Pipeline**: ItineraryForwarderSendReceive

3. Click on **Filters** for this port and configure the following filters; these deliberately use the same context properties as the Off-Ramp we created earlier:

   ○ Microsoft.Practices.ESB.Itinerary.Schemas.ServiceName == SMCOffRampDynamicTwoWay

   ○ Microsoft.Practices.ESB.Itinerary.Schemas. IsRequestResponse == true

   ○ Microsoft.Practices.ESB.Itinerary.Schemas.ServiceState == Pending

   ○ Microsoft.Practices.ESB.Itinerary.Schemas.ServiceType == Messaging

4. Now we will examine the itinerary **SMCOneWayBroker**, which we specified we would use in our On-Ramp. Open the SMCSupplyChain. ItineraryLibrary project that is contained within the solution. Open SMCOneWayBroker.Itinerary; your screen should look like the following screenshot:

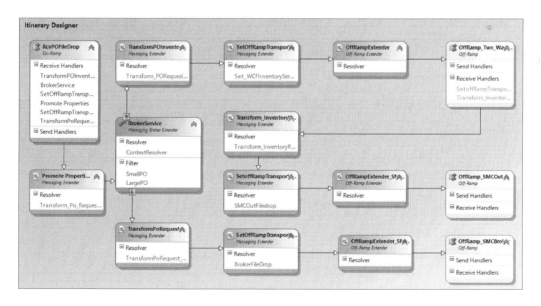

5. The first part of the itinerary broadly consists of the following points, the function of which is provided alongside each point:

   ○ **On-Ramp**: **RcvPOFileDrop** receives the message.

   ○ **Messaging Extender**: **PromoteProperties** executes a map that maps itself, for example, **PORequest** to **PORequest**. This was implemented as a workaround to make the promoted property `TotalDue` accessible to the **Context Resolver** used by the **BrokerService**.

   ○ **Messaging Broker Extender**: The **Broker Service** evaluates the value of `TotalDue`, a promoted property within **PORequest**. This is implemented using two filters, **SmallPO** and **LargePO**. Filters are added using the **Itinerary Broker Outport** toolbox shape. **SmallPO** matches less than or equal to 500; **LargePO** matches `TotalDue` greater than 500. The first filter that evaluates true will be executed in the same way as a Switch statement in C#.

6. If the **LargePO** filter evaluates true, the following will occur in order to return a rejected **POResponse**:

   ○ **Messaging Extender**: **TransformPORequest_POResponse** executes a map that generates the appropriate **POResponse** indicating that it has been rejected

   ○ **Messaging Extender**: **SetOffRampTransport_Broker** uses a static resolver to specify the output location of `C:\filedrops\SMCBroker\%MessageID%.xml`

   ○ **Off-Ramp Extender**: **OffRampExtender_SMCBroker** is a required component to invoke **Off_Ramp**

   ○ **Off-Ramp**: **OffRamp_SMCBroker** specifies the one-way Dynamic Send port that we created earlier (our Off-Ramp)

7. If the **SmallPO** filter evaluates true, the following will occur in order to check the inventory and return an appropriate **POResponse**:

   ○ **Messaging Extender**: **TransformPOInventoryRequest** executes a map that generates an **InventoryRequest** based on the details of the inbound **PORequest**

   ○ **Messaging Extender**: **SetOffRampTransport** uses a static resolver to configure the WCF properties

- ○ **Off-Ramp Extender**: **OffRampExtender** is a required component in strict mode to invoke **Off_Ramp**

- ○ **Off-Ramp**: **OffRamp_Two_Way_WCF_Inventory** specifies the two-way Dynamic Send port we created earlier and uses this to call the Inventory WCF Service

- ○ **Messaging Extender**: **Transform_InventoryResponse_POResponse** executes a map to generate the appropriate **POResponse**

- ○ **Messaging Extender**: **SetOffRampTransport_SMCOut** uses a static resolver to specify the output location of `C:\filedrops\SMCOut\%MessageID%.xml`

- ○ **Off-Ramp Extender**: **OffRampExtender_SMCOut** is a required component in strict mode to invoke **Off_Ramp**

- ○ **Off-Ramp**: **OffRamp_SMCOut** reuses the one-way Dynamic Send port that was used for the **LargePO** filter to send the **POResponse** to the folder specified in the resolver configuration previously

As described, this itinerary uses the Itinerary Broker Service to implement the functionality of the `PurchaseOrderBroker` orchestration. Before running this sample, we will first examine some of the configuration properties and common "gotchas" required to make this type of scenario work, which are as follows:

- To configure the **Filter** for the **Itinerary Broker Service**, one **Itinerary Broker Outport** per filter is required. To access the context properties you should configure the **Expression** value to be: `//Property[@name='TotalDue']<=500`.

- When changing the value of **Export Mode** from **Default** to **Strict**, ensure that you have an **Off-Ramp Extender** before any **Off-Ramp**. **Strict** mode requires this.

- **Static Resolver** is configured to call the WCF Inventory Service as follows:

  - ○ **Transport Name**: `WCF-WSHTTP`

  - ○ **Target Namespace**: `http://tempuri.org/IInventoryCheckService/`

  - ○ **Action**: `GetInventoryData` (this specifies the operation from the **Service Contract** we wish to execute)

  - ○ **Transport Location**: `<Path to the .SVC file>` (path not included for brevity purposes)

- The **Is Request Response** property of the **SMCOneWayBroker** itinerary is set to `true`. Even though we are using a one-way receive location, by setting this, the runtime promotes the `TransmitWorkID` property to the **Message Context**. This is used by the **Itinerary Cache** component, which is contained within the `ItinerarySendPassthrough` pipeline as specified on our `SMCDynamicTwoWay` Off-Ramp. This enables the appropriate itinerary instance to be matched to the response.

- The `ItineraryForwarderSendReceive` is used in our `SMCDynamicTwoWay` Off-Ramp. When a message is received through a two-way receive port, an instance subscription is created. This consists of the `EpmRRCorrelationToken` promoted property and a `RouteDirectToTP` promoted property. The Forwarder component contained within this pipeline sets the `RouteDirectToTP` property to `false` in the message content, thus ensuring that the itinerary can process the message; this is required in our scenario because we use a two-way Off-Ramp. Once the itinerary is completed, it will set the property to `true`; if we had used a two-way On-Ramp, the response would, therefore, have been returned.

Now, we will test our itinerary and ESB tracing functionality to examine what is happening under the covers:

1. Open the `SMCSupplyChain.ItineraryLibary` project that is contained within the solution. Open `SMCOneWayBroker.Itinerary`.

2. Export the itinerary by clicking on the **Itinerary Designer** surface and selecting **Export Model**. Save this in a convenient location as `SMCOneWayBroker.xml` and verify that it exports successfully.

3. We will now deploy this by opening a command prompt and changing to the directory `C:\Program Files (x86)\Microsoft BizTalk ESB Toolkit 2.2\Bin`.

4. We will use the tool **ESBImportUtil** that is provided to deploy itineraries. Run the following command:

   ```
   EsbImportUtil.exe /f:"<Path to folder with Itinerary>\
   SmcOneWayBroker.xml" /c:deployed
   ```

5. Verify that you get the message `The Itinerary <Itinerary location xml> was imported successfully to database ....`

6. Now check whether the receive locations, send ports, and required hosts have been started.

7. Now, we will enable tracing for the ESB Toolkit. Open your `BTSNTSvc.exe.config` file that is located by default under `C:\Program Files (x86)\Microsoft BizTalk Server 2013\`.

8. Add the following section to your `<Configuration>` block to configure a listener for the ESB Toolkit Version 2.2, which will write to the event log:

```
<system.diagnostics>
<sources>
   <source name ="BizTalk ESB Toolkit 2.2" />
</sources>
<switches>
   <add name="BizTalkESBToolkit20" value="4"/>
</switches>
<trace autoflush="true" indentsize="4">
   <listeners>
   <add name="myListener"
      type="System.Diagnostics.EventLogTraceListener"
      initializeData="BizTalk ESB Toolkit 2.2" />
   </listeners>
</trace>
</system.diagnostics>
```

9. From the BizTalk Administration Console, open the **SMCSupplyChain** application, expand **Receive Locations**, right-click on `SMCOnRamp.File`, and select **Properties**.

10. Click on the configuration ellipsis button for the **ItinerarySelectReceiveXML** pipeline. Set the **ResolverConnectionString** value to `ITINERARY:\\` `name=SMCOneWayBroker`.

11. We will now demonstrate how the Itinerary Broker Service filter functionality works. First, copy the `PORequest_small.xml` file, which contains a `TotalDue` value less than 500, from the `SampleMessages` directory, and then copy it to `C:\Filedrops\SMCIn`.

12. Within the `C:\Filedrops\SMCOut` directory should be a new PORequest with a Status code of 200 for approved.

13. Copy the `PORequest_large.xml` file, where `TotalDue` is greater than 500, from the `SampleMessages` directory to `C:\filedrops\SMCIn`.

14. Within the `C:\Filedrops\SMCOut` directory should be a new PORequest with a Status code of 400 for rejection.

15. Open the **Event Viewer Application Log** and you will see events with the source BizTalk ESB Toolkit Version 2.2. Each particular event is referenced by a service ID and it corresponds with the `SMCOffRampDynamicOneWay` Off-Ramp that is defined in our itinerary.

Using the combination of ESB tracing and the exported XML file enables you to determine which route your itinerary took and where it stopped if a failure occurred.

Lessons learned

We walked through how to implement a supply chain scenario using either an inflexible monolithic approach or an ESB-based approach by leveraging the ESB Toolkit 2.2 for the BizTalk Server 2013. In particular, we demonstrated the Itinerary Broker Service functionality, which enables routing and can remove the need for orchestrations in some simplistic scenarios. We demonstrated the reuse of previously generated artifacts within different ESB itineraries. We deployed the itineraries easily without recompilation or redeployment of the solution code.

We have scratched the surface here on the ESB Toolkit functionality. It provides many additional capabilities including the abilities to use orchestrations within itineraries, resolve itineraries based on **Business Rules Engine** (**BRE**) policies, a complex exception-handling framework and management portal.

XML web services that required using WSDL and SOAP could be quite complex, and in the mid-2000s, RESTful services became very popular as a simpler alternative. We shall discuss the REST architecture in the next half of this chapter.

RESTful services

Representational State Transfer (**REST**) was originally introduced in the dissertation of Roy Thomas Fielding in the year 2000. The most important principles of REST are as follows:

- **REST builds on client-server architecture**: REST clients send requests to services that provide responses. In other words, services always serve clients, and not the other way around.

- **REST uses HTTP methods explicitly**: In a sense, REST mimics CRUD operations: POST for creating data, GET for reading data, PUT for updating data, and DELETE for deleting data. The usage of other HTTP methods, such as HEAD or TRACE, is not that well-defined in REST. Generally, they should be used as defined in HTTP.

- **REST is a stateless architectural style**: Statelessness means that no client context is stored on the server between requests. All context, parameters, and data needed for the server to generate the response are included in the request. This significantly improves scalability and simplifies the architecture.

- **REST has a uniform interface**: Each resource is referenced via a global identifier (for example, URI). This is probably the main difference between RESTful and web services. REST suggests Resource-Oriented Architecture, while SOAP web services focus on operations.

It is important to understand that REST is a set of principles (or best practices) and not a standard. A service that uses REST is called a **RESTful service**.

Use case – shopping cart

Happy Biking Inc. is a retail organization that has several dozen stores all over North America. However, their business is still local in nature: each store works with the local market only. They have a set of warehouses that are used by a few stores in the same area. The company has decided to expand their business and start delivering bikes to individual customers in the region using small trucks. They want to start selling from their web page, which is currently serving only informational purposes.

At the moment, they think of simply taking orders on the Web and performing further phone calls to the customers to collect payments. In other words, the initial web page has to support just the catalog and the shopping cart.

Happy Biking does not have software developers on staff. Usually, the company prefers to buy existing products, as they did for their accounting software, the CRM, and inventory management tools. But when it comes to the web presence, the company decides to do some custom work. The shopping cart is no exception; its look and feel has to be customized.

Happy Biking decided to hire a software development company focusing on delivering solutions in e-business. The developers are very experienced with Microsoft technologies and the .NET platform in particular. The customer has no doubt that the development will be done on time and with high quality. Their only concern is that they have to maintain the solution and expand it when there is a business need.

Starting to sell from their website is the primary goal for the company today. Let's look at the key requirements for this challenge.

Key requirements

Since Happy Biking Inc. does not have developers and their IT department is very small, the solution should be easily maintainable. It has to solve the purposes of an online store, that is, have the following set of features:

- An ability to present the list and details of the products to customers on the website
- An ability to select products to buy
- A shopping cart that would enable adding, removing, and changing some parameters of customer orders
- A simple database maintenance solution

This solution would start as a pilot with a limited number of capabilities. In the future, it will connect to a payment system and possibly to an accounting system. However, the company has no plans of making significant investments in IT in the foreseeable future.

Additional facts

The management of Happy Biking suggests that if their experience with the online shopping cart is successful, they would like to expand the system by adding a few new features:

- Connecting the shopping cart to a payment system
- Integrating it with the accounting system
- Making data management easy for a non-technical employee

Pattern description

REST deals with resources and applies actions to them. Web pages, images, shopping cards—all of them are resources. Resources can be reached by their **unified resource identifiers (URIs)**. For example, `http://www.thesitename.com/shoppingcart/3421` can be the URI of a shopping cart.

Reaching resources by their URIs is done using the GET method of HTTP. On web pages, this would be presented as a link. The GET call should be used for queries only and never change the server state.

Note that the response for the GET method is not specified in REST. The client has to know what the server will send as a response. Responses can be in XML, in JSON, or in any other format. The server also sends status codes defined in the HTTP standards.

Deleting a resource also refers to it using its URI. For example, deleting item 3421 from the shopping cart can be addressed with the DELETE method as follows:

```
DELETE shoppingcart/3421
```

The server can reply with the status codes as follows:

```
200 OK
202 Accepted
204 No content
```

Code 202 means that the resource is marked for deletion, and codes 200 and 204 mean that the resource is actually deleted.

POST and PUT methods are in fact a little tricky. They don't map directly to CRUD operations, which is understandable because REST and CRUD serve different purposes. REST is designed for sending actions over the Web, and CRUD is designed for direct data operations.

Creating a new resource on the server is done using the POST method of HTTP. For example, adding a new item to the shopping cart can be presented as follows:

```
POST /item
<item>
    <name>bicycle</name>
    <units>3</units>
    <price>$1000</price>
</item>
```

The server replies with a standard HTTP response and a status code 201, which means **created**.

Updating a resource is also done using the PUT HTTP method. For example, changing the number of units to 3 in the shopping cart can be done, for example, with the following line of code:

```
PUT shoppingcart/3421/units=3
```

Candidate architecture – RESTful WCF Services

WCF had the ability to expose and consume RESTful services since it was first released as a part of .NET 3.0. Building RESTful services in .NET 3.0 was not easy, but .NET 3.5 simplified the process by adding a few new classes in the framework. Today, in .NET 4.5, building RESTful services is as easy as building traditional SOAP web services. And in fact, this is the native implementation of the REST style, and we shall not consider another candidate.

For this solution, our database will be managed by SQL Server. For working with the data, SQL Server Management Studio will be used.

Solution design aspects

Building a shopping cart requires developing a few operations that perfectly correspond with HTTP methods:

- Adding a new item to the shopping cart requires the POST method
- Viewing items in the shopping cart requires the GET method
- Deleting items from the shopping cart requires the DELETE method
- Updating an item should be done with the PUT method

Designing the services will be a straightforward task.

Solution implementation aspects

The software company that Happy Biking hired has a staff of .NET developers and has experience developing complex solutions on the .NET platform. .NET WCF provides a general approach to WCF services, and developing RESTful services would not be a challenge for that company.

Solution operations aspects

The suggested design separates the functionality at the level of service operations. This enables IT to identify problems easily. SQL Server Management Studio is a perfect tool for maintaining the database. There is some learning curve for the IT department, but the operations are straightforward and database maintenance should not present a risk.

Organizational aspects

The organization takes a slight risk by adding a developed solution to their business instead of buying an off-the-shelf package. Hiring the team of professional developers mitigates the risk and guarantees that the solution will be maintainable. The design separates different methods that make the entire solution easy to upgrade.

However, since the organization does not have developers in their IT team, they may need to outsource future development as well.

Solution evaluation

We have some concerns with regard to the organizational aspects of the solution. Other than that, it's all thumbs up, as shown in the following table:

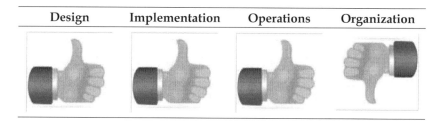

Design	Implementation	Operations	Organization

Building the solution

We will build the solution with a simple user interface, focusing mostly on the REST service. We shall consider a more sophisticated interface later in this book.

Solution components

The solution will contain a RESTful service that accesses an SQL Server database. In order to run it, one needs to have IIS and SQL Server 2012 installed. We will build the RESTful service that will be running on IIS. We will also build a simple test program.

The following diagram depicts the main components of our solution:

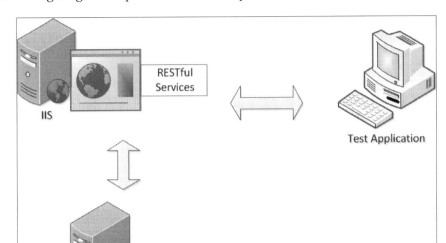

For this example, we assume that IIS and SQL Server 2012 are installed on the same computer.

Solution setup

After the installation is done, let us now proceed to the setup:

1. Copy the example files for this chapter in a separate folder.

2. Open SQL Server Management Studio and run the following scripts from the setup folder in order to create the `HappyBikes` database and the `Items` table:

   ```
   create_database.sql
   create_items.sql
   ```

3. Add test items by running the following script:

   ```
   add_test_items.sql
   ```

4. Run Visual Studio 2013.

5. Open the `RESTService` solution and go to the `RESTService` folder in the folder samples. You will see two projects already developed for you: the `RESTService` project and the `TestUI` project as shown in the following screenshot:

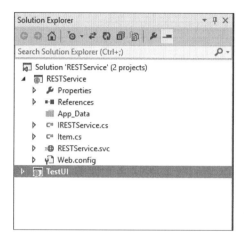

6. Right-click on the `RESTService` project. Select **Publish...** and publish it on the local IIS. Use `localhost` for the Server.

7. Right-click on the `TestUI` project. Select **Publish...** and publish it on the local IIS. Use `localhost` for the Server.

WCF RESTful service description

Follow the steps in this subsection in order to explore the WCF RESTful service:

1. For our example, we are using the `Item` class to store and change information about items in the store catalog. Double-click on the `Item.cs` file of the `RESTService` project to see the class as shown in the following code snippet:

```
namespace RESTService
{
  [DataContract (Name = "Item")]
  public class Item
  {
    [DataMember(Name = "itemID")]
    public string itemID {get; set; }
    [DataMember(Name = "stateMSG")]
    public string stateMSG { get; set; }
    [DataMember(Name = "name")]
    public string name {get; set; }
```

```
    [DataMember(Name = "description")]
    public string description { get; set; }
    [DataMember(Name = "id")]
    public int id {get; set; }
    [DataMember(Name = "quantity")]
    public int quantity { get; set; }
    [DataMember(Name = "price")]
    public double price { get; set; }
  }
}
```

2. Double-click on the `IRESTService.cs` file in the `RESTService` project. Let's analyze the service contract. The service contract is specified by the public interface `IRESTService`. Each operation contract describes one REST operation.

3. The first operation returns the list of items. It utilizes the GET method of HTTP, as shown in the following code snippet:

```
[OperationContract]
    [WebGet(
        ResponseFormat = WebMessageFormat.Xml,
        BodyStyle = WebMessageBodyStyle.Bare,
        UriTemplate = "/list")]
    List<Item> getItemsList();
```

The `WebGet` attribute defines the operation as the GET operation. It does not require the `Method` parameter always defaulting to the GET method.

The response format is defined as XML in our example. Another possible choice would be JSON.

When invoked, the method returns a list of items.

4. Let's run the Test UI. Right-click on the `TestUI` project in the **Solution Explorer** and select **Set as StartUp Project**.

5. Run the application by pressing on the green arrow on the toolbar in Visual Studio. If the Standard toolbar is selected, this green arrow is shown along with the name of the default browser (Internet Explorer in our case), as shown in the following screenshot:

6. Click on the **List** button on the page. The result screen will show the items currently in the database as shown in the following screenshot:

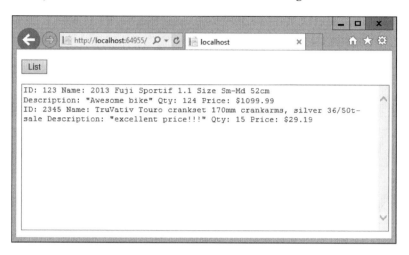

7. Let's find out what raw XML is returned by the method. In order to do that, right-click on the `RESTService.svc` file of the `RESTService` project. Click on **Browse with...** and select a browser. Click on the **Browse** button, and you will get a screen similar to the following screenshot:

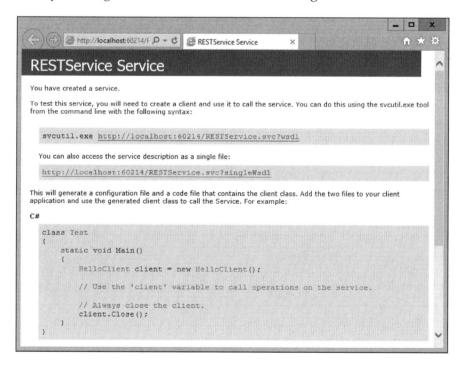

8. In the address bar of the browser, add /listItems to the end of the service address in order to invoke the GET method as described in the operation contract. Hit the *Enter* key. The result will be the raw XML returned by the method, as shown in the following screenshot:

```xml
<?xml version="1.0"?>
<ArrayOfItem xmlns:i="http://www.w3.org/2001/XMLSchema-instance"
xmlns="http://schemas.datacontract.org/2004/07/RESTService">
  <Item>
      <description>Awesome bike</description>
      <id>1</id>
      <itemID>123</itemID>
      <name>2013 Fuji Sportif 1.1 Size Sm-Md 52cm</name>
      <price>1099.99</price>
      <quantity>124</quantity>
      <stateMSG i:nil="true"/>
  </Item>
  <Item>
      <description>excellent price!!!</description>
      <id>3</id>
      <itemID>2345</itemID>
      <name>TruVativ Touro crankset 170mm crankarms, silver 36/50t-sale</name>
      <price>29.19</price>
      <quantity>15</quantity>
      <stateMSG i:nil="true"/>
  </Item>
</ArrayOfItem>
```

9. Let's explore other operations in the IRESTService.cs file of the RESTService project.

10. To add an item, we'll be using the POST method of HTTP. The operation contract is defined in the IRESTService.cs, as shown in the following code snippet:

```
[OperationContract]
[WebInvoke(
  RequestFormat = WebMessageFormat.Xml,
  ResponseFormat = WebMessageFormat.Xml,
  BodyStyle = WebMessageBodyStyle.Bare,
  UriTemplate = "/addItem")]
Item AddItem();
```

11. The Method parameter is not specified and refers to POST by default.

12. The [WebInvoke] attribute uses the Method parameter that defaults to POST. For all other methods, that is, PUT and DELETE, the values have to be specified. Notice that the request format is specified as XML, which means that the details of the added item have to be passed as an XML in the request message body. Another option to specify the request format is JSON.

13. The XML passed in the message body may look like the following code snippet:

```
<Item>
    <id>0</id>
    <description>Awesome bike<description>
    <itemID>123</itemID>
    <name>2013 Fuji Sportif 1.1 Size Sm-Md 52 cm</name>
    <price>1099.99</price>
    <quantity>124</quantity>
<Item>
```

14. To delete an item, we'll be using the DELETE method of HTTP. The [OperationContract] attribute is defined in IRESTService.cs, as shown in the following code snippet:

```
[OperationContract]
[WebInvoke(Method = "DELETE",
   ResponseFormat = WebMessageFormat.Xml,
   BodyStyle = WebMessageBodyStyle.Bare,
   UriTemplate = "delete/{id}")]
string DeleteItem(string id);
```

15. Notice that the Method parameter in the [WebInvoke] attribute is DELETE. The value of UriTemplate is delete/{id}. It means that the URL will look like http://service_uri/delete/{id}, for example, http://localhost:60214/RESTService.svc/delete/1.

16. To update an item, we'll be using the PUT method of HTTP. The [OperationContract] attribute is defined in the IRESTService.cs file, as shown in the following code snippet:

```
[OperationContract]
[WebInvoke(Method = "PUT",
   RequestFormat = WebMessageFormat.Xml,
   ResponseFormat = WebMessageFormat.Xml,
   BodyStyle = WebMessageBodyStyle.Bare,
   UriTemplate = "/updateItem")]
Item AddItem();
```

17. And finally, let's look at the Web.config file. In order to make the WCF Service work as a RESTful service, one needs to specify webHttpBinding for the service endpoint as well as webHttp for the endpoint behavior, as shown in the following code snippet:

```
<system.serviceModel>
  <services>
```

```xml
      <service behaviorConfiguration="ServiceBehaviour"
name="RESTService.RESTService">
      <endpoint address="" behaviorConfiguration="web"
binding="webHttpBinding"
        contract="RESTService.IRESTService" />
    </service>
    </services>

    <behaviors>
     <serviceBehaviors>
      <behavior name="ServiceBehaviour">
      <!-- To avoid disclosing metadata information, set the value
below to false and remove the metadata endpoint above before
deployment -->
        <serviceMetadata httpGetEnabled="true"/>
        <!-- To receive exception details in faults for debugging
purposes, set the value below to true. Set to false before
deployment to avoid disclosing exception information -->
        <serviceDebug includeExceptionDetailInFaults="false"/>
      </behavior>
     </serviceBehaviors>
     <endpointBehaviors>
      <behavior name="web">
       <webHttp/>
      </behavior>
     </endpointBehaviors>
    </behaviors>
    <serviceHostingEnvironment multipleSiteBindingsEnabled="true" />
    </system.serviceModel>
```

Lessons learned

In this example, we learned how to build RESTful services using Visual Studio 2013. RESTful services are a lightweight alternative to web services and may be chosen if services do not require sophisticated server logic. RESTful services are based on the HTTP protocol, which makes them ideal for using on the Web.

A comparison of RESTful services and SOAP web services is presented in the following table:

	RESTful services	**SOAP web services**
Architectural pattern	Resource-oriented architecture.	Service-oriented architecture.
Methods	Typically addresses create/delete/update methods applied to resources.	Any method can be addressed by service operations.
Interface	Uses generic HTTP methods: GET, DELETE, PUT, and POST.	The interface has to be defined every time.
Standards	Uses standards at the higher level: HTTP and URI. REST itself is not a standard. No mandatory standard for GET responses; however, the usage of XML or JSON is recommended.	Uses SOAP, WSDL, and UDDI. Using XML is standard de facto. Also WS-* standards can be applied.
Performance	Less overheads.	SOAP requires more data to be sent.
Communication	This is stateless.	Can be stateless or stateful.
Security	Uses transport-level security (SSL/TLS).	Can use both transport-level and message-level security (WS-*).

Future of RESTful services

WCF is a unified programming model for building communication in systems. It supports many protocols and communication patterns. It is also the framework of choice for building service-oriented applications. It allows building secure, reliable, and transaction-oriented solutions. One can use WCF to build SOAP Web services as well as RESTful services.

Another framework, **ASP.NET Web API**, makes it easy to build HTTP services and has become an ideal platform for building RESTful services. The following table provides a comparison between the two frameworks:

WCF	ASP.NET Web API
Services built on the WCF platform can support multiple protocols, such as HTTP, TCP, or UDP.	Supports HTTP only.
Services built on the WCF platform can support multiple encodings, such as Text, MTOM, or Binary.	ASP.NET Web API supports a variety of media types with XML and JSON being the most popular.
Supports WS-* standards and higher-level protocols.	Supports only basic protocol and formats.
Supports request-reply, one-way, and duplex message exchange patterns.	HTTP is request-response in nature. Additional patterns can be supported using SignalR.
Ships with .NET.	Also ships with .NET but is open source.

Microsoft suggests that "support for REST in ASP.NET Web API is more complete and all future REST feature improvements will be made in ASP.NET Web API."

We shall present an example of an ASP.NET Web API application in *Chapter 12, Presentation Layer Patterns*.

Summary

In this chapter, we introduced web services and their evolution to WCF services. We talked about the main principles of Service-oriented Architecture and its most popular implementation—Enterprise Service Bus. We touched on RESTful services and provided examples of those.

In the next chapter, we will move to Enterprise Information Integration and discuss Data Exchange patterns.

10
Data Exchange Patterns

We started our discussion of integration patterns in the preceding two chapters. We considered several architectural patterns to support Enterprise Application Integration. In this chapter, we'll discuss architectural patterns for **Enterprise Information Integration (EII)**.

The purpose of EII is to make data originated in one system available in other systems. The reasons for it may be as follows:

- To process original data with a different set of tools to achieve a new result; for example, taking data from HR and accounting systems to print paychecks.

- To create a copy of the original data in order to offload the system while performing noncritical operations. A typical example would be creating daily reports for a system with a heavy load, such as a banking system.

- To combine data originated in several systems to query or to analyze aggregated data. The data sources can be heterogeneous and distributed over several locations.

- To retrieve data from different sources in order to present a combined view.

- To migrate data from a legacy system in a newly developed or acquired system. This type of data migration is often performed once, and the original data is retired.

- To support backup and disaster recovery requirements.

Heterogeneous data sources present an additional challenge of data transformation into one agreed-upon data format for presentation or further processing. One of the tasks of an architect is to suggest a data format that can become a canonical data model.

A canonical data model in an integration solution is the data model that describes the standard view of the data in the solution. The canonical data model can exist just in the solution, or it can reflect the entire enterprise view of the data. The latter enables consistent use of data across the enterprise. For the canonical data model pattern in integration design, please refer to the book *Enterprise Integration Patterns: Designing, Building, and Deploying Messaging Solutions*, *Gregor Hohpe* and *Bobby Wolf, Addison Wesley.*

Typically canonical data models are represented by canonical schemas in the middle-tier of the solutions. In order to promote loose coupling of the solution components, data transformations are developed between schemas of individual components and canonical schemas.

However, structural inconsistencies between the data are not the only (and probably not the major) challenge of heterogeneous systems. A more significant challenge is **semantic inconsistencies**.

Imagine the integration of customer data belonging to different financial systems of a large bank. Over many years of business, the systems have been grown inconsistently; the data has been entered and reentered many times. Loan origination systems, a core banking system, a customer relationship management system, all may have data related to the same customers. And what's more important, the data is not necessarily exactly the same. A customer might call himself Bob or Robert, and his name would be recorded in different systems in different ways. The customer may have changed his address several times but forgotten to update all systems (or he would not even care, assuming that keeping data in a consistent way would be the bank's business). A teller or a financial advisor could make a typo, misspell words, or make another mistake.

In any case, when it comes to integrating data and presenting it in a consistent view, semantic transformations have to be performed. We'll talk about the challenges of sematic transformation later in this chapter.

And last, but not least, data validation and data cleansing are part of EII. Addresses and postal codes can be validated against the postal services database; social security numbers or bank account numbers should conform to a specific pattern; and some data is mandatory and some dependent on other data. There are many techniques of data validation and data cleansing that could be performed against the entire database or on the fly, every time the data is on the move.

In this chapter, we shall consider different patterns of data exchange, whether it involves data replication, migration, or integration. We'll go over some contradicting approaches in data integration and discuss why and when each of them should be used.

File transfer

In an ideal world, organizations have enough time, resources, and desire to perform proper planning. They consider the business growth and constraints, and can predict what software applications and systems they will buy in the next five years.

In the real world, organizations may grow by doing mergers and acquisitions, change software vendors, and do no proper planning until it's too late. And this is how it has always been.

Originally, business applications did not allow any integration. Accounting packages, HR software, and CRM applications worked independently. But after a while, the need to be able to use data in another application started looking more and more important.

As an example, let's consider a program that is used to send faxes. The program would have an ability to work with different fax modems, potentially perform fax broadcasting, and would certainly need some sort of address book. It may need to process different types of documents and even be able to embed recipients' names and titles into them. Each of those tasks is a major challenge, and the company cannot focus on all of them. If they become, for example, experts in fax processing, they will need to focus on it to stay ahead of the competition. They may want, for example, to deal with more fax modems. In the mid-1990s, when faxing was considered a major way of communication, there were thousands of different fax modems in the world, and the data transmission standards were far from complete. Just to cover the majority of the fax modems, the companies during those days would have needed to spend more effort on the faxing components of the software and less on everything else.

At the same time, other companies may find their niche in building address books, which started simply as digital copies of their paper ancestors. Later, more information and features were added to the address book application, turning them into contact management programs. Eventually, contact managers gave birth to very powerful customer relationship management systems.

But long before it happened, companies realized the need for focusing on specific features building their competitive advantage and integrating with other applications. The very first method of integrating data was exporting it from one application as a file and importing it into another application.

In order to understand each other's data, applications have to use a common data format. Some of the formats that originated back in the 1980s and 1970s are still around. **Comma-separated values (CSV)**, for example, are still around and used by many programs. CSV files don't really imply any semantics; the content of them is completely up to the designers. The semantics of the data are usually driven by the industry; as a result, many industry-specific data formats have emerged. HL7 in healthcare, ISO 8583 in the financial industry, GJXDM in law enforcement and justice, and many others specify details of the data transferred. Some of them have become more than just data formats, adding business semantics or extensibility rules.

Once data is extracted and stored in the form of a file, it often cannot be immediately consumed by another program. In many cases, it does not even have to be. That made the file transfer approach quite useful. If the decision about when the file has to be delivered can be made by a human, the delivery can be also controlled by a human. An operator can move the file to another destination using any copy program or can even copy the file on a floppy disk and courier it to another office.

The following diagram presents a file transfer with a man in the middle when the file is delivered manually. In olden days, this method was so popular that it even got a name—**netwalk**.

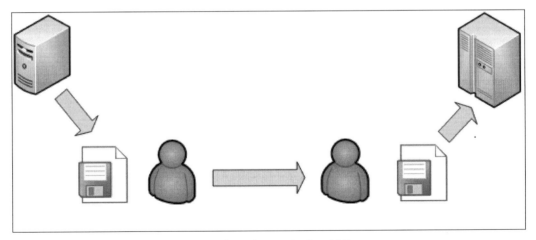

File transfer with a man in the middle

The approach has become so popular that, even with the advance of computer technologies and the invention of the Internet, organizations continued exchanging data in the form of files.

To facilitate the process, many file transfer standards have been invented. File transfer protocols, such as **FTP**, **rsync**, **FTPS**, and many others, had only one goal—to transfer files. The file transfer pattern started losing the man in the middle and became fully automated, as shown in the following diagram:

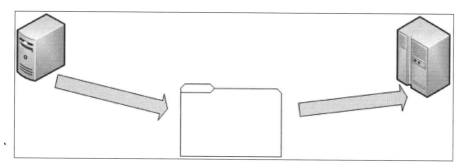

Automated file transfer

With the automation, the following problems arose:

- The main usage of the pattern has been exchanging information between disconnected systems, for example, sending daily database updates. Consider, for instance, a multiple listing service (MLS) that holds information about property listings. Such a system is updated every day by real estate brokers, and all brokers and realtors are interested in getting the updates. Because the entire database is significant, only the updates are downloaded by interested parties. The updates are usually combined into one file at the end of the day, but brokers and realtors don't know when exactly this file will be ready each day—MLS operates independently. The file is often created under the same name all the time and placed on the FTP site for download. To make sure that they download the new and not the old file, brokers and relators have to synchronize their effort with the MLS. It can be achieved by several means, for example, providing an indication of the file creation time or suggesting a time window for the new file to be created.

- Another architectural challenge that you may not find significant, but nevertheless has to be dealt with, is the decision about which party has to remove the file after it is downloaded. If the file is not overwritten, as in the previous case, the file storage area will have to be cleaned up periodically. Ideally, the process has to be automated, and which side takes responsibility for that depends on factors such as availability, security, and data retention.

- When the file is moved from one party to another party, what happens if there are processing or network errors? If the errors are related to the network and the file cannot be retrieved properly, an alternative method of communication between parties has to be established. If the errors are related to the quality of the data, the feedback has to be given to the party from where data originated. It can be though just one-way communication with no ability to send feedback. In that case, an alternative mechanism should be used as well, that can simply be a phone call to the other party administrator.

- Providing proper security is also a challenge. Remember that not only the traffic has to be secured, which is usually done by means of a secure protocol such as FTPS, but the file holding area should be secured as well. This can be achieved by IP filtering, for example.

The file transfer pattern is one of the simplest, and it can be very useful when it comes to exchanging data between two applications. However, overuse of it in the environment where much more data has to be exchanged results in the point-to-point anti pattern (*Chapter 8, Integration Patterns and Antipatterns*).

A shared database

In the previous pattern, we assumed that the data moves in one direction; one application prepares the data and another uses it. What if the data traffic is more complex?

Consider an organization that does a lot of sales. Dozens of people in the sales department are on the phone every day following leads that can come from different locations. They can exchange the leads or even follow up with someone else's leads of complete sales started by another person. The organization uses many different applications:

- **A lead management application**: This application keeps all information about leads and ongoing sales from the opportunity to the completed sale stage. The lead management server can be accessed remotely when an employee is on the move.

- **A customer relationship management application**: This is used for maintaining all information about customers, from their name and address to their product preferences and communication notes.

- **A Bookkeeping and accounting application**: This is where all money transactions are recorded.

- **A marketing application**: This builds marketing campaigns based on the historic information and distributes materials to all potential customers.

All of these applications use and update customer information. Different people from different departments (sales, marketing, or accounting) use them. At the end of each day, the applications need to exchange updated customer information. If we use the **File Transfer** pattern to do that, first of all, we'll have too many files to fly around. Secondly, what is the proper sequence of the file exchange? We don't want to overwrite changes made by one program by the older data coming from another program. Each program has to perform a proper update of customer information, and the entire procedure does not look very simple.

On top of that, there are structural and semantic inconsistencies of data. Every time the data is transferred, it has to be formatted in order to be used by another application. But formatting may not be enough to solve semantic inconsistencies between the applications. In the worst-case scenario, the inconsistencies may be so large that we would talk about **semantic dissonance**. In the case of semantic dissonance, the meaning of the same objects is different in different systems. A customer from a sales point of view is a person who would potentially buy the product. From a marketing point of view, the customer may be the entire family, all members of which have to be targeted at the same time.

An alternative solution for this conundrum is using the **Shared Database** pattern as illustrated in the following diagram:

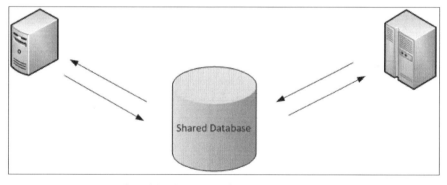

A shared database accessible from all applications

The shared database should be easily accessed by any application at any time. All conflicts that arise as a result of simultaneous access should be resolved seamlessly. In other words, we are looking into using a client-server approach. On a Microsoft platform, a natural choice would be MS SQL Server. All other Microsoft database applications, such as Visual FoxPro or Access, would not easily support our requirements.

In order to let applications access the database, some interface should be provided. The history of such APIs cannot be called uneventful. Over a couple of decades, Microsoft has developed DB-Library, DAO, RDO, ODBC, OLE DB, ADO, and so on, which were more or less performing a decent job of interfacing with databases.

The **Open Database Connectivity (ODBC)** specification was released by Microsoft in September 1992. In essence, ODBC is a 50+ function call level API that usually builds another layer of abstraction. Additional level of abstraction would certainly decrease the performance of any solution. However, for SQL Server, Microsoft has developed a native ODBC driver that replaced SQL Server API — **DB-Library**. The performance did not suffer but rather was improved.

ODBC got momentum in the database developers' community, and the number of ODBC drivers increased over years. Microsoft, however, almost abandoned the API, recommending OLE DB instead, only to return to ODBC recently. SQL Server 2012 is the last one to include SQL Server provider for OLE DB. All OLE DB approaches are recommended to be converted to other solutions.

Today, ODBC is in its Version 3.8, introduced with the release of Windows 7 and improved with the release of Windows 8.

Another popular API, **ActiveX Data Object (ADO)**, was released in October 1996. With the introduction of .NET, the conceptual model of ADO was presented by ADO.NET. Its major classes include `SqlConnection`, `SqlCommand`, `DataReader`, `DataSet`, and `DataTable` (along with server controls for ASP.NET applications). We provided a brief overview of ADO.NET in *Chapter 2, The .NET Framework Primer*.

- With the advance of ADO.NET, another approach that was quite popular before in-database development tools, such as FoxPro, for instance, came to life. This approach, called **Language Integrated Query (LINQ)**, extends programming languages by the addition of query expressions very similar to SQL. The resulting source code looks consistent and significantly improves its maintainability.

- The Shared Database pattern, most certainly, has enough technological support, and does not present a large challenge from a developer's point of view. However, for architects, using the pattern sometimes is not easy at all.

- The challenges are pretty much the same as with other data exchange patterns: structural and semantic differences. With the Shared Database pattern they got a new twist—architects had to design a view of the data that covers all views of all connected applications. Even if the software vendors are willing to cooperate and align their schemas to the shared database schema and even if they are willing to develop data transformations, some problems may still appear. Imagine, for example, software applications designed in different countries. In some countries, there is a notion of the first, second, and last names. Some countries use first name, father's name, and last name instead. Some other countries may consider more than two names for an individual, and some would insist on having a middle name (which is not a second name, by the way). Creating a data schema that satisfies all these applications could turn into a nightmare task for an architect.

- If the software applications cannot be changed, using this pattern is quite questionable. However, if applications can be modified, if building a shared database schema is possible, and if transformations don't present a huge challenge; in other words, if using the pattern is feasible, it's certainly a viable solution.

- A disadvantage of this pattern is that the shared database represents a single point of failure. That's why, while using this pattern, architects must pay additional attention to high availability and disaster recovery. As we have discussed in *Chapter 3*, *The SQL Server Primer*, Microsoft has a long history of perfecting these capabilities of SQL Server.

Data replication and synchronization

Keeping data in one place so that all applications can access it may work just fine if the data load is not high. When the number of applications increases, it would be a natural decision to separate them in such a way that they don't access the data source simultaneously.

One of the solutions is to create an exact copy of the data source, a replica. The process of creating a replica is called **replication**.

Consider, for example, a database that is constantly being updated. It could be a financial database with information about customer accounts and transactions. It could be an inventory database that reflects the status of merchandise in several stores. Every hour the organizations need to perform analysis to understand the trends, they need to run reports, or to perform other tasks on data, which could be quite resource-consuming. If these operations are performed on the live database, they may interrupt regular access to the database by other applications.

If a replica (secondary database) is created every hour, the reports or data analysis tasks can be run off it, which will not increase the load to the main database.

Another typical example of data replication can be seen in remote applications. Consider a sales person who travels with his/her laptop and does not always have the means to connect to the company database. When the connection is established, the main database (or its relevant part) is copied on the sales person's laptop, reflecting the changes since the last connection.

The replication pattern has a couple of challenges.

First, we have to add a data replicating application to the mix. This will increase the load on the database, which means that we want to do it in the most efficient manner.

We may also want to keep the database copies almost identical. The more often we perform operations on the secondary database, the more often we want to do replication. This becomes especially important if the replication also serves the need of database backup.

It's important to understand that replication is a constant process that does not require stopping operations on the main database. Replication should be performed without significantly decreasing the performance or data availability.

Replication can be performed synchronously, when replicas (in theory, more than one) are updated all at once as a part of one atomic transaction. This, without a doubt, requires much more resources to keep up the performance and transaction response times. For the purposes of maintaining a copy of the main data to perform additional operations on it once in a while, asynchronous replication is usually performed. If the asynchronous replication method is chosen, only the main database is updated with the original transaction; replicas are updated after that. For systems with disconnected databases, only the asynchronous method would work.

The replication pattern has a very limited usage when the entire data or its subset has to be duplicated. It cannot be used as a Swiss Army knife for all integration purposes. Doing so, especially in service-oriented architecture, creates very tight coupling between integration participants and all of a sudden turns into an antipattern. An excellent analysis of the replication antipattern in the SOA environment was performed in the *Data Replication as an Enterprise SOA Antipattern* article by *Tom Fuller* and *Shawn Morgan* (http://msdn.microsoft.com/en-us/library/bb245678.aspx).

The SQL Server replication

SQL Server 2012 has the following three different types of replication:

- **Transactional replication**: During transactional replication, each transaction performed on the main database is copied to the secondary database. There is a certain measurable latency that can be decreased with proper optimization.

- **Snapshot replication**: This is most appropriate when the data changes infrequently and it is acceptable to have non-synchronized database copies for a period of time.

- **Merge replication**: This enables autonomous changes to different databases. At the end of the process, all databases are synchronized.

 Starting from SQL Server 2005, another similar feature was added to the Microsoft offering, targeting specifically disaster recovery scenarios. **Database mirroring**, such as replication, supports a copy of the main database. However, the secondary copy of the database is not available during the mirroring process, which enables higher performance. The secondary copy becomes available only when disaster recovery procedures kick in. During mirroring, unlike during replication, not only the data but database schema changes as well are being copied to the secondary database.

Data synchronization using Sync Framework

If the solution allows using two SQL Server databases similar in nature, then SQL Server replication is a good choice for data synchronization. However, if the databases are heterogeneous, their nature is quite different, or the data exchange requires data transformation, then we should consider approaches other than SQL Server replication.

 Note that the current replication feature enabling the publishing of data from Oracle to SQL Server or from SQL Server to non-SQL Server subscribers will be removed in future versions of SQL Server. Microsoft recommends avoiding this feature in new development work and is planning to modify applications that currently use this feature.

Developers would appreciate that Microsoft has also come up with **Sync Framework**—a comprehensive platform for synchronizing data in a variety of scenarios. In addition to simply performing database replication, it also allows the following:

- Synchronizing a database with a database in the Azure cloud
- Performing bulk changes using a table-valued parameter feature of SQL Server to apply multiple updates, inserts, or deletes by using a single stored procedure call
- Controlling data to be synchronized with parameter-based filters

Sync Framework, in fact, allows much more than just database replication. It can also provide synchronization of files and folders as well as web feeds such as RSS or Atom.

However, the future of the Microsoft Sync framework is unknown at the moment. Version 2.1 was released as RTM in 2010. Later, in October 2010, Version 4.0 CTP was announced, skipping Version 3. In 2011, the Sync Framework Toolkit was launched, and it provides all features enabled in the Sync Framework October CTP. There has not been much activity related to the framework since then.

Data synchronization using messaging

Every message is data. So, why not use messages for data replication, especially when the usage of regular data replication tools is limited?

Once upon a time, one of the authors of this book was consulting an organization that had two DB/2 databases that required replication. The organization realized that buying DB/2 native replication tools would be much more expensive than building a solution using Microsoft BizTalk.

In fact, Microsoft BizTalk can work as a perfect tool for data replication and synchronization, especially when you can leverage BizTalk features, such as different adapters or the ability to build data transformation or an orchestration in the middle.

However, you should realize that implementing data synchronization using BizTalk requires development, which can be quite expensive and time-consuming. Therefore, for SQL Server databases developing a solution using native SQL Server replication would be our preferred method.

Data migration

A special case of data exchange—**data migration**—became quite popular with the passing of a few decades of IT history. Software and hardware became old and needed replacement. However, over the course of business, a lot of important data had been gathered and processed. This data had to be moved from legacy systems to new systems.

When more systems became outdated, data migration became a common operation, in the last decade. Merges and acquisitions also played a significant role when merged companies running different software wanted to create a consistent approach to their information.

It is important to note that the main difference between data migration and data integration is that data migration procedures are performed once and the data in the old system is retired. This does not mean though that the data migration will not be repeated in future. If the data migration is simply the result of replacing the aging hardware, the same procedures may be repeated in four to five years.

Data migration between complex systems can be a real challenge. Data migration projects may take 6 to 12 months and require an extensive analysis of legacy as well as new systems, very thorough design, complex programming, and many test runs. An additional challenge that many organizations have is that the migration process should not significantly affect the system in production. Assuming that systems in production constantly update their data, most organizations decide to interrupt the work of legacy systems at least for a few hours in order to migrate the data.

With a significant amount of data, manual data migration can become a tedious and very time-consuming process. Special tools were developed, and one of the major techniques became **extract, transform, and load** (ETL). The ETL pattern was already used in data warehousing, and we look at it in more detail later in this chapter.

The extract, transform, and load pattern for centralized data aggregation

The **extract, transform, and load** (ETL) pattern proved very useful in different architectural solutions. In data warehousing, it is used even more often than in data migration.

A **data warehouse** is a large data store constructed from several data sources and is intended to be used for reporting and analysis purposes. Data warehouses are constantly updated by feeding data from the data sources.

A part of a data warehouse that focuses on a specific area of interest is called a **data mart**.

First systems using data aggregation in a single source were developed in the early 1970s. For example, AC Nielsen, a global marketing research firm, used what they called "data mart" around that time to provide aggregated information for their customers.

The data warehouses as we know them today became a reality only in the late 1980s. The term **data warehouse** was originally used in the 1988 article *An architecture for a business and information system* by B.A. *Devlin* and P.T. *Murphy*.

Data warehouses are built primarily for reporting and analytical purposes. Applications and technologies used for analyzing data in order to make better businesses is called **business intelligence (BI)**. First BI systems evolved from decision-making systems in the 1980s. In Microsoft offerings, BI tools are delivered on the **SQL Server Analysis Services (SSAS)** platform. The OLAP Services were released as a part of SQL Server 7; with the addition of data mining tools, Analysis Services were released in the 2000. Reporting tools in the Microsoft BI offering are represented by **SQL Server Reporting Services (SSRS)**.

There are the following obvious benefits of aggregating data in a data warehouse from different sources:

- Enabling data analysis operations that would be nonfeasible otherwise, by bringing data together from different sources
- Creating reports on aggregated data
- Being able to log transaction history even if the source system does not maintain it
- Improving the overall data quality by performing data validation and data cleansing
- Presenting business information at a higher level required by decision makers

Creating a full-blown data warehouse is not necessarily a right solution. Often, building a centralized aggregated database requires gathering some, but most vital, information.

Use case – master patient index

Valley Health Services Authority operates on the territory of the Diagon Valley. There are seven hospitals, a health agency, and a medical lab providing health care to the people in the Valley.

Every time a patient comes to a medical facility, his/her information is entered or updated in the system. Initially, all patient data was kept in the form of paper files, but eventually everything was digitized. Now, all facilities run software to keep track of the patients' history. However, each facility has its own software, and the information is not centralized.

Over decades of operation, each facility collected gigabytes of patient data, but most of them never performed data cleansing consistently. As a result, some patient information has errors, and some is missing. Many patients moved and never updated their records, especially if they visited hospitals or clinics once, for example, in need of emergency care.

Needless to say, even if all information were entered correctly all the time, there is still room for inconsistencies. For example, Margaret Smith could've called herself Peggy when she was 20 years old, but later decided to use her full name, Margaret. She could also have got married and changed her last name to Brown. Therefore, there could be records of that patient that use the name of Peggy Smith as well as Margaret Brown.

In addition to the data inconsistency, another major concern of the Valley Health Services Authority is that the patient data is decentralized. When a new patient is admitted by a hospital, it would be extremely beneficial to know the patient's medical history that is recorded in other facilities. Today, there is no way to retrieve this information in a quick, preferably nonmanual manner.

An added complexity to the problem is that there is no single reliable method to identify patients. The Valley requires patients to have a **Patient Health Number (PHN)** but, in reality, there is no 100 percent guarantee that every patient would have one. First of all, the process of getting the PHN is a few months long, and even if a person who moved to the Valley applied for the PHN immediately, she still may be admitted to the hospital before getting the number. Secondly, the patient could be brought to emergency care without having the PHN on her, or even unconscious.

For similar reasons, any other government-issued identifier would not be 100 percent reliable.

In order to maintain consistent patient data, including their demographics and medical history, the Valley Health Authority decided to build a **master patient index** (**MPI**). The MPI will consist of major patient information that will be constantly updated by new data from all medical facilities. Initially, the MPI will consist of minimal information, such as the patient's demographic and abstracts of medical history, including brief descriptions of visits to medical facilities. The MPI will be available to all doctors in the Valley and later will have capabilities to be updated by general practitioners as well.

To start the initial phase, building the MPI database, an ETL process has to be established. One of many challenges that the Health Authority faces is figuring out what technology they want to use. Currently, they have a very strong skillset in Microsoft SQL Server, but the ETL process is something new to them. They are also not familiar with the BI offering from Microsoft, with SSIS in particular.

The architects' team is challenged to design the proper approach and select the technology for its implementation.

Pattern description

The extract, transform, and load (ETL) pattern, as its name suggests, consists of three major steps. Each of them is described in the next sections

Extraction

The first step assumes the extraction of data from a source system in order to be used later in the data warehouse. Data extraction is unique for each data source and often considered the most complex step in ETL. Source systems, as in our use case, could exist for many years, and unfortunately, could be poorly documented. Many old systems don't have a convenient API, and extraction can be done only by exporting a file. Data formats in these systems are not flexible and not configurable.

The extraction process has to be aligned with the usage of the source system. It is common that the extraction occurs only once a day when the source system is not busy, for example, at night. However, there are also systems that require much more frequent updates of the central database. At any rate, extraction is a periodic process that has to be scheduled to run automatically.

 In the ETL for data migration, extraction can be run manually, since it is performed once (or a very limited number of times). In the ETL for data warehouses, extraction has to run automatically, since it is has to be performed periodically, sometimes several times in one hour.

The data can be extracted completely every time. If the amount of data is not significant, this does not pose a problem. The extracted data can overwrite the old data or can be filtered in order to bring just recent changes during the process of data load. The extraction can be also incremental, when only the latest changes are extracted. With legacy systems and simplified extraction mechanisms, such as data export, only full extraction is possible.

A very common approach to incremental extraction is having timestamps of each record in the source system and using them to identify new records. Unfortunately, many legacy systems don't have timestamps and don't allow adding them.

After the data is extracted, it has to be transferred to the centralized system for performing transformation and load. Data transfer can be triggered by the end of the extraction operation or scheduled for a specific time of the day.

As we mentioned before, the data in the source systems is often gathered over decades in an inconsistent manner. The extracted data has to be validated, which can be performed either before the transformation or as a part of the transformation process. Other tasks, such as data cleansing or data deduplication should be also done after the extraction. The decision whether these tasks are a part of the transformation or supposed to be executed separately primarily depends on the ETL tools and detailed procedures. For example, if the target database has an ability to work with the up-to-date postal database, validating addresses separately at each data source would not make much sense. On the other hand, if the extraction procedure allows performing some initial data cleansing such as truncating leading spaces, using it would be advantageous and may even improve the performance of subsequent operations.

Transformation

Any data transformation requires some initial mapping. The mapping process is an activity that often needs more time than developing the transformation itself. It involves specialists with enough business as well as technical knowledge and, for large data schemas, may require weeks.

As mentioned before, the major challenges in transformation (and data mapping) are structural and semantic inconsistencies.

The transformation stage usually consists of separate steps, especially if it includes data cleansing and data deduplication. Modern ETL tools, including SSIS, enable building ETL packages as a set of components. The components can even be executed in parallel. Componentizing the data transformation process improves the overall clarity and makes the implementation achievable with fewer errors. Tools such as SSIS help in visualizing the components and their sequence.

Data manipulations during the transformation can be quite extensive. Some of the data manipulations include the following:

- Changing data fields to conform to a specific pattern, for example, 999-999-9999 for phones, or X9X 9X9 for postal codes

- Dealing with inconsistencies, such as removing leading and trailing spaces, unifying different characters used for field separation, or bringing all names to a standard form

- Validating data against reference tables

- Using fuzzy matching algorithms to match incoming data against stored data

- Removing duplicate records

- Translating free-form values to enumerations, for example, "White" and "Caucasian" to a single numeric value

- Dividing fields into a few, for example, dividing a string with the first, middle, and last names into three fields

- Combining fields together

- Building a calculated value, for example, creating a sale amount out of quantity and price

- Building new records as a result of aggregating several other records, for example, total number of transactions per month

- Building pivot tables

- Transposing columns into rows and the other way around

Loading

This is the last stage in the ETL process. Once the data is validated, cleaned, and transformed to the target schema, it can be loaded in the target database (data warehouse). Data loading requirements differ for different organizations. The schedule of data loading is not necessarily the same as the schedules for data extractions. Extracted data can be kept in a staging area and updated several times before transformation. However, it is common that data transformation and loading are aligned, and often the latter is simply triggered by the former.

During all of the ETL stages, some additional tasks are performed. The most important are logging and exception processing. Very often, the data cannot be processed automatically, but may re-enter the system after some manual correction.

Key requirements

The analysis of the use case of the master patient index for the Diagon Valley Health Authority brings up several requirements. some of which are as follows:

- The MPI system must receive admission, discharge, and transfer information on a daily basis from all participating systems
- Data extraction has to be performed with the least impact on the performance of the source systems
- The system should have the ability to add a significant number of new sources in the future, such as general practitioners' databases
- The matching procedures must support exact patient match as well as fuzzy matching
- Matching fields may include the following:
    - First name
    - Middle name
    - Last name
    - Date of birth
    - Sex
    - Patient health number (PHN)
    - Address
    - Daytime phone number
    - Evening phone number
    - Social security number
- In the case of achieving a fuzzy match, the operator's (human) decision is final
- The matching procedure should allow for some data validation and cleansing, for example, validating phone numbers against a proper template and excluding numbers that belong to first responders
- The aggregated information has to be securely stored
- In the first stage, we want to build a prototype of the future ETL process that gives us a foundation for architecture selection

Candidate architecture #1 – SQL Server

Building a data-intensive solution, potentially a data warehouse, on the Microsoft platform, gives us the natural suggestion of using SQL Server for storing data. Let's discuss what it would take to use SQL Server engine and the power of T-SQL in order to develop ETL.

Solution design aspects

SQL Server capabilities make it an excellent candidate for a highly reliable solution. In an environment with 24/7 operations and a large number of transactions, the high availability feature of SQL Server and its disaster recovery capabilities would make it a definite winner. However, for an ETL solution that will be run on a daily basis, this does not give any advantage.

The usage of T-SQL provides excellent performance. But at the first stages of the project with less than a dozen data sources and with data processed once a day, performance is not critical. If it ever becomes an issue, SQL Server could be the solution.

Solution implementation aspects

The organization has a very strong skillset in SQL Server. Performing the development would not be any problem for them.

The T-SQL solution requires coding everything by hand. Some capabilities, such as logging, would require an additional design and implementation effort. Using heterogeneous sources can become a real challenge. And finally, implementing the data flow can become a challenge, for example, when managing the state between steps is needed.

Solution operations aspects

The organization has a very strong skillset in maintaining other SQL Server solutions. Adding another SQL Server solution would not create an operational concern.

Organizational aspects

As the organization already has experience with SQL Server, no additional training is required.

Since the ETL solution is totally new to the organization, and its nature is different from all other solutions, the implementation should be better separated from other SQL Server installations. Additional licenses will be required.

Solution evaluation

As you see, there are pros and cons: the operations and organization evaluation gives us a thumbs up, but the design and development evaluation gives us a thumbs down as shown in the following diagram:

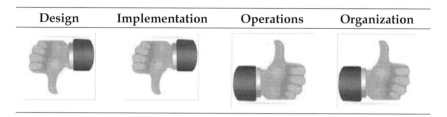

Design	Implementation	Operations	Organization

Candidate architecture #2 – SSIS

SSIS is designed for ETL. Let's see how it fits into our solution.

Solution design aspects

Since all data required for processing is brought over into the SSIS memory space, performance may become an issue for complex operations. Certain operations, such as the ones requiring data merge or lookup, would work faster in the T-SQL solution. However, at the first stages of our MPI project, performance is not an issue. In fact, with SSIS, it can become an issue only when the amounts of data start approaching terabytes. If that happens, at the future stages we can create a mixed solution, where some specific cases would be processed by SQL Server itself instead of SSIS.

SSIS is designed specifically for ETL purposes. Many operations can be easily done in SSIS compared to other tools. A visual approach to the design and implementation is a significant advantage of SSIS.

SSIS provides logging capabilities, which is an advantage of this approach as well.

SSIS allows accessing heterogeneous data sources, including SQL Server, Oracle, Teradata, DB2, ODBC, or text files. It can integrate data from business workflows in ERP or CRM applications.

Solution implementation aspects

Currently, the organization does not have a lot of skills in SSIS, but has a lot of experience in developing and maintaining SQL Server solutions. As the target data will be stored in a SQL Server database, building the schema for it should not be a challenge for the Valley Health Authority IT team. On the other hand, SSIS has an easy-to-learn interface; with the deep knowledge of data intensive solutions, the SSIS learning curve for the team should be insignificant.

Additional tasks, especially nondatabase-related tasks, can be coded using C# or Visual Basic. Using Execute SQL Task in SSIS, one can also run T-SQL code. In order to understand the SSIS Object Model, please refer to the following description from Microsoft at `http://technet.microsoft.com/en-us/library/ms136025.aspx`.

Solution operations aspects

Currently, the organization does not have SSIS solutions, but maintains many SQL Server databases. Since SSIS is not a complex tool and the target MPI database is stored in SQL Server, maintaining the SSIS solution should not create a problem for the IT team.

Organizational aspects

Some investment in SSIS training is required since the organization does not currently have SSIS skills. However, with extensive SQL Server knowledge, the learning curve should not be steep.

In the future, the Health Authority plans to extend the solution by adding many more data sources. Since there is not much knowledge of the technologies used to maintain these data sources, SSIS is an excellent choice, as it provides very good coverage of different data sources. The ability to extent the code by using C# or T-SQL is also a plus point.

SSIS does not require licenses other than SQL Server licenses. Compared to the previous candidate architecture, the number of licenses would be the same.

Solution evaluation

All thumbs up as shown in the following table:

Design	Implementation	Operations	Organization
👍	👍	👍	👍

Candidate architecture #3 – BizTalk

Even if BizTalk is primarily an EAI tool rather than an EII tool, with heterogeneous data sources, it is a very strong candidate.

Solution design aspects

BizTalk is a reliable technology that is based on the foundation of SQL Server. It has several capabilities that help easily achieve high availability and design for high volume. It has a data persistence mechanism that prevents data from disappearing. However, as it was with the pure SQL Server approach, for an ETL solution that will be run on a daily basis and can be repeated if needed, this does not give any advantage.

A significant advantage of BizTalk is its large library of adapters. Data can be read from literally any source. With the high possibility of expanding the solution in the future, this certainly is a pro.

Solution implementation aspects

BizTalk has native mapping and transformation capabilities that will reduce the development time.

The visual interface helps with implementation, but the learning curve for the team will still be steep. BizTalk is a complex tool and learning it from scratch would take some significant time.

Solution operations aspects

Currently, the organization does not have any BizTalk experience. Its maintenance will require some learning, not only BizTalk itself, but potential maintenance tools as well, such as BizTalk 360.

Organizational aspects

Implementing BizTalk will require buying licenses on top of SQL Server licenses, which will be more expensive compared to the previous approaches.

Solution evaluation

Well, it's certainly not a winner, as shown in the following table:

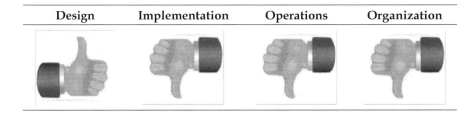

Design	Implementation	Operations	Organization

Architecture selection

The benefits and risks of all solutions are presented in the following table:

Solution	Benefits/risks
SQL Server	**Benefits** • Highly reliable solution, designed for scalability • Existing in-house staff to develop, to maintain, and to support the solution **Risks** • Significant amount of code to be developed • Use of heterogeneous sources is challenging

Solution	Benefits/risks
SSIS	**Benefits**
	• Perfectly fits the solution from the design perspective
	• Extensible solution; will satisfy future needs
	• Enables easy integration with heterogeneous data sources
	Risks
	• No in-house expertise with SSIS
BizTalk Server	**Benefits**
	• Reliable and extensible technology
	• Enables easy integration with heterogeneous data sources
	Risks
	• No in-house expertise with BizTalk
	• Additional licensing and training costs

With a lot of heterogeneous data sources, both BizTalk and SSIS look like strong candidates. Both are extensible solutions and require a learning curve. However, SSIS does not require an additional license, it is designed for ETL, and therefore it is our choice.

Building the solution

For the first phase of the ultimate integration solution, we will build an SSIS package that extracts information from a mixed data source. The data will be imported from an Excel file and a text file and merged together. The files contain new records, and are updated on a daily basis. The resultant merged information is loaded into the target MPI database.

Data structures

The files and the database are presented in the sample folder for the book.

The Excel file has the following structure:

- Name
- Gender
- Race
- Street Address
- City
- State
- ZIP
- SSN
- HRN
- DOB
- Comments

The text file is a CSV (comma-separated) file with the following fields:

- HRN
- First Name
- Last Name
- MI
- Date of Birth
- Gender
- Race
- Social Security Number
- Street Address
- City
- State
- ZIP

Notice that some data is presented in different ways in these two files. For example, the Excel file has two name fields (first and last) and the text file has three name fields (first, last, and middle initial). Before merging the data, such fields have to be transformed into a consistent format.

The resultant MPI patients data table has a structure similar to the one shown in the following screenshot:

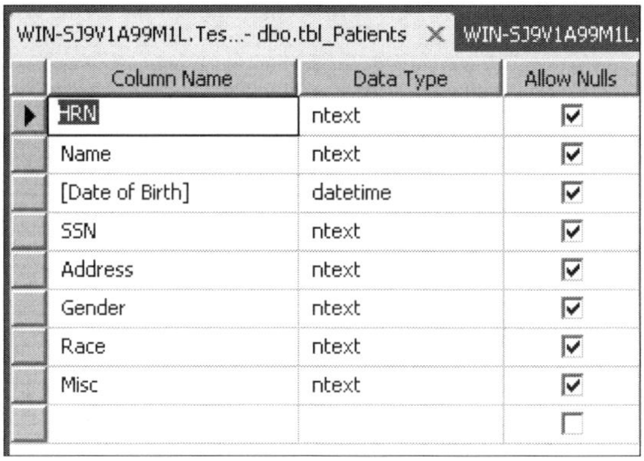

Column Name	Data Type	Allow Nulls
HRN	ntext	☑
Name	ntext	☑
[Date of Birth]	datetime	☑
SSN	ntext	☑
Address	ntext	☑
Gender	ntext	☑
Race	ntext	☑
Misc	ntext	☑
		☐

In order to create the database and its tables (Patients, States, and Cities) run the following SQL scripts from the book samples:

- `create_database.sql`
- `create_patients.sql`
- `create_states.sql`
- `create_cities.sql`

In order to achieve loading data into the target table, the following SSIS operations have to be performed.

1. Build the data flow for the Excel data source using the following steps:

   1. Use the Excel Connection Manager to specify the data source, including the filename, Excel sheet name, and columns. You can also specify the output in the event there is an error.

   2. Create the full name as a concatenation of the `First Name` and the `Last Name` fields.

   3. Create the output address field as a combination of the `Street Address`, `City`, `State`, and `ZIP` fields.

4. Sort the data by the HRN (Health Record Number) and Name fields. Now the data flow will look like the following:

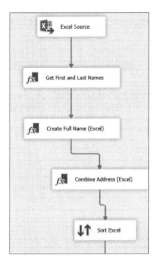

2. Build the data flow for the text data source using the following steps:

1. Use the Flat File Connection Manager to specify the data source, including the filename, Excel sheet name, and columns. You can also specify the output in case of an error.

2. Replace empty fields with NULL values.

3. Create the full name as a concatenation of the First Name, MI, and the Last Name fields.

4. Sort the data by the HRN (Health Record Number) and Name fields. Now the data flow will look like the following:

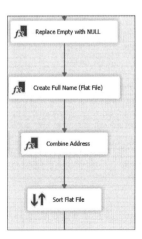

3. Now we have our two sources (flat file and Excel file) ready to be merged. In the next step we'll merge records from two sources, as shown in the following screenshot:

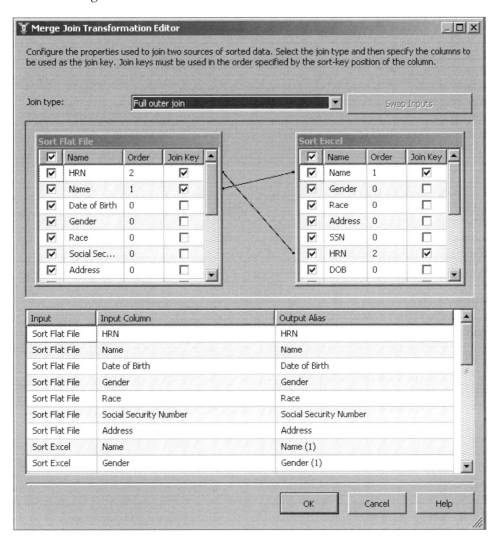

4. After merging the sources, we need to perform data validation. In order to validate states and cities, we shall use the Lookup shape, as shown in the following diagram:

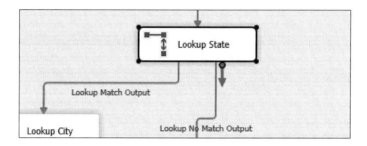

5. Double-click on any Lookup shape in the data flow, and the **Lookup Transformation Editor** will pop up, as shown in the following screenshot:

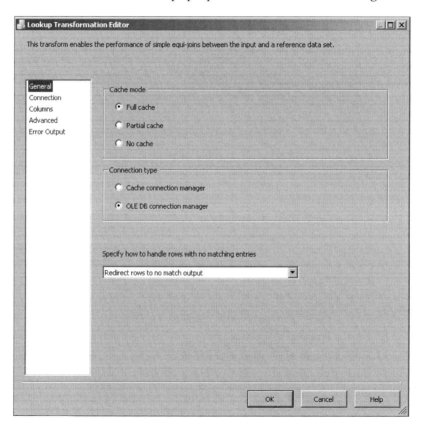

6. Use the Transformation Editor to match a field in the input record to reference data. In case of a match, the data output will be different from when the match is not achieved.

 In addition to Lookup Transformation, SSIS provides the Fuzzy Lookup Transformation shape. Lookup Transformation retrieves only matches or nonmatches; Fuzzy Lookup retrieves records that are similar and not necessarily exact matches.

7. When all lookups are performed, we direct correct data to the destination file and erroneous data to the logfile, as shown in the following diagram:

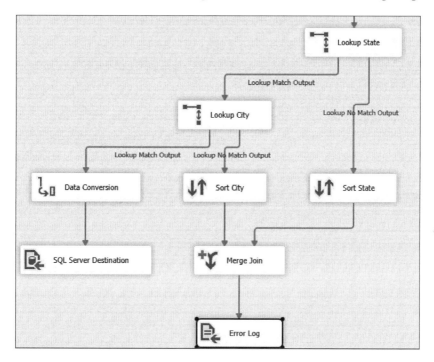

Lessons learned

We have built an ETL solution for the initial phase of a very complex data integration project. We used SSIS to bring the data into the future data warehouse.

In the next pattern, we consider a slightly different approach. We will bring together, from several sources, only the key elements of the data — the master data. The data will be brought in a centralized hub. We will use the data to search across the entire enterprise.

Multiple master synchronization

It is a rare business that has one and only one version of truth for all of the data that it maintains. Instead, businesses rely on a hodgepodge of diverse systems, all of which will identify the critical nouns of a business differently, and will often contain radically different versions of the definition of those nouns.

For example, in one system, one of our authors might be labeled "Mike", in another "Michael", and in a third "That funny-smelling, old guy." When one attempts to manage and reconcile these discrepancies, one is presented with the same issue Humpty Dumpty presented to Alice in *Through the Looking-Glass*.

"When I use a word," Humpty Dumpty said in a rather scornful tone, "it means just what I choose it to mean—neither more nor less."

When trying to integrate and resolve these issues, you are potentially dealing with dozens of Humpty Dumpties, all of whom have attached different, nuanced meanings to the nouns they track. In this section, we will review a use case for a fictitious company, World Wide Widgets, and evaluate and review portions of a potential solution.

The resolution of these issues will be complex and involve multiple, diverse technologies, even within the Microsoft stack. Here, we will provide a glimpse into the large world of master data management and the multiple methods for arriving at a single version of truth within a large diverse organization.

Use case – master data management for WWW

World Wide Widgets (WWW) developed and patented multiple types of widgets for use in the brake and acceleration systems of automobiles and light trucks. They currently manufacture these system components in factories in North America, South East Asia, and Europe for sale to several auto manufacturers. Each manufacturer has insisted on slightly different designs of these components. WWW has sold the Widge-O-Stop brake system and the Widge-O-Go acceleration system, with modifications to the Toy O D'oh car company.

It was recently announced that Toy O D'oh will recall all 2009 and 2010 models for faulty brakes and gas pedals. Each of these systems uses WWW's patented Widge-O units. Regulatory authorities in Asia, North America, and Europe have all announced investigations and the legal department has warned management to expect long and protracted litigation around these issues.

You have been assigned the task of designing and building a system that will gather and characterize all of the company's records on the development of this system as well as the sales and marketing of this system to Toy O D'oh. You must get all of the records, including unstructured and semi-structured data.

Key requirements

The system must correctly identify staff over time and correctly assign to them the roles they were in during particular times. This was a quite a long-term effort. People left or joined the company, were promoted or changed roles, or changed names because of marriage or divorce. The project itself went through many code names. The trade name "Widge-O" was coined by the marketing department. The engineers, patent lawyers, and others involved in the research development and patents used numerous other terms.

Third-party consultants were also used as part of the development efforts. These include safety testing labs, software developers, and outside law firms for patent and regulatory work, all of whom should have left (but perhaps did not) copies of their work product with WWW. Your system should identify gaps if they exist.

The company requires each staff person to maintain documents and work products on their local hard drives for seven years. Some staff have found this to be an onerous requirement, so they have moved data onto other media. They will make that media available to you for searching and indexing.

Structured data that must be searched can be found in both Oracle systems and SQL Server systems. You must identify employees involved with Widge-O. Data concerning these assignments can be found in the Oracle HR system. Data concerning safety testing can be found in SQL Server-based systems.

One of the biggest issues with any forensics type of project is the human factor. Here, the lawyers are involved, and you must expect that everyone will be running for cover. They will be deleting documents and e-mails, moving material to USB devices and engaging in every imaginable effort to **Confound Your Assessment (CYA)**. Additionally, employees are not attempting to cover up or hide data, but they may inadvertently improperly store data.

During the normal course of events, data and documents are altered over time. Versioning and the explanations for changes can be key evidence in law. You will need to track versions, dates, and revisions of data as part of any solution.

Additional facts

Given the risks and issues that would arise should this project fail, including legal liabilities and damage to the business's good name, we can assume that we will have more than adequate staffing and technical capabilities for this project. Moreover, this is an engineering company that understands the need for good design and competent software development, so they hire superior talent for both development and operations.

Pattern description

Like most enterprises, WWW has multiple databases, each of which controls data for its specific area or business purpose, each of which is master of its own domain. Like most enterprises, WWW has no minimal tools in place to monitor and resolve differences between these data sources. For the purposes of this litigation, these differences must be identified and brought to the attention of the business so that they can be resolved or explained.

In **master data management (MDM)** situations such as this one, we gather the key data, often called the key nouns of an organization, identify data disparities, and reconcile those disparities. For example, a key noun for any organization would be "customers". The same customer might be identified as "Mike" in one system and "Michael" in another or may have different mailing addresses and phone numbers in those systems because of a move. One would reconcile these disparities in any MDM system using appropriate business rules so that the company can properly service the customer and have an accurate picture of its customer base. One rule might be "the most recently reported address is deemed to be the correct address", for example.

MDM, in this situation, serves the key role of gathering evidence for analysis by the legal team.

WWW needs to gather all of its data concerning its interactions with Toy O D'oh, identify any discrepancies, and then reconcile those discrepancies or feed them into a human workflow so that they can be investigated.

Candidate architecture

There are the following tools that we need to handle the issues presented:

- We must extract existing data from multiple relational systems and load it into a clean environment where we will track data access and changes.

- We must manage the definitions of key business nouns across multiple environments.

- We must track metadata concerning various documents, spreadsheets, and other objects.

- We must use unstructured and semi-structured data as a source for data mining and data analysis tasks by storing metadata concerning these objects in SQL Server.

- We must search through and index semi-structured and un-structured data across the enterprise. This will include every server, every laptop, and all of the miscellaneous storage devices.

These needs cannot be met with any single product or technology in the Microsoft catalog. Rather, we will need to incorporate several technologies into our solution to gather, index, store, and present data to end users.

Solution design aspects

In the following list, we will review all of the technologies that we can bring to bear on the problem at hand:

- **SSIS**: We have already discussed the use of SSIS before. Here we have *classic* ETL issues — the very issues SSIS was designed to deal with — as well as extracting data from "nontraditional" sources, such as documents, e-mails, and spreadsheets. SSIS does not typically come up on an architect's radar when faced with these data sources. Nevertheless, SSIS is an excellent tool to extract metadata and other information from these objects, as we saw in the previous pattern.

- **Master Data Services**: The key functionality of Master Data Services that we will illustrate here is the creation of a master data hub — a single source for all master data regardless of source system. We will ensure data consistency by treating each master data change as a transaction and logging the date and time, and the user making the change.

- **Search Server 2010 Express**: We must search and index documents across the enterprise. These documents can be in numerous formats. The Express edition is limited to a standalone installation but, generally, provides all functionality as the full version. It provides the functionality we seek here and has the advantage of being free.

Solution operations aspects

WWW already has SQL Server in place. At most, we are simply leveraging the functionality of the latest release of SQL Server. While Search Server Express may be a new technology for this enterprise, it has an easy, light, and intuitive administrative interface and should not provide any significant issues for WWW operations staff.

Organizational aspects

Simply put, this project must get done and must get done correctly. The risks to the very existence of the company should they lose any litigation, along with the adverse publicity arising from taking the blame for product failures, is simply too great. The organization will get the resources needed to be successful. In this case, that should be a simple task. For the most part, we are extending products already in use with a staff very familiar with the Microsoft stack.

Solution evaluation

Unlike other scenarios that we have discussed throughout this book, here we have no single magic bullet technology that can solve all of our issues. Instead, we will need to deploy multiple technologies that can meet the wide-ranging requirements presented here.

Results of our assessment is as shown in the following table (all thumbs up):

Design	Implementation	Operations	Organization

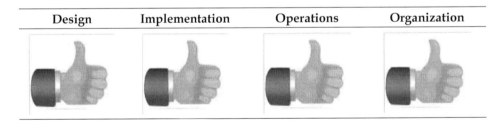

Architecture selection

Let's consider the components that make up this candidate architecture:

Components	Benefits/risks
SQL Server, Master Data Services, and SSIS	**Benefits** • Easily deployed as an extensible ETL tool • Designed to handle batch processing of large files, exactly the task at hand. • No additional licensing costs—comes with SQL Server • Can be built and maintained by current staff • Can build business rules to resolve data conflicts **Risks** • Need to build a sophisticated error handling system • Does not handle unstructured data well
Search Server	**Benefits** • Indexes unstructured data • Can review administrative shares (such as C$) on desktops **Risks** • Not clear whether staff has the skills to support the product • Still possible for users to "hide" relevant documents on portable devices

This is an extraordinarily complex data management task as it touches on all of the data held by the organization in every possible format in which the organization holds it. You must get data in both the organizations' "approved" formats as well as in any format that might be held by a key staff person that they obtained from outside sources (such as through Internet research). In this case, the combination of a SQL Server-based solution along with Search Server will serve this organization.

Building the solution

We will need to deal with both structured data stored in relational databases and unstructured data stored in filesystems of various sorts (for example, marketing documents and engineering design drawings). We will manage conflicts between the relational systems using Master Data Services, ETL using SSIS, and filesystem indexing using Search Server and SSIS.

The Electronic Discovery Reference Model (`http://edrm.net/`) refers to the following six phases of handling data:

1. Information management
2. Identification
3. Preservation and collection
4. Processing, review, and analysis
5. Production
6. Presentation

The six phases are presented in the following diagram:

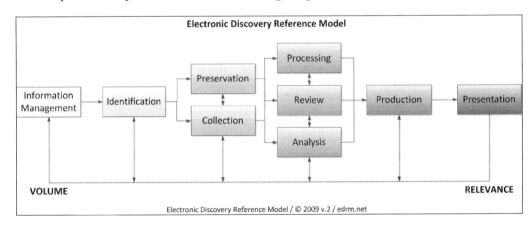

Our tasks focus on steps 1 through 3 while providing a firm foundation for steps 4 through 6, which can be handled using SharePoint, SQL Server Reporting Services, and Power Pivot.

In order to execute these tasks, we will need to have two data constructs, one for the document and other source metadata, and a second to hold relational data for analysis. While we could use two schemas for this purpose, we have elected to go with two separate databases. First, this will optimize performance for what is expected to be two very different reporting criteria. Second, it will minimize confusion for both users and system operators. Third, it will allow us to secure the data properly, particularly if we need to extend the metadata system to include comments or other attorney work product that should not be distributed outside the organization.

From a high-level logical view, our system will look like the following diagram:

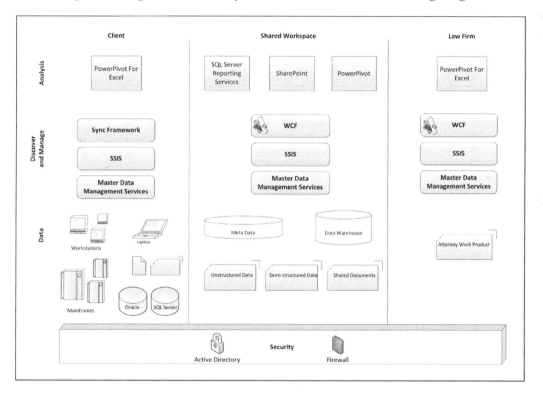

Fetching relational data

First, we will need to know the who, what, when, where, and how of the development and production of the Widge-O. The "who" can be ascertained from the HR system. Here, we will use the HR schema provided to us in the Oracle 10*g* Express Edition as it is already populated with data. We have written out the `Employees` and `Department` tables to comma-separated files. We have created two parallel data flows, each of which pulls data from a comma-delimited ASCII file, converts the data to an appropriate datatype, and loads the data into the correct tables in the HR schema of the metadata database we previously created, as shown in the following screenshot:

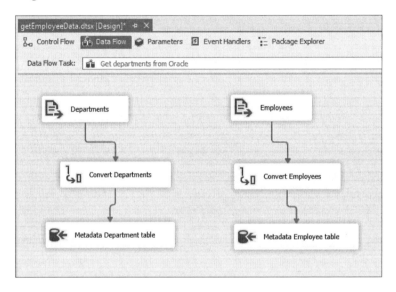

Master data services

To install MDS, follow the instructions given on the Microsoft Developer Network at `http://msdn.microsoft.com/en-us/library/ee633752.aspx`.

Once you have completed the installation and configuration, your next step will be to create a model around the key "nouns" or entities you will be tracking. MDS creates a hierarchy around each noun and its properties. This is a hierarchical structure that organizes the data. In our scenario, one key entity that needs to be tracked would be the Widge-O product line. We might, therefore, use the following model:

- WidgeO Litigation
- Auto products

- Brake products
- Widge-O Stop
- Acceleration products
- Widge-O Go

We will need to create an application; we'll do so using the following steps. Make sure the WWW service allows Windows authentication.

1. Open the MDS configuration manager and select **Web Configuration** from the left-hand side panel.

2. Choose **Default Web Site** and select **Create Application** to bring up the **Create Web Application** dialog. Fill in the configuration fields and select OK, as shown in the following screenshot:

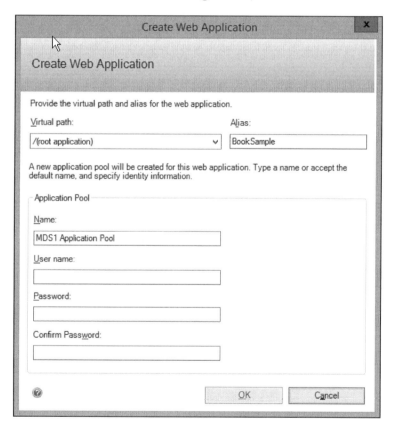

3. Next, you will need to select a database for the application. Click on the **Select** button that appears under the **Database** group box to bring up the **Connect to Database** dialog. Make the appropriate selections for your database's security context and select **OK**, as shown in the following screenshot:

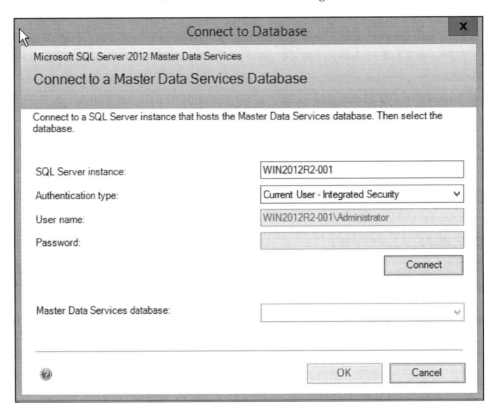

4. Your configuration manager should now appear similar to the following screenshot:

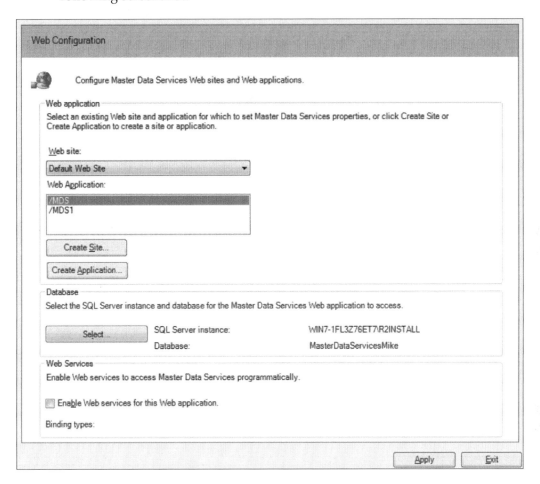

5. On the **Web Configuration** screen, select **Apply**. You should see the success dialog box. Select the **Launch Application in browser** checkbox to begin the actual work, as shown in the following screenshot:

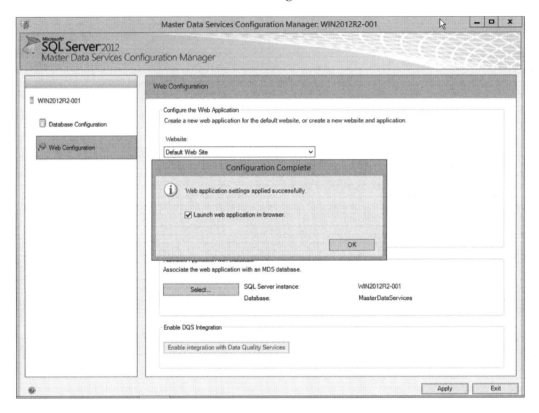

6. This will bring you to the default management page in your browser, as shown in the following screenshot:

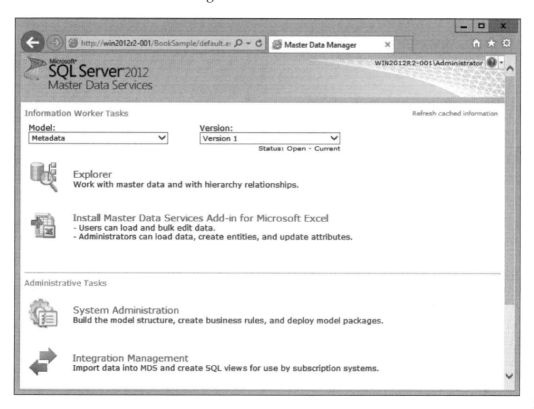

7. It will quickly become apparent that navigation through the MDS interface is not particularly intuitive. A cheat sheet is available at `http://msdn.microsoft.com/ en-us/library/ee633735(SQL.105).aspx`. Open the **System Administration** link. We need to create a new model as described previously, so click on **Models**, and then click on the icon with the + symbol, as shown in the following screenshot:

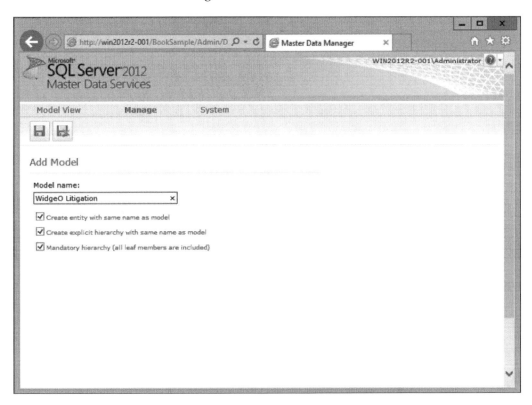

8. Enter `WidgeO Litigation` in the textbox, leave the defaults, and click on the Save icon.

9. We will now need to add entities to our model. You can think of entities as levels in the hierarchy or as dimensions in a snowflake schema. Select the **Manage** menu item then select **Entities**.

10. Once again, select the green **+** icon, add `Auto products`, and select **No** from the **Enable explicit hierarchies and collections** drop-down list, as shown in the following screenshot:

11. Save the entity and repeat the process for `Brake products`, `Widge-O Stop`, `Acceleration products`, and `Widge-O Go`.

12. Entities have attributes that are well... attributes. They are similar to attributes in an XML file or the fields in a table. Once you have completed the creation of the entities, you should see the Manage screen, looking like the following screenshot:

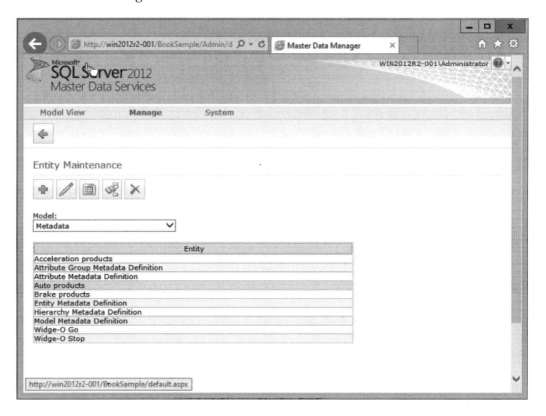

13. When you select one of the entities, a number of icons will appear, as you can see displayed in the previous screenshot. We will limit our attribute creation to the `Widge-O Go` and `Widge-O Stop` leaf levels.

14. Highlight `Widge-O Go` and click on the Pencil icon. You will be taken to the edit entity page. Note that there are already two attributes, `name` and `code`. We will add `version` and `data source` to the attributes.

15. Click on the green **+** symbol. The **Add Attribute** page will appear.

16. Type `data source` in the **Name** field and accept the remaining defaults.

17. Repeat the process for `version`, and then repeat these steps for the `Widge-O Stop`.

18. Click back through the Save icons to reach the **Entity Maintenance** page and save your work.

19. Next, we will need to relate the entities through domain-level attributes. So, for the `Brake Product` entity, add a `Widge-O Stop` domain attribute and tie it with the `Brake Product` entity.

20. For the acceleration products entities, add a `Widge-O Go` domain attribute and tie it to the acceleration products. For the `auto products` entities, add a `brake products` and `acceleration products` domain attribute and tie it to `auto products`, as shown in the following screenshot:

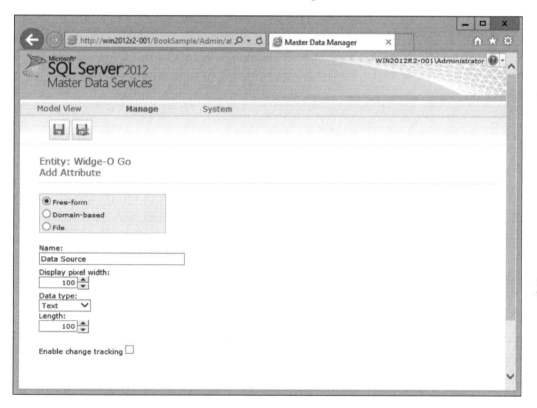

21. In order to complete our hierarchy, add a domain-based attribute `Products` to the `WidgeO Litigation` entity and point it towards the `WidgeO Litigation` entity in the **Entity** drop-down list.

22. Navigate back to the main menu. You can use the breadcrumbs path appearing next to the SQL Server graphics in the upper-left corner of the page. You will need to make sure that the correct model appears in the model menu, and then select **Version 1** from the **Versions** drop-down list.

23. Now (finally) we'll create our hierarchy. Select **System Administration** from the home page and then manage derived hierarchies from the menu. The derived hierarchy is derived from relating domain attributes.

24. Select **WidgeO Litigation** from the drop-down list, and click on the green **+** icon. Name the hierarchy `WidgO ToyOdoh 1 Litigation` and click on **Save**. The hierarchy editing page will appear.

25. Simply drag the auto products line from the left-hand side to the right-hand side, and the hierarchy is created. We have now completed our hierarchical structure to use to manage relational data concerning the product lines.

Next, we will need to create the infrastructure required to manage unstructured and semi-structured data, such as the material contained in Word files, e-mail, PDF files, or spreadsheets.

Unstructured data

A significant portion of a company's data is not held in structured relational databases. Instead, it is held in multiple, unstructured, or semi-structured formats. Think of how much day-to-day activity you, dear reader, carry out using relational databases and how much is carried out with e-mail. Indeed, you might even consider code and comments to fit the definition of semi-structured data.

Here the litigation teams need all of the documents concerning the Widge-O lines of products. "All" does not mean "most"—so every document, marketing graphic, engineering design, and sales spreadsheet must be found and indexed.

For the purposes of this exercise, we want to capture the metadata concerning all relevant documents. We will create a single directory to crawl. In the real world, you would need to crawl the administrative partitions and associated directories of each computer on the network (for example, `\\computer1\ C$`, `\\computer1\D$`, and `\\ComputerN\C$`) searching for any file with a relevant extension (for example, `.docx`, `.xlsx`, `.pdf`).

1. Create a directory labeled `WidgeO`, and then open your SSIS project for this chapter. For the purposes of illustrating this effort, simply load it with a random assortment of files you now have on your system. Create a variable named `path` with a string datatype, and then drag a `Foreach` container onto the package, as shown in the following screenshot:

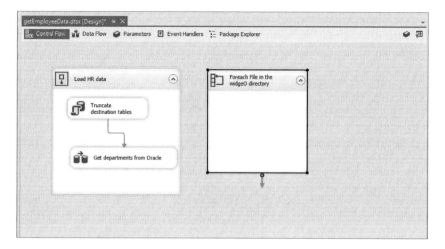

2. Open the `Foreach` loop container and select the **Collection** dialog from the left-hand side. We will be using a `Foreach file` enumerator. Browse the `WidgeO` directory you created earlier, as shown in the following screenshot:

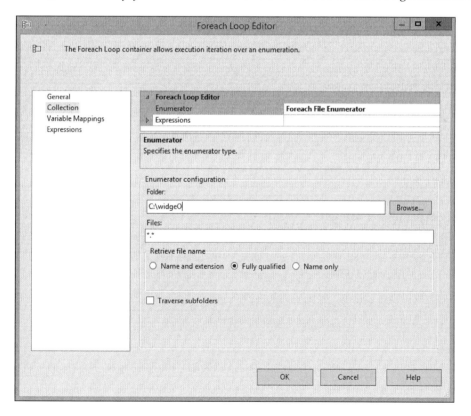

3. Next, select the variable mapping and select the User::path variable we created earlier. This should be mapped to the 0 index. Click on **OK**, as shown in the following screenshot:

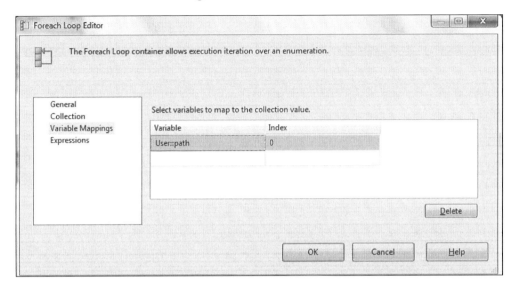

4. Click on **OK** to accept your work. The Foreach loop will loop through each file in this directory. We will create a script to fetch the metadata and load the results into our database.

5. In order to handle that task, create additional string variables: createDate to track the date of creation, DocName for the document name, and lastModDate to track the last modification date. You can create other variables to track other properties as you choose.

6. Drag a script task into the Foreach container and label it getDocData. You can create some artificial data for the purposes of this exercise by copying random files into the widge0 directory.

7. Open the execute script object. We need to map the variables correctly. The path variable should be entered as read only, while the DocName, createDate, and LastModDate variables are mapped as read-write. Select the values from the drop-down lists.

8. There are many ways we can get this data from the DTS variables collection into the database. Here, we will choose to build an `insert` statement string and pass it to an execute SQL task. To that end, create a variable `insertSQL` and add it as a read-write variable. We will then simply concatenate the string to create the `insert` statement.

9. You will need to add a `using System.IO` line, and then the following code in the `Main()` method, as shown in the following code snippet:

```
public void Main()
{
string path = Dts.Variables["path"].Value.ToString(); //remember
that the variable name is case sensitive.
//for test
//MessageBox.Show(path, "path", MessageBoxButtons.OK);
System.IO.FileInfo fileInfo = new FileInfo(path);
Dts.Variables["CreateDate"].Value = fileInfo.CreationTime.
ToString();
Dts.Variables["lastModDate"].Value = fileInfo.LastWriteTime.
ToString();
Dts.Variables["DocName"].Value = fileInfo.Name.ToString();
//MessageBox.Show(Dts.Variables["DocName"].Value. ToString(),
"DocName", MessageBoxButtons.OK);
//build the sql
string SQL = "INSERT INTO Documents.DocumentTrace (DocName,DocPath
,CreateDate,LastModifedDate,CreatedBy, ComputerID) VALUES ( " + "'
"; SQL = SQL + Dts.Variables["DocName"].Value + "' " + ", " + "' "
+ path + "' " +", ";
SQL = SQL + "' " + Dts.Variables["CreateDate"].Value + "' , " + "'
" + Dts.Variables["lastModDate"].Value + "' ,";
SQL = SQL + "133, 1)";
//MessageBox.Show(SQL, "SQL", MessageBoxButtons.OK);
Dts.Variables["insertSQL"].Value = SQL;
Dts.TaskResult = (int)ScriptResults.Success;
}
```

Note that we did not include any error handling as a best practice for this example shell.

10. Once your code is complete, drag and execute the SQL task into the `Foreach` loop. We will use the same connection as the one we used earlier in the chapter. Select **Variable** from the **SQL Source Type** drop-down list, and select **User::insertSQL** as the **Source Variable**, as shown in the following screenshot:

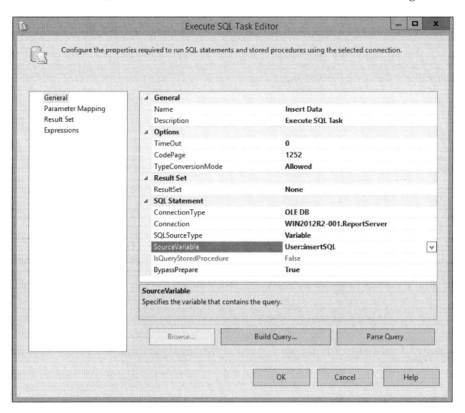

11. We have previously populated some of the tables with data using SQL inserts included in the source code. This statement will insert the data into the `DocumentTrace` tables so that we have the correct metadata for the relevant documents. You can now run the code and test it by selecting the `DocumentTrace` table.

Setting up a search

As is the case with most companies, the "working knowledge" at WWW is often not contained in formal, relational data structures. Instead, it is in documents, e-mails, spreadsheets, and a host of other types of files that are used in every company for day-to-day interaction and collaboration.

You will need to work with a system that has SharePoint installed. Download and install Search Server 2010 Express from Microsoft using the install wizards. We will only work with crawling data on the local machine hosting SharePoint, as most of our corporate masters would take a dim view of us crawling production networks and colleagues' computers as a training exercise. We will also focus on Search Server Express, as it allows you to familiarize yourself with the basic tasks associated with indexing and searching for unstructured data without incurring any licensing costs. Free is good.

Perform the following steps to set up a search:

1. Once you have Search Server installed, open the **Search Administration** page and then select **Content Sources** and **Add a Content Source**:

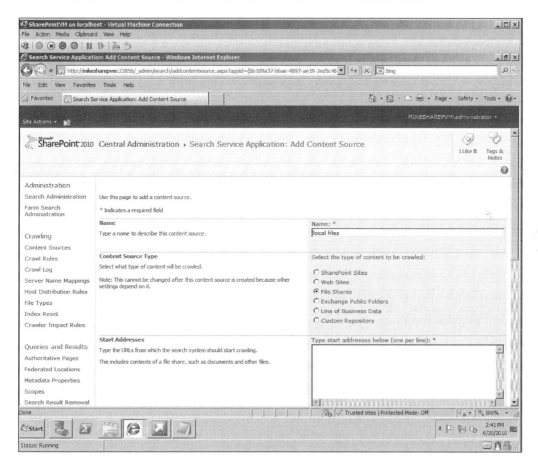

2. Name the crawled local files and select the **File Shares**. For **Start Address**, enter the absolute path for the machine you are working with, along with the directory you wish to crawl (for example, `\\MyMachine\SomeShare`). Select **Crawl the folder and all subfolders of each start address**, and, if you wish, create a schedule for both the full and incremental crawls. Check **Start full crawl of this content source**, click on **OK**, and away you go. You will be brought back to the **Manage Content Sources** page where you will see the status of your crawl.

Once the crawl is complete, you can check the results in the crawl log. You can also enter a search term in the SharePoint site and see the results. For our particular scenario, this makes the content available quickly and easily to the lawyers and others who will need to work with it.

Lessons learned

Here, we have scratched the surface of the myriad issues surrounding master data management and the use of unstructured data in enterprise data management systems. There are, of course, additional tools and methods that we simply do not have the space to cover. Here we have used the basic tools of Master Data Services and SSIS to handle some of the tasks associated with this problem.

Data sharing and federation

Data warehouses have a long history. From the 1970s to the 1990s, more data warehousing tools and methods were developed and, by the 2000s, data warehouses were a real success. A lot of books and articles were written; many organizations invested a lot of money in data warehouses and solutions from Oracle, Microsoft, and other software vendors.

Some organizations believed that data warehouses were the only solution for a complex data integration problem. However, some of them faced challenges. Let's look at a use case that will show us some typical challenges and concerns.

Use case – real-time data retrieval from highly sensitive data sources

The Republic of Prudonia as any other country has law enforcement and justice organizations. The crime level in this county is very low, and the government once even suggested converting all police forces to forestry workers, but it never happened. As of 2014, Prudonia has 15 police departments, courts, and a gaol. Each police department has dozens of sworn officers, investigators, and other personnel.

With the addition of courts and gaol employees, there are more than a thousand people who use law enforcement databases on a daily basis.

Each police department, as well as the courts and the gaol, has its own record management system. Some of them, especially small ones, started transferring paper files into computer databases just recently, but now each and every employee has access to the digitized data. Police officers even have laptops or tablets with satellite connectivity to access the databases from any place in the country.

In addition to that, the country has some centralized information that belongs to state departments, but this information is minimal.

As all law enforcement systems in the country grew inconsistently, they use different software that are not totally integrated. Some information, for example, driver license information, comes from the State Department of Licensing and is available to anyone in the law enforcement. But the country does not have a centralized system with criminal records or other related information. If a police officer stops a car for speeding, the only criminal information that they can get comes from the databases of their own department.

Police officers certainly appreciate the fact that they can find out whether the driver license of the stopped person is valid. They can also find out whether the car is stolen; this information also comes from one of the state databases. However, if the person has criminal records in another police department, the police officer would not be able to know it.

Prudonian law enforcement and justice organizations realized the deficiency of the system a long time ago. Even with the launching of the first record management systems, some of the IT professionals suggested making that effort consistent across the entire country. But since all police departments had their own agendas, the suggestion was never heeded.

Now the need for integration of the criminal records is obvious, and data exchange sounds like a reasonable solution.

Data warehouse challenges

First, the IT consultants recommended creating a data warehouse and feeding it with the data from record management systems on a daily basis. With the known advantages and the successful history of data warehouses, the technology choice sounded very feasible. Each police officer would be given an application running on their laptop that would enable real-time search in the data warehouse. Now, if a suspect were stopped on the street, the officer could get everything that has been known about the suspect in the entire country.

But as usual, the human factor was much more critical than technologies.

The first obstacle appeared when business analysts and subject matter experts from different police departments started meeting to work on data mapping. In order to understand each other's data better, the organizations were asked to present examples of actual data. But the actual data contained sensitive information, and sharing this data required a written permission from chiefs of the involved departments. Getting the papers signed took a few weeks, and the entire process stopped.

When some department chiefs were puzzled by the request to share data with other organizations, they realized that, in the proposed solution, they would have to give away their data in order for this data to be aggregated in the data warehouse. Most of them did not appreciate the idea.

Working in law enforcement has its consequences. Seeing criminal problems every day is a challenging experience. Many law enforcement officers have seen many people whom they would never trust. Not only criminals, but many other people, including fellow officers, sometimes lost their trust. After a couple of decades working there, some of them created a habit of being suspicious, even paranoid, at least in the very beginning.

And when they heard that now they were supposed to give their data away for someone else to manage it on a daily basis, that idea was not much supported. Even if they still would have control of the original data, the data was very precious to be also stored somewhere else.

Some police chiefs decided to look closer at the solution. And since they were already prejudiced against the approach, they started finding more concerns that were not thought of initially.

One of the concerns was the fact that the data warehouse was planned to be updated everyday. ETL processes usually take time and interfere with the sources systems; therefore, the updates are usually done as infrequently as possible. For Prudonia, with a relatively low crime rate, the systems were not enormously busy, and the number of daily transactions was not huge, but still doing the updates as frequent as every 5 minutes, as some of the police departments suggested, was not possible.

Really, combining real-time updates with the data warehousing approach was not feasible.

Another concern brought up by the participants was the fact that the data warehouse solution would be too much for their needs. Their immediate requirements specify real-time search functionality only. They never requested any aggregated reports or business analysis. Certainly, having analytical tools sounded nice in the very beginning, but the effort was considered too extensive when the approach came under scrutiny.

The whole solution now looked too heavy and, with the trust problems, did not look feasible at all.

Another approach – data federation

Let's take a look at the following diagram of the data warehouse, originally proposed by IT experts:

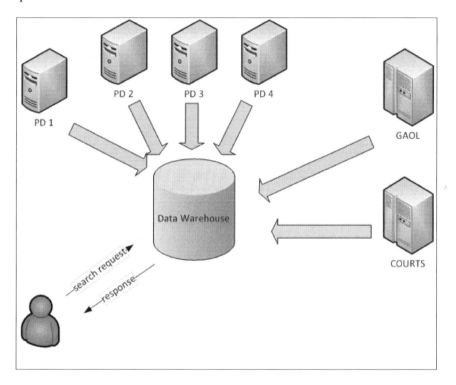

The workflow on this diagram has two big steps. First, all information from data sources is uploaded to the data warehouse where it is aggregated. Secondly, a user issues a search request and gets back a response with the aggregated result.

What if we retrieve the data from the source systems and aggregate it every time a search request is issued? In that case, we replace the data warehouse with a middle-tier system that retrieves the data from the source systems and aggregates it, as shown in the following diagram:

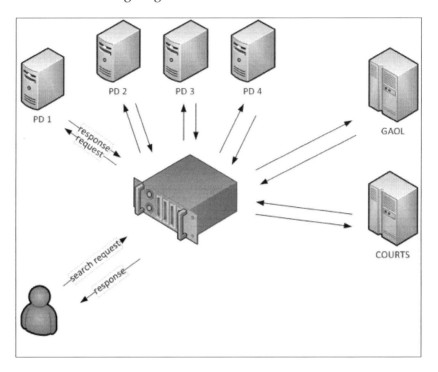

The proposed approach is called **data federation**.

Pattern description

A federated database is a set of distributed databases that can be accessed through a level of abstraction. The data can be accessed through a unified interface every time the request is sent. Aggregated data does not have to be stored longer than for the time of the transaction.

> Another term used equally with the federated database, is **virtual database**.

The pattern has the following features:

- The data sources can be (and usually are) heterogeneous and distributed. Each source's system has to provide an interface that does not have to be unified. It is critical though that the data retrieval time from each individual data source is insignificant. With legacy systems, to improve this characteristic, a staging area can be added to the slow source system. This mixed model is sometimes called the **Embassy Model**.

- The data is owned and controlled by the source systems. The retrieval mechanism at the source system can implement business rules deciding what data should be returned and when. It can implement an appropriate privacy approach, returning more confidential data, only to requests with higher privileges. Some data can be completely hidden if necessary.

- The data in the middle tier is not persisted. The data is aggregated on the fly and never stored. Data encryption may be somewhat a challenge as with any aggregation.

- The data sources can be (and are better) accessed asynchronously. This significantly improves the performance of the overall system. Some requirements may state that retrieving just some data would be still valuable. In that case, the timeout for accessing the data sources can be minimized.

- Data traffic should be encrypted. The level of encryption is dictated by the industry. Transport-level encryption, such as SSL/TLS, is mandatory.

- The middle tier should imply a canonical data schema that is exposed to the clients. Depending on the requirements, the canonical schema may represent the union as well as the intersection of the data. Data transformation operations in the middle tier can be as complex as the ones we discussed while talking about data warehouses.

Key requirements

The project is interdepartmental, which means that the implementation of it will be done by either a government IT department or by a group created under the state CIO.

The IT department does not have a lot of history and, most likely, will hire external contractors for design and development.

The pilot project has to be developed fast, in six to eight months. The demonstration of the pilot project should convince all organizations to participate in the project.

The largest organizational problem is establishing trust between integration participants. The technology selection will barely affect this challenge.

Candidate architecture #1 – BizTalk Server

Every data request-response is an individual message. Therefore, BizTalk Server, the middle tier that deals with messages, is our first candidate.

Solution design aspects

BizTalk Server has several advantages that make it a strong candidate for this solution from the design perspective:

- BizTalk perfectly works with heterogeneous data sources. The number of included and third-party adapters is large, which enables working with different, even legacy data sources.

- BizTalk is a reliable technology that is based on the foundation of SQL Server. It has several capabilities that help easily achieve high availability; it is designed for high volume.

 Note that data persistence in BizTalk is quite a disadvantage in this case since the data owners don't want the sensitive data to be persisted anywhere in the middle tier.

Solution implementation aspects

The visual interface helps with implementation, but the learning curve for the team will still be steep. BizTalk is a complex tool and learning it from scratch would take a significant time.

However, BizTalk has native mapping and transformation capabilities, which will reduce the development time.

Solution operations aspects

BizTalk is not an easy tool to deal with. It requires some training and potentially buying third-party maintenance tools.

Organizational aspects

BizTalk solutions are built on top of SQL Server, which means buying additional licenses. In order to provide high availability, for example, by means of clustering, even more additional licenses are required.

Solution evaluation

If the organization were a BizTalk shop with a lot of experience with BizTalk, using BizTalk could have been advantageous. However, high licensing costs and a steep learning curve make it less attractive. The following table shows the results of our assessment:

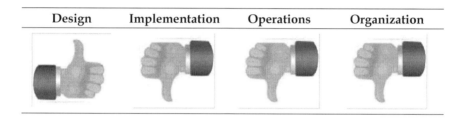

Design	Implementation	Operations	Organization

Candidate Architecture #2 – .NET

Another approach that we would consider is developing the middle tier from scratch using .NET and C#. An external development team should be hired since the IT department does not have enough resources.

Solution design aspects

Designing a high-availability, high-performance solution from scratch can be a challenge. However, in the .NET community, many patterns and best practices have been established to help with these tasks. Data extraction from sources would be a real challenge since all data connections have to be developed (no adapters as in the BizTalk case).

Solution implementation aspects

With a proper design and a highly skilled team, writing the code does not sound extremely difficult. However, this is a time-consuming task and very likely expensive.

Solution operations aspects

Running the application and performing its maintenance and support would require building additional tools.

Organizational aspects

In order to develop the solution, the IT department has to hire external contractors. It may also need to invest in the Visual Studio licenses.

However, solving the biggest challenge of the solution — trust concerns — might be easier with the solution whose development is under control.

Solution evaluation

The most challenging part of the work is the solution design. Performance, security, and reliability don't come as a part of a package. However, writing .NET code has the advantage of having complete control of the solution, which is important when the integration participants have very limited trust in each other. Have a look at the following table:

Design	Implementation	Operations	Organization

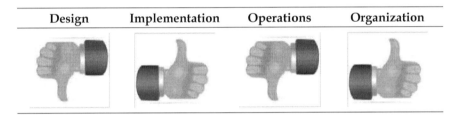

Architecture selection

Making a decision in this case is a very difficult process. All candidate architectures have probably more disadvantages than advantages.

However, since there are many unknowns, complex organizational dynamics, and the need to have more control over the solution, we recommend developing the solution as a .NET application.

The components are described in the following table:

Component	Benefits/Risks
BizTalk	**Benefits** • Has an extensive library of adapters and enables integration with heterogeneous data sources • Reliable and extensible technology • Has a native mapping and transformation capability **Risks** • No previous expertise • Needs significant investment of time and resources • Persists data in the middle tier
.NET development	**Benefits** • With a proper design, business logic can be easily implemented • Total control over the solution • Does not persist data in the middle tier **Risks** • Designing high-availability, high-performance solutions can be a challenge

Download the code of the WCF service that works as a middle tier and provides some basic security and two data sources, to see the sample implementation. The code can be downloaded from the Packt site at `www.packtpub.com`.

Lessons learned

• In a very complex, organizational situation, when integration participants feel a lack of trust in each other, data warehouses are not the ideal solution for data aggregation. Using data federation for data-sharing tasks is preferred when there is no actual need of persisting data in the middle tier.

Summary

In this chapter, we talked about many facets of information integration architecture. We discussed file transfer, shared databases, data migration, and data synchronization. We looked into the ETL pattern and data federation. We have chosen leading technologies and provided working examples for some patterns.

With this chapter, we completed the discussion on integration patterns. In the next chapter, we'll talk about workflows, both with and without human intervention.

11
Workflow Patterns

In business process automation and system integration, often you may hear about workflows. However, if you asked several professionals what workflows are, you will get a number of different answers. And this is no surprise since the concept of workflow is decades old and is used in many industries. In software-intensive systems, workflows can be as simple as steps to complete and approve a document or as complex as tasks involved in managing a long-running process between different departments or organizations.

Nevertheless, there are some commonalities in all these approaches to workflow systems, which are described as follows:

- Workflows are composed of a series of steps. Each step represents a task or an activity that has to be performed under some circumstances.
- The steps can be performed in parallel or in sequence.
- Execution of a specific step may depend on the input to that step.
- Action in each step may use some rules specific to that step.
- These rules can determine which step should be executed next.
- Each step may produce an output. The output may be used as an input for other steps.
- Workflows can be stateful as well as stateless.

In this chapter, we'll consider two different types of workflows: fully automated workflows and workflows that require human intervention.

Fully automated workflows

The idea of automatic execution of software components is as old as computer programming itself. In a sense, every computer program executes a workflow running its modules step-by-step. However, this execution does not require additional tools and methods.

In system integration, every time one system passes the control to another system, there is a chance of building a general workflow system. Steps executed in this workflow can be run completely independent of human intervention. The decision about executing a certain step can be made based on configuration, business rules, and the output of previous steps.

Let's take another look at data federation discussed in the previous chapter. We shall focus on the required workflow rather than data exchange.

Use case – a single dashboard view

Sam MacColl Financial is a financial services organization based in Perth, Scotland. They focus on providing quality individual and corporate financial services with a special attention to individual retirement planning. They employ over 3,000 employees in Scotland. The majority of their branches are in Scotland, but they are slowly expanding into England and parts of Ireland and Wales.

The company's focus on long-term buy-and-hold investments has meant that their retirement and investment products fared comparatively well in the subprime downturn due to limited exposure. This means that they have grown rapidly over the last 18 months and anticipate further growth. They found that many customers take multiple products from the Sam MacColl portfolio; they want to encourage this as it increases "stickiness".

They have had online banking available for checking and savings account products since their inception, but they now want to add their other products to enable self-service. Users increasingly expect an available, self-service portal that provides a consolidated view across all products. Their current Internet Bank application is coded in ASP and calls ASMX Web services from the application tier to access savings and checking account information. The current portal does not provide a summary view for checking, savings, and retirement account information as users have to log in to a separate portal to access this information.

Recently, customer complaints have risen, and the company wants to take action to provide the best possible customer experience. They want to expand and provide a consistent dashboard for their checking, savings, and retirement account information. They would like a platform that provides extensibility; specifically, the ability to add new products and accounts to the dashboard with minimal code changes. A flexible solution will enable the company to provide a better portal, which in turn, will enable customers to get a fast and real-time view of their financial products, thereby improving customer satisfaction.

Sam MacColl's major systems run on the Windows platform and have a web service facade to which they can connect. As part of this project, they will be upgrading these to WCF. They do have a sizeable number of .NET developers and own some of Microsoft's major server platforms such as SharePoint Server and Exchange Server. The downstream systems that hold financial information are standardized on SQL Server backend databases and have the same security model; for example, they restrict each customer to have access only to their own data and provide internal employees with minimum possible information necessary to perform their job.

Sam MacColl has adopted a **buy versus build** strategy, where they prefer using existing, well-tested frameworks and products with extensibility points instead of custom-building their own solutions from the ground up. They try to structure their solutions in a very loosely coupled manner using a common, open standard wherever possible to minimize development effort and the ongoing supportability burden that comes from maintaining custom code. This is relevant in this use case as it is expected that the Internet Bank application will need to expand and add additional systems integration as the number of self-service products increases. As a first step, the Sam MacColl architecture team has asked to see a critical comparison of different architectures against their requirements. In the recommended approach, they would like to see a proof of concept, which demonstrates a sample dashboard with an end-to-end implementation.

Key requirements

The following are the key requirements for a new software solution:

- A single dashboard view for all financial service products that the customers have.

- An online banking application that is easier to maintain and requires less custom code.

Additional facts

There are some additional details gathered after the initial use case was shared with the technical team. The requirements derived from this include the following:

- The frontend does not have to know where the information comes from; it should only contact a single point.
- All calls should be made in a service-oriented fashion.
- The system needs to be able to scale to more than one million users over a 24-hour period, which equates to approximately 12 users per second.
- During peak usage, which occurs at the beginning of a day and during the evening, the maximum number of users is 25 per second.
- The response time is critical for the dashboard page as this is the page used by 90 percent of customers every day. They would like 95 percent of users to receive a response within three seconds and 99 percent of them to receive a response within five seconds.
- The bank would like to have a consistent workflow platform that supports synchronous, asynchronous, short, and long-running workflows.
- The system must provide tracking and monitoring capabilities.
- The system must provide exception management at every stage.
- Initially, the system must not only address the dashboard requirement, but also must provide the capabilities necessary to add additional services to the Internet Bank, including the following services:
  - **Handling transactional workflows**: This is a requirement for Sam MacColl Financial to implement workflows that require guaranteed once-only delivery (for example, payment workflows).
  - **Long-running asynchronous workflows**: The bank is considering implementing an end-to-end mortgage application; in future, many of the transactions required in these types of processes can be long running and may require human intervention or approval. The system should be able to support these capabilities.
  - **Real-time updates**: The system must be capable of providing real-time updates if payments are implemented on the system.

The Scatter-Gather pattern

In this scenario, we need to receive a single inbound request. Then, based on the content in that request call, several backend services gather information about the customer and then correlate the responses, aggregate them, and finally send them in a single response message. The web application will then display their personalized information to them.

The logical choice is to use an aggregator, which is responsible for the collection of requests, performing transformations (if they are required), and returning the response. All of this also needs to be done in the shortest possible time, as users are not willing to wait more than three to five seconds for this type of information. This pattern is commonly referred to as the **Scatter-Gather pattern**.

In the Scatter-Gather pattern, information is broadcast to multiple recipients and then the responses are reaggregated into a single message. An aggregator component is responsible for receiving the initial request message, broadcasting in an appropriate format to all the target systems, and finally, combining the results of these individual but related messages and returning them as a single response so that they can be processed as a whole. Typically, in this pattern, the aggregator is implemented as a separate tier, so it can abstract the logic necessary to maintain the overall message flow and handle any exceptions from any of the systems queried.

This pattern is particularly successful if you follow service-oriented concepts and require a loosely coupled, scalable aggregator that can be reused by different applications across your organization. As the calling application only calls a single method on the aggregator, the source of the information and how it is extracted is abstracted from that tier. This enables additional targets or sources of information to be added with no update required on the client side. The following diagram depicts a high-level representation of what this could look like for Sam MacColl Financial. As is evident from the diagram, separating the aggregator from the consumer of the aggregator (the Internet Bank application) creates a layer of abstraction between them and the endpoints, if properly designed. It also means that the consumers need not worry about implementing any logic that is specific to the interface that the backend systems provide. The aggregator in this example makes calls to the three target systems in parallel:

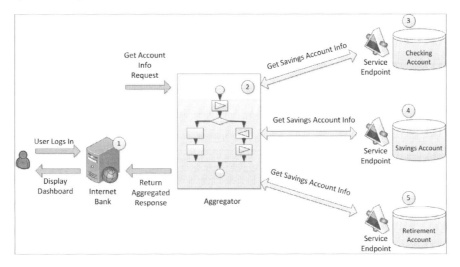

Factors affecting implementation details

As we have discussed so far in this chapter, there are many key factors that need to be taken into consideration while implementing this pattern. Here, we are going to outline the ones that we consider important, while evaluating solutions for this type of problem with customers. The factors that we consider important are as follows:

- **Completeness**: This determines when we are ready to publish the aggregated response message. Whether returning of partial data is useful or not is perhaps the most important factor to consider while implementing this pattern. This will depend on the scenario and the client's requirements. For example, in a price-comparison engine that queries hundreds of sources, partial data is likely to be valuable and relevant. In cases where results from multiple sources need to be merged to one coherent response, partial data may not be useful.

- **Aggregation strategy**: The strategy you use depends primarily on the completeness criteria and SLAs that the aggregator needs to meet. The two most common scenarios we have seen are **Timeout**, where the aggregator waits for a specified duration of time for responses and then either returns the response or an exception to the client, and **Wait for all**, which is used when an incomplete order is not meaningful. Typically, it is important that the aggregator knows the expected number of responses and has appropriate exception handling capabilities. An exception to this is where the aggregation concludes based on some external event; for example, the end of a trading day may conclude the aggregation of the value of all stock trades in that period.

- **Aggregation algorithm**: Typically, there will be a requirement to sort or condense the data in some way. Factors that affect this include the size of the aggregated response that is to be returned and whether the user is interested in all of the responses or a small subset of the responses. One extreme would be if there is a single best answer; for example, in an auction site, the seller may only be interested in the highest confirmed bid. If a larger amount of data is being returned, it may need to be sorted by one or more criteria; hotel booking websites are a good example of this. Factors for consideration include price, facilities, and distance from local amenities. Whether the data should be condensed depends on the type of data being returned — numeric data is best suited for this. For example, while analyzing sales data, it is often the volume and average order value that is of interest. If you decide to condense the data and only return a subset, you should consider whether you wish to archive the complete selected data for later evaluation.

- **Exception handling and appropriate timeout**: Implementation of this factor depends on the aggregation strategy algorithm and completeness criteria for your system. Even in a **wait for all** aggregation strategy, it is unlikely that waiting indefinitely is the desired behavior, especially in a synchronous request-response scenario. A timeout and exception handler should be implemented so that the aggregator can handle all possible scenarios, including one of the endpoints being unavailable; for example, due to system outage. If an exception occurs, it must return an appropriate response message to the client, and you should also log this in the appropriate log.

- **Monitoring and tracing**: This is distinct from exception handling; it provides the ability to monitor and trace the aggregator. If implemented correctly, this can be used in a number of ways, such as providing average processing times for the aggregator over a 24-hour period, or enabling system administrators to determine the progress of in-process operations. This can be provided by the following platforms: Microsoft AppFabric for Windows Server provides monitoring capabilities, so does BizTalk Server, which enhances this further with the option of implementing **Business Activity Monitoring (BAM)**.

- **Type of response to return (the data format)**: How you represent the data to consumers is an important consideration. Using WCF ensures that you make appropriate use of message contracts, data contracts, and the bindings it provides so that you get the right trade-off among performance, client-side operations that are available on the dataset, and interoperability.

- **Number of calls versus expected usage**: Returning smaller datasets typically places less load on the backend systems that are queried, requires a smaller payload size, less CPU overhead, and can provide better performance as measured by response time. However, if implementing this approach requires that each user now make multiple calls to the aggregator component's operations, this may actually place more overhead on the system and provide a poorer perceived performance. Consider the scenario where someone logs in to their online bank, views their summary page of all account balances, and then looks at the detailed statement of one account, for example, their credit card account. There are two succinct operations that are performed here. Whether all this information should be returned by the aggregator in a single response or it could require two calls, is an important design decision to make. Typically, this depends on the normal usage of the system and the customer requirements. Sometimes, historical usage or trending data shows that a majority of logged-in customers will examine only the dashboard view and then log out. In that case, by only returning the condensed summary data, you will be able to minimize the load on the backend systems and improve response time.

- **Correlation**: This is handled implicitly in the platform; for example, if you are calling synchronous two-way services using a request-response port in BizTalk, you will need to define this yourself based on the Message ID or some other unique value.

- **Processing (parallel or sequential)**: Unless sequential processing is a typical requirement, an aggregator should perform all backend calls in parallel to minimize the processing time and latency.

- **Durability of data**: You should determine whether the data is transient or transactional. Normally, in the Scatter-Gather pattern, the data is transient; for example, if the user does not receive a response, they will simply retry. This pattern is intended to service, primarily, read requests from multiple systems. If you are performing a transaction such as a payment, you might want to consider implementing this as a separate component and requiring the client to call this. The Internet Bank system, mentioned previously, opted to take this approach. They implemented a single orchestration as their Scatter-Gather aggregator, and then had separate messaging components if any stock trade or funds transfer was initialized. If transactional processing semantics are required, you should determine whether the platform supports this; for example, the BizTalk orchestration engine that guarantees no loss of messages.

Candidate architecture #1 – BizTalk Server

BizTalk is Microsoft's Enterprise Integration tool and has a robust messaging and workflow (orchestration) engine. MacColl bank is already, largely a Microsoft-based technology firm. BizTalk provides full and complete integration with Microsoft and other heterogeneous technology through its adapter framework. For the purpose of this analysis, the assumption will be that BizTalk is not already in use within the organization.

We can take a look at the decision framework as it relates to BizTalk to see whether a BizTalk-based solution is a fit for this use case.

Solution design aspects

The system needs to be capable of processing one million messages over a 24-hour period. The peak load represents 25 messages per second. While dealing with requirements like this, it is always good to have a margin of safety in terms of throughput ceiling. Therefore, this system will require a robust and proven host, which can scale to meet these throughput requirements and beyond. To implement this pattern, we would require the **BizTalk Orchestration Engine**, which can easily be used for service aggregation and provide support for correlation. BizTalk also has the ability to expose an orchestration through a SOAP or WCF endpoint.

Each call to the backend services could be implemented in an inline fashion using a .NET helper class to instantiate a WCF channel factory or call the service and retrieve the response. The more traditional approach is to use the logical request or response ports that BizTalk server provides to do this. Making the calls in an inline fashion may be beneficial in this scenario, as it reduces the number of persistence points required and also the round trips via MessageBox.

From a performance perspective, recent benchmarks by the Microsoft BizTalk Customer Advisory Team demonstrated that BizTalk can scale to process tens of millions of messages per day using well-tuned middle-tier hardware. Specifically, for two-way calls they have obtained over 60 messages per second for a Scatter-Gather pattern that made five backend calls. These tests were performed on mid-tier Enterprise hardware, which is available to the customer. This gives us a sufficient margin of safety as it is more than double our peak requirements. BizTalk Server also provides a comprehensive monitoring infrastructure with out-of-the-box built-in capabilities and the Business Activity Monitoring framework, which can be used to provide a customized, business-centric monitoring solution.

Solution implementation aspects

Sam MacColl Financial is predominantly a Microsoft technology-based organization. The assumption here is that they do not already have BizTalk running; therefore, if the decision was made to use this particular product, they would also have to bear the additional infrastructure and solution support necessary to support a system like this.

Given that they have already made extensive use of other Microsoft technologies, they have some of the platform skills required. However, BizTalk is quite a complicated product to understand and maintain; therefore, they would need to invest in training some key staff to establish one or more **subject matter experts (SMEs)** within their architect, development, and operations teams. Given that they currently do not have the in-house expertise and the amount of money that would be required for training, unless they have planned broader needs and uses of BizTalk, it would be a negative factor in this use case.

Solution operations aspects

As stated, Sam MacColl Financial does not have an existing BizTalk implementation. Therefore, they would need to invest in training their operational team, putting processes in place to support BizTalk as well as the necessary infrastructure. Supporting BizTalk requires a rather unique set of skills.

Solution operations are a negative factor in using BizTalk for this use case.

Organizational aspects

Sam MacColl Financial does not already have an existing BizTalk platform that they can leverage, and they do not have the experience in running and maintaining this system. Therefore, this is a negative factor in using BizTalk for this use case.

Solution evaluation

As our evaluation shows, this solution has a lot of weaknesses in implementation and operations. There are also some negative organizational aspects, as shown in the following table:

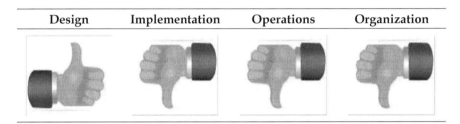

Design	Implementation	Operations	Organization

Candidate architecture #2 – .NET WF service

Microsoft AppFabric for Windows Server provides a rich host for **Windows Communication Foundation (WCF)** and **Windows Workflow Foundation (WF)** applications. The AppFabric host provides supporting services, tools, and diagnostics to make hosting and managing services simpler. The WF service would leverage the existing capabilities that Sam MacColl has in .NET. WCF is something they are already planning to use for their backend services; WF is capable of providing the durable workflow tier that they need in order to implement the aggregator.

The aggregator could be implemented as a workflow service. In .NET 4, workflow services have been expanded to provide more features and easier integration with WCF endpoints. WCF supports several out-of-the-box bindings, and additional bindings are available through several sources, including the BizTalk Adapter Pack. Standardizing on WCF would, therefore, allow them to communicate with their existing backend services (which will move to a WCF interface), and it will also add connectivity to other systems that they want to aggregate in the future.

Adding additional services would be done in a visual drag-and-drop design environment, minimizing the development time. Any required message transformation could be done in custom activities. The **Parallel Actions** shape provides the capabilities to call systems in a synchronous manner, and a timeout can be implemented within the shape to enforce SLAs for maximum client-wait duration. In addition to this, persistence is provided in the .NET Framework through the SQL Workflow Instance Store. This allows durability requirements to be met if required at a later date, for example, if transactional data such as payments is to be processed by AppFabric.

Now, we will look at the decision framework and evaluate the workflow service as an implementation fit for this use case.

Solution design aspects

As stated previously, the throughput requirements equate to a peak load of 25 messages per second. Implementing this pattern would require a single aggregator workflow service that must fulfill the following tasks:

- Expose a request-response endpoint to the client
- Call the backend systems and aggregate the responses
- Perform any necessary translation
- Implement timeouts to ensure that client SLAs were met
- Send the aggregated responses back to the original client

The backend services that need to be integrated are WCF based; by adding service references to these endpoints, the logic is automatically encapsulated into a WF activity, which can be used within the aggregator workflow. Adding service references is a straightforward process and means that if additional WCF endpoints need to be added, it can be done quickly and easily. WF also provides the ability to write code-based activities that can also be used to encapsulate any specific code, such as code transformation. Any code-based activities can be defined in a separate assembly, which allows this functionality to be reused across different workflows and applications.

By utilizing AppFabric as a host, one can take advantage of the scale-out capabilities that it provides. This would enable Sam MacColl Financial to scale-out their aggregator tier if it became necessary due to throughput requirements.

Solution implementation aspects

Sam MacColl Financial develops complex solutions on .NET, and they will be moving their backend services to WCF as a part of their new Internet Bank project. They already have a large installed base of Windows Server 2008 R2 and have gradually, over the last six months, begun rolling out Windows Server 2012. AppFabric, available as a free download, is an extension on top of IIS/WAS, and the development team already has extensive experience in developing web solutions on the .NET platform.

Workflow services will reduce the coding effort required to build this application as the aggregator can be implemented without a lot of custom code. This will speed up development and reduce testing time compared to what it would be if they were to fully customize all this logic and hosting capability in C#.

Solution operations aspects

Sam MacColl Financial already has an existing Windows Server infrastructure on which they can deploy AppFabric. Supporting workflow systems are paradigm shifts for many operations staff, so training will be required.

Organizational aspects

As stated, Sam MacColl Financial already has an existing Windows infrastructure that can support AppFabric and .NET workflow services development. While this is a new technology and will require some training, it is not expected that this will be a significant burden. Therefore, this solution represents a good fit for the organization.

Solution evaluation

This approach looks much better. There are some operational concerns, but otherwise it looks great, as shown in the following table:

Design	Implementation	Operations	Organization

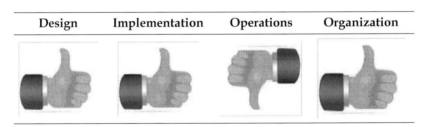

Architecture selection

Let's look at how these candidate architecture technologies stack up against each other. We can break down the primary benefits and risks of each choice in the following manner:

Technology	Benefits/risks
BizTalk Server	**Benefits** • This has many out-of-the-box adapters, which means connecting to the majority of systems is only a configuration task • This provides durability throughout with the Message Box • This is an enterprise-class hosting infrastructure **Risks** • There are perceived large server footprints • There are significant upfront costs
.NET workflow service	**Benefits** • This is a lightweight, high throughput feature, and a rich host for .NET 4.5 Windows Workflow • This has debugging, monitoring, and exception handling capabilities of AppFabric • This provides load-balancing capabilities • This has implicit and explicit correlation capabilities • This provides persistence through a workflow persistence provider **Risks** • This is a perceived large server footprint • There are significant upfront costs

There are a number of key benefits of .NET 4.5 workflow services in this scenario. It meets all the requirements with no additional upfront cost over and above Windows license fees. BizTalk provides a lot of additional features, which are not necessarily required in this scenario, where the priority is on processing transient data. These include BAM, the Business Rules Engine, and the host of adapters it provides. These are valuable features, but at present, this scenario does not require them.

Therefore, in evaluating these options against the problem scenario, the .NET WF service is the most appropriate choice. Although both BizTalk Server and a .NET WF service meet the necessary solution and design aspects, the organization already has the infrastructure necessary to support the latter scenario with no additional licensing costs. As they have no firm plans to use BizTalk and do not require any of the additional functionality, such as BAM or complex mapping, the latter solution becomes the prominent and chosen candidate.

Building the solution

For this solution demonstration, we will implement three WCF backend services that represent the checking, payment, and retirement account systems; these services will have data contracts, but will be "stubbed out". We will then implement a workflow service, which will be our aggregator, and also a sample ASP.NET page which will represent our web tier. A key aspect of this solution architecture is to follow service-oriented principles and keep our design as loosely coupled as possible. Within the organization, passing data by a data contract is acceptable; if we were interfacing with external systems, we would implement message transformation. The components of the solution are listed as follows:

- **Internet Bank**: the ASP.NET page
- **Aggregator**: the .NET workflow
- **Checking Account**: the WCF service
- **Savings Account**: the WCF service
- **Retirement Account**: the WCF service

You can see the main components of the solution depicted on the diagram in the *The Scatter-Gather pattern* section.

Implementing this solution demonstration will allow us to evaluate .NET capabilities to implement the Scatter-Gather pattern. For simplicity purposes, we will not implement a timeout in this workflow.

Setup

Initial setup is needed to simulate the backend services. For demo purposes, the backend checking, saving, and retirement account services will be implemented as separate projects, each containing a single WCF service contract with an arbitrary operation implementation to return an object representing the account. A separate data contracts project has been used to define the `Customer` and `Account` classes that we will use to exchange data between different parts of the application. The `DataContract` attribute of these classes allows WCF to serialize the objects and pass them efficiently between different tiers.

It is good practice to deploy common data contracts and types to separate assemblies so that they can be reused within different applications in an organization.

This project also contains an empty aggregator project, which will host our workflow service, and a web tier project, which will host our ASP.NET page. In this solution demonstration, you will deploy the backend WCF services that have been provided and then implement a workflow service that serves as our aggregator. Finally, we will create an ASP.NET page that will consume our aggregator service. Perform the following steps:

1. First, let's begin with the setup. Before starting, you will need to ensure you have the following software on your machine:

    ◦ Visual Studio 2012

    ◦ The Microsoft .NET 4.5 framework

    ◦ AppFabric 1.1 for Windows Server. For the detailed description of AppFabric installation, refer to `http://msdn.microsoft.com/en-us/library/hh334245(v=azure.10).aspx`

2. Launch Visual Studio and open the `SammMaccolBank.sln` solution from the book sample code. You will see the following projects:

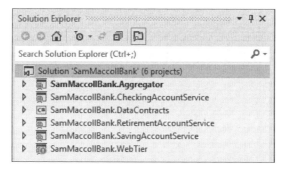

3. Build and publish each of the following projects:

    ◦ `SamMaccollBank.CheckingAccountService`

    ◦ `SamMaccollBank.RetirementAccountService`

    ◦ `SamMaccollBank.SavingAccountService`

4. The setup is now complete.

For testing, you can use the WCF Test Client located under `Program Files\ Microsoft Visual Studio 11.0\Common7\IDE` (or `Program Files (x86)\ Microsoft Visual Studio 11.0\Common7\IDE` for 64-bit systems).

Building the service aggregator workflow service

So, you have successfully deployed the backend WCF services and utilized the WCF Test Client tool to test and verify the functionality of each of these. We will now implement the service aggregator workflow service.

Setting up the project

Perform the following steps to set up the project:

1. Launch Visual Studio 2012 and open the `SamMaccollBank.sln` solution from `<Installation Directory>\SamMaccollBank\`.

2. Right-click on **References** for the `SamMaccollBank.Aggregator` project, and add a reference to `SamMaccollBank.DataContracts`. This will allow you to use the data contracts defined within this project while exchanging data with the backend WCF services.

3. Now, you need to add a service reference to each of our backend WCF services. Right-click on the `SamMaccollBank.Aggregator` project and select **Add Service Reference**. The address should be `http://localhost/CheckingAccountService/CheckingAccount.svc`, and the namespace should be `CheckingAccountService`. Click on **OK** to add the reference.

Repeat the previous process, adding service references for the retirement and savings account services using the following details:

Service	Address	Namespace
Retirement	`http://localhost/retirementaccountservice/retirementaccount.svc`	`RetirementAccountService`
Savings	`http://localhost/SavingAccountService/SavingAccount.svc`	`SavingAccountService`

Implementing the AccountAggregator workflow

Perform the following steps to implement the AccountAggregator workflow:

1. Once you have added these service references, and you have rebuilt the project, open the `AccountAggregator.xamlx` workflow. In the toolbox, you should see three new custom activities, which have been generated and can be used to call the backend services.

2. Now we shall implement the required logic for the `AccountAggregator.` `xamlx` workflow. Within the workflow, click on the **Imports** tab and enter the `SamMaccollBank.DataContracts` namespace.

3. Now drag-and-drop a **Sequence** shape onto the empty workflow space. Change the display name from **Sequence** to `AccountAggregatorScope`.

4. Our service will receive an object of the `Customer` type and will return a sorted dictionary of the `<String, Account>` type. Because all objects are modeled using our common base class `Account`, we will use a single instance of the `System.Collections.Generic.SortedDictionary` class to return the aggregated account information to the consumer of the service. To create these two objects, click on **AccountAggregatorScope**, then click on the **Variables** tab, and create the following two objects. Note that to create both of these objects, you will need to select **Browse for type...** while selecting the variable type.

Name	Variable Type	Scope	Default
current Customer	Customer (Browse for SamMaccollBank.DataContracts to select)	AccountAggregat orScope	
account Dictionary	Dictionary <String, Account> (Type in Dictionary in the **Type Name** to select the System.Collections.Generic.Dictionary class)	AccountAggregat orScope	New Dictionary (Of String, Account)

5. We will also need variables for the request and response messages to the three backend services that the account aggregator is consuming. The types were already created for us when we added the service reference. By clicking on **Browse for type ...**, you can see the following:

   ° `SamMaccollBank.Aggregator.CheckingAccountService`

   ° `SamMaccollBank.Aggregator.RetirementAccountService`

   ° `SamMaccollBank.Aggregator.SavingAccountService`

   For each of these, there is a request message type, which is of the `<OperationName>Request` format and a response message type with the `<OperationName>Response` format.

6. As we have a project reference and access to the data contracts assembly, our generated classes use these types. This enables us to pass the `currentCustomer` object to each of the backend service-request operations as an input variable. This is one of the advantages of having a shared data contracts assembly. We can also create some variables of the `Account` type to represent the responses. Now create the following variables by clicking on **AccountAggregatorScope**:

Name	Variable Type	Scope
checkingResponse	Account	AccountAggregatorScope
savingResponse	Account	AccountAggregatorScope
retirementResponse	Account	AccountAggregatorScope

7. Now add a **Parallel** shape to `AccountAggregatorScope` and change its display name to `Aggregate Call`.

8. Within the **Aggregate Call** shape, add three sequence shapes, which should be side by side. From left to right, name them `Checking Account`, `Saving Account`, and `Retirement Account`, respectively.

9. Within the `Checking Account` shape, add a `GetCheckingAccount` activity from the toolbox.

10. You now need to define the input parameters. Click on the `GetCheckingAccount` activity you just added. In the **Properties** window, you will see a couple of parameters that need to be configured, including `Customer`, which allows you to specify the input object for this parameter. `GetCheckingAccountResult` allows you to specify where the result of this service operation call will be stored. We will use the variables that we defined earlier. Configure them as shown in the following table:

Name	Variable Type
Customer	currentCustomer
GetCheckingAccountResults	checkingResponse

11. This should look like the following screenshot:

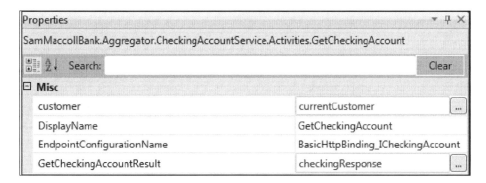

12. Below the `GetCheckingAccount` activity, add an `InvokeMethod` activity and name it `Add Checking to Dictionary`. Assign the `accountDictionary` value to the **TargetObject** property. Assign the `Add` value to the **MethodName** property. To configure **Parameters**, click on the ellipsis button. Add the parameters as shown in the following table:

Direction	Type	Value
In	String	checking
In	Account	checkingResponse

13. Within the `Saving Account` shape, add a `GetSavingAccount` activity from the toolbox.

14. You now need to define the input parameters. Click on the `GetSavingAccount` activity you just added. In the **Properties** window, you will see a couple of parameters that need to be configured. `Customer` allows you to specify the input object for this parameter. `GetSavingAccountResult` allows you to specify where the result of this service operation call will be stored. We will use the variables that we defined earlier. Configure them as shown in the table:

Name	Variable Type
Customer	currentCustomer
GetSavingAccountResult	savingResponse

15. Below the GetSavingAccount activity, add an InvokeMethod activity and name it Add Saving to Dictionary. Assign the accountDictionary value to the **TargetObject** property. Assign the Add value to the **MethodName** property. To configure the **Parameters** click on the ellipsis button. Add the parameters as shown in the next table:

Direction	Type
In	String
In	Account

16. Within the Retirement Account shape, add a GetRetirementAccount activity from the toolbox.

17. You now need to define the input parameters. Click on the GetRetirementAccount activity you just added. In the **Properties** window, you will see a couple of parameters that need to be configured including Customer, which allows you to specify the input object for this parameter. GetRetirementAccountResult allows you to specify where the result of this service operation call will be stored. We will use the variables that we defined earlier. Configure them as shown in the following table:

Name	Variable Type
Customer	currentCustomer
GetRetirementAccountResults	retirementResponse

18. Below the GetRetirementAccount activity, add an InvokeMethod activity and name it Add Retirement to Dictionary. Assign the accountDictionary value to the **TargetObject** property. Assign the Add value to the **MethodName** property. To configure **Parameters**, click on the ellipsis button. Add the parameters as shown in the following table:

Direction	Type
In	String
In	Account

19. Now drag-and-drop a ReceiveAndSendReply activity at the top of your workflow just inside the AccountAggregatorScope. This will add a new **Sequence** activity, which contains a Receive and a SendReplyToReceive activity.

20. Create a new variable called `handle` with the following property:

Name	Variable Type	Scope
handle	CorrelationHandle	AccountAggregatorScope
savingResponse	Account	AccountAggregatorScope
retirementResponse	Account	AccountAggregatorScope

21. Drag the `Receive` and `SendReplyToReceive` activities above the **Sequence** activity (but still within `AccountAggregatorScope`). Now, delete the empty **Sequence** activity.

22. Drag the `SendReplyToReceive` activity to the bottom of the workflow, and place it just outside the `Aggregate Call` parallel activity.

23. Click on the **Receive** activity and change **DisplayName** to `Receive Customer Request`. Set the following properties, which represent the WCF service, operation, and parameter information for consumers of this workflow service. You should follow sensible naming conventions as you would while defining properties for code-based WCF services.

Property	Value
ServiceContractName	http://tempuri.org/IAccountAggregator
OperationName	GetCustomerAccount

24. To define the parameter information that the consumer will see, click on the ellipsis button of the **Content** property of the `Receive Customer Request` activity. Then, click on the **Parameters** radio button and set the following parameter:

Name	Type	Assign to
Customer	SamMaccollBank.DataContracts.Customer	currentCustomer

25. On the `Receive Customer Request` activity, you also need to make sure that the **CanCreateInstance** property is checked true. If this is not selected, the **Receive** activity will not be able to instantiate the workflow service. Then, click on the ellipsis button for the **CorrelationInitializers** property. Make sure that the initializer is set to the `handle` variable that we defined earlier.

26. Click on the `SendReplyToReceive` activity, and click on the ellipsis button of the **Content** property. Here, select the **Message** radio button and define the following properties. This defines the return type that consumers of the workflow service will receive for the operation we defined with the earlier `Receive` activity.

Property	Value
Message Data	accountDictionary
Message Type	System.Collections.Generic.Dictionary<System.String,SamMaccollBank.DataContracts.Account>

Your workflow is now complete.

Consuming the service aggregator workflow service with ASP.NET

We will now finish the implementation of the ASP.NET page using the following steps, which will take entry of customer details, consume our service, and then from the returned `Dictionary` object, will display those results to the end user:

1. You should now open the `SamMaccollBank.WebTier` project. This contains a stub implementation of the page we will implement.

2. Right-click on `Default.aspx` and select **View in Browser**. You should see a page similar to the following screenshot:

3. The page has implemented a number of `<asp:TextBox>`, `<asp:Button>`, and `<asp:Label>` objects. The `<asp:>` tag prefix indicates that there is either a local script or server-based dynamic content that needs to be processed; for example, the user will see the output of this dynamic ASP.NET call in their browser as standard HTML. You can see this by right-clicking on the `Default.aspx` page and selecting **View Markup**.

4. The `getAccountInfo` button has an `OnClick()` method call with `getCustomer_Click` specified. If you right-click on the `Default.aspx` page and select **View Code**, you can see the empty implementation of this method. If you view the page in the browser again and click on the **Get Account Details** button, you will see that nothing changes.

5. Add a reference in this project to `SamMaccollBank.DataContracts`. This will allow us to access the `Customer` and `Account` objects that we will need.

6. Also, add a service reference to the `Account` aggregator workflow service you just deployed and tested. The following are the settings:

Property	Value
Address	`http://localhost/aggregator/accountaggregator.xamlx`
Namespace	`AccountAggregator`

7. In the `Default.aspx.cs` file, add the following `using` statement:

```
Using SamMaccollBank.DataContracts;
```

8. In the `Default.aspx.cs` file, add the following implementation of `getCustomer_Click`:

```
public void getCustomer_Click(object sender, EventArgs e)
{
//Create the customer object
Customer customer = new Customer();
//Get the values from the text boxes and assign them to the
customer object properties
customer.FirstName = FirstName.Text;
customer.LastName = LastName.Text;
customer.CustomerID = CustomerID.Text;
customer.Address1 = Address1.Text;
customer.Address2 = Address2.Text;
customer.City = City.Text;
customer.State = State.Text;
customer.Zip = ZIP.Text;
//Create the client using the classes generated by our Service
Reference
```

```
AccountAggregator.AccountAggregatorClientsvcClient = new
AccountAggregator.AccountAggregatorClient();
AccountAggregator.GetCustomerAccounts request = new
AccountAggregator.GetCustomerAccounts();
request.customer = customer;
//Create dictionary object to store results
Dictionary<string, DataContracts.Account>accountDictionary =
svcClient.GetCustomerAccounts(request);
//Update Text boxes for each of the accounts
CheckingBalance.Text = accountDictionary["checking"].
CurrentBalance;
CheckingID.Text = accountDictionary["checking"].AccountID;
RetirementID.Text = accountDictionary["retirement"].AccountID;
RetirementBalance.Text = accountDictionary["retirement"].
CurrentBalance;
SavingBalance.Text = accountDictionary["saving"].CurrentBalance;
SavingID.Text = accountDictionary["saving"].AccountID;
}
```

9. Right-click again on `Default.aspx` and select **View in Browser**. Enter the customer details as was done previously and then click on the **Get Account Details** button. The account will be found and the account values will be populated.

Lessons learned

This solution, using Microsoft AppFabric 1.1 for Windows Server, WCF, and WF from .NET 4.5, demonstrated how workflow services can be used to orchestrate communication between backend service endpoints with minimal code. There was no need to tightly couple any of the components, and any of them could be reused by other applications. By utilizing well-defined data contracts, we can follow service-oriented practices and deploy loosely coupled applications. The Scatter-Gather pattern is a powerful pattern to implement if you want to provide a dashboard view for users from multiple sources. As well as for financial services, this can also be used to provide a single view about an individual across corporate systems: payroll, vacation, and so on. AppFabric is a very powerful host, and with some of its additional features such as persistence, it is something you should consider for use within your organization.

Human workflows

Some workflows cannot be fully automated and require people to participate. People can perform certain tasks, can initiate an automated step, or can assign a task to another person. Workflows with human intervention, or human workflows, have some specific features rarely or never found in fully automated workflows, which are described as follows:

- Automated steps are usually executed in a predictable timeframe. The workflow can have a timeout assigned to specific steps. Steps executed by humans have unpredictable latency.

- Some steps may require escalation if they cannot be completed. For example, if a person cannot execute a workflow task in a given time, it can be reassigned to another person.

- In some businesses, there is a possibility of long-running workflows. For example, insurance claim systems can run workflows for years waiting for human responses from certain steps.

- Execution of some steps may be triggered by humans and may not necessarily follow business rules.

Use case – repair/resubmit with human workflow

Bowl For Buddies is a nonprofit organization that sets up bowling parties to raise money for charity. As part of this effort, people raise money by going around houses and asking for donations. The donations are based on the number of pins the participants knock down during the bowling party (for example, $0.05 for each pin knocked down). During the house visit, donors give an e-mail address to which a donation request can be sent after the bowling event is over. In this e-mail, the donors receive the amount they need to pay and a link to the secure payment processor. Once the payment is made, Bowl For Buddies is notified.

Currently, much of this process is done manually. Data is collected on paper forms and entered into an Excel spreadsheet. Once the bowling event is over, a volunteer calculates the amount owed by each person and sends them an e-mail requesting payment. The existing Excel solution is being replaced by an internal SharePoint 2010 implementation.

Bowl For Buddies currently has a co-located website that runs on an ISP-supported Windows instance. Eventually, they want to be able to collect donations on the website. This will be a separate system similar to the way payments are currently collected and tracked. In terms of collection, donations through the website should follow the same process as donations though the house-to-house method.

The end-to-end payment collection process needs an overhaul. Bowl For Buddies is looking at developing e-mail and payment services to add automation to the collection process. As part of this process, they would like to develop a defined set of guidelines for the payment collection process with a goal of automating whatever is possible. The solution will need to work with the SharePoint 2010 site and should allow easy modification later to work with the website.

Bowl For Buddies does not have a large IT department or IT budget. The website they currently have is ASPX based and the e-mail and payment services they are building will be done through WCF services. They are willing to make investments in areas that aid in the donation collection process and that can be expanded to other branches if the company expands.

Key requirements

The following are the key requirements for a new software solution:

- Automate the process for processing donation pledges
- Include proactive notifications to staff for delinquent payments or data errors
- Work with an organization's future strategy around SharePoint and .NET solutions

Additional facts

We've identified some additional solution aspects that may help us decide on the right solution:

- SharePoint 2010 is used to maintain lists of customers, including their e-mail addresses and donation amounts.
- When an e-mail is invalid or returned, or a donor does not pay within a set period of time, a person will call to verify the intent of the donor.

- When the website is able to accept donations, it will use SQL Server to store user information.

- A general process for donation collection will include sending the user an e-mail, evaluating the results of sending the e-mail, waiting for payment, notifying manually if data needs to be corrected, updating the data for resubmission, and updating the system once payment is received.

Pattern description

Workflows are a series of steps that are related to each other. These steps may require interaction with outside resources. Typically, these resources are other systems, and the interaction can complete in an automated fashion without any human intervention. In some cases, the workflows require human intervention to fix and correct data, or the workflows are totally related to human processes such as a document approval process. When a workflow is related to human activity, it is known as a **human workflow**.

Human workflows can interact with people in several ways. Some of these include SharePoint, e-mail, text messaging, instant messenger, and web forms. What makes human workflows different from nonhuman workflows is the variability introduced by the human factor. People can be slow while they respond, out of town, unwell, or have other factors that prevent them from interacting with the workflow as expected. This adds a degree of uncertainty to all human workflows and ensures that they are typically long running.

Using automated workflows to model a business process allows for that process to be applied in the exact same way, time and again. This is difficult in a manual, people-driven progression of data collection and processing. In addition to repeatability, using a central environment to process these workflows provides a way to monitor many types of workflows. This allows you to analyze the collective results of all the workflows and increase efficiency by removing bottlenecks or streamlining unnecessary steps.

Modeling the Bowl For Buddies payment process in a workflow will help them apply the same business activity over and over in the same manner. This workflow can be exposed as a service to allow many different outside entities to interact with it. The service layer hosting the e-mail and notification service will provide the abstraction from specific destination systems.

The logical architecture of the solution is as follows:

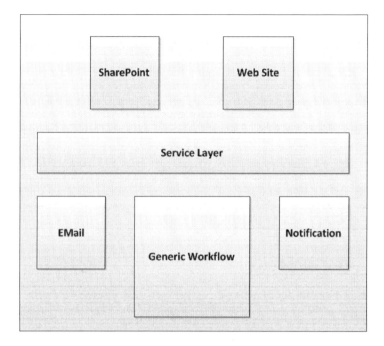

Candidate architecture #1 – BizTalk Server

BizTalk is Microsoft's enterprise integration tool, which could be used to help Bowl For Buddies coordinate the payment collection process. The previous releases of BizTalk Server had basic built-in human workflow support. This was not widely adopted nor used in the marketplace, and hence is no longer part of the latest version of the product.

Even without the specific human workflow components, BizTalk does have a robust orchestration engine that can be easily used to model a business process such as the payment collection process. BizTalk has built-in adapters for SharePoint and SQL, which makes it an ideal candidate for consideration.

The next sections provide a detailed review of BizTalk's role in this scenario.

Solution design aspects

A BizTalk orchestration can model the payment collection process. BizTalk can expose this orchestration to outside consumers through a WCF service adapter, SQL Server adapter, or SharePoint adapter. Any or all of these adapters can be used to activate a new instance of the payment collection process.

Once started, the orchestration makes external calls to the e-mail service to send the e-mail to the donor. If an invalid response is received, the notification service will be used to update SharePoint and wait for corrected data to be sent back to the long-running orchestration. If the response from the e-mail transmission is successful, the orchestration will wait for the response for payment service and update SharePoint with the results. If the payment result is not received, the process will wait for updated information from SharePoint and try again.

The SharePoint adapter will be used to read and write information to SharePoint. When the SQL Server-based solution is added later, the SQL Server Adapter can easily be added. BizTalk's extensive routing ability will be used as needed to route messages between SQL Server, SharePoint, and external services.

Solution implementation aspects

Bowl For Buddies does not have a large IT staff. Using a full-blown enterprise integration tool such as BizTalk Server might be a large undertaking for a small IT organization. In addition, learning to develop BizTalk-based solutions requires additional training and effort. This is probably something Bowl For Buddies cannot undertake given the small staff.

Solution operations aspects

Bowl For Buddies does not have BizTalk running nor do they have servers for BizTalk to run on. In addition to BizTalk, they would require SQL Server. Both of these carry heavy licensing costs and require extensive operation monitoring in order to have a successful implementation. Also, monitoring BizTalk requires training on how to handle suspended messages and how to reprocess them. This is something likely to be outside the scope of what the existing IT staff can handle.

Organizational aspects

Bowl For Buddies is not a large organization. Using an enterprise server tool such as BizTalk would not be a good fit for them. Even though they have expansion plans that could add additional offices, the need for BizTalk in areas other than payment collection is unknown.

Solution evaluation

Well, this does not look like an acceptable solution. All thumbs down except for the design, as shown in the following table:

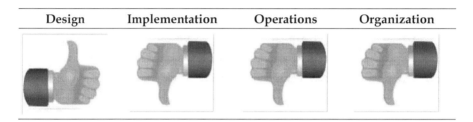

Design	Implementation	Operations	Organization

Candidate architecture #2 – .NET workflow and SharePoint

The solution would leverage .NET 4.5 technologies to support this use case. We would use a .NET workflow service to expose endpoints to a SharePoint workflow. In order to meet the scenario and enable reuse outside a pure SharePoint-hosted process workflow, putting core logic inside a service-exposed .NET workflow allows for reuse by other systems.

Solution design aspects

SharePoint 2010 has a built-in workflow engine. This uses .NET 3.5 workflow technologies to provide out-of-the-box workflow templates for common scenarios and to support extensive customization. This could provide a complete solution if the solution would be totally contained in SharePoint. Given the addition of a future web-based solution, moving the core workflow logic out of SharePoint is a better alternative.

Moving the business process out of SharePoint allows for the use of .NET 4.5 and Microsoft AppFabric 1.1 for Windows Server to host the solution. This provides a single point of tracking and monitoring with new features of the .NET 4.5 workflow.

Our solution would use a simple SharePoint workflow to call into a .NET workflow service. The .NET workflow would be a workflow service—a workflow exposed as a WCF service. This workflow would have the payment collection process modeled to include sending an e-mail, waiting for a payment response, and sending notifications. Custom service calls would be needed for interaction with external systems for e-mail, payment processing, and notifications.

Solution implementation aspects

Bowl For Buddies does not have a tight timeline. The adoption of workflow technology and workflow services through WCF will speed up the delivery process, reducing the amount of testing needed versus a custom-coded solution.

Solution operations aspects

Using .NET 4.5 and AppFabric provides a lot of features out of the box, including logging, monitoring, and troubleshooting support. This is done through a plugin into IIS; something that many IT resources know well. As Bowl For Buddies already has an ASPX-based website, its IT staff is already accustomed to this interface.

Organizational aspects

Adoption of .NET 4.5 and Microsoft AppFabric for Windows Server will not require significant investment in software licenses as these technologies are all included with the price of Microsoft Windows. The existing intranet-based server that runs the SharePoint site could be used for this solution. Adoption of this technology is a low-risk endeavor, given the fact that it is built into the Windows framework.

Solution evaluation

As shown in the following table, we have all thumbs up! This is definitely our choice.

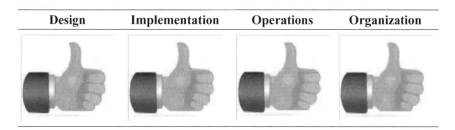

Design	Implementation	Operations	Organization

Architecture selection

Let's look at how these candidate architecture technologies stack up against each other. We can break down the primary benefits and risks of each choice as follows:

Technology	Benefits/risks
BizTalk Server	**Benefits** • This has out-of-the-box adapters for SQL Server and SharePoint • This has robust enterprise-class hosting infrastructure for processes exposed as WCF services • This has a built-in admin tool and a variety of third-party tools with extensive monitoring information **Risks** • This has additional licensing costs • There is a large learning curve for development, monitoring, and operations • This needs large infrastructure requirements
The .NET workflow and SharePoint	**Benefits** • There is a robust hosting environment • There are easy configuration-based tracing and monitoring options, including detailed message bodies • This has low cost of ownership • This leverages existing hardware **Risks** • New technology could face some breaking issues • Large learning curve for development, monitoring, and operations

A key benefit of using .NET 4.5 and Microsoft AppFabric for Windows Server is its lightweight solution without extensive additional software expenditures. This release of the .NET framework has significant changes compared to past .NET releases, and it supports AppFabric as a rich hosting environment. While this new technology introduces a certain level of risk in the solution, this is acceptable, given the overall benefits gained from this technology. While BizTalk can do exactly what is needed for this scenario, it would be overkill. Given the small size of Bowl For Buddies and the lack of need for BizTalk in other areas of the company, it is not a right fit in this case.

For this scenario, the .NET workflow with SharePoint is the best choice.

Building the solution

This solution has two key areas: a .NET workflow solution and a SharePoint solution. An ideal layout of the physical architecture is shown in the following diagram:

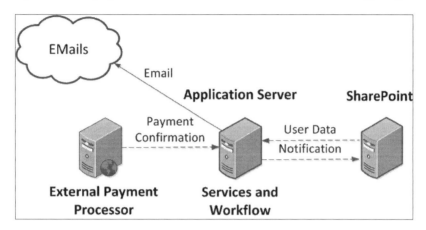

While it is possible to run all the applications on a single server, separation of the application server running workflow services and SharePoint components is ideal.

SharePoint 2010 runs with a .NET 3.5 workflow, and workflow services use .NET 4.5. While these can co-exist on the same server, the solution is cleaner when separated.

Setup

Our sample is broken down into two sections. The first section walks through the creation and testing of the .NET workflow to process payments. The second section creates a SharePoint customer list. SharePoint is not needed for the first section, and a testing tool is provided to test the workflow. To run an end-to-end solution, SharePoint 2010 needs to be installed.

This solution has several parts. The key areas are as follows:

- Various existing services for sending e-mail, processing credit card payments, and updating the SharePoint list
- An AppFabric-hosted workflow—called from the SharePoint workflow or the test application—to manage the flow of payment processing and data correction
- A SharePoint site to host the Bowl For Buddies list of customers
- A SharePoint workflow triggered from additions and changes to the customer list

Some initial setup is required. These steps assume that SharePoint 2010, InfoPath 2010, and AppFabric are all installed on the same server. Even if you are just running the workflow section, you are required to complete the following steps because the solution is built around the website names used in them.

Prepare your environment by performing the following steps:

1. When installed, SharePoint 2010 takes over both port 80 and the default website as an ASP.NET 2.0-based site. Create a new website inside the IIS running on port 1234. This will host the external services and core workflow. Ensure the default application pool is running .NET 4.5. Name the website `HumanWorkflow` and point it to the `C:\HumanWorkflow` folder, as shown in the following screenshot:

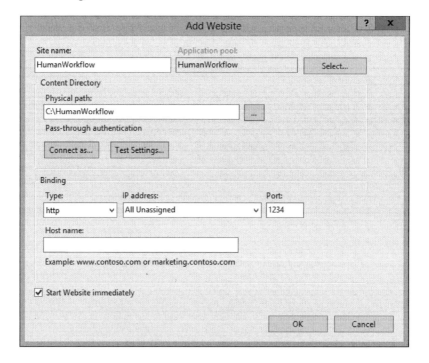

2. Launch Visual Studio and open `HumanWorkflow.sln` in the `<Installation Directory>\HumanWorkflow` folder. When prompted to create the virtual directories, click on **OK**.

3. Once the virtual directories are created, the `HumanWorkflow.Notification` service must run in an application pool with access to the SharePoint site. For this demo, create an application pool that runs .NET 4.5, as an administrator, and name it `WF4-SPAccess`. Change the application pool for this service to use the one we have just created.

4. Depending on the operating system, you may need to create event log sources used by this code. Add the following sources inside the server's application log: `ProcessPayments`, `EmailService`, and `NotificationService`.

The following projects are included in the `HumanWorkflow` solution:

* `HumanWorkflow.CoreWorkflow`: This is the main project that will contain the process payments workflow called by external systems.

* `HumanWorkflow.EmailSvc`: This service is used to simulate sending an e-mail. Pass in an e-mail address that starts with an "F" to test the failure logic.

* `HumanWorkflow.Notification`: This service is used to update SharePoint on the status of a record. For this demo, this defaults to writing to the event log. See the service comments on how to switch this to write to SharePoint.

* `HumanWorkflow.Tester`: This is a Windows form to test the workflow without SharePoint.

* `HumanWorkflow.HelperDocs`: This is a folder with helper text files used for creating the SharePoint workflow and SharePoint list.

Building the core workflow

First off, the Process Payments .NET workflow will be built and deployed to AppFabric. This workflow will receive a payment request message that starts the process. The first step is to call an e-mail service to notify the donor. If the response is successful, the process moves to the payment service. If the process returns an error, a notification is sent, and the workflow waits to receive updated information. Once the updated information is received (note that only e-mail address update is shown in the demo), the e-mail is sent again. Once moved to the Receive Payment Notice flow, the workflow waits to receive payment information. This must be done using the supplied testing application, and the user ID must match with that of the submitted record. Once the payment is received, a success notification is made. If payment errors occur, the process sends a notification and waits for the updated user information.

In this section, the following tasks will be accomplished:

* Adding a new workflow service to an existing project

* Building request-response contracts for SharePoint integration

* Building a flowchart workflow logic for the process payment procedure

- Calling several external services and evaluating the response
- Setting up content correlation for payment and the updated data to be sent back to the same running workflow instance
- Deploying the solution to AppFabric

Checking the environment

This solution starts with a workflow service project already created and includes existing service references for e-mail (called `Send Email`) and notification (called `Send Notification`) external services. The project has been set up to run on port 1234 at `http://localhost:1234/HumanWorkflow.CoreWorkflow/ ProcessPayment`. This solution also includes a helper custom activity for writing information to the event log. This will be used for some basic process-flow tracking. The tracking features of AppFabric can be used for this, but for simplicity, the event log will work for this demo. Perform the following steps:

1. Launch Visual Studio 2012 and open `HumanWorkflow.sln` in the `<Installation Directory>\HumanWorkflow` folder.

2. A project named `HumanWorkflow.CoreWorkflow` already exists.

3. Right-click on **Project** and select **Properties**. Select the **Web** tab. Ensure the **Use Local IIS Web Server** radio button is selected. Click on **Create Virtual Directory** to ensure the directory exists in IIS.

Implementing the top-level workflow

Perform the following steps to implement the top-level workflow:

1. Right-click on the project and select **Add New Item**. Select the workflow templates under **Visual C#**, and add a new **WCF Workflow Service** called `ProcessPayment.xamlx`.

2. Click on the top-level **Sequential Service** option and click on the **Variables** tab at the bottom-left corner of the screen. Delete the data variable (this is created by default and not used).

3. Add variables to the workflow as per the following table:

Name	Type
ListHandle	CorrelationHandle this is the correlation variable used to receive payment confirmation and updated user data if needed, located under System.ServiceModel.Activities)
listID	Int32

Name	Type
listName	String
listEmail	String
listBowlingScore	Double
listDonationAmount	Double
listTotalDonation	Double

4. Click on the **ReceiveRequest** activity. Click on the ellipsis next to the **Content** property.

5. Select the **Parameters** radio button and enter parameters as per the following table:

Name	Type	Assign to
ID	Int32	listID
Name	String	listName
BowlingScore	Double	listBowlingScore
DonationAmount	Double	listDonationAmount
EmailAddress	String	listEmail

6. With **ReceiveRequest** selected, click on the **CorrelationInitializes** property (if the **Properties** window is not visible, press the *F4* key). Select **Add initialize**. Add **ListHandle**. Select **Query correlation initializer** from the drop-down list. In the **XPath Queries** drop-down list, select **ID: Int32**. Click on **OK**. This will set up a correlation value that can be used by other receive activities to get information back into this same workflow instance.

7. With **ReceiveRequest** selected, ensure the **CanCreateInstances** checkbox is checked. This is located under the properties of the activity. Press the *F4* key if they are not visible.

8. Click on the **SendResponse** activity. Click on the ellipsis next to the **Content** property. Select the **Parameters** radio button and enter the following parameters:
   - Name: Result
   - Type: Boolean
   - Value: True

9. With **SendResponse** selected, ensure the **PersistBeforeSend** checkbox is checked. This is located under **Properties**.

10. Drag the custom activity called **EventLogHelper**, located under `HumanWorkflow.CoreWorkflow` in the toolbox. Place it between the **ReceiveRequest** and **SendResponse** activities. Set the value of **TextEventLog** property to `Received GETDATA Message`. If this activity is not available, build the solution, and it should be seen in the toolbox.

11. Drag an **Assign** shape from the **Primitives** section of the toolbox, and place it under the **EventLogHelper** activity. Set the **To** value to `listTotalDonation`. Set the **Value** to `listDonationAmount * listBowlingScore`. IntelliSense should recognize these values.

Implementing the flowchart workflow logic

Perform the following steps to implement the flowchart logic:

1. Drag a flowchart shape from the **Flowchart** section of the toolbox. Place it under **SendResponse**. The workflow should look like the following screenshot:

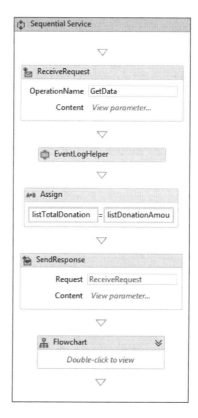

2. Double-click on the **Flowchart** activity to drill down to the flowchart surface.

3. The end result of the next few steps will be a flowchart for the payment collection process. The final result will look like the following screenshot:

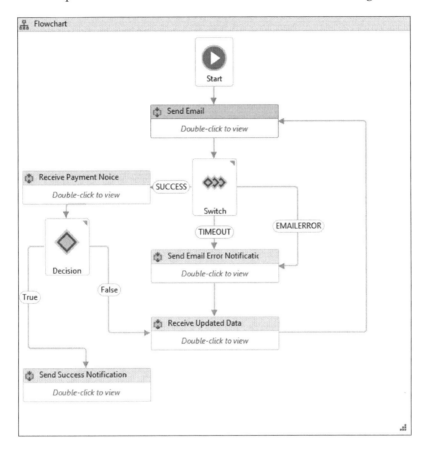

4. Click on the top-level flowchart, and click on the **Variables** tab at the bottom left. Add variables as shown in the following table. These will be within the flowchart scope:

Name	Type
EmailResult	String
paymentReceived	Boolean
errorMessage	String

5. Drag a **Sequence** activity from the **Control Flow** section of the toolbox onto the flowchart surface under the **Start** arrow. Rename this to Send Email. This activity will call the external e-mail service to send the user an e-mail. The result of this call will determine the next step in the flow.

6. Draw a line from the **Start** shape to the **Send Email** sequence activity.

7. Under the **Send Email** activity, add a **FlowSwitch** activity from the **Flowchart** section of the toolbox. Select the type to be `String` while adding the shape to the surface. Set the **Expression** property to `Email Result`. The name on the activity shape displays **Switch**.

8. Draw a line from the **Send Email** sequence activity to the **Switch** activity.

9. Drag a **Sequence** activity from the **Control Flow** section of the toolbox onto the flowchart surface, which is to the left of the **Switch** activity. Rename this to `Receive Payment Notice`. This activity will wait for a payment message from an external source for a fixed amount of time. Sending the payment notice can be done using the provided Tester Windows forms tool located under the tester project.

10. Draw a line from the left-hand side of the **Switch** activity to the **Receive Payment Notice** sequence. Uncheck the **IsDefaultCase** checkbox in the properties. Set the value of **Case** to `SUCCESS`.

11. Drag a **Sequence** activity from the **Control Flow** section of the toolbox onto the flowchart surface to the bottom right from the **Switch** activity. Rename this to `Send Email Error Notification`. This activity will send error message information back out of the workflow — in this case, back to SharePoint.

12. Draw a line from the bottom of the **Switch** activity to the **Send Email Error Notification** sequence. Uncheck the **IsDefaultCase** checkbox in the properties. Set the **Case** value to `TIMEOUT`.

13. Draw a line from the right-hand side of the **Switch** activity to the **Send Email Error Notification** sequence. Uncheck the **IsDefaultCase** checkbox. Set the **Case** value to `EMAILERROR`.

14. Drag a **Sequence** activity from the **Control Flow** section of the toolbox onto the flowchart surface under the **Send Email Error Notification** sequence activity. Rename this to `Receive Updated Data`. This activity will wait for updated user data from the external data provider — in this case, SharePoint.

15. Draw a line from the bottom of the **Send Email Error Notification** sequence activity to the **Receive Updated Data** sequence.

16. Draw a line from the right-hand side of the **Receive Updated Data** sequence activity to the **Send Email** sequence activity.

17. Moving to the left-side of the flowchart, under the **Receive Payment Notice** activity, add a **FlowDecision** activity from the **Flowchart** section of the toolbox. Set the **Condition** property to `paymentReceived`. The name on the activity shape displays **Decision**.

18. Draw a line from the bottom of the **Receive Payment Notice** sequence activity to the top of the **Decision** activity.

19. Drag a **Sequence** activity from the **Control Flow** section of the toolbox onto the flowchart surface, under the **Decision** activity. Rename this to `Send Success Notification`. This activity will update the external data provider with a success message—in this case, SharePoint.

20. Draw a line from the left-hand side of the **Decision** activity to the top of the **Send Success Notification** sequence activity. This represents the true result.

21. Draw a line from the right-hand side of the **Decision** activity to the left-hand side of the **Receive Updated Data** sequence activity. This represents the false result. Note how once an activity is defined for an event, such as **Receive Updated Response**, it is easy to reuse that logic.

22. Now the basic flow of the flowchart is complete. The solution should now build with no errors. Verify this by right-clicking on the project and selecting **Build**. The next steps will add logic to the five sequence shapes that were added to the flowchart.

23. On the main flowchart surface, double-click on the **Send Email** activity. This set of activities will compose the request and response messages to the external e-mail service, evaluate the response message, and generate error messages if needed.

Implementing the Send Email activity

Perform the following steps to implement the Send Email activity:

1. Click on the top-level **Send Email** sequence activity, and click on the **Variables** tab on the bottom-left corner. Add the following variables:

Name	Type	Default
emailRequest	EmailRequest	NewHumanWorkflow. CoreWorkflow.SendE- mail.E-mailRequest()
emailResponse	EmailResponse	nil
emailCount	Int32	nil
emailResultLocal	String	nil

2. Drag the custom activity called **EventLogHelper** located under `HumanWorkflow.CoreWorkflow`. Place it as the first activity in the sequence. Set the **TextEventLog** property to **Started Send Email**.

3. Drag an **Assign** shape from the **Primitives** section of the toolbox, and place it under the **EventLogHelper** activity. Set the **To** value to `emailCount`. Set the **Value** as `emailCount + 1`.

4. Drag an **Assign** shape from the **Primitives** section of the toolbox, and place it under the previous **Assign** activity. Set the **To** value to `emailRequest.AmountDue`. Set the **Value** to `listTotalDonation`.

5. Drag an **Assign** shape from the **Primitives** section of the toolbox, and place it under the previous **Assign** activity. Set the **To** value to `emailRequest.EmailAddress`. Set the **Value** to `listEmail`.

6. Drag an **Assign** shape from the **Primitives** section of the toolbox, and place it under the previous **Assign** activity. Set the **To** value to `emailRequest.ID`. Set the **Value** to `listID`.

7. Drag the **Send Email** service reference from the toolbox, and place it under the last **Assign** activity. If this is not present in the toolbox, rebuild the solution. Set the values of **Email** to `emailRequest` and of **SendEmailResult** to `emailResponse`. So far, the **Send Email** process should look like the following screenshot:

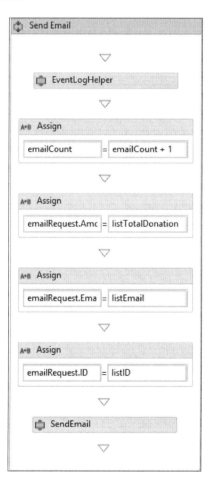

8. Drag an **If** activity from the **Control Flow** section of the toolbar under the **Send Email** activity. Set the **Condition** property to `emailResponse.Response`.

9. Drag an **Assign** shape from the **Primitives** section of the toolbox, and place it inside the **Then** side of the **If** activity. Set the **To** value to `emailResultLocal`. Set the **Value** to `SUCCESS`.

10. Drag an **If** activity from the **Control Flow** section of the toolbar, and place it inside the **Else** side of the **If** activity. Set the **Condition** property to `emailCount =< 3`.

11. Drag a **Sequence** activity from the **Control Flow** section of the toolbox into the **Then** side of the **If** activity. Set the **DisplayName** property to `Email Error`.

12. Drag an **Assign** shape from the **Primitives** section of the toolbox and place it inside the **Email Error** sequential activity. Set the **To** value to `errorMessage`. Set the **Value** to `"The email process returned an error sending the message"`.

13. Drag an **Assign** shape from the **Primitives** section of the toolbox, and place it below the previous **Assign** activity. Set the **To** value to `emailResultLocal`. Set the **Value** to `"EMAILERROR"`.

14. Drag a **Sequence** activity from the **Control Flow** section of the toolbox into the **Then** side of the **If** activity. Set the **DisplayName** property to `Timeout`.

15. Drag an **Assign** shape from the **Primitives** section of the toolbox, and place it inside the **Timeout** sequential activity. Set the **To** value to `errorMessage`. Set the **Value** to `"The e-mail process has hit more than 3 errors"`.

16. Drag an **Assign** shape from the **Primitives** section of the toolbox, and place it below the previous **Assign** activity. Set the **To** value to `emailResultLocal`. Set the **Value** to `"TIMEOUT"`.

17. Drag an **Assign** shape from the **Primitives** section of the toolbox, and place it outside of the **If** activities as the last activity of the workflow. Set the **To** value to `emailResult`. Set the **Value** to `emailResultLocal`. The process should look like the following screenshot:

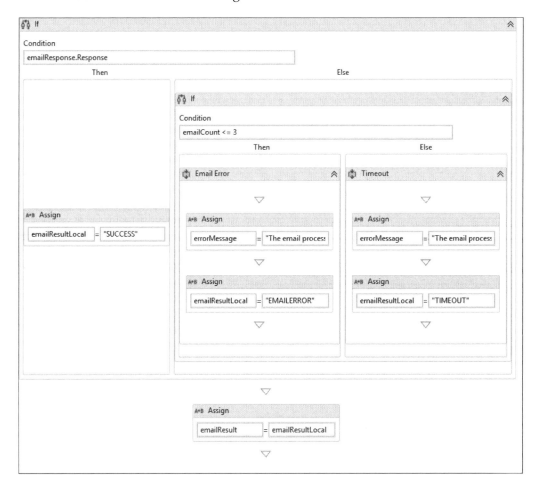

Implementing the Receive Payment Notice activity

Perform the following steps to implement the Receive Payment Notice activity:

1. Return to the main flowchart surface by using the breadcrumbs on the top of the workflow surface. Double-click on the **Receive Payment Notice** activity. This set of activities will wait for a response from the payment service, evaluate the response message, and generate an error message based on the response or a timeout. This set of activities is reached only if `"SUCCESS"` is returned from the **Send Email** sequence.

2. Drag the custom activity called **EventLogHelper** located under `HumanWorkflow.CoreWorkflow`. Place it as the first activity in the sequence. Set the **TextEventLog** property to `"Started Receive Payment Notice"`.

3. Drag a **Parallel** activity from the **Control Flow** section of the toolbox right under the **EventLogHelper** activity.

4. With the **Parallel** activity selected, click on the **Variables** tab on the bottom-left corner of the screen. Add the following variable at the **Parallel** scope:
    ◦ Name: `hitDelay`
    ◦ Type: `Boolean`
    ◦ Default: `False`

5. With the **Parallel** activity selected, set the value of **CompletionCondition** to `hitDelay`. This will allow the parallel shape to complete even when all the branches have not finished.

6. Drag a **Sequence** activity from the **Control Flow** section of the toolbox onto the flowchart surface inside the **Parallel** activity. Set the value of **DisplayName** to `NotPaidTimeout`.

7. Drag **ReceiveAndSendReply** from the **Messaging** section of the toolbox and place it to the right of the last sequence activity inside the parallel activity. This will add a new sequence activity to the flow. Set the value of **DisplayName** of the new right **Sequence** activity to `PaymentReceived`.

8. Working in the **NotPaidTimeout** sequence, drag a **Delay** activity from the **Primitives** section of the toolbox. Set the **Duration** property to `New TimeSpan(0, 2, 0)`. This will set in a delay of two minutes. While in real life this would be longer, we do not want to have to wait for a few days to run the demo.

9. Drag an **Assign** shape from the **Primitives** section of the toolbox, and place it below the **Delay** activity. Set the **To** value to `paymentReceived`. Set the **Value** to `False`.

10. Drag an **Assign** shape from the **Primitives** section of the toolbox, and place it below the previous **Assign** activity. Set the **To** value to `errorMessage`. Set the **Value** to `No payment was received in the set amount of time`.

11. Drag an **Assign** shape from the **Primitives** section of the toolbox and place it below the previous **Assign** activity. Set the **To** value as `hitDelay`. Set the **Value** to **True**. This will cause the parallel activity to complete rather than wait for the payment response.

12. Working in the **PaymentReceived** sequence activity, click on the **Receive** activity. Rename **Operation** to `GetPaymentConfirmation`. Under **Content**, click on **View parameter...**. Select the **Parameters** radio button and enter the following parameters:

Name	Type	Assign to
paymentID	Int32	nil
paymentResult	Boolean	paymentReceived

13. With **Receive** selected, click on the **CorrelatesWith** property. Set this to `ListHandle`. Click on **CorrelatesOn**. Select **paymentID** from the dropdown and click on **OK**. This will set the receive activity to follow the correlation based on the ID of the donor record.

14. Click on the **SendReplyToReceive** activity. Under **Content**, click on **Define...** and select the **Parameters** radio button. Enter the following parameters:

    ○ Name: `Result`, type: `Boolean`, value: `True`

15. With **SendReplyToReceive** selected, ensure the **PersistBeforeSend** checkbox is checked.

16. Drag the custom activity called **EventLogHelper** located under `HumanWorkflow.CoreWorkflow`. Place it between the receive and send activities. Set the **TextEventLog** property to `Received Payment Message`.

17. Drag an **If** activity from the **Control Flow** section of the toolbar, and place it under the **SendReplyToReceive** activity. Set the **Condition** property to `paymentReceived`.

18. Drag an **Assign** shape from the **Primitives** section of the toolbox, and place it inside the **Then** side of the **If** activity. Set the **To** value to `errorMessage`. Set the **Value** to `Payment Received`.

19. Drag an **Assign** shape from the **Primitives** section of the toolbox, and place it inside the **Else** side of the **If** activity. Set the **To** value to `errorMessage`. Set the **Value** to `The Payment System returned an error in the payment`.

20. Drag an **Assign** shape from the **Primitives** section of the toolbox, and place it below the previous **If** activity; ensure it is outside the **If** block. Set the **To** value equal to `hitDelay`. Set **Value** to `True`. This will cause the parallel activity to complete rather than wait for the delay.

21. Drag the custom activity called **EventLogHelper** located under
    `HumanWorkflow.CoreWorkflow`. Place it outside the parallel shape.
    Set the **TextEventLog** property to the `errorMessage` variable.

Implementing the Send Success Notification activity

Perform the following steps to implement the Send Success Notification activity:

1. Navigate to the main flowchart surface; double-click on the
    SendSuccessNotification activity.

2. With the **Send Success Notification** sequence activity selected, click on the
    Variables tab on the bottom-left corner of the screen. Add the following
    variables:

    - Name: `notificationRequest`, type: `NotificationRequest`
      (under the **Send Notification** reference type), type: `New
      HumanWorkflow.CoreWorkflow.SendNotification.
      NotificationRequest()`

    - Name: `notificationResponse`, type: `NotificationResponse`
      (under the **Send Notification** reference type)

3. Drag the custom activity called **EventLogHelper**, located under
    `HumanWorkflow.CoreWorkflow`. Place it as the first activity in the sequence.
    Set the **TextEventLog** property to `Started Send Success Notice`.

4. Drag an **Assign** shape from the **Primitives** section of the toolbox, and
    place it below the **TextEventLog** activity. Set the **To** value equal to
    `notificationRequest.ID`. Set the **Value** to `listID`.

5. Drag an **Assign** shape from the **Primitives** section of the toolbox,
    and place it below the previous **Assign** activity. Set the **To** value to
    `notificationRequest.NotificationType`. Set the **Value** to `SUCCESS`.

6. Drag the custom activity called **SendNotification**, located under
    `HumanWorkflow.CoreWorkflow.SendNotification`. Place it under the
    Assign activity. Set the **Notification** property to `notificationRequest`. Set
    the **SendNotificationResponse** property to `notificationResponse`.

7. Navigate back to the main flowchart surface; double-click on the **SendEmail
    Error** Notification activity.

Implementing the Send Email Error Notification activity

Perform the following steps to implement the Send Email Error Notification activity:

1. With the **Send Email Error Notification** sequence activity selected, click on the **Variables** tab on the bottom-left corner of the screen. Add the following variables at the **Parallel** scope:

   ° Name: `notificationRequest`, type: `NotificationRequest` (under the `SendNotificationreference` type), default: `NewHumanWorkflow.CoreWorkflow.SendNotification. NotificationRequest()`

   ° Name: `notificationResponse`, type: `NotificationResponse` (under the **SendNotification** reference type)

2. Drag the custom activity called **EventLogHelper** located under `HumanWorkflow.CoreWorkflow`. Place it as the first activity in the sequence. Set the **TextEventLog** property to `Started Send Email Error Notification`.

3. Drag an **Assign** shape from the **Primitives** section of the toolbox, and place it below the **TextEventLog** activity. Set the **To** value to `notificationRequest. ErrorMessage`. Set the **Value** to `errorMessage`.

4. Drag an **Assign** shape from the **Primitives** section of the toolbox, and place it below the previous **Assign** activity. Set the **To** value equal to `notificationRequest.ID`. Set the **Value** to `listID`.

5. Drag an **Assign** shape from the **Primitives** section of the toolbox, and place it below the previous **Assign** activity. Set the **To** value equal to `notificationRequest.NotificationType`. Set the **Value** to `ERROR`.

6. Drag the custom activity called **SendNotification** located under `HumanWorkflow.CoreWorkflow.SendNotification`. Place it under the **Assign** activity. Set the **Notification** property to `notificationRequest`. Set the **SendNotificationResponse** property to `notificationResponse`.

7. Navigate back to the main flowchart surface; double-click on the **Receive Updated Data** activity.

Implementing the Receive Updated Data activity

Perform the following steps to implement the Receive Updated Data activity:

1. Drag the custom activity called **EventLogHelper**, located under `HumanWorkflow.CoreWorkflow`. Place it as the first activity in the sequence. Set the **TextEventLog** property to `Started Receive Updated Data`.

2. Drag **ReceiveAndSendReply** from the **Messaging** section of the toolbox, and place it under the **EventLogHelper** activity. This will add a new sequence activity to the flow. Set **DisplayName** of the new **Sequence** activity to `Update Data`.

3. Working in the **Update Data** sequence activity, click on the **Receive** activity. Rename **Operation** to `GetUpdatedData`. Under **Content**, click on **View parameter....** Select the **Parameters** radio button and enter the following parameters:

    ○ Name: `ID`, type: `Int32`, assign to: `listID`
    ○ Name: `Email`, type: `String`, assign to: `listEmail`

4. With **Receive** selected, click on the **CorrelatesWith** property. Set this to `ListHandle`. Click on **CorrelatesOn**. Select **ID** from the dropdown. Click on **OK**. This will set up this **Receive** activity to follow the correlation based on the ID of the donor record.

5. Click on the **SendReplyToReceive** activity. Under **Content**, click on **Define....** Select the **Parameters** radio button and enter the following parameters:

    ○ Name: `Result`, type: `Boolean`, value: `True`

6. With **SendReplyToReceive** selected, ensure the **PersistBeforeSend** checkbox is checked.

7. Drag the custom activity called **EventLogHelper** located under `HumanWorkflow.CoreWorkflow`. Place it between the receive and send activities. Set the **TextEventLog** property to `Received GETUPDATEDDATA Message`.

8. Save the workflow. Right-click on the project and select **Build**. The workflow service will now be available to be called from within IIS.

Testing the workflow

1. The preceding tasks can be tested using the supplied `Tester.exe` application included in the `HumanWorkflow` solution.

2. In order to build the SharePoint 2010 solution to test the workflow, please follow the instructions included in the `BuildSharePointSolution.doc` file.

Lessons learned

In this pattern, we looked at how to build an AppFabric hosted workflow service for a human workflow. Using a workflow external to SharePoint allows for reuse of the business process by other systems. Using Microsoft AppFabric for Windows Server gives us a single processing environment that reduces the complexity of monitoring and administration.

Summary

In this chapter, we considered workflows with and without human intervention. We looked again in the case of federated data search and focused on its workflow. We compared different technologies that Microsoft offers in this domain.

One of the main conclusions we can make is that BizTalk is not positioned to be the core software for workflow systems despite its excellent orchestration engine. Its main capabilities lie in the area of message exchange, data transformation, and an easy connectivity to a myriad of systems through its extensive set of adapters. Using it just to support workflows is like using a sledgehammer to crack a nut.

In the next chapter, we move the focus of our discussion to the presentation layer of multilayered software systems.

12
Presentation Layer Patterns

The evolution of user-oriented devices has been happening so fast that we could call it a revolution. Some of the authors of this book remember piles of punch cards and magnetic tapes, yet today we discuss video cameras embedded into contact lenses. Despite the rapid changes, some ideas are so fundamental that they seem to have been around forever. For example, one of the most influential factors in this area was the invention of the computer mouse by Douglas Engelbart in the 1960s, along with the hypertext and rectangle-like screen presentations called **windows**.

In this chapter, we will discuss the technologies that support interaction with the end user; this is commonly called the **presentation layer**. We will talk about web and desktop applications; Silverlight, ASP.NET, and WPF; and we'll focus on three major patterns: MVC, MVP, and MVVM.

The term "presentation layer" may be a little deceiving, since in information technology, it is used in two different senses. First, the presentation layer is the sixth layer in the **Open Systems Interconnection** (**OSI**) model, which presents data from network layers to the application layer and vice versa. Second, the presentation layer is the layer that interacts with users in the multilayered application model. The latter is used in this chapter.

A typical, somewhat simplified, multilayered approach to the application architecture is depicted in the following the diagram:

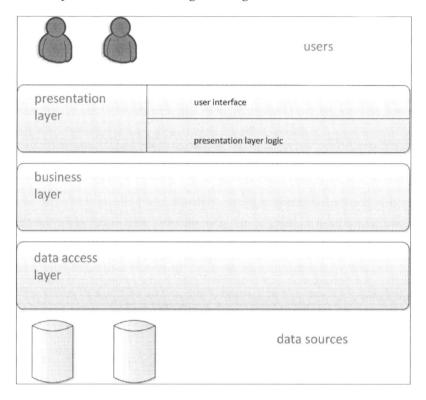

It is important to notice that the presentation layer is not an equivalent of the **User Interface (UI)**. In addition to UI components, presentation layers may also have data validation rules, business rules, and other presentation logic. Having major business logic coded in the presentation layer is generally an antipattern; however, some business logic (for example, navigation rules) often resides there for performance reasons.

User interfaces and related presentation layers are implemented by a broad spectrum of technologies, targeting applications from Xbox to mobile. In this chapter, we will focus on a relatively small class of business applications that can usually be architected using the multilayered paradigm.

Building presentation layers

Enterprise systems that require more or less elaborate presentation layers often present challenges to the architects. To understand these challenges, let's take a look at typical implementations. Architects usually consider three main approaches: desktop applications, web applications, and mobile applications. This separation reflects the history of end user technologies. Desktop applications provided much richer functionality compared to the first web applications; browser-based clients could not satisfy most business needs. However, with the advance of the Internet, web applications also changed and browser-based clients became common, delivering intranet solutions for enterprise users. The variety of mobile devices caused a burst of new technologies that created some chaos in the developers' minds for a little while. Even today, if the software vendor does not want to deliver a browser-based mobile application, they still have to develop a few "native" applications (usually one for each major brand).

This taxonomy is based on tradition rather than on technical features. However, it gives us a basis for discussion.

Desktop applications

Applications that interact with end users via personal computer desktops are historically the first class of applications with a graphical user interface.

Originally, this major class of applications, which provided graphical UI and interaction with end users, was developed in one of the available programming languages to communicate with the backend on the same computer or on the same network. These applications have been providing rich functionality, and therefore, are often called **rich client applications**.

Before the active use of the multilayered (initially, three-layered) paradigm in software architecture, the functionality of the presentation layer did not necessarily just support interactions with end users. Many applications (for example, the ones built on MS Access) supported very tight connection of the user interface with the database. Modules responsible for presenting the user interface also sometimes implemented business logic.

After separating system functionality into several layers, the presentation layer still continued to carry a lot. With the introduction of web clients, which could initially implement a very minimal set of features, the notion of thick clients versus thin clients was suggested.

Rich client applications are also called **fat clients** or **thick clients**, and the term was introduced as a comparison to thin clients, or web applications. Thin clients had very little overhead, being completely browser-based.

Today, Microsoft has a variety of technologies supporting rich clients (you can read our evaluation of some of these APIs in *Chapter 2, The .NET Framework Primer*).

Windows Forms

Windows Forms (WinForms) is the original API used to develop the user interface of Windows desktop applications with the .NET framework. A **form** is a visual surface to display information to end users. **Controls** are added to the forms and respond to user actions. A large number of controls have been introduced since WinForms was released in the very first version of .NET. Typical controls include textboxes, buttons, radio buttons, drop-down boxes, and others.

Today, WinForms is clearly showing its age, particularly when its capabilities are compared to those of WPF and WinRT, but it is still a viable API for applications that exclusively target the desktop and where a sophisticated modern UI is not necessary.

In .NET 4.5, Microsoft positions WinForms as a tool for developing smart clients. A **Smart client** is a client application that can synchronize local data to a remote server but does not require an Internet connection for the majority of its functions. In our taxonomy described in this chapter, smart clients could be positioned between desktop and web applications.

Windows Presentation Foundation

Windows Presentation Foundation (WPF) is an API, introduced in .NET 3.0, to develop rich user interfaces for .NET applications, with no dependencies on legacy Windows APIs and with support for GPU-accelerated 3D rendering, animation, and media playback. Today, WPF is a mature, stable API optimized for performance.

WPF has significantly more features than WinForms, enabling easy animation, template-driven UI design, and different object embedding. In WPF Version 4.5 (in .NET 4.5), a powerful **Ribbon** control was introduced that allowed building an MS Office-like interface.

However, most importantly, WPF clearly supports the usage of architectural patterns, which we'll discuss in this chapter.

Designing the UI in WPF can be done using one of the existing visual tools, but any UI is always presented in **eXtensible Application Markup Language** (**XAML**)—a declarative XML-based language. XAML code to some extent can be reused in Silverlight (`http://msdn.microsoft.com/en-us/library/cc903925(VS.95).aspx`).

WPF is getting constant improvements that provide a far simpler upgrade path to WinRT compared to Windows Forms.

Microsoft Office VBA applications

From the very beginning of its existence, Microsoft Office applications provided some abilities for programming. Excel macros, WordBASIC, all such development tools were eventually organized in the form of **Visual Basic for Applications** (VBA). The presentation layer in this class of applications is the host MS Office application itself. Adding VBA code typically does not extend the UI features but rather adds some business logic.

VBA was not designed as a full-blown development tool. It lacks certain significant features, for example, proper security. For that reason, VBA applications usually don't have enterprise quality and are intended to be used by a limited group of users.

However, VBA is the perfect tool for its purposes. One can significantly extend the capabilities of the MS Office presentation using VBA.

InfoPath

InfoPath initially was a part of Microsoft Office and provided an ability to build and control forms. Probably the main use of InfoPath is providing a presentation layer for SharePoint. In 2014, Microsoft discontinued InfoPath, but the roadmap for SharePoint forms is not clear. Very possibly, that will be replaced with other Office applications.

Web applications

With the evolution of the Internet and particularly the World Wide Web, another type of client emerged as an alternative to desktop applications. The applications were hosted in a browser and used comparatively primitive methods to present the user interface.

The advance of the communication tools resulted in developing the ability to host data and business layers remotely and in the ability to support constant communication between clients and servers. Web applications went through a series of improvements. Their capabilities became comparable to desktop applications and enabled full-blown browser-based applications on internal enterprise networks.

ASP.NET

ASP.NET applications are server-side applications that can be run on Microsoft Internet Information Server (IIS). Code for ASP.NET can be developed using Microsoft languages, such as Visual Basic or C#, or other languages, such as Python or Ruby.

ASP.NET has several programming models targeting the presentation layer development, available as templates for developers in Visual Studio 2013. Some of them are as follows:

- **ASP.NET Web Forms**: This provides developers with a rich set of controls, and it is somewhat similar to Windows Forms. ASP.NET has been developed in parallel with .NET and currently is in Version 4.5. The ASP.NET Web Forms API consists of the `System.Web.Forms` namespace, as we described in *Chapter 2, The .NET Framework Primer*.

- **ASP.NET MVC**: This is designed to facilitate pattern-based development, and we will talk about it in detail later in this chapter. The API consists of the `System.Web.Mvc` namespace as described in *Chapter 2* as well.

- **Single Page application template**: This is intended to create applications that use HTML 5 and JavaScript. It supports AJAX for asynchronous data exchange with the server.

- **Facebook template**: This was introduced in Visual Studio 2013 in order to build Facebook applications.

Silverlight

Silverlight applications are developed as a combination of .NET code and XAML. Silverlight applications are client-side applications, and therefore, are independent of the web server. They can be independent or integrated into ASP.NET websites. Silverlight uses a small subset of .NET that has to be downloaded and installed on the client.

Silverlight was initially named WPF/E and was a subset of WPF targeting web applications. However, they have many differences, and the original intention of massive code sharing does not seem to be feasible, at least for most projects.

Scripting with JavaScript and jQuery

JavaScript is an open standard that is commonly used in web development to add functionality to applications. Visual Studio has a JavaScript debugging feature that enables stepping through the client-side as well as the server-side code. As well as Silverlight, JavaScript code can be included in ASP.NET applications.

In the last two years, Microsoft has been promoting TypeScript, an open source programming language that was developed to help enable the building of large-scale JavaScript applications. It is a strict superset of the JavaScript language. For more information about TypeScript, please visit the site `http://www.typescriptlang.org/`.

While JavaScript is a client-side scripting language, **jQuery** is an open source toolkit built on JavaScript. Microsoft made a significant contribution to the jQuery project.

In 2005, a new approach emerged, based on a set of technologies such as Asynchronous JavaScript, CSS, DOM, and XML. The approach was called **Ajax**—short for Asynchronous JavaScript + XML. Ajax quickly gained popularity as a group of techniques that provides asynchronous data interchange with the server.

Mobile development

From Windows CE and Pocket PC, Microsoft mobile development had a long path to the modern **Windows Phone**. Its latest release, Version 8.1, was launched in April 2014, and it was a major improvement over the previous version. The version number was kept as 8.1 to align with the desktop version.

Also, with the advance of hardware and increasing popularity of tablet devices, Windows RT was introduced as the OS for tablets.

Mobile development in the last 15 years has been very active and the terminology has changed several times. Let's list a few major incarnations:

- **Windows Phone OS**: This is a successor to Windows Mobile and is designed to work on smartphones.

- **Windows RT (WinRT) OS**: This is an edition of Windows 8 designed for mobile devices that use the 32-bit ARM architecture.

- **Microsoft Design Language**: Formerly known as "Metro," this is the main design language for Windows 8, Windows Phone, and Xbox One.

- **Windows Store**: This is an application store with the primary role to distribute "Metro-style" applications.

- **Windows Phone Store**: This is a distribution vehicle for Windows Phone applications.

  As of the end of 2013, developers need one account for both Windows Store and Windows Phone Store;; however, these two marketplaces are still separate.

- **Windows Phone Store Application model**: This is a new application model based on Windows RT. This model is a direct result of the effort that Microsoft has been making in order to achieve convergence with desktop applications.

- **Windows Phone Silverlight 8 Application model**: This is the application model that was used until the release of 8.1. You can continue using this application model for Windows Phone 8.1 development.

- **Windows Phone Silverlight 8.1 Application**: This is the newest major version despite the minor increase in the version number.

- **Windows Phone 8.1 SDK**: This enables development using any of the three models mentioned in the preceding points on this list.

MVC, MVP, and MVVM

With the advance of the multilayered approach and object-orientation in computer programming, new best practices emerged. One of them was formulated as the **Separation of Concerns** design principle. The principle suggests that computer application code should be separated into distinct sections, each addressing a separate concern. In fact, Separation of Concerns is an old principle that forced the modularity of programs even in the very old days of software development. However, with the advance of the OO design, this principle caused the development of several patterns.

We should note that architectural patterns that we discuss in this chapter are not strictly presentation layer patterns. They suggest architecture that covers other layers as well. However, the main reason these patterns were developed is the need to properly structure the presentation layer.

In this chapter, we will talk about the most popular patterns that found their way into Microsoft tools and technologies. We will talk about the MVC pattern, the central pattern for the ASP.NET MVC framework; about the MVP pattern, which is often used with Windows Forms; and about the MVVM pattern, which got its popularity with the introduction of WPF.

The model-view controller pattern

The first architectural pattern that was suggested to separate the concerns of designing application with a UI was the **model-view-controller** (**MVC**) pattern. This pattern was introduced in 1978 in the Smalltalk community. (The Smalltalk community is actually responsible for introducing a number of patterns and for productive discussions on this very topic).

The MVC pattern gives us an answer to the question "How do we structure code for a program with UI?" The pattern divides the code into the following three components:

- **Model**: This component represents the business model/data. Model does not know about View or Controller. Model can be as simple as a database with a simple data access object. For more complex projects, it can include an ORM layer, a file set, or other components.

- **View**: This component handles the user interface or the output with which the user interacts. It can also include validation code or other parts of the presentation layer. In fact, separating this component (layer) from others was the main intention of the pattern.

- **Controller**: This component changes the model as a result of the events in View. Controller can work with multiple views, and it determines which view to display.

Component communication in the MVC pattern is depicted in the following diagram:

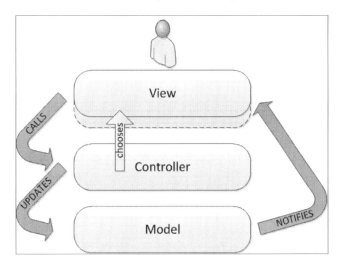

The implementations of MVC can be quite different. Often, there is only one view per controller; notifications can be implemented using pull or push models. Communication between components typically uses the **Observer design pattern** (http://en.wikipedia.org/wiki/Observer_pattern).

The model-view-presenter pattern

The model-view-presenter **(MVP)** pattern was originally introduced in an article by Mike Patel, in 1996 (*MVP: Model-View-Presenter. The Taligent Programming Model for C++ and Java*).

The MVP pattern also separates View from Model, which has the same meaning as in the MVC pattern. The separation is done with the component called **Presenter**, as illustrated in the following screenshot:

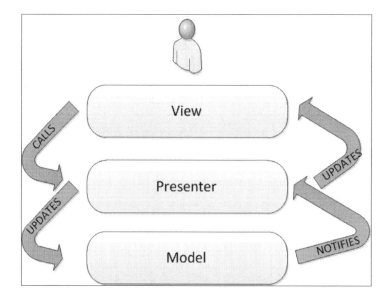

Presenter is quite different from Controller. First off, Presenter has a two-way communication with View. Presenter truly separates View and Model. Secondly, Presenter (a single instance) deals with only one View.

Most commonly, this pattern is used with Windows Forms.

Model-View-View Model

The **Model-View-ViewModel (MVVM)** pattern was introduced in .NET 3.0 with WPF and Silverlight. Today, the pattern is used with other technologies. For example, a JavaScript implementation of it is **knockout.js**.

The MVVM pattern is based on the Presentation Model pattern introduced by Martin Fowler in 2004 (`http://martinfowler.com/eaaDev/PresentationModel.html`). The MVVM pattern was introduced to leverage the core features of WPF and Silverlight (WPF/E).

Model and View in MVVM have the same meaning as in the previous patterns. The third component is called **ViewModel**, shown in the following diagram:

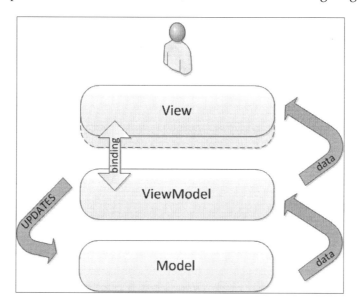

It may look somewhat similar to the MVP pattern but, unlike Presenter in the MVP pattern, ViewModel in the MVVM pattern does not need a reference to View. View binds to the properties in ViewModel using the internal binding mechanism of WPF. In terms of WPF, ViewModel is set as the **DataContext** of View. It is also possible to handle several View instances with one ViewModel instance.

Working with a use case – a user interface for the shopping cart

We are going to use the example that we have developed in *Chapter 9*, *Web Services and Beyond*. Just to refresh your memory, we will briefly describe the use case. Then we will focus on the UI development for the solution.

As you remember, we built a shopping cart for Happy Biking Inc., a company that sells bikes, parts, and related equipment all over North America. The company decided to hire a software development team to build the shopping cart service that would be connected to a payment system, and later to the internal inventory system and other applications.

In *Chapter 9*, *Web Services and Beyond*, we built RESTful services to support the shopping cart but, on the client side, we connected it only to the test user interface. Now, we need to develop a proper user interface. Let's discuss the key requirements.

Key requirements

The key requirements were as follows:

- Happy Biking decide to extend its market reach to Internet users. Therefore, they want to build an online system that will be accessible via Internet browsers, which limits the client development to browser-based applications.

- At this moment, the company does not have the intention of building mobile applications, considering it a much lower priority.

- Since the company does not have its own developers and has hired a software development company, the development should be performed relatively quickly and in an organized manner. To achieve that, the development team needs to use an existing framework for the UI development.

- The solution should work on all major browsers, which means that it has to be coded in the most generic way. No usage of browser-specific tools is allowed.

- The shopping cart is only one task in a whole bunch of enhancements that the company wants to make to their online system. They envisage a large multipurpose website that serves end users efficiently and in a consistent manner.

Candidate architecture #1 – Silverlight

The rich set of features available for the user interface makes Silverlight very attractive to organizations.

Solution design aspects

Designing a user interface in Silverlight is certainly fun, but the overall design may suffer a little. First, Silverlight needs a subset of .NET to be downloaded and run on the client, which limits the capabilities of the solution. Too many dependencies on the client software limit the target user base. Second, expanding the solution will be limited to using Silverlight or will require significant redesign.

An advantage of Silverlight would be the ability to use the MVVM pattern, which helps structuring the implementation.

Solution implementation aspects

Thanks to the toolset (Blend for Visual Studio 2013), the implementation is simpler than for other solutions. However, without enough experience, the implementation could be slow; the learning curve for Silverlight is quite steep.

Solution operations aspects

Solution operations would have additional problems since the solution depends on the client software. The performance may also suffer.

Organizational aspects

The biggest problem that the organization sees is that there is no clear roadmap for Silverlight. Since Silverlight Version 1 was released in 2007, Microsoft has released a new version of Silverlight every year. Now the product has not been discontinued, but the latest release was in 2011. Another concern is the inability to run on several platforms.

Solution evaluation

The following table shows the solution evaluation:

Design	Implementation	Operations	Organization

Candidate architecture #2 – ASP.NET MVC

From the variety of different ASP.NET templates, we should consider the MVC template as the most advanced one. The Single Page Application template would be a nice choice if the company did not plan to expand the features of their website. Web Forms is probably too old as a technology and has the possibility of being discontinued. It also does not force any pattern to be used for rapid development.

Solution design aspects

ASP.NET design has a few advantages over Silverlight. First, the resulting code can be run on any browser, including mobile browsers. Secondly, it can be enhanced with JavaScript and the usage of jQuery. And finally, it enforces the use of the MVC pattern that is well understood, presumably better than MVVM, because of its history.

Solution implementation aspects

The implementation of the ASP.NET MVC project may look a little difficult, but it is significantly simplified in Visual Studio. The initial default project covers many implementation aspects. It may look complex for a small solution but certainly pays off in the big run.

However, compared to Silverlight, the development and testing would certainly have more challenges. Given the complexity of the final solution, we would give the implementation aspects a "thumbs down".

Solution operations aspects

Generally, the solution does not rely on complex components. On the server side, it relies on Microsoft IIS, which has been a proven web server solution for many years. On the client side, it relies on the code that can be very clean if the design pattern is followed properly. Constant improvements to the ASP.NET MVC model help developers build cleaner and more maintainable code.

Organizational aspects

The ASP.NET solution can be expanded and seamlessly merged with other websites. Since it can be used on any browser, it is a definite win when it comes to discussions on the end user base.

Solution evaluation

As shown in the following table, we have three out of four thumbs up! This is definitely our choice:

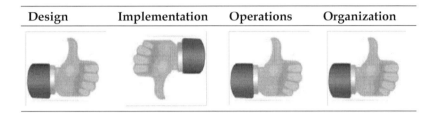

Design	Implementation	Operations	Organization

Architecture selection

Selection between these technologies does not seem to be a problem. If we consider all aspects, the ASP.NET MVC is a much better choice compared to Silverlight. However, if we analyze the details, we would notice that the biggest advantage is given by the fact that the ASP.NET client can run on any browser and does not depend on the downloadable runtime component. If the end user profile were more predictable, for example, an employee on the internal network, Silverlight would look much more attractive. For intranets, Silverlight definitely has more advantages.

The framework description

In order to perform rapid development and satisfy key requirements, the development team has chosen ASP.NET MVC as a framework for developing the user interface.

The ASP.NET MVC framework was released in 2009 as Version 1 and reached Version 5 in 2013. Over several years, it has passed through a series of improvements, and currently runs on .NET 4.5 and 4.5.1 and Visual Studio 2013.

User interface development

Let us consider the following steps to develop the user interface:

1. Copy the example files for *Chapter 9, Web Services and Beyond*, into a separate folder.

2. Run Visual Studio 2013 and open the RESTService solution.

3. We have already created the ASP.NET MVC project for you. In order to explore it, you may double-click on the **Shopping MVC UI** project. It will expand, showing its components.

4. However, let's take a look at how you would create a new ASP.NET MVC project and what steps are involved.

5. Click on **File** in the main menu, then **New**, and then **Project**.

6. Under the language of development (in our case **Visual C#**) select **Web**, and then **ASP.NET Web Application**.

> Notice that, if you have selected Visual Studio 2012, under the **Web** item, you would be able to choose from a bunch of different ASP.NET templates. In Visual Studio 2013, the selection happens in the next step.

7. Select the MVC template. You can add references to Web Forms or WEB API as well. You can also add a unit test project, as shown in the following screenshot:

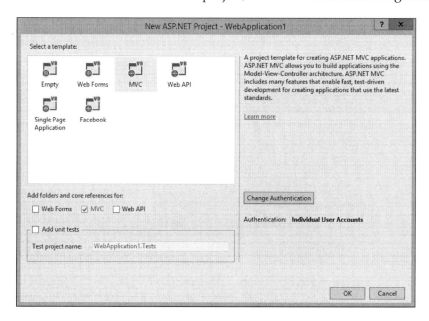

8. In ASP.NET MVC 5, there is a new **Change Authentication** mechanism. Click on the button, and you will have a choice of the following:

    ° **No Authentication**: This is the minimal selection. There will be no support for login or registration in the resultant template.

    ° **Individual User Account (default)**: This selection will force the application to use the ASP.NET identity that lets users create a username and password or use authentication via Facebook, Google, Microsoft, or Twitter.

    ° **Organizational Accounts**: This option should be selected if you want to use Windows Identity Foundation for Windows **Active Directory (AD)** or Azure AD.

    ° **Windows Authentication**: This option is intended for intranet sites.

    For our case, we need to choose the **Individual User Account** option.

9. 'The following screenshot shows the Shopping MVC UI project that we have already created as an ASP.NET MVC application:

10. The project is a typical MVC project with a few pages already in the template. We simply changed the look and feel of the default pages and connected the interface to the services we have developed before.

11. Right-click on the **Shopping MVC UI** project and select **Set as** a **StartUp Project**.

12. Run the application.

The ASP.NET MVC project

For a default ASP.NET MVC project, Visual Studio creates several default folders that we saw previously. This helps developers separate Models, Views, and Controllers, as well as giving some structure to additional files. The default folders are described in the following list:

- `Controllers`: This folder contains controller classes. The classes are written in C# or another programming language. The framework requires that all controller filenames end with "the word `Controller`", for example, `PurchaseOrderController.cs`.

- `Models`: This folder contains classes that represent models.

- `Views`: This folder stores the HTML files that are required for the user interface. The `Views` folder contains subfolders—one per controller. If you want to create views shared between controllers (for example, master view and layout pages), you should place them in a separated `Shared` subfolder.

- `App_Data`: This folder is used for storing application data, for example, the database used in the project.

- `Content`: This folder is used for static files, such as CSS files.

- `Images`: This folder is used for images. In previous versions of ASP.NET, the images were stored under the `Content` folder (often in a separate subfolder).

- `Scripts`: This folder stores JavaScript files.

Lessons learned

In this example, we considered the development of components of the online retail system, starting with the shopping cart. We compared the Silverlight and ASP.NET technologies and came to the conclusion that deployment restrictions that Silverlight has could make it a good choice for intranets. For the Internet application, we have chosen ASP.NET MVC.

Having an initial project template based on a well-known pattern without a doubt helps streamline the design and development of the solution.

Working with a use case – a desktop time billing application

Accents Software Inc. is a company that develops accounting and CRM software for small- and medium-size organizations. Today, they have several thousand clients with almost fifty thousand end users. They realized that many of their clients provide professional services to other organizations, and therefore, have specific needs.

The company decides to enhance their offer with another software package, **Bill Your Time**. The main purpose of this new application is to perform time tracking of clients' employees and to effectively schedule the tasks that they work on.

All Accents Software's programs are built on the Microsoft platform. Their accounting software can be configured to use Microsoft SQL Server as well as Microsoft Access databases for the backend. It is multiuser software; typically, users work on their workstations connected to the central database. The MS Access solution is not used much; it also has certain security problems, and it is scheduled to be discontinued this year.

All Accents Software applications are desktop apps developed using Windows Forms. The major language of development always has been C#, but some original applications were developed in Visual Basic (even before .NET) and later migrated to VB.NET.

Accents Software is also planning to improve its offerings by redesigning the user interface for existing applications. For new applications, they want to achieve a high level of user interface configuration. Ideally, the interface should be template-driven, and the templates should be reusable for many Accents' applications.

Key requirements

The key requirements are as follows:

- The Bill Your Time application should be able to use the databases from the XYZ accounting software. Since the support for MS Access will be discontinued, all new applications should be configured to access MS SQL Server databases.

- Accents Software clients use different editions of SQL Server, including SQL Server Express.

- The user interface should be configurable to fit the needs and preferences of end users. The configuration should be template-driven, as Accents Software wants to distribute new templates for a fee.

- Accents Software applications should have a roadmap targeting a consistent user interface and shared databases.

Candidate architecture for the desktop accounting application #1 – intranet with Silverlight

Developing an intranet application is a very attractive decision. There are many advantages of intranet applications: convenient and well-known navigation techniques, an ability to build the same solution for internal and external users, easy integration at the presentation level, and many more. Silverlight also adds rich user interface capabilities, and we decided to make it our candidate number one.

Solution design aspects

Designing a Silverlight UI for an intranet application has a lot of advantages. Using Silverlight, developers can build a feature-rich user interface. The MVVM pattern streamlines the development. Using XAML gives the ability to build a very configurable user interface.

At first glance, it seems that the intranet solution mitigates the challenge that we would have building an Internet application. One may say that intranet users are predictable and manageable. This might be true if Accents Software developed a product for one large enterprise. However, this is not our case.

Since the end users of the new product belong to many different organizations, their environment and their habits are unknown. We don't know all their browsers; we cannot control any of their settings. Therefore, the intranet approach really does not give us any advantage. The end users in our use case are as unpredictable as Internet users.

In addition, connecting to the database from Silverlight is not trivial, and would need an additional layer, for example, in the form of web services.

Solution implementation aspects

A great toolset (Blend for Visual Studio 2013) makes development relatively simple. It makes development easier even if we take a very steep learning curve into consideration.

Solution operations aspects

For the product development, most operational problems show up during support. Supporting a browser-based solution that can be run in different environments is a difficult task. An additional concern is adding a web server into the architecture. This is a new component that can be different in different organizations. Accent Software deals with each customer individually, and adding a component of that sort might create deployment and support nightmares. Remember that Accents Software's customers are small- and medium-sized organizations that often don't have their own IT department.

Organizational aspects

As we mentioned earlier in this chapter, the biggest organizational problem in our opinion is the fact that there is no clear roadmap for Silverlight. It is not clear whether or when Microsoft will launch its next version.

Solution evaluation

Despite the rich set of Silverlight features and the temptation to move to an intranet solution, this does not seem to be our preferred solution, and the evaluation shown in the following table illustrates the fact:

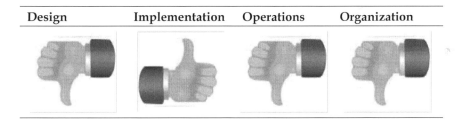

Design	Implementation	Operations	Organization

Candidate architecture for the desktop accounting application #2 – Desktop WPF app

What if we want to keep the richness of Silverlight but don't want to run an intranet application? The answer is WPF. In fact, in terms of functionality, WPF is even richer than Silverlight because it is not limited to being a subset of .NET.

Solution design aspects

First, WPF gives us the ability to design an application with an extremely sophisticated UI and even supports our requirement to make the UI template-driven. Secondly, WPF (like Silverlight) supports MVVM, which makes designing the application easier and the development more disciplined.

In fact, WPF seems to be the right choice to support our roadmap. It is an essential part of .NET and has been evolved with it. It is not too old (like, for example, Windows Forms). And it seems to have all necessary capabilities for developing consistent user interfaces for all Accents Software applications.

Solution implementation aspects

WPF has a steep learning curve, and certainly it suggests the new development paradigm. However, once learned, WPF becomes a powerful tool in the developers' hands. A lot of features and effects (including the template-driven interface) can be coded easily once the developers build enough skills.

Solution operations aspects

WPF can access the database management system directly. It does not need an additional layer (as is the case with Silverlight). It also does not need IIS, an additional component that would make the entire architecture a little more complex.

Being a desktop application, it is more manageable compared to a web application (that might behave differently under different browsers).

There are also such means of application deployment as **ClickOnce**, which enables web-style deployment for non-web applications. It takes away a lot of the hassle in a typical deployment process.

Organizational aspects

WPF, being a part of .NET, has a clear roadmap, and it will be supported and enhanced by Microsoft for many years. It has a rich feature set that will allow Accents Software to migrate all of their applications to the new platform, while keeping a consistent look and feel.

Solution evaluation

The evaluation is all thumbs up, as shown in the following table:

Design	Implementation	Operations	Organization

Architecture selection

Comparing the risks and benefits of the Silverlight solution with the WPF solution, we see that the latter is definitely a winner, as shown in the following table:

Solution	Benefits/risks
Intranet solution with Silverlight	**Benefits** • Feature-rich user interface • Usage of MVVM pattern • Great toolset **Risks** • Too many potential end user environments. More complicated support • Architecture seems to be more complex (additional layer to communicate with database and a web server) • Steep learning curve • No clear roadmap
Desktop solution with WPF	**Benefits** • Very feature-rich user interface • Usage of MVVM pattern • Simpler architecture • Clear roadmap **Risks** • Steep learning curve

Pattern implementation description

Let's discuss the major features of the MVVM implementation in WPF in the following list:

- Data binding is a process that establishes a connection between View and ViewModel. Data binding can be established in one of three directions: one way, two ways, or one way to source.

- Binding can be also established as a one time activity, updating View only when the data context of ViewModel changes.

- The communication between View and ViewModel is done using the `INotifyPropertyChanged` interface.

- The View is coded in XAML. Ideally code behind does not exist—other than the default created by Visual Studio (it never happens, though).

- Model, as in MVC or MVP, is the least formalized component. It can be data from a database or a totally different object. For example, one UI control can change its appearance based on the behavior of another control. In this case, the second control plays the role of Model.

- In our example, the MVVM pattern can be presented as the following:

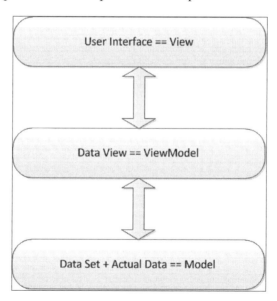

User interface development

Building a full-blown WPF application is a long but very exciting journey. In this chapter, we will present a complete solution for one screen: the Client Management screen of the **Bill Your Time** application. We will focus on the most important aspects of building a WPF application using the MVVM pattern.

You may notice that we use Visual Basic.NET in the following example and not C# as before. Really, it does not make any difference!

1. In Visual Studio 2013, open the `BillYourTime.sln` solution. In the **Solution Explorer** screen you will see one project, **BillYourTime**, as shown in the following screenshot:

2. Click on the **Start** arrow or press the *F5* key and run the project.

3. Navigate to **View | Clients** from the menu or click on the **Clients** button ().

4. On the main screen, you will see two parts. The left-hand part represents a list of clients. Click on any client, and you will see the details on the right-hand part, as shown:

5. Let's look into the code and see what is involved in this presentation. We will explore different components of the MVVM pattern and their relationship.

6. First off, let's open the XAML of the main screen (`formMain.xaml`) and explore the code representing a control. For this exercise, let's look at the `Address` textbox:

```
<TextBox Grid.Column="1" Name="_c_txbAddress" Height="Auto"
HorizontalAlignment="Stretch" TextWrapping="Wrap"
IsEnabled="False" Foreground="Black">
    <TextBox.Text>
        <MultiBinding Converter="{StaticResource
cnvAddressConverter}">
            <Binding Mode="OneWay" Path="Street1" />
            <Binding Mode="OneWay" Path="City1" />
            <Binding Mode="OneWay" Path="State1" />
            <Binding Mode="OneWay" Path="Country1" />
            <Binding Mode="OneWay" Path="ZIP1" />
        </MultiBinding>
    </TextBox.Text>
</TextBox>
```

Notice a couple of things. First of all, this is multibinding, which means that one UI control is bound to several data fields. Second, every time the binding runs, it activates the `cnvAddressConverter` function, which creates the presentation properly. This is not necessary but, in many cases, it gives developers the freedom to change the default binding.

7. The textbox (part of View) is linked to ViewModel by means of binding. All controls on the right-hand side of the screen (grouped in the grid `grdClientProperties` container) are (re)bound to the dataset every time a new line is selected on the left-hand side of the screen. The binding is done with literally one line of code, which is as follows:

```
grdClientProperties.DataContext = currentClientDataRow
```

8. Every time the user selects a line in the client list, the value of `currentClientDataRow` changes. `currentClientDataRow` is a data row view defined as the following:

```
Friend currentClientDataRow As DataRowView
```

When the application goes through its initialization cycles or when the data changes, the data row view is updated from the underlying dataset.

9. Therefore, in order to go on displaying all details of the client record, only the following steps are needed:

    1. Load the dataset.

    2. Create a view from a dataset table. You can create several views from one table. Each view can, for example, present different subsets of the dataset table using different filtering.

    3. Design the UI, binding each control to one or more fields in the view.

    4. During runtime, change the data context of the control container. This will change the binding for each field in the container.

    5. Enjoy the new view!

10. Let's take a look at another example of mighty binding. On the same client properties screen (on the right-hand side of the main window), click on the **Admin** tab , as shown in the following screenshot:

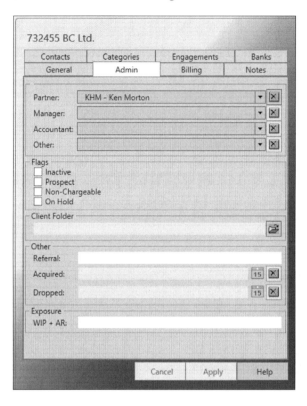

11. Click on the **Partner** combo box, and you will see the list of people coming from the Employee table of the database.

12. If you look in the code of the combo box, you will see the binding again, as shown:

```
<ComboBox Grid.Row="0" Grid.Column="1" Name="_c_cmbPartner"
Text="{Binding Path=EmployeeID1, Mode=OneWay,
Converter={StaticResource cnvEmployeeNameConverter}}"
>
<ComboBox.ItemsSource>
    <Binding Source="{StaticResource collEmployees}" />
</ComboBox.ItemsSource>
</ComboBox>
```

In this case, the entire source of the combo box is bound to the Employees data view.

Let's see how the notification in the MVVM model works using the following example:

1. Select one of the clients from the list on the left-hand side of the screen, as shown:

2. In the client properties window on the right-hand side, click on the **Inactive** checkbox in the **Admin** tab, as shown:

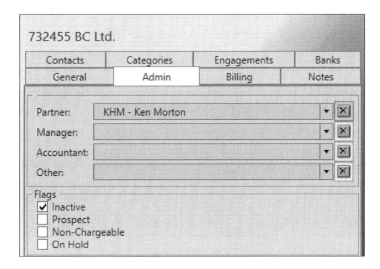

3. You will notice that the **Inactive** icon immediately appeared next to the client name in the list on the left-hand side of the screen, as depicted in the following screenshot:

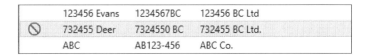

4. The trick is in the fact that both client information on the right-hand side of the screen and the record in the client list on the left-hand side of the screen are bound to the same ViewModel. (Notice, that you can bind the checkbox values as well as the icon). Changing View would affect ViewModel, which will affect another View instance as well. The first View instance has to be bound in two ways, which are as follows:

```
<CheckBox Grid.Row="0" Name="_c_chbInactive" Content="Inactive"
IsChecked="{Binding Path=InActive, Mode=TwoWay}"
```

Lessons learned

We compared solution implementations using Silverlight and WPF. Despite the fact that they both use MVVM pattern and .NET (Silverlight uses a subset of .NET), the constraints for these two technologies are quite different.

We have briefly looked into the MVVM pattern implementation in WPF. We learned that, if we simply follow the pattern, we can achieve very powerful effects.

Summary

In this chapter, we looked into different presentation layer technologies on the Microsoft platform: desktop, web, and mobile development. We compared major patterns for the presentation layer development, such as MVC, MVP, and MVVM. In the next chapter, we'll wrap up our discussion of patterns. There are certainly more architectural patterns than we have talked about in this book. We hope that this book will give you some ideas and useful approaches for your own scenarios and use cases.

13
Conclusion

In this book, we presented several technologies on the Microsoft platform, discussed their capabilities, and tried to position them so that they can be used in different solutions. Although we mostly focused on middle-tier architecture and integration, we also touched on some other layers, including the presentation layer. Among the Microsoft products that we discussed, the major focus was on SQL Server, SharePoint, and BizTalk.

Because most of the solutions include some coding, we provided an overview of capabilities of the .NET platform. Currently in Version 4.5, .NET is a very powerful tool that can solve major problems. In our solution discussion, we assessed architectures using .NET where applicable.

Microsoft provides architects and developers with a variety of tools and technologies. Using them in solutions requires knowledge of patterns and best practices, which have originated and solidified through the delivery of many hundreds of projects. Many books have been written on this topic; however, most of the books discussed design patterns. This book focuses on patterns for architects, specifically, solution architects.

Patterns for software-intensive systems

The notion of patterns is centuries, if not millenniums, old. Patterns existed in different industries, in architecture, and even in folklore. The entire discussion of patterns in software that started in the late 1980s was influenced by the books of Christopher Alexander, a famous architect who worked on many buildings in several countries.

The first book on software design patterns, *Design Patterns: Elements of Reusable Object-Oriented Software* was published in 1994 by *Addison-Wesley Professional*, authored by *E. Gamma*, *R. Helm*, *R. Johnson*, and *J. Vlissides* (often referred to as the Gang of Four). Since then, the discussions of patterns never stopped. Authors presented patterns for user interfaces, databases, and so on.

One of the most significant attempts to describe patterns and to build pattern catalogs is the Martin Fowler signature series of books. The books in these series present patterns of enterprise application architecture, integration patterns, service design patterns, and others. If you are serious about patterns, you should have one or two books from this series on your desk (`https://www.informit.com/imprint/ series_detail.aspx?ser=2629220&sorttype=3&dir=1&page=1`).

We would also like to mention the significant efforts of Thomas Erl, who collected and presented dozens of patterns for service-oriented architecture in his book.

In the Microsoft world, there is a tremendous ongoing effort by the Microsoft **patterns & practices** team, which has made a lot of recommendations related to specific products (`http://msdn.microsoft.com/en-us/library/ff921345.aspx`).

Where to go next

This book is not a tutorial on the Microsoft technologies, nor does it provide some code that you can copy and paste to your solution, and everything will start working miraculously.

We rather hope that this book will provoke some thoughts and encourage you, as architects, to consider a few things while designing your solutions:

- **Look into the requirements**: This is your final target; this is what you want to achieve. Pay additional attention to nonfunctional requirements.

- **Consider different technologies for your solution**: See how much configuration and development each of the technology requires.

- **Apply the framework that we discussed in our book**: Remember to always consider all aspects of the solution when you perform technical evaluation. Take into account design, implementation, and operational aspects as well as the organizational context.

- **Try applying weight to your criteria**: If there is no clear winner in the evaluation, try applying weight to your criteria. For example, when your organizational context presents nonnegotiable constraints, it really does not matter that the performance of one solution is slightly better than another.

Writing this book was a valuable exercise for us. We hope that reading it will be a valuable experience for you.

Index

Customers database 113
custom list 130
custom Web Parts, SharePoint
   URL 133

D

data access layer (DAL) 51
data aggregation
   benefits 280
Database availability group (DAG) 150
database design, payroll processor
      application 77
Database Engine 64
Database Engine Tuning Advisor 65
database mirroring 277
Database Recovery Advisor 67
Database Server role, SharePoint 126
DataContext 393
data federation
   about 325, 326
   features 327
   pattern description 326, 327
Data Flow task 96
data integration
   about 160
   differentiating, with data migration 279
data mart 280
data migration
   about 279
   differentiating, with data integration 279
Data Processing 82
data publisher
   configuring 205-210
Data Quality Services. *See* DQS
data replication
   about 275, 276
   challenges 276
   SQL Server replication 277
data sharing
   .NET 329
   about 322
   architecture selection 330, 331
   BizTalk 328
   key requisites 327
   real-time data retrieval use case 322, 323

data synchronization
   about 275, 276
   performing, messages used 278
   performing, Sync Framework used 277, 278
Data Transformation Services (DTS) 89
data warehouse
   about 280, 322
   challenges 323, 324
DB-Library 274
derived (architectural) requirements,
      solution decision framework 11
desktop applications
   about 385
   desktop time billing application 401
   InfoPath 387
   Microsoft Office VBA applications 387
   Windows Forms 386
   Windows Presentation Foundation
      (WPF) 386
desktop operating systems
   about 146
   using 146
desktop time billing application
   about 401
   architecture selection 405
   building, with Silverlight 402
   building, with WPF 403
   key requisites 401
   pattern implementation description 406
   user interface, developing 407-412
Developer edition, BizTalk Server 2013 104
development foundation
   setting up 193, 194
development tools, SharePoint
   about 139
   Napa 141
   SharePoint Designer 139
   Visual Studio 140
DNR database 113
document library, SharePoint 132
Domain name registration (DNR)
      service 107, 113
DQS 70
DQS Client 65
DQS Cleansing transformation 90

E

publisher 217
Publishing Approval workflow 134
Publishing category, site templates 129
Publish/Subscribe pattern
about 217
publisher 217
subscriber 217
subscription 217
Publish/Subscribe pattern, BizTalk 101
PurchaseOrderBroker orchestration
implementing 245, 246
pushing 217

R

Razor syntax 57
receiver 164, 166
release candidate (RC) 41
reliability, BizTalk Server 105
Reliable Payroll Pro Inc.. *See* RPP
Remote Procedure Calls (RPCs) 138
replication. *See* data replication
Reporting Services 64
Representational State Transfer. *See* REST
Resolver service 230
REST
about 252
principles 252, 253
RESTful services
about 253
facts 254
future 265
key requisites 254
pattern description 254, 255
RESTful WCF Services 256
shopping cart use case 253
solution, building 257
versus, SOAP web services 265
RESTful WCF Services
organizational aspects 257
solution design aspects 256
solution evaluation 257
solution implementation aspects 256
solution operations aspects 256
reusable workflows, SharePoint 134
revision-control system. *See* source
control systems

Ribbon control 386
rich client applications 385
RPP
about 71
details, adding to 91
requirements analysis 91, 92
rsync 271

S

sandbox solutions 136
scalability, BizTalk Server 106
Scatter-Gather pattern 336, 337
Scripts folder 400
Search Server
benefits 303
risks 303
security, BizTalk Server 107
selective XML index feature 69
semantic dissonance 273
semantic inconsistencies 268
sender 164, 166
Separation of Concerns (SoC) 48, 390
sequencing 106
service abstraction 223
service aggregator workflow service
AccountAggregator workflow,
implementing 348-353
implementing, with ASP.NET 354-356
project, setting up 348
service applications, SharePoint 135
service autonomy 223
service encapsulation 223
service granularity 223
service orientation 223
service-oriented architecture. *See* SOA
service reusability 223
services, cloud computing
Infrastructure as a Service (IaaS) 154
Platform as a Service (PaaS) 154
Software as a Service (SaaS) 154
services, ESB Toolkit
about 229
BizTalk Operations service 230
Exception handling service 229
Itinerary services 229
Resolver service 230

Thank you for buying
Applied Architecture Patterns on the Microsoft Platform
Second Edition

About Packt Publishing

Packt, pronounced 'packed', published its first book "Mastering phpMyAdmin for Effective MySQL Management" in April 2004 and subsequently continued to specialize in publishing highly focused books on specific technologies and solutions.

Our books and publications share the experiences of your fellow IT professionals in adapting and customizing today's systems, applications, and frameworks. Our solution based books give you the knowledge and power to customize the software and technologies you're using to get the job done. Packt books are more specific and less general than the IT books you have seen in the past. Our unique business model allows us to bring you more focused information, giving you more of what you need to know, and less of what you don't.

Packt is a modern, yet unique publishing company, which focuses on producing quality, cutting-edge books for communities of developers, administrators, and newbies alike. For more information, please visit our website: www.packtpub.com.

About Packt Enterprise

In 2010, Packt launched two new brands, Packt Enterprise and Packt Open Source, in order to continue its focus on specialization. This book is part of the Packt Enterprise brand, home to books published on enterprise software – software created by major vendors, including (but not limited to) IBM, Microsoft and Oracle, often for use in other corporations. Its titles will offer information relevant to a range of users of this software, including administrators, developers, architects, and end users.

Writing for Packt

We welcome all inquiries from people who are interested in authoring. Book proposals should be sent to author@packtpub.com. If your book idea is still at an early stage and you would like to discuss it first before writing a formal book proposal, contact us; one of our commissioning editors will get in touch with you.

We're not just looking for published authors; if you have strong technical skills but no writing experience, our experienced editors can help you develop a writing career, or simply get some additional reward for your expertise.

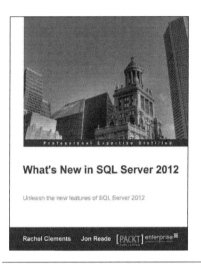

What's New in SQL Server 2012

ISBN: 978-1-84968-734-8   Paperback: 238 pages

Unleash the new features of SQL Server 2012

1. Upgrade your skills to the latest version of SQL Server.

2. Discover the new dimensional model in Analysis Services.

3. Utilize data alerts and render reports to the latest versions of Excel and Word.

Oracle Application Integration Architecture (AIA) Foundation Pack 11gR1: Essentials

ISBN: 978-1-84968-480-4   Paperback: 274 pages

Develop and deploy your Enterprise Integration Solutions using Oracle AIA

1. Full of illustrations, diagrams, and tips with clear step-by-step instructions and real-time examples to develop full-fledged integration processes.

2. Each chapter drives the reader right from architecture to implementation.

3. Understand the important concept of Enterprise Business Objects that play a crucial role in AIA installation and models.

Please check **www.PacktPub.com** for information on our titles

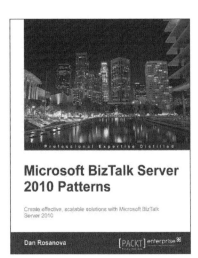

Microsoft BizTalk Server 2010 Patterns

ISBN: 978-1-84968-460-6   Paperback: 396 pages

Create effective, scalable solutions with Microsoft BizTalk Server 2010

1. Provides a unified example from the beginning to end of a real-world solution.

2. A starter guide expecting little or no previous BizTalk experience, but offering advanced concepts and techniques.

3. Provides in-depth background and introduction to the platform and technology.

BizTalk Server 2010 Cookbook

ISBN: 978-1-84968-434-7   Paperback: 368 pages

Over 50 recipes for developers and administrators looking to deliver well-built BizTalk solutions and environments

1. Enhance your implementation skills with practically proven patterns.

2. Written by a BizTalk expert and MVP, Steef-Jan Wiggers, the book is filled with practical advice.

3. Learn best practices for deploying BizTalk 2010 solutions.

Please check **www.PacktPub.com** for information on our titles

Made in the USA
San Bernardino, CA
23 February 2015